CASE CLOSED

VOLUME 47

Gosho Aoyama

Case Briefing:

Subject: Jimmy Kudo, a.k.a. Conan Edogawa
Occupation: High School Student/Detective
Special Skills: Analytical thinking and deductive reasoning, Soccer
Equipment: Bow Tie Voice Transmitter, Super Sneakers, Homing Glasses, Stretchy Suspenders

The subject is hot on the trail of a pair of suspicious men in black when he is attacked from behind and administered a strange substance which physically transforms him into a first grader. When the subject confides in the eccentric inventor Dr. Agasa, they decide to keep the subject's true identity a secret for the safety of everyone around him. Assuming the new identity of first-grader Conan Edogawa, the subject continues to assist the police force on their most baffling cases. The only problem is that most crime-solving professionals won't take a little kid's advice!

Table of Contents

CONFIDEN

CASE CLOSED

Volume 47
Shonen Sunday Edition

Story and Art by GOSHO AOYAMA

MEITANTEI CONAN Vol. 47
by Gosho AOYAMA
© 1994 Gosho AOYAMA
All rights reserved.
Original Japanese edition published by SHOGAKUKAN.
English translation rights in the United States of America, Canada,
the United Kingdom and Ireland arranged with SHOGAKUKAN.

Translation
Tetsuichiro Miyaki

Touch-up & Lettering
Freeman Wong

Cover & Graphic Design
Andrea Rice

Editor
Shaenon K. Garrity

Printed in Canada

Published by VIZ Media, LLC
P.O. Box 77010
San Francisco, CA 94107

10 9 8 7 6 5 4 3 2 1
First printing, July 2013

FILE 1: A SUSPICIOUS DEDUCTION

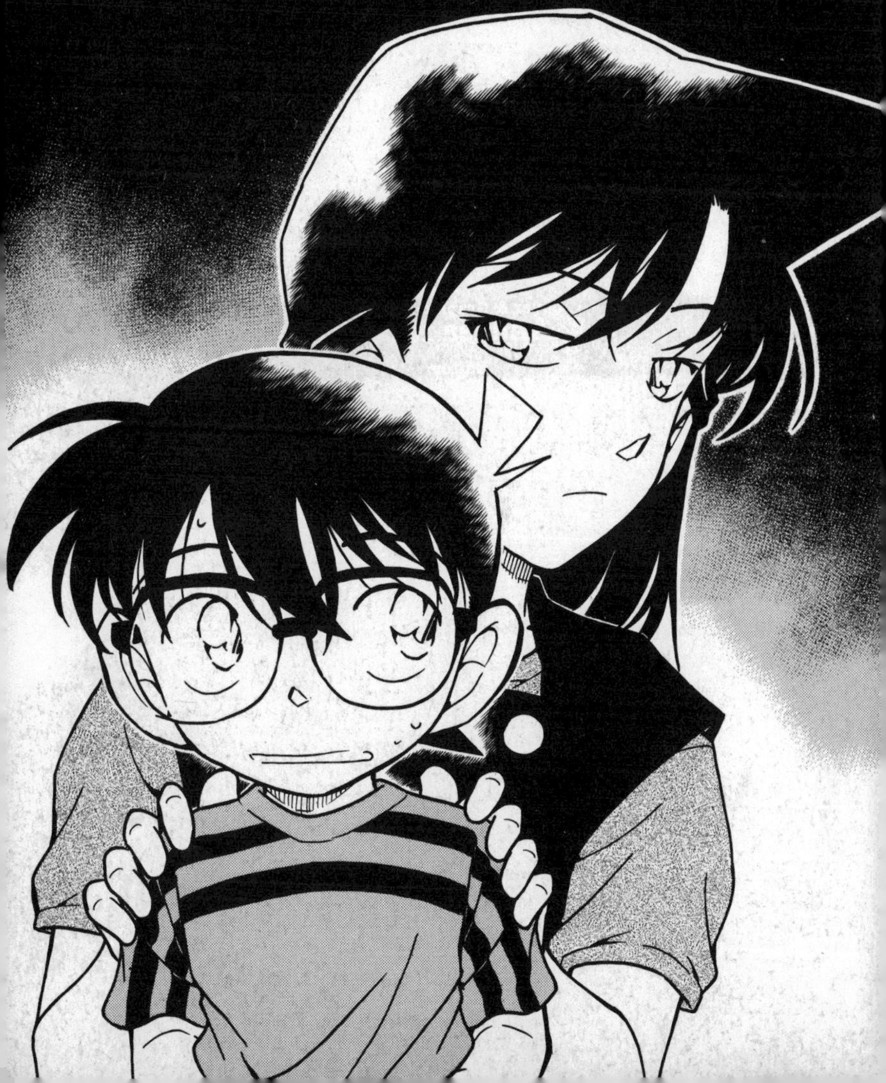

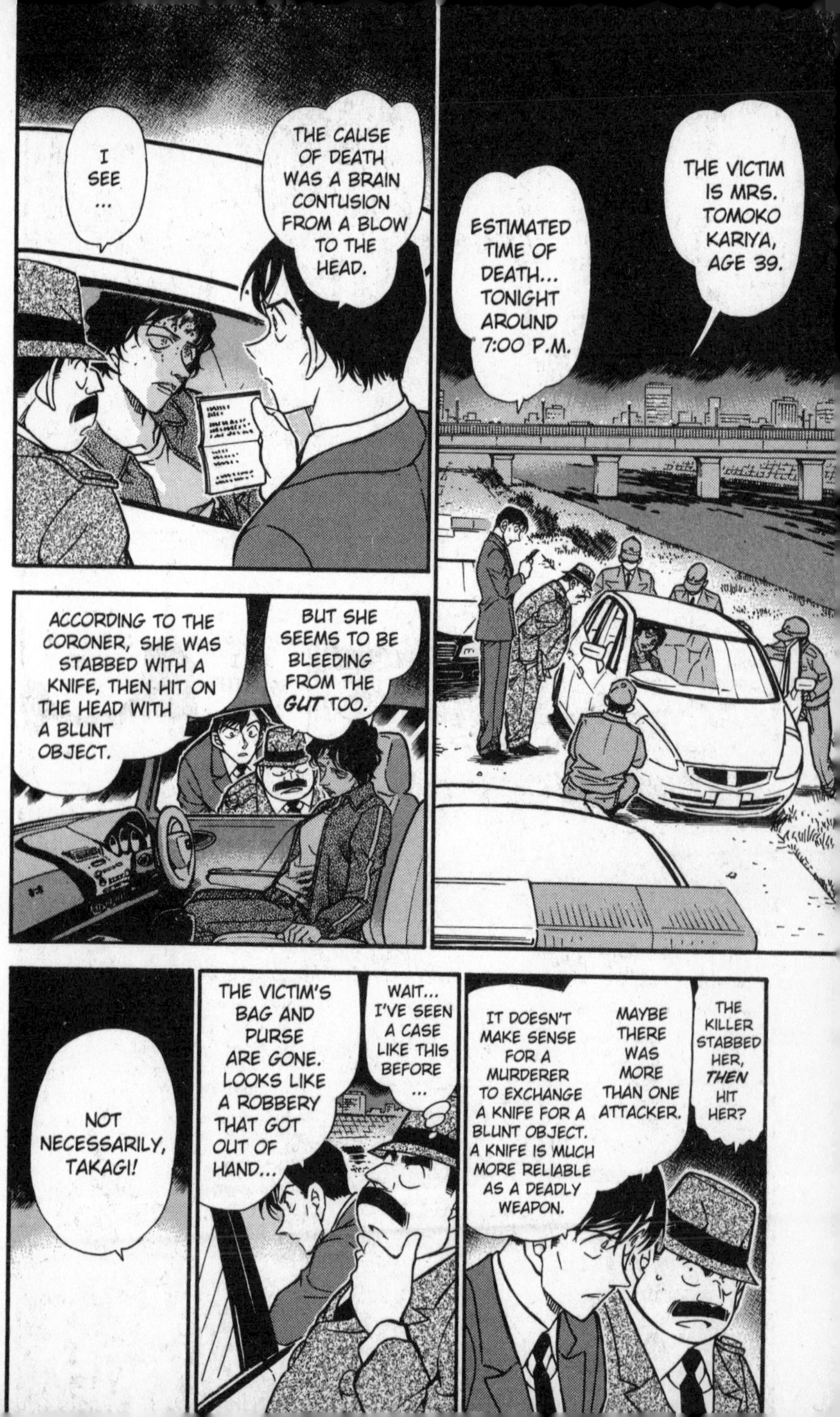
THE VICTIM IS MRS. TOMOKO KARIYA, AGE 39.
ESTIMATED TIME OF DEATH... TONIGHT AROUND 7:00 P.M.
THE CAUSE OF DEATH WAS A BRAIN CONTUSION FROM A BLOW TO THE HEAD.
I SEE ...
BUT SHE SEEMS TO BE BLEEDING FROM THE *GUT* TOO.
ACCORDING TO THE CORONER, SHE WAS STABBED WITH A KNIFE, THEN HIT ON THE HEAD WITH A BLUNT OBJECT.
THE KILLER STABBED HER, *THEN* HIT HER?
MAYBE THERE WAS MORE THAN ONE ATTACKER.
IT DOESN'T MAKE SENSE FOR A MURDERER TO EXCHANGE A KNIFE FOR A BLUNT OBJECT. A KNIFE IS MUCH MORE RELIABLE AS A DEADLY WEAPON.
WAIT... I'VE SEEN A CASE LIKE THIS BEFORE ...
THE VICTIM'S BAG AND PURSE ARE GONE. LOOKS LIKE A ROBBERY THAT GOT OUT OF HAND...
NOT NECESSARILY, TAKAGI!

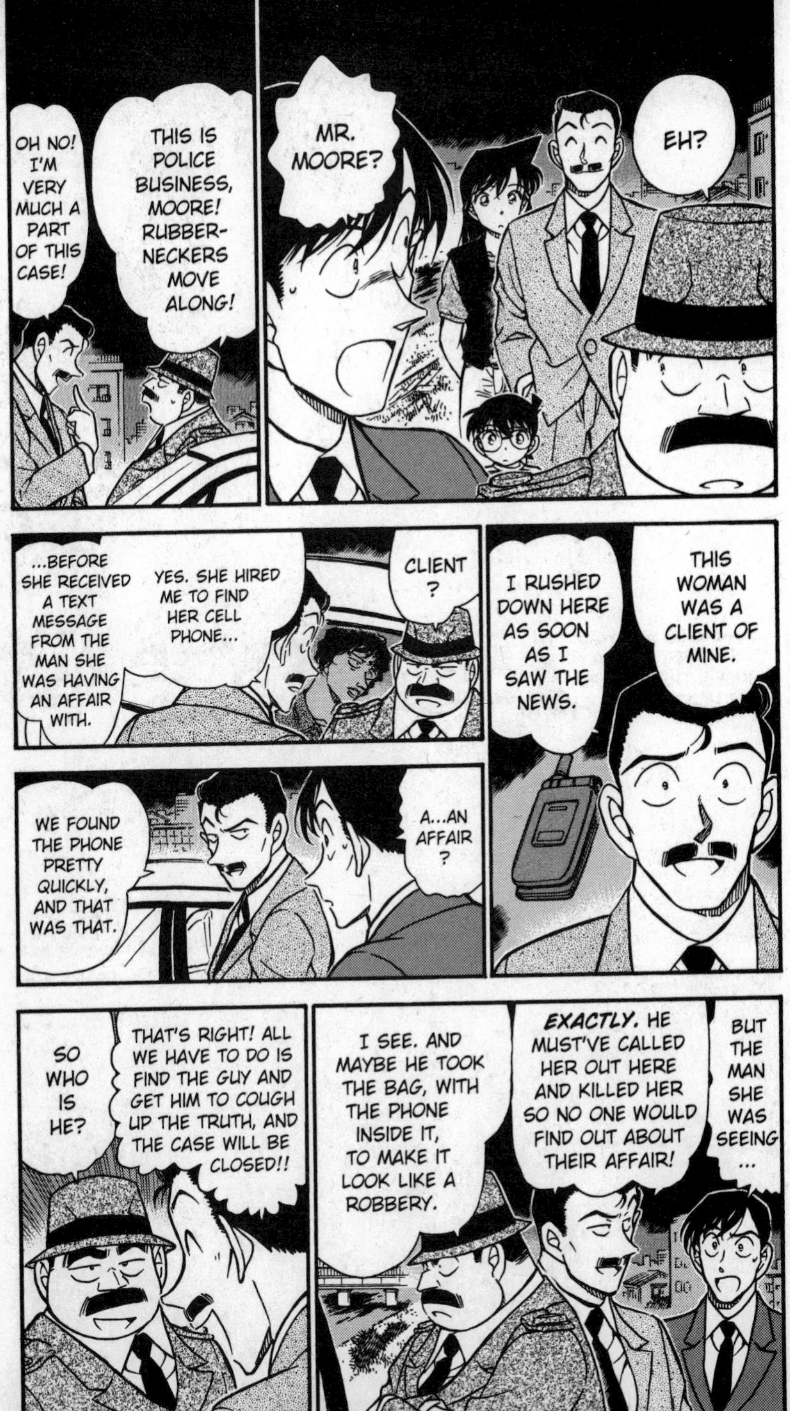
EH?
MR. MOORE?
THIS IS POLICE BUSINESS, MOORE! RUBBER-NECKERS MOVE ALONG!
OH NO! I'M VERY MUCH A PART OF THIS CASE!
THIS WOMAN WAS A CLIENT OF MINE.
I RUSHED DOWN HERE AS SOON AS I SAW THE NEWS.
CLIENT ?
YES. SHE HIRED ME TO FIND HER CELL PHONE...
...BEFORE SHE RECEIVED A TEXT MESSAGE FROM THE MAN SHE WAS HAVING AN AFFAIR WITH.
A...AN AFFAIR ?
WE FOUND THE PHONE PRETTY QUICKLY, AND THAT WAS THAT.
BUT THE MAN SHE WAS SEEING ...
EXACTLY. HE MUST'VE CALLED HER OUT HERE AND KILLED HER SO NO ONE WOULD FIND OUT ABOUT THEIR AFFAIR!
I SEE. AND MAYBE HE TOOK THE BAG, WITH THE PHONE INSIDE IT, TO MAKE IT LOOK LIKE A ROBBERY.
THAT'S RIGHT! ALL WE HAVE TO DO IS FIND THE GUY AND GET HIM TO COUGH UP THE TRUTH, AND THE CASE WILL BE CLOSED!!
SO WHO IS HE?

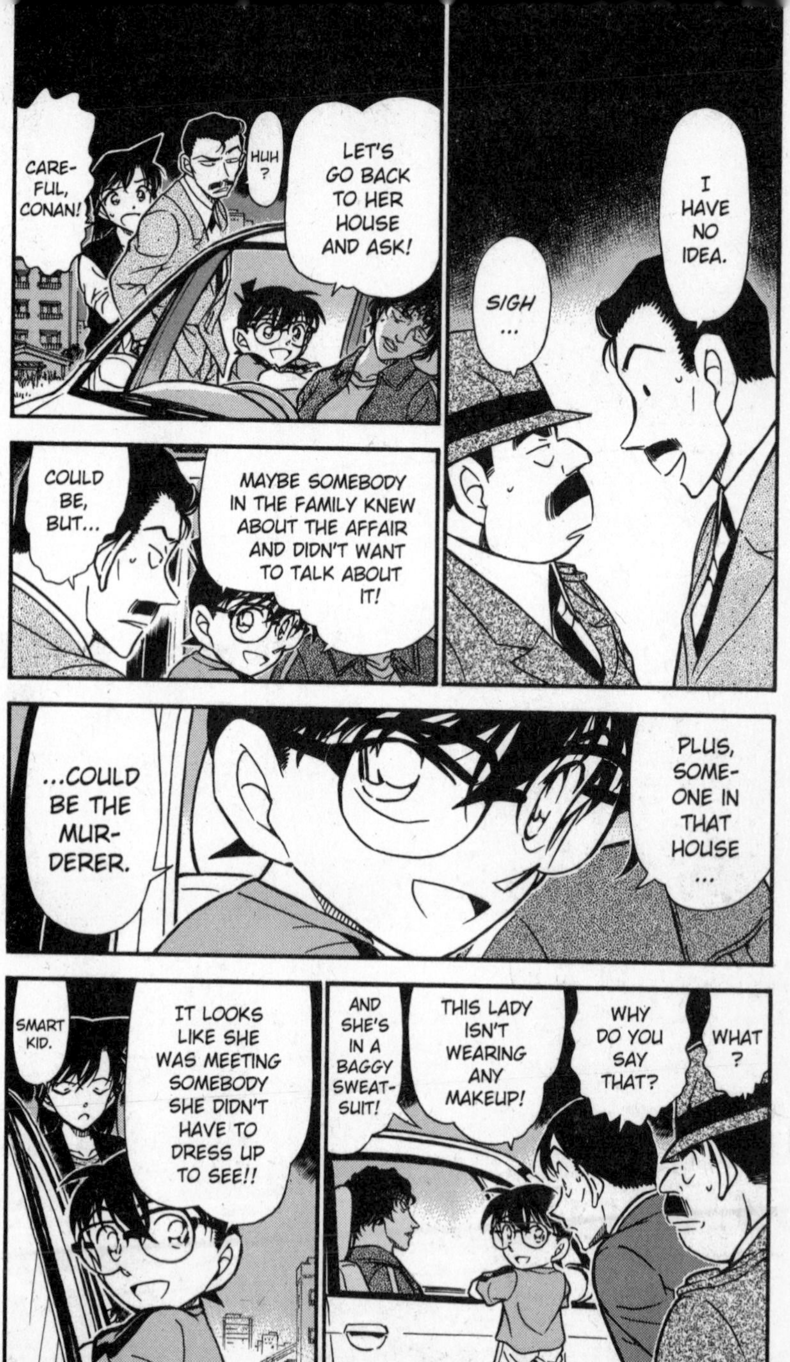
I HAVE NO IDEA.
SIGH...
LET'S GO BACK TO HER HOUSE AND ASK!
HUH?
CARE-FUL, CONAN!
MAYBE SOMEBODY IN THE FAMILY KNEW ABOUT THE AFFAIR AND DIDN'T WANT TO TALK ABOUT IT!
COULD BE, BUT...
PLUS, SOME-ONE IN THAT HOUSE...
...COULD BE THE MUR-DERER.
WHAT?
WHY DO YOU SAY THAT?
THIS LADY ISN'T WEARING ANY MAKEUP!
AND SHE'S IN A BAGGY SWEAT-SUIT!
IT LOOKS LIKE SHE WAS MEETING SOMEBODY SHE DIDN'T HAVE TO DRESS UP TO SEE!!
SMART KID.

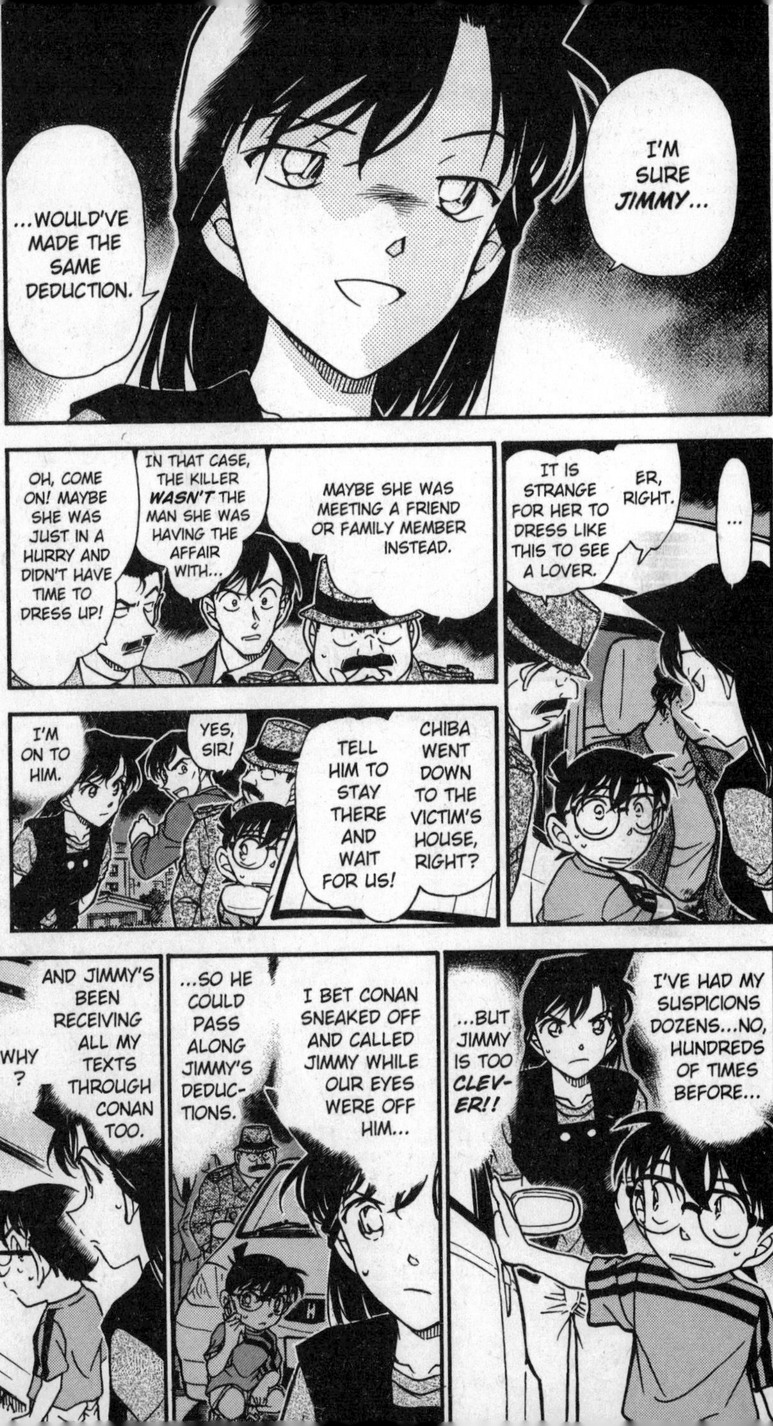
I'M SURE JIMMY...
...WOULD'VE MADE THE SAME DEDUCTION.
...
ER, RIGHT.
IT IS STRANGE FOR HER TO DRESS LIKE THIS TO SEE A LOVER.
MAYBE SHE WAS MEETING A FRIEND OR FAMILY MEMBER INSTEAD.
IN THAT CASE, THE KILLER WASN'T THE MAN SHE WAS HAVING THE AFFAIR WITH...
OH, COME ON! MAYBE SHE WAS JUST IN A HURRY AND DIDN'T HAVE TIME TO DRESS UP!
CHIBA WENT DOWN TO THE VICTIM'S HOUSE, RIGHT?
TELL HIM TO STAY THERE AND WAIT FOR US!
YES, SIR!
I'M ON TO HIM.
I'VE HAD MY SUSPICIONS DOZENS...NO, HUNDREDS OF TIMES BEFORE...
...BUT JIMMY IS TOO CLEVER!!
I BET CONAN SNEAKED OFF AND CALLED JIMMY WHILE OUR EYES WERE OFF HIM...
...SO HE COULD PASS ALONG JIMMY'S DEDUCTIONS.
AND JIMMY'S BEEN RECEIVING ALL MY TEXTS THROUGH CONAN TOO.
WHY?

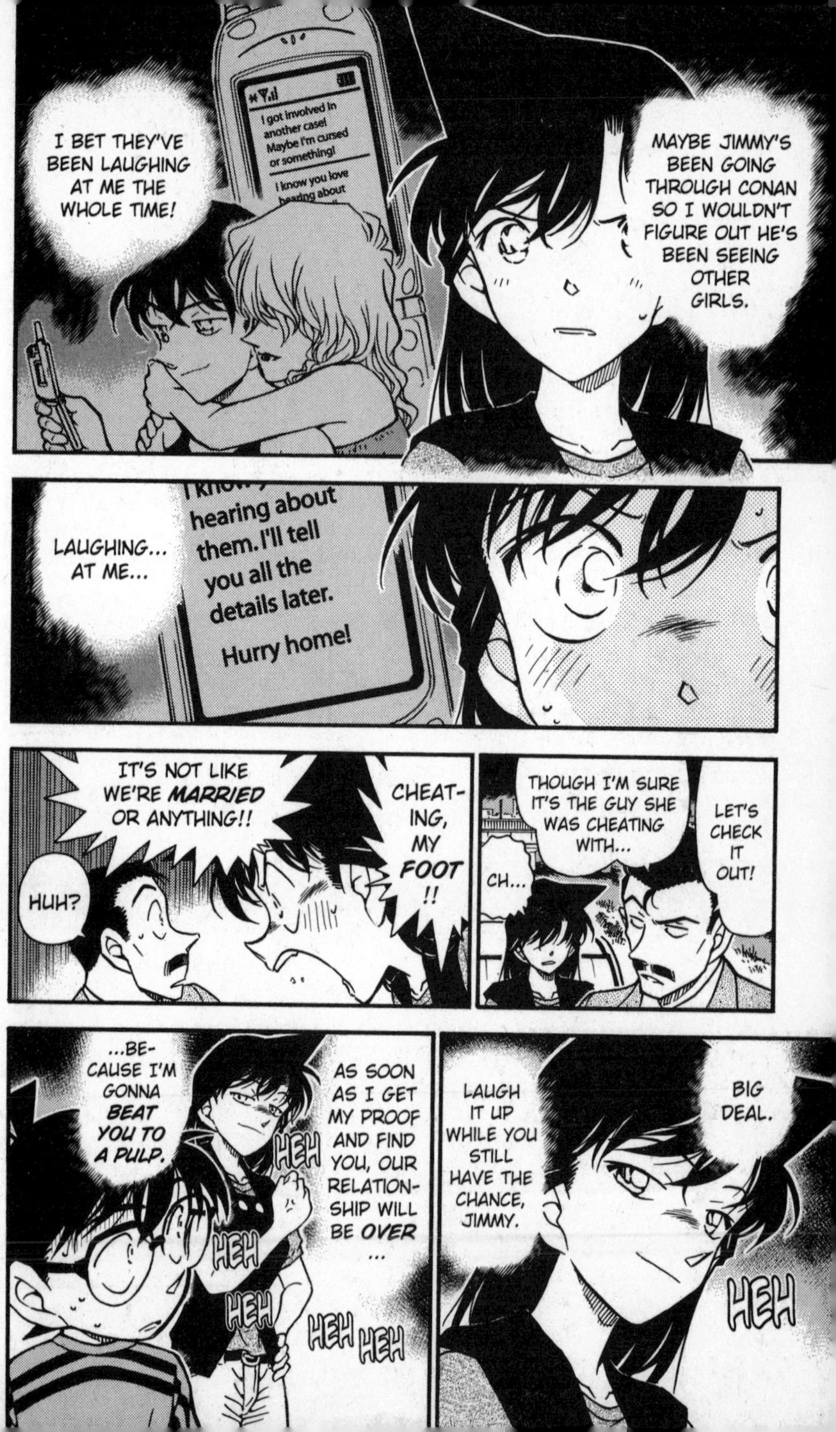
MAYBE JIMMY'S BEEN GOING THROUGH CONAN SO I WOULDN'T FIGURE OUT HE'S BEEN SEEING OTHER GIRLS.
I got involved in another case! Maybe I'm cursed or something!
I know you love
I BET THEY'VE BEEN LAUGHING AT ME THE WHOLE TIME!
hearing about them. I'll tell you all the details later.
Hurry home!
LAUGHING... AT ME...
LET'S CHECK IT OUT!
THOUGH I'M SURE IT'S THE GUY SHE WAS CHEATING WITH...
CH...
CHEAT-ING, MY FOOT!!
IT'S NOT LIKE WE'RE MARRIED OR ANYTHING!!
HUH?
BIG DEAL.
LAUGH IT UP WHILE YOU STILL HAVE THE CHANCE, JIMMY.
HEH
AS SOON AS I GET MY PROOF AND FIND YOU, OUR RELATION-SHIP WILL BE OVER...
...BE-CAUSE I'M GONNA BEAT YOU TO A PULP.
HEH
HEH
HEH
HEH
HEH

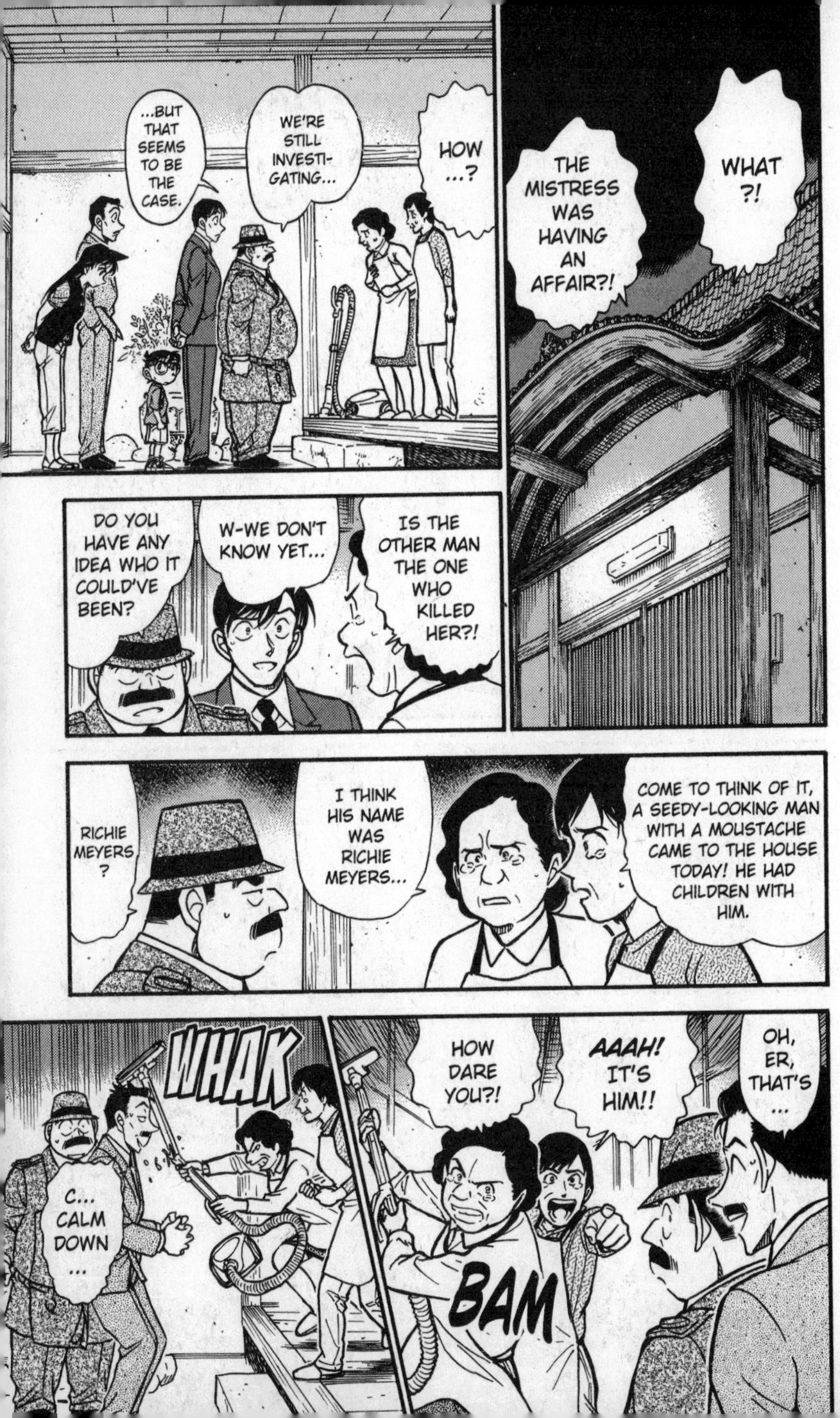
WHAT?!
THE MISTRESS WAS HAVING AN AFFAIR?!
HOW ...?
WE'RE STILL INVESTI-GATING...
...BUT THAT SEEMS TO BE THE CASE.
IS THE OTHER MAN THE ONE WHO KILLED HER?!
W-WE DON'T KNOW YET...
DO YOU HAVE ANY IDEA WHO IT COULD'VE BEEN?
COME TO THINK OF IT, A SEEDY-LOOKING MAN WITH A MOUSTACHE CAME TO THE HOUSE TODAY! HE HAD CHILDREN WITH HIM.
I THINK HIS NAME WAS RICHIE MEYERS...
RICHIE MEYERS?
OH, ER, THAT'S...
AAAH! IT'S HIM!!
HOW DARE YOU?!
BAM
WHAK
C... CALM DOWN...

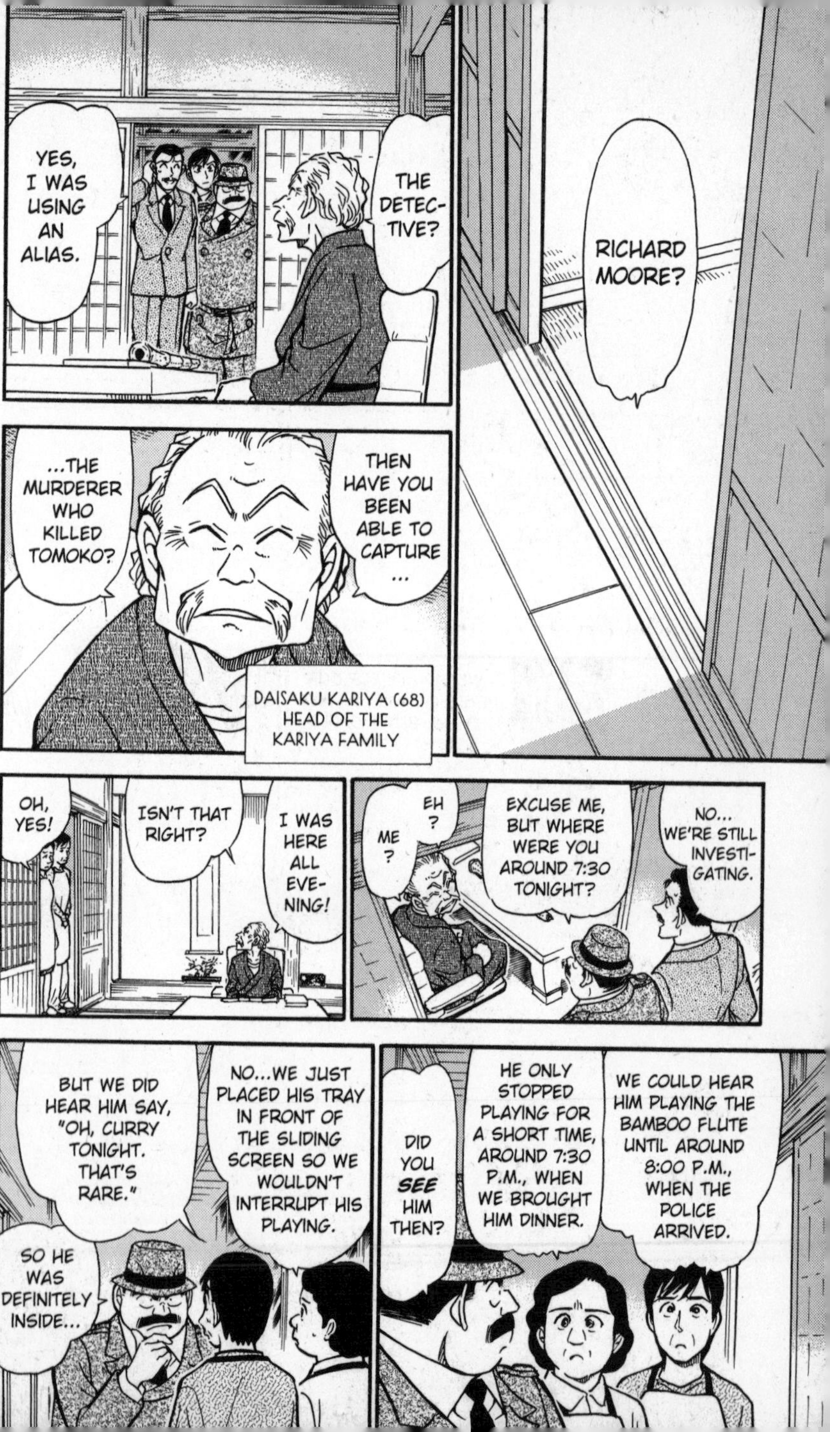
RICHARD MOORE?
THE DETECTIVE?
YES, I WAS USING AN ALIAS.
THEN HAVE YOU BEEN ABLE TO CAPTURE ...
...THE MURDERER WHO KILLED TOMOKO?
DAISAKU KARIYA (68) HEAD OF THE KARIYA FAMILY
NO... WE'RE STILL INVESTIGATING.
EXCUSE ME, BUT WHERE WERE YOU AROUND 7:30 TONIGHT?
EH?
ME?
I WAS HERE ALL EVENING!
ISN'T THAT RIGHT?
OH, YES!
WE COULD HEAR HIM PLAYING THE BAMBOO FLUTE UNTIL AROUND 8:00 P.M., WHEN THE POLICE ARRIVED.
HE ONLY STOPPED PLAYING FOR A SHORT TIME, AROUND 7:30 P.M., WHEN WE BROUGHT HIM DINNER.
DID YOU *SEE* HIM THEN?
NO...WE JUST PLACED HIS TRAY IN FRONT OF THE SLIDING SCREEN SO WE WOULDN'T INTERRUPT HIS PLAYING.
BUT WE DID HEAR HIM SAY, "OH, CURRY TONIGHT. THAT'S RARE."
SO HE WAS DEFINITELY INSIDE...

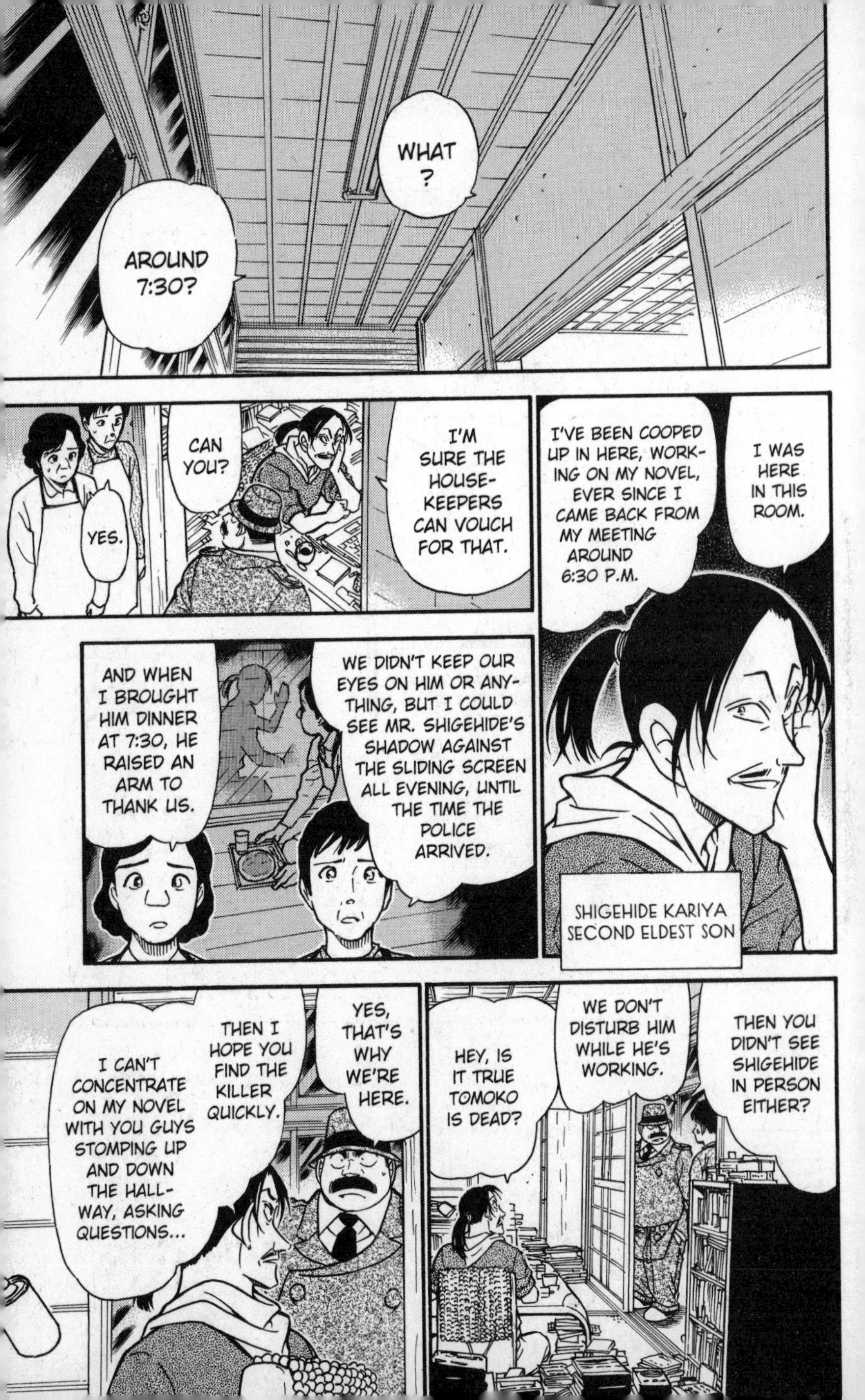
WHAT ?
AROUND 7:30?
I WAS HERE IN THIS ROOM.
I'VE BEEN COOPED UP IN HERE, WORKING ON MY NOVEL, EVER SINCE I CAME BACK FROM MY MEETING AROUND 6:30 P.M.
SHIGEHIDE KARIYA SECOND ELDEST SON
I'M SURE THE HOUSEKEEPERS CAN VOUCH FOR THAT.
CAN YOU?
YES.
WE DIDN'T KEEP OUR EYES ON HIM OR ANYTHING, BUT I COULD SEE MR. SHIGEHIDE'S SHADOW AGAINST THE SLIDING SCREEN ALL EVENING, UNTIL THE TIME THE POLICE ARRIVED.
AND WHEN I BROUGHT HIM DINNER AT 7:30, HE RAISED AN ARM TO THANK US.
THEN YOU DIDN'T SEE SHIGEHIDE IN PERSON EITHER?
WE DON'T DISTURB HIM WHILE HE'S WORKING.
HEY, IS IT TRUE TOMOKO IS DEAD?
YES, THAT'S WHY WE'RE HERE.
THEN I HOPE YOU FIND THE KILLER QUICKLY.
I CAN'T CONCENTRATE ON MY NOVEL WITH YOU GUYS STOMPING UP AND DOWN THE HALLWAY, ASKING QUESTIONS...

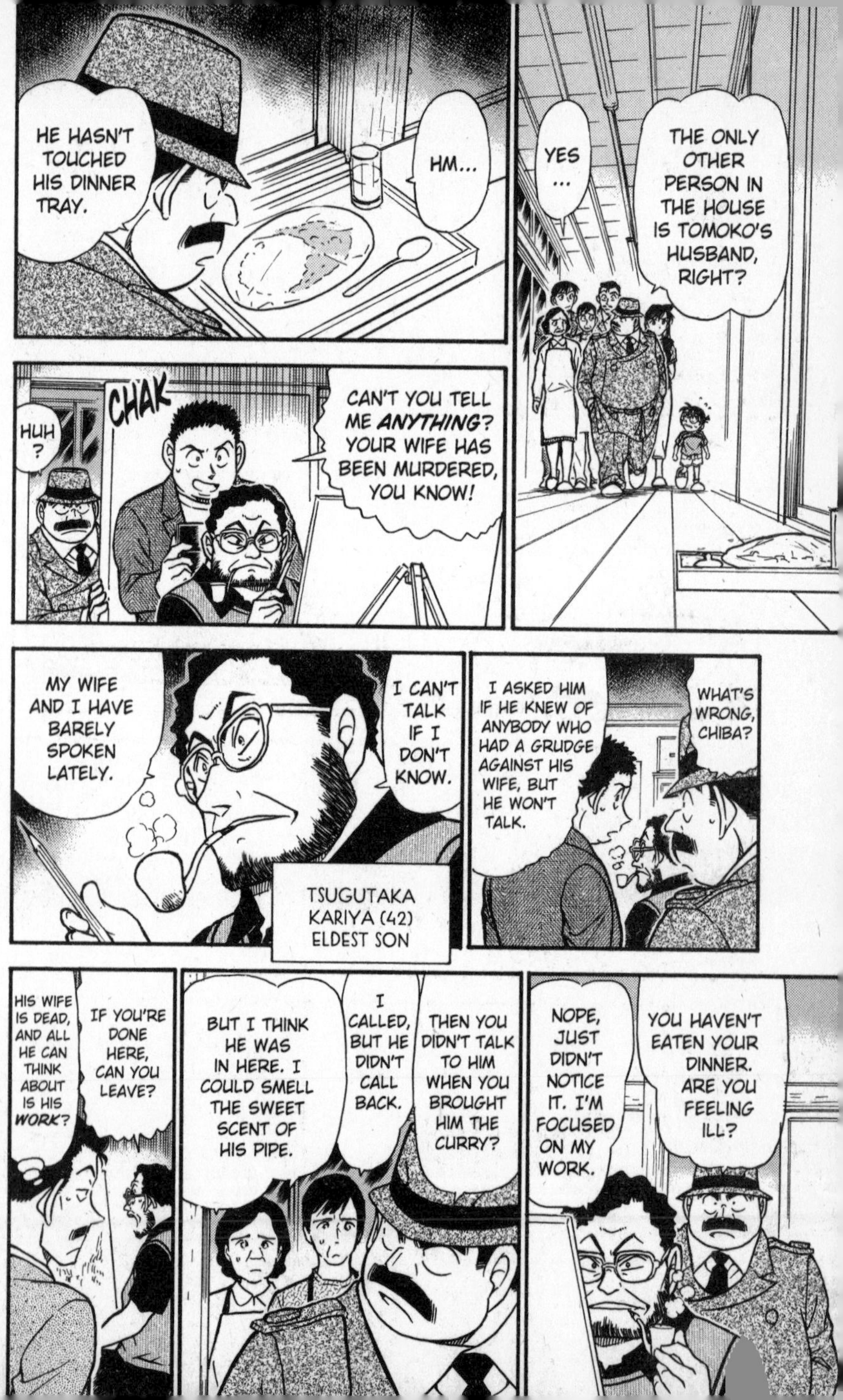
THE ONLY OTHER PERSON IN THE HOUSE IS TOMOKO'S HUSBAND, RIGHT?
YES ...
HM...
HE HASN'T TOUCHED HIS DINNER TRAY.
CAN'T YOU TELL ME *ANYTHING*? YOUR WIFE HAS BEEN MURDERED, YOU KNOW!
CHAK
HUH?
WHAT'S WRONG, CHIBA?
I ASKED HIM IF HE KNEW OF ANYBODY WHO HAD A GRUDGE AGAINST HIS WIFE, BUT HE WON'T TALK.
I CAN'T TALK IF I DON'T KNOW.
MY WIFE AND I HAVE BARELY SPOKEN LATELY.
TSUGUTAKA KARIYA (42) ELDEST SON
YOU HAVEN'T EATEN YOUR DINNER. ARE YOU FEELING ILL?
NOPE, JUST DIDN'T NOTICE IT. I'M FOCUSED ON MY WORK.
THEN YOU DIDN'T TALK TO HIM WHEN YOU BROUGHT HIM THE CURRY?
I CALLED, BUT HE DIDN'T CALL BACK.
BUT I THINK HE WAS IN HERE. I COULD SMELL THE SWEET SCENT OF HIS PIPE.
IF YOU'RE DONE HERE, CAN YOU LEAVE?
HIS WIFE IS DEAD, AND ALL HE CAN THINK ABOUT IS HIS *WORK*?

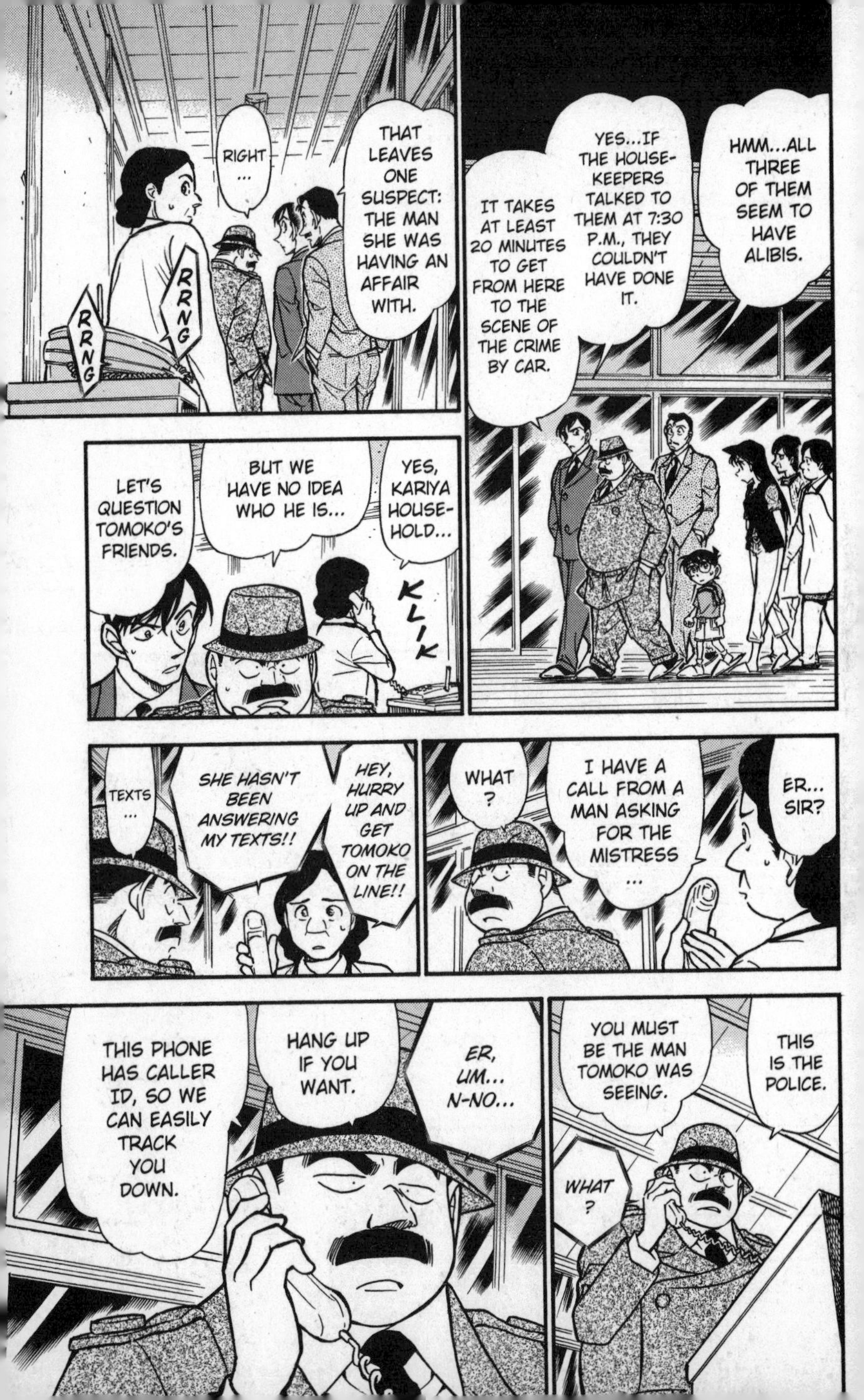
HMM...ALL THREE OF THEM SEEM TO HAVE ALIBIS.
YES...IF THE HOUSE-KEEPERS TALKED TO THEM AT 7:30 P.M., THEY COULDN'T HAVE DONE IT.
IT TAKES AT LEAST 20 MINUTES TO GET FROM HERE TO THE SCENE OF THE CRIME BY CAR.
THAT LEAVES ONE SUSPECT: THE MAN SHE WAS HAVING AN AFFAIR WITH.
RIGHT...
RRNG
RRNG
YES, KARIYA HOUSE-HOLD...
KLIK
BUT WE HAVE NO IDEA WHO HE IS...
LET'S QUESTION TOMOKO'S FRIENDS.
ER... SIR?
I HAVE A CALL FROM A MAN ASKING FOR THE MISTRESS...
WHAT?
HEY, HURRY UP AND GET TOMOKO ON THE LINE!!
SHE HASN'T BEEN ANSWERING MY TEXTS!!
TEXTS...
THIS IS THE POLICE.
YOU MUST BE THE MAN TOMOKO WAS SEEING.
WHAT?
ER, UM... N-NO...
HANG UP IF YOU WANT.
THIS PHONE HAS CALLER ID, SO WE CAN EASILY TRACK YOU DOWN.

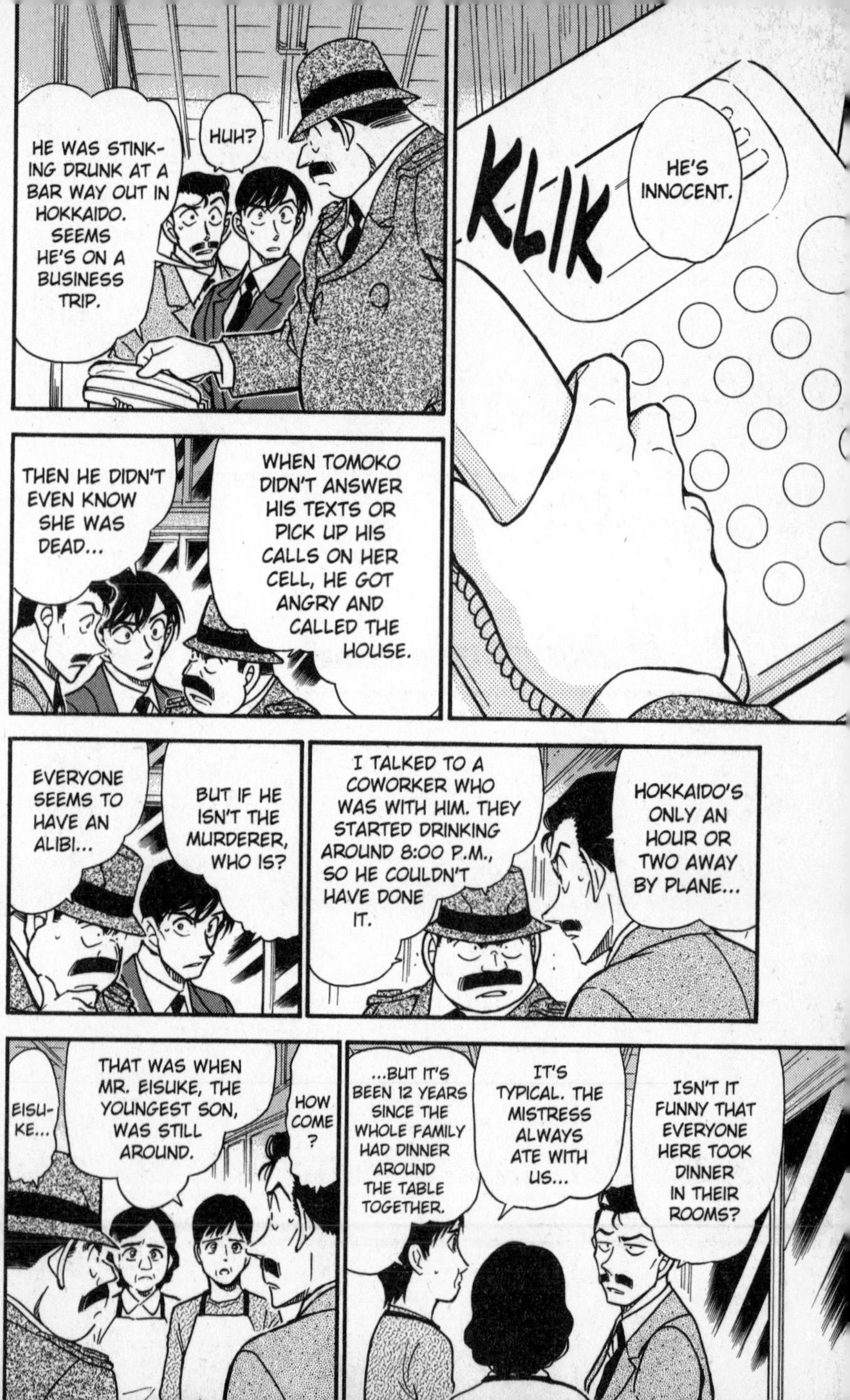
KLIK
HE'S INNOCENT.
HUH?
HE WAS STINKING DRUNK AT A BAR WAY OUT IN HOKKAIDO. SEEMS HE'S ON A BUSINESS TRIP.
WHEN TOMOKO DIDN'T ANSWER HIS TEXTS OR PICK UP HIS CALLS ON HER CELL, HE GOT ANGRY AND CALLED THE HOUSE.
THEN HE DIDN'T EVEN KNOW SHE WAS DEAD...
HOKKAIDO'S ONLY AN HOUR OR TWO AWAY BY PLANE...
I TALKED TO A COWORKER WHO WAS WITH HIM. THEY STARTED DRINKING AROUND 8:00 P.M., SO HE COULDN'T HAVE DONE IT.
BUT IF HE ISN'T THE MURDERER, WHO IS?
EVERYONE SEEMS TO HAVE AN ALIBI...
ISN'T IT FUNNY THAT EVERYONE HERE TOOK DINNER IN THEIR ROOMS?
IT'S TYPICAL. THE MISTRESS ALWAYS ATE WITH US...
...BUT IT'S BEEN 12 YEARS SINCE THE WHOLE FAMILY HAD DINNER AROUND THE TABLE TOGETHER.
HOW COME?
THAT WAS WHEN MR. EISUKE, THE YOUNGEST SON, WAS STILL AROUND.
EISUKE...

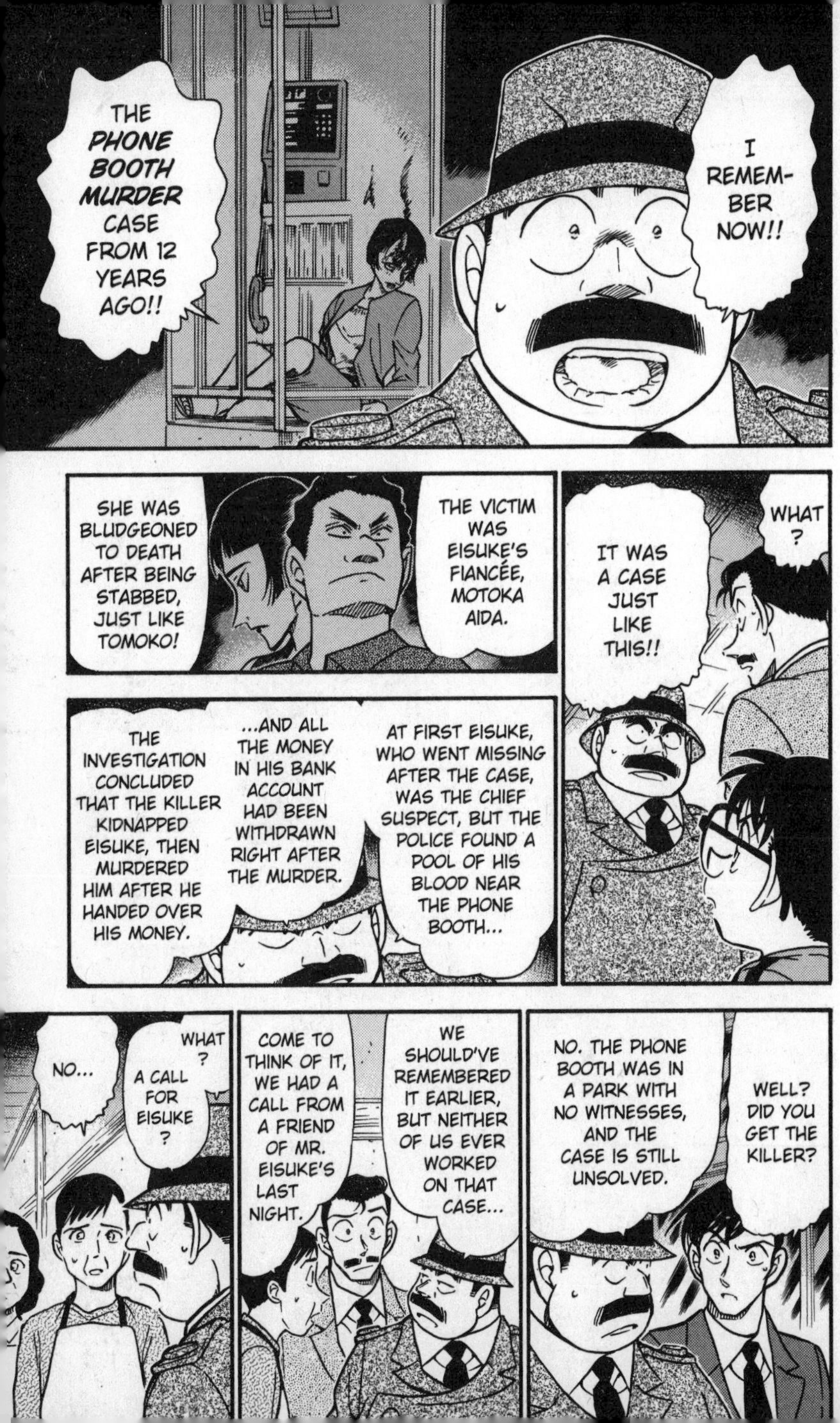
I REMEMBER NOW!!
THE PHONE BOOTH MURDER CASE FROM 12 YEARS AGO!!
WHAT?
IT WAS A CASE JUST LIKE THIS!!
THE VICTIM WAS EISUKE'S FIANCÉE, MOTOKA AIDA.
SHE WAS BLUDGEONED TO DEATH AFTER BEING STABBED, JUST LIKE TOMOKO!
AT FIRST EISUKE, WHO WENT MISSING AFTER THE CASE, WAS THE CHIEF SUSPECT, BUT THE POLICE FOUND A POOL OF HIS BLOOD NEAR THE PHONE BOOTH...
...AND ALL THE MONEY IN HIS BANK ACCOUNT HAD BEEN WITHDRAWN RIGHT AFTER THE MURDER.
THE INVESTIGATION CONCLUDED THAT THE KILLER KIDNAPPED EISUKE, THEN MURDERED HIM AFTER HE HANDED OVER HIS MONEY.
WELL? DID YOU GET THE KILLER?
NO. THE PHONE BOOTH WAS IN A PARK WITH NO WITNESSES, AND THE CASE IS STILL UNSOLVED.
WE SHOULD'VE REMEMBERED IT EARLIER, BUT NEITHER OF US EVER WORKED ON THAT CASE...
COME TO THINK OF IT, WE HAD A CALL FROM A FRIEND OF MR. EISUKE'S LAST NIGHT.
WHAT? A CALL FOR EISUKE?
NO...

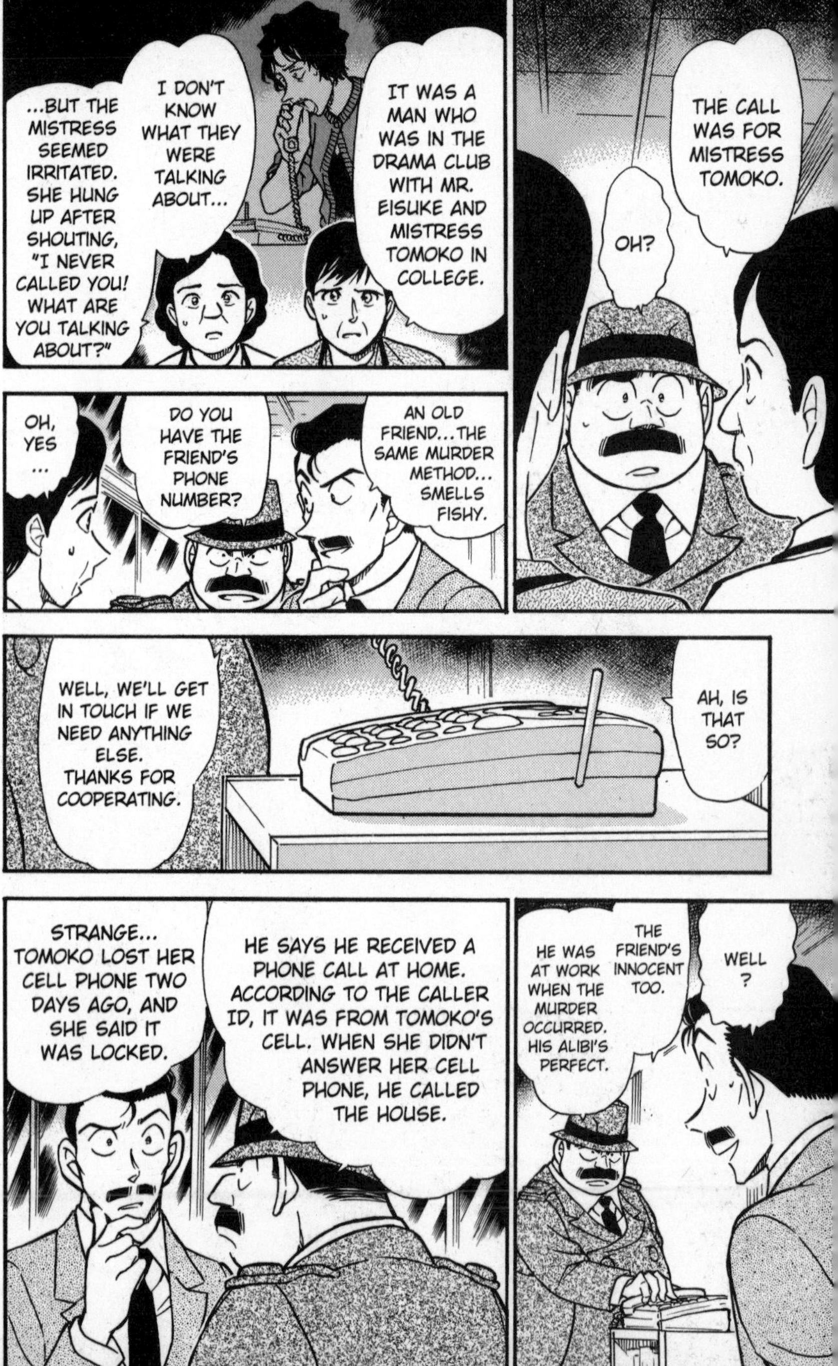
THE CALL WAS FOR MISTRESS TOMOKO.
OH?
IT WAS A MAN WHO WAS IN THE DRAMA CLUB WITH MR. EISUKE AND MISTRESS TOMOKO IN COLLEGE.
I DON'T KNOW WHAT THEY WERE TALKING ABOUT...
...BUT THE MISTRESS SEEMED IRRITATED. SHE HUNG UP AFTER SHOUTING, "I NEVER CALLED YOU! WHAT ARE YOU TALKING ABOUT?"
AN OLD FRIEND...THE SAME MURDER METHOD... SMELLS FISHY.
DO YOU HAVE THE FRIEND'S PHONE NUMBER?
OH, YES ...
AH, IS THAT SO?
WELL, WE'LL GET IN TOUCH IF WE NEED ANYTHING ELSE. THANKS FOR COOPERATING.
WELL ?
THE FRIEND'S INNOCENT TOO.
HE WAS AT WORK WHEN THE MURDER OCCURRED. HIS ALIBI'S PERFECT.
HE SAYS HE RECEIVED A PHONE CALL AT HOME. ACCORDING TO THE CALLER ID, IT WAS FROM TOMOKO'S CELL. WHEN SHE DIDN'T ANSWER HER CELL PHONE, HE CALLED THE HOUSE.
STRANGE... TOMOKO LOST HER CELL PHONE TWO DAYS AGO, AND SHE SAID IT WAS LOCKED.

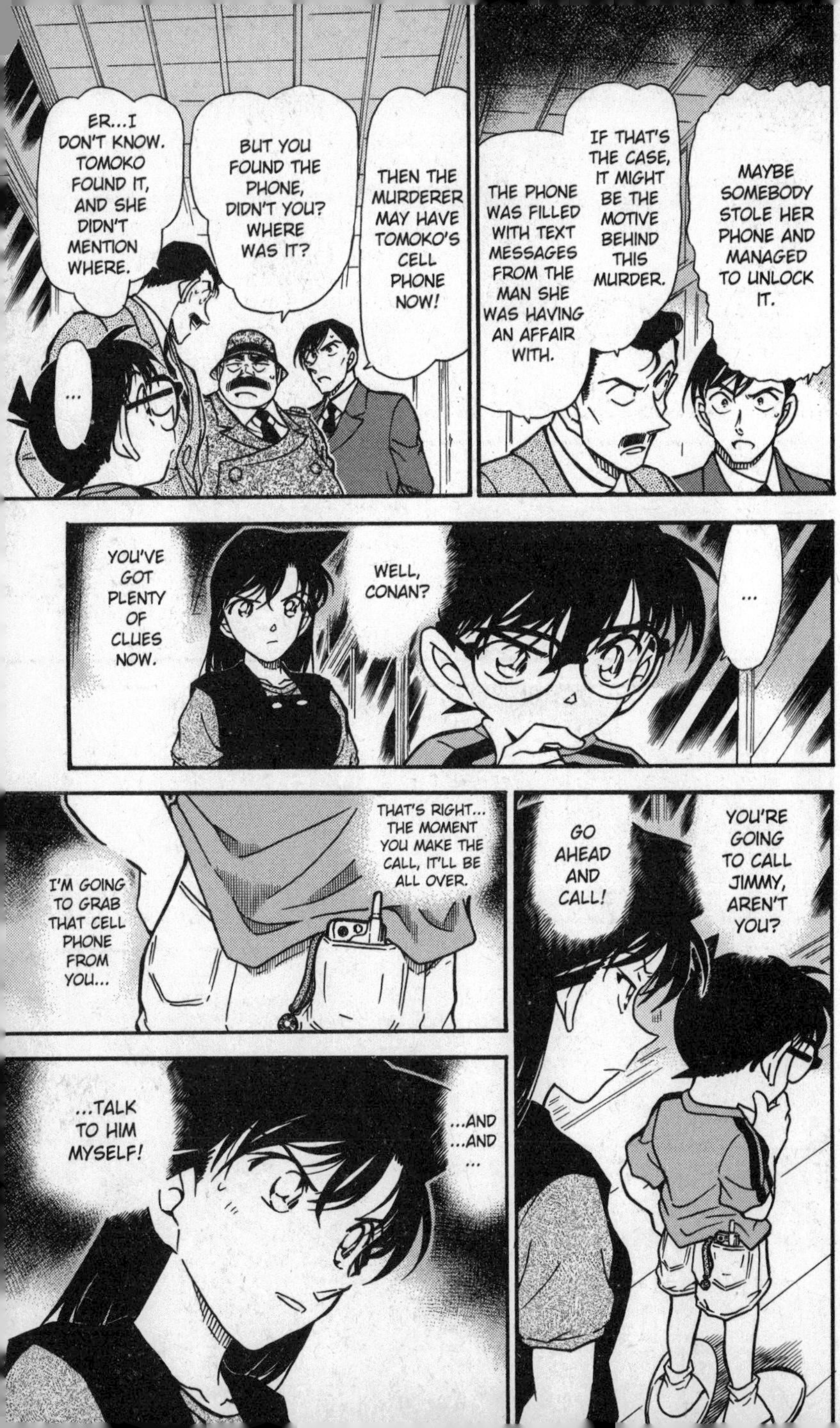
MAYBE SOMEBODY STOLE HER PHONE AND MANAGED TO UNLOCK IT.
IF THAT'S THE CASE, IT MIGHT BE THE MOTIVE BEHIND THIS MURDER.
THE PHONE WAS FILLED WITH TEXT MESSAGES FROM THE MAN SHE WAS HAVING AN AFFAIR WITH.
THEN THE MURDERER MAY HAVE TOMOKO'S CELL PHONE NOW!
BUT YOU FOUND THE PHONE, DIDN'T YOU? WHERE WAS IT?
ER...I DON'T KNOW. TOMOKO FOUND IT, AND SHE DIDN'T MENTION WHERE.
...
...
WELL, CONAN?
YOU'VE GOT PLENTY OF CLUES NOW.
YOU'RE GOING TO CALL JIMMY, AREN'T YOU?
GO AHEAD AND CALL!
THAT'S RIGHT... THE MOMENT YOU MAKE THE CALL, IT'LL BE ALL OVER.
I'M GOING TO GRAB THAT CELL PHONE FROM YOU...
...AND ...AND ...
...TALK TO HIM MYSELF!

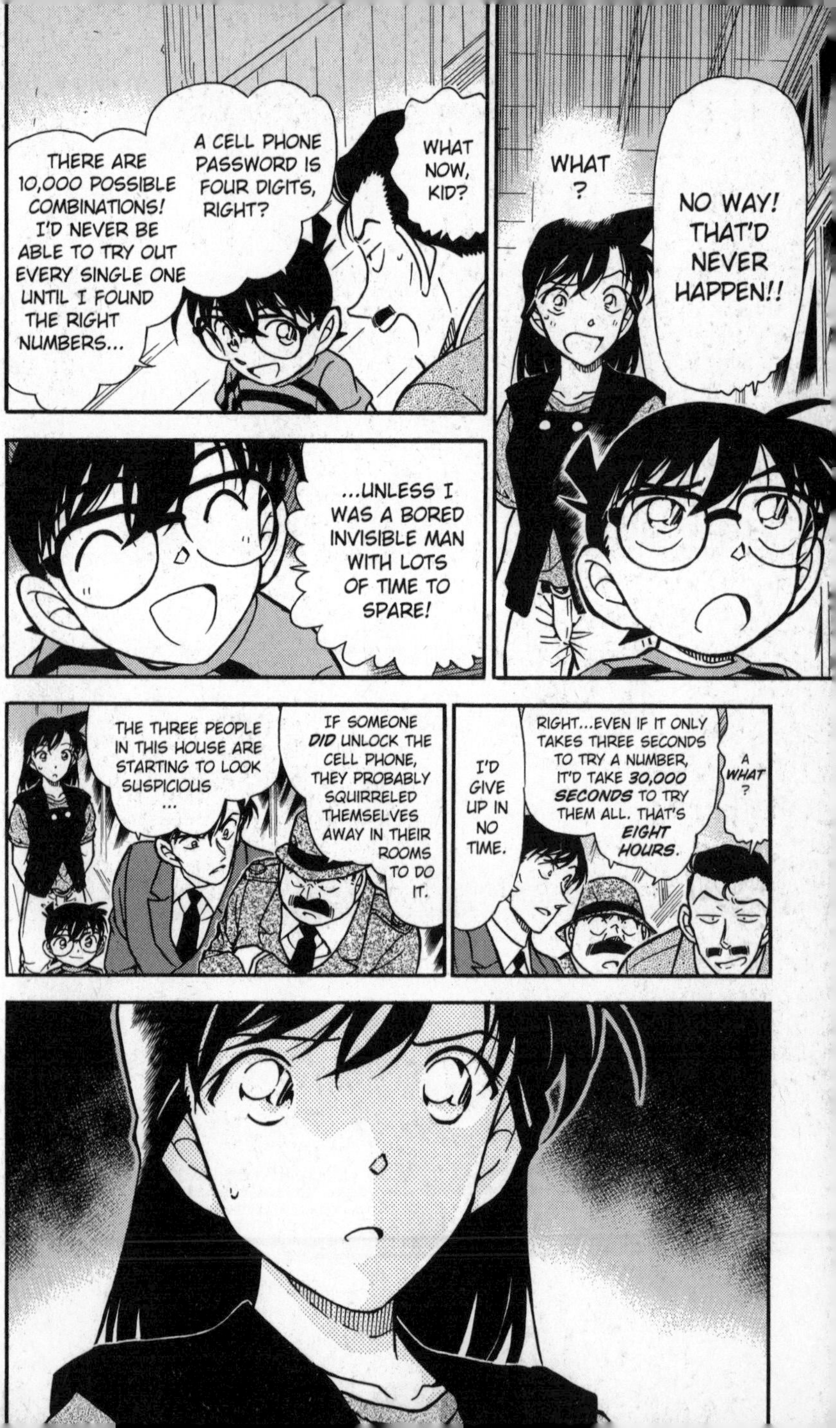
WHAT ?
NO WAY! THAT'D NEVER HAPPEN!!
WHAT NOW, KID?
A CELL PHONE PASSWORD IS FOUR DIGITS, RIGHT?
THERE ARE 10,000 POSSIBLE COMBINATIONS! I'D NEVER BE ABLE TO TRY OUT EVERY SINGLE ONE UNTIL I FOUND THE RIGHT NUMBERS...
...UNLESS I WAS A BORED INVISIBLE MAN WITH LOTS OF TIME TO SPARE!
A *WHAT* ?
RIGHT...EVEN IF IT ONLY TAKES THREE SECONDS TO TRY A NUMBER, IT'D TAKE **30,000 SECONDS** TO TRY THEM ALL. THAT'S ***EIGHT HOURS***.
I'D GIVE UP IN NO TIME.
IF SOMEONE ***DID*** UNLOCK THE CELL PHONE, THEY PROBABLY SQUIRRELED THEMSELVES AWAY IN THEIR ROOMS TO DO IT.
THE THREE PEOPLE IN THIS HOUSE ARE STARTING TO LOOK SUSPICIOUS ...

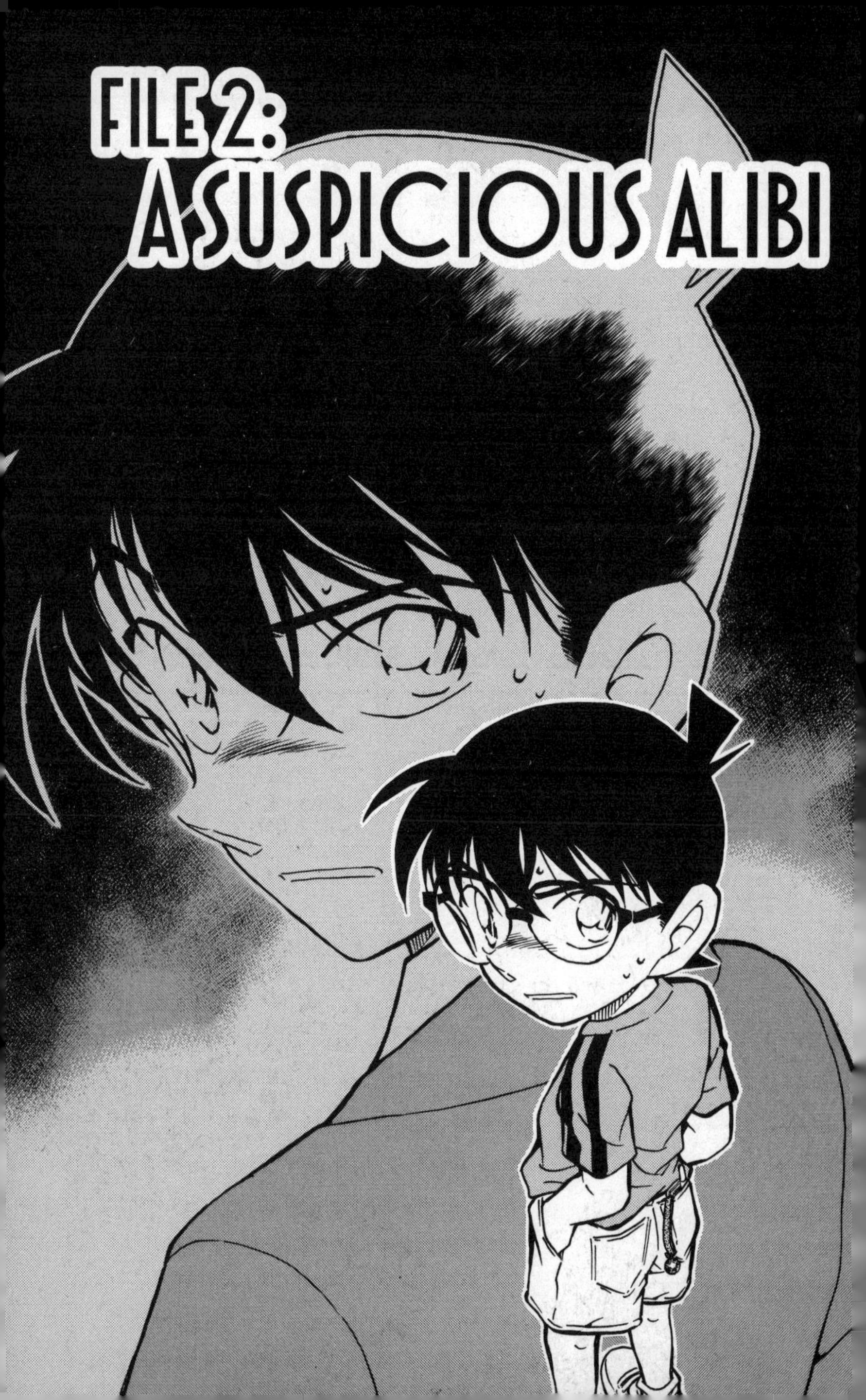
FILE 2:
A SUSPICIOUS ALIBI

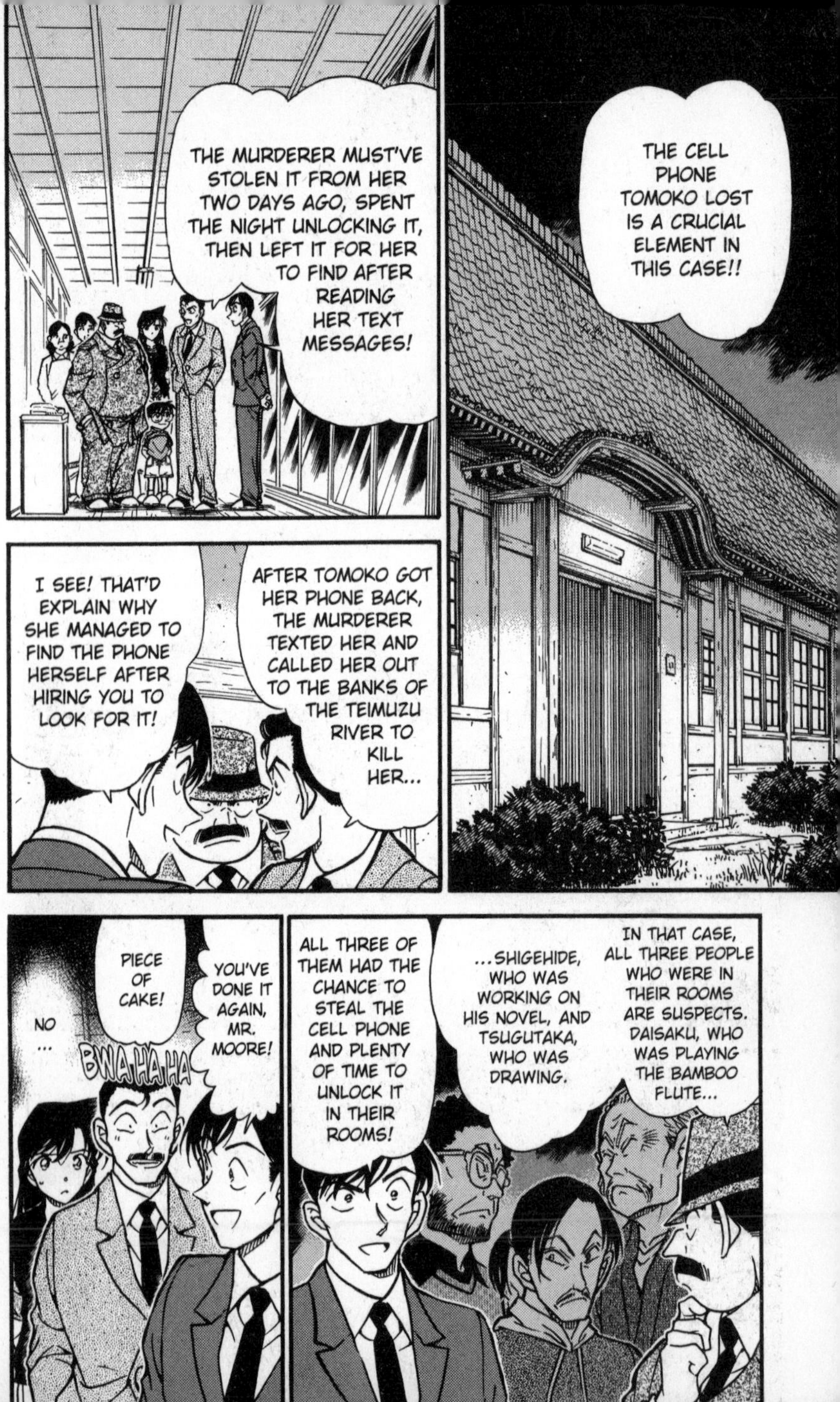
THE CELL PHONE TOMOKO LOST IS A CRUCIAL ELEMENT IN THIS CASE!!
THE MURDERER MUST'VE STOLEN IT FROM HER TWO DAYS AGO, SPENT THE NIGHT UNLOCKING IT, THEN LEFT IT FOR HER TO FIND AFTER READING HER TEXT MESSAGES!
AFTER TOMOKO GOT HER PHONE BACK, THE MURDERER TEXTED HER AND CALLED HER OUT TO THE BANKS OF THE TEIMUZU RIVER TO KILL HER...
I SEE! THAT'D EXPLAIN WHY SHE MANAGED TO FIND THE PHONE HERSELF AFTER HIRING YOU TO LOOK FOR IT!
IN THAT CASE, ALL THREE PEOPLE WHO WERE IN THEIR ROOMS ARE SUSPECTS. DAISAKU, WHO WAS PLAYING THE BAMBOO FLUTE...
...SHIGEHIDE, WHO WAS WORKING ON HIS NOVEL, AND TSUGUTAKA, WHO WAS DRAWING.
ALL THREE OF THEM HAD THE CHANCE TO STEAL THE CELL PHONE AND PLENTY OF TIME TO UNLOCK IT IN THEIR ROOMS!
YOU'VE DONE IT AGAIN, MR. MOORE!
PIECE OF CAKE!
BWAHAHA
NO ...

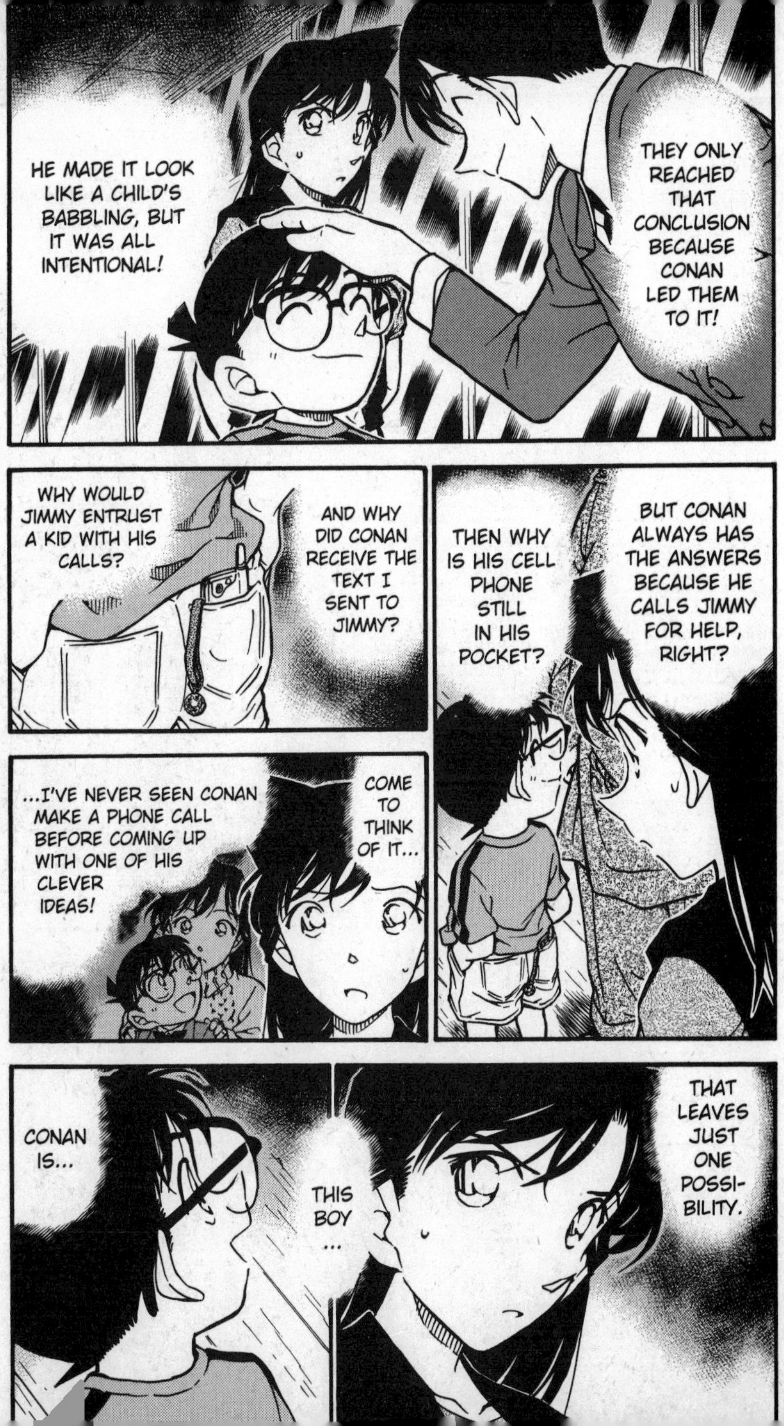
THEY ONLY REACHED THAT CONCLUSION BECAUSE CONAN LED THEM TO IT!
HE MADE IT LOOK LIKE A CHILD'S BABBLING, BUT IT WAS ALL INTENTIONAL!
BUT CONAN ALWAYS HAS THE ANSWERS BECAUSE HE CALLS JIMMY FOR HELP, RIGHT?
THEN WHY IS HIS CELL PHONE STILL IN HIS POCKET?
AND WHY DID CONAN RECEIVE THE TEXT I SENT TO JIMMY?
WHY WOULD JIMMY ENTRUST A KID WITH HIS CALLS?
COME TO THINK OF IT...
...I'VE NEVER SEEN CONAN MAKE A PHONE CALL BEFORE COMING UP WITH ONE OF HIS CLEVER IDEAS!
THAT LEAVES JUST ONE POSSIBILITY.
THIS BOY...
CONAN IS...

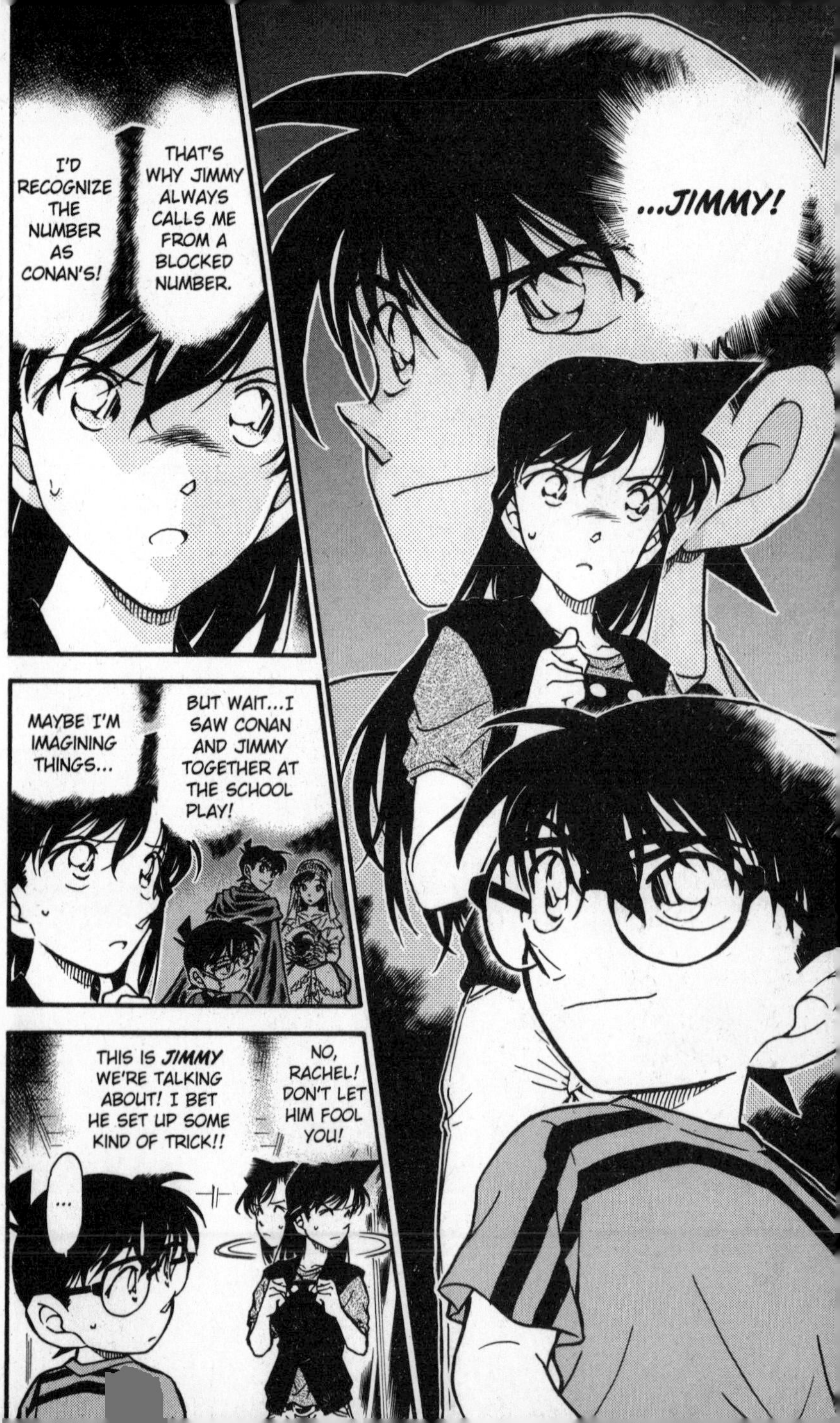
...JIMMY!
THAT'S WHY JIMMY ALWAYS CALLS ME FROM A BLOCKED NUMBER.
I'D RECOGNIZE THE NUMBER AS CONAN'S!
BUT WAIT...I SAW CONAN AND JIMMY TOGETHER AT THE SCHOOL PLAY!
MAYBE I'M IMAGINING THINGS...
NO, RACHEL! DON'T LET HIM FOOL YOU!
THIS IS *JIMMY* WE'RE TALKING ABOUT! I BET HE SET UP SOME KIND OF TRICK!!
...

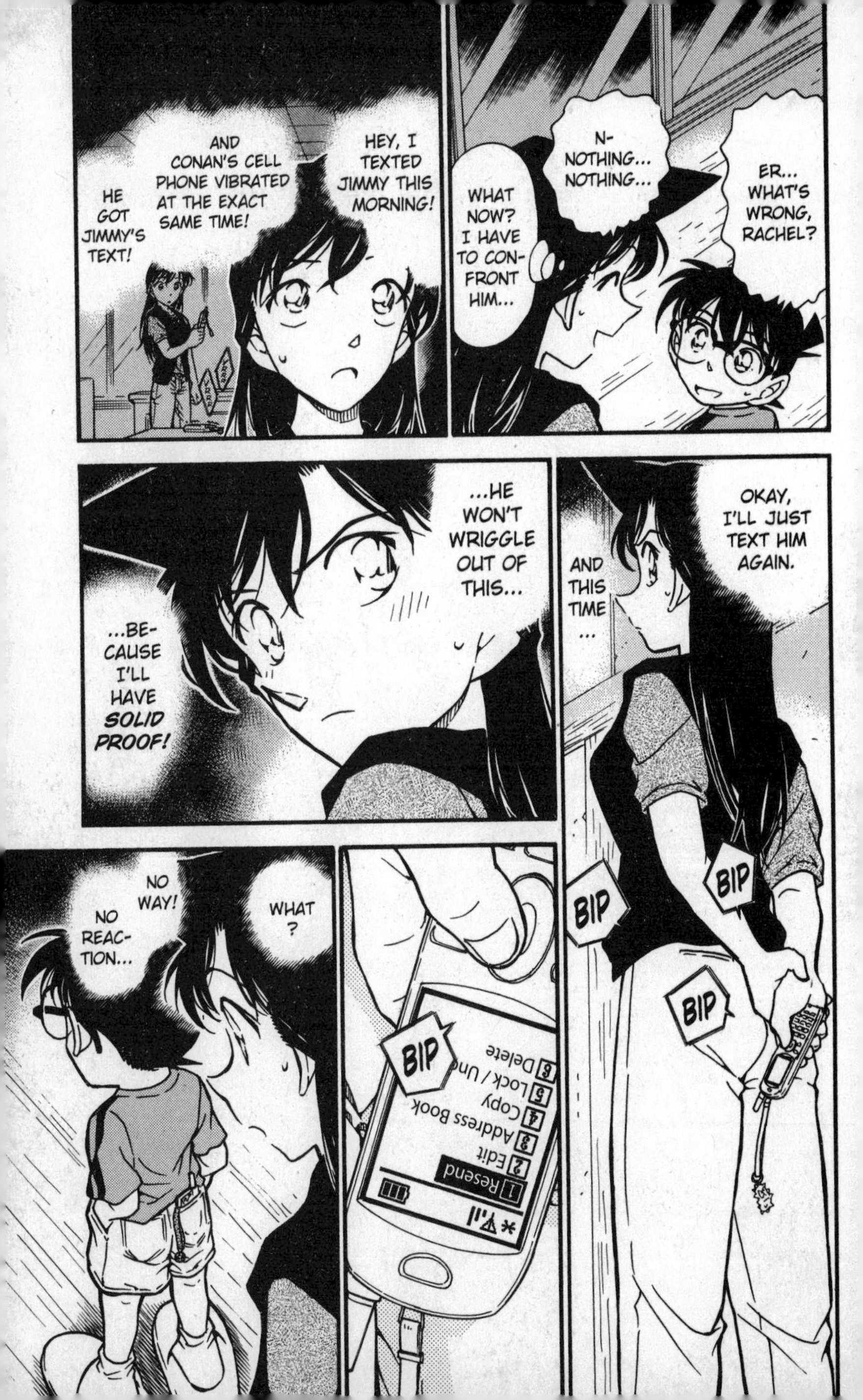

ER... WHAT'S WRONG, RACHEL?
N-NOTHING... NOTHING...
WHAT NOW? I HAVE TO CON-FRONT HIM...
HEY, I TEXTED JIMMY THIS MORNING!
AND CONAN'S CELL PHONE VIBRATED AT THE EXACT SAME TIME!
HE GOT JIMMY'S TEXT!
OKAY, I'LL JUST TEXT HIM AGAIN.
AND THIS TIME...
BIP
BIP
BIP
...HE WON'T WRIGGLE OUT OF THIS...
...BE-CAUSE I'LL HAVE SOLID PROOF!
BIP
1 Resend
2 Edit
3 Address Book
4 Copy
5 Lock / Un
6 Delete
WHAT?
NO WAY!
NO REAC-TION...

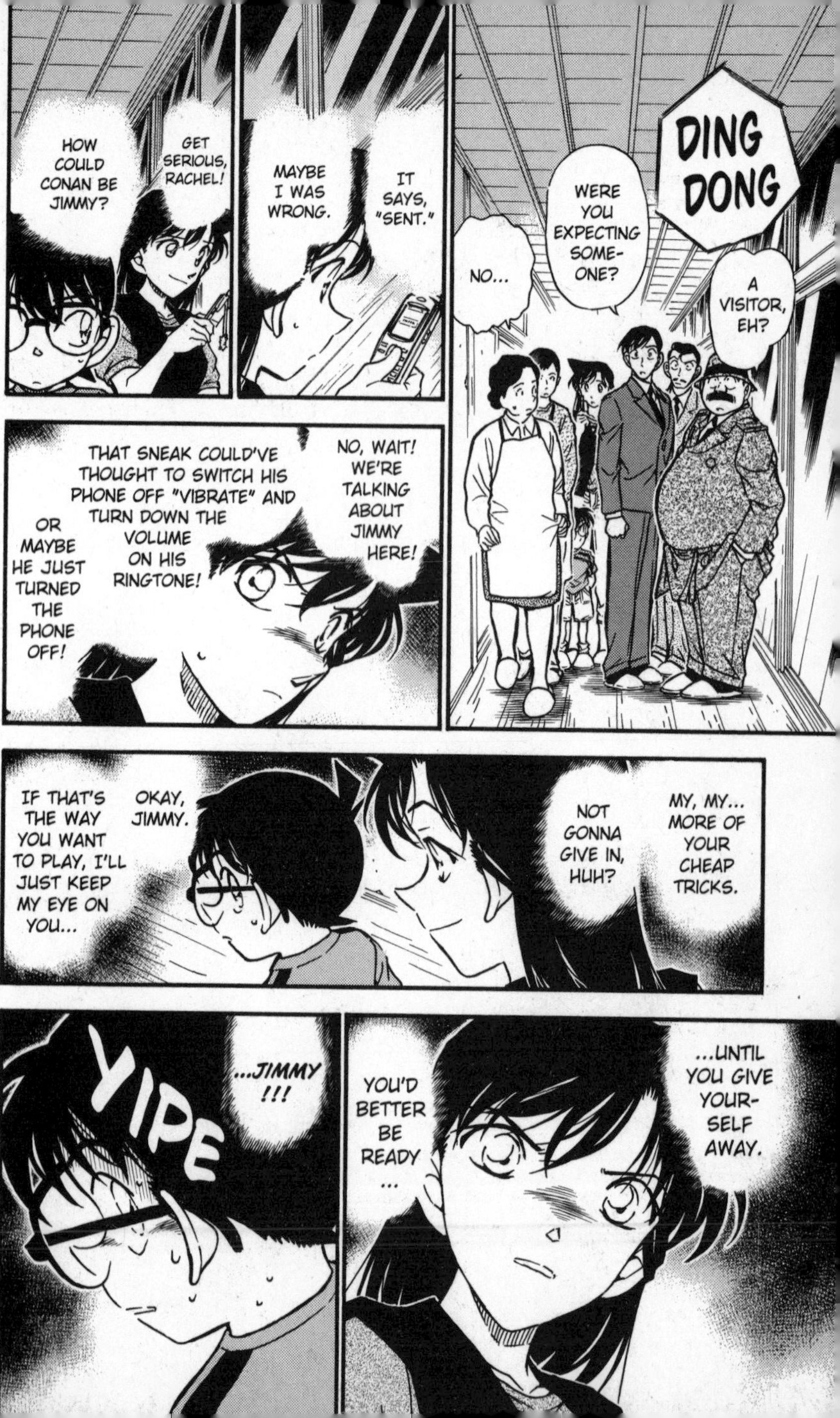
IT SAYS, "SENT."
MAYBE I WAS WRONG.
GET SERIOUS, RACHEL!
HOW COULD CONAN BE JIMMY?
NO, WAIT! WE'RE TALKING ABOUT JIMMY HERE!
THAT SNEAK COULD'VE THOUGHT TO SWITCH HIS PHONE OFF "VIBRATE" AND TURN DOWN THE VOLUME ON HIS RINGTONE!
OR MAYBE HE JUST TURNED THE PHONE OFF!
DING DONG
A VISITOR, EH?
WERE YOU EXPECTING SOME-ONE?
NO...
MY, MY... MORE OF YOUR CHEAP TRICKS.
NOT GONNA GIVE IN, HUH?
OKAY, JIMMY.
IF THAT'S THE WAY YOU WANT TO PLAY, I'LL JUST KEEP MY EYE ON YOU...
...UNTIL YOU GIVE YOUR-SELF AWAY.
YOU'D BETTER BE READY ...
...JIMMY !!!
YIPE

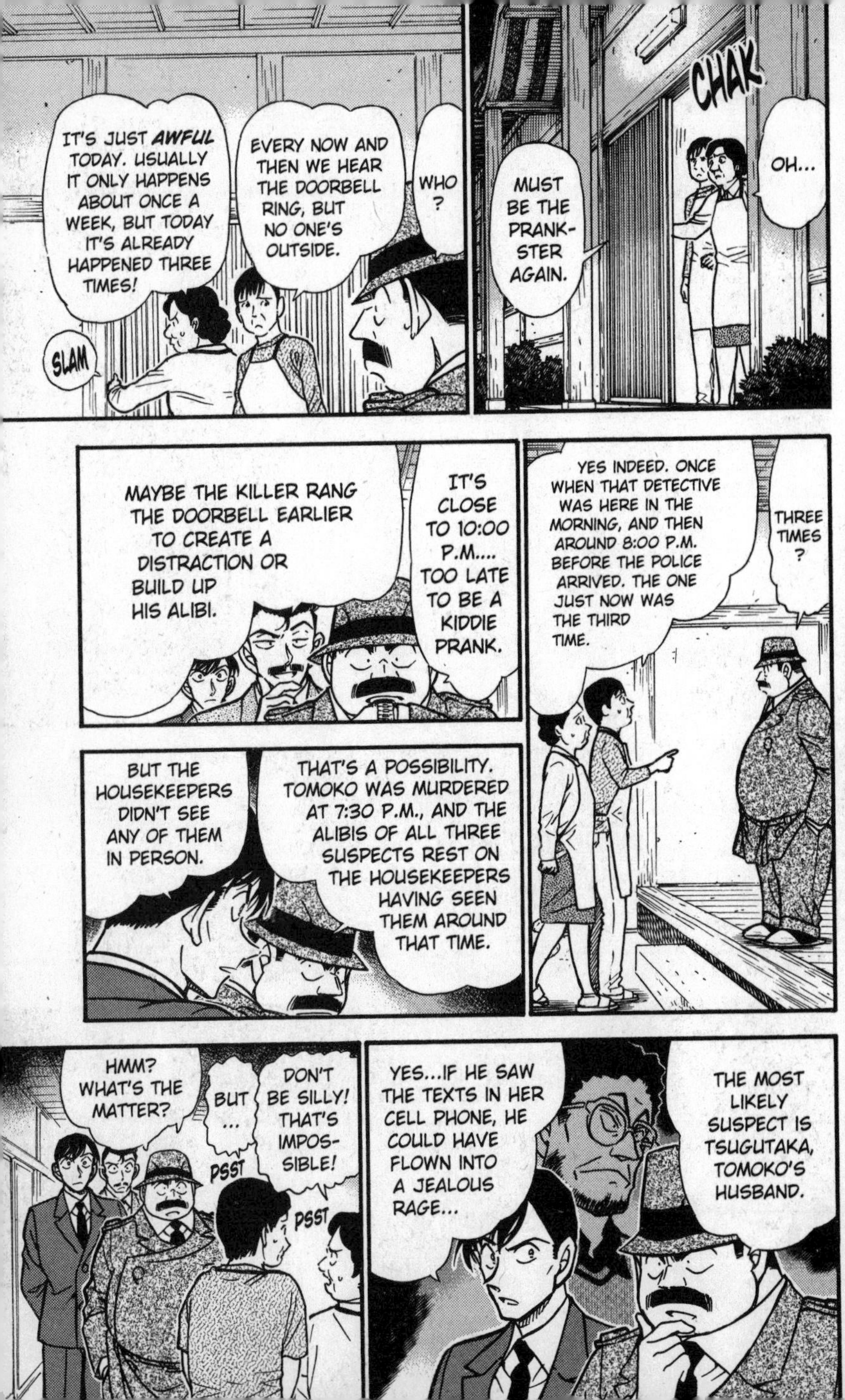
CHAK
OH...
MUST BE THE PRANK-STER AGAIN.
WHO?
EVERY NOW AND THEN WE HEAR THE DOORBELL RING, BUT NO ONE'S OUTSIDE.
IT'S JUST AWFUL TODAY. USUALLY IT ONLY HAPPENS ABOUT ONCE A WEEK, BUT TODAY IT'S ALREADY HAPPENED THREE TIMES!
SLAM
THREE TIMES?
YES INDEED. ONCE WHEN THAT DETECTIVE WAS HERE IN THE MORNING, AND THEN AROUND 8:00 P.M. BEFORE THE POLICE ARRIVED. THE ONE JUST NOW WAS THE THIRD TIME.
IT'S CLOSE TO 10:00 P.M.... TOO LATE TO BE A KIDDIE PRANK.
MAYBE THE KILLER RANG THE DOORBELL EARLIER TO CREATE A DISTRACTION OR BUILD UP HIS ALIBI.
THAT'S A POSSIBILITY. TOMOKO WAS MURDERED AT 7:30 P.M., AND THE ALIBIS OF ALL THREE SUSPECTS REST ON THE HOUSEKEEPERS HAVING SEEN THEM AROUND THAT TIME.
BUT THE HOUSEKEEPERS DIDN'T SEE ANY OF THEM IN PERSON.
THE MOST LIKELY SUSPECT IS TSUGUTAKA, TOMOKO'S HUSBAND.
YES...IF HE SAW THE TEXTS IN HER CELL PHONE, HE COULD HAVE FLOWN INTO A JEALOUS RAGE...
DON'T BE SILLY! THAT'S IMPOS-SIBLE!
BUT ...
PSST
PSST
HMM? WHAT'S THE MATTER?

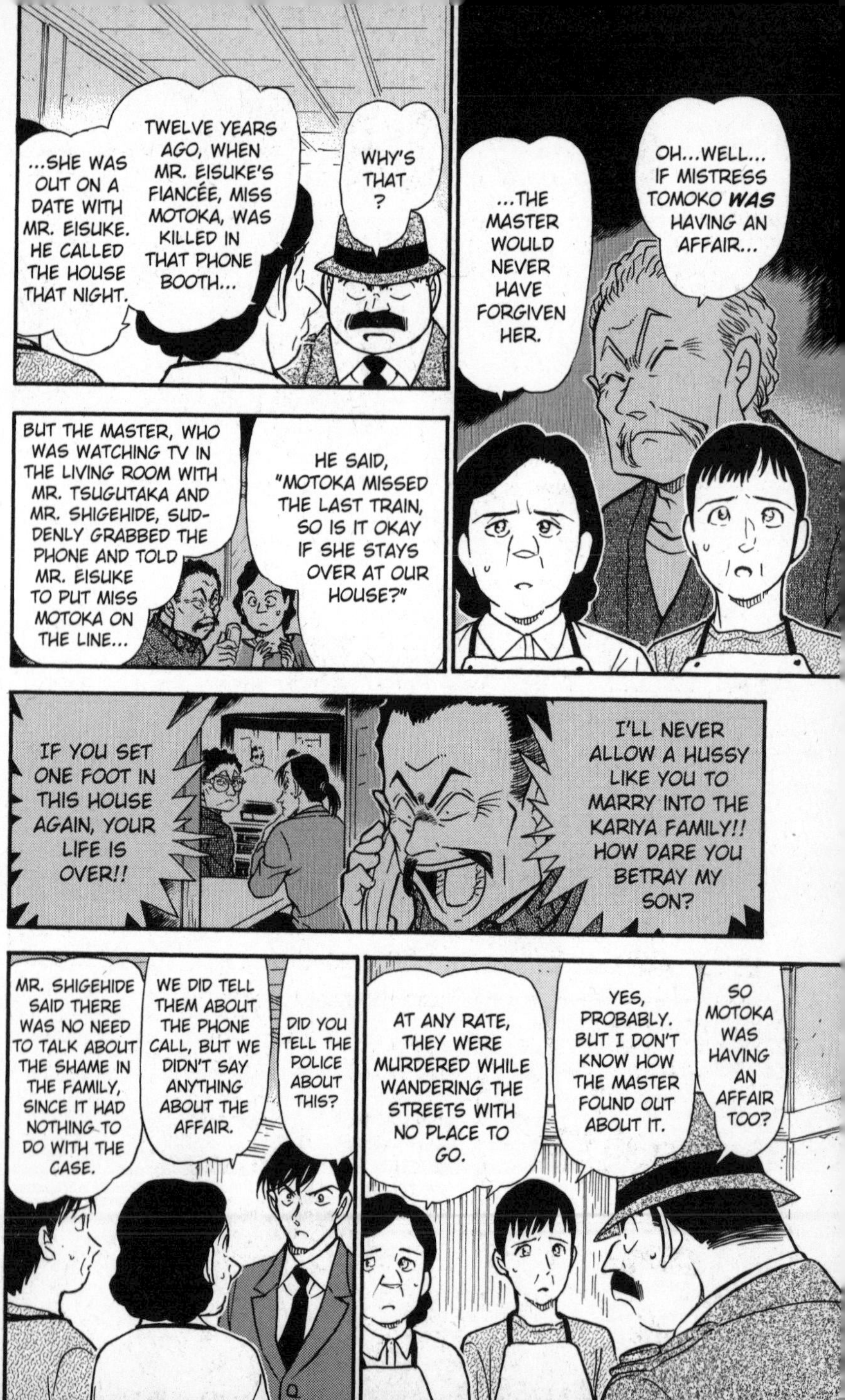
OH...WELL... IF MISTRESS TOMOKO **WAS** HAVING AN AFFAIR...
...THE MASTER WOULD NEVER HAVE FORGIVEN HER.
WHY'S THAT?
TWELVE YEARS AGO, WHEN MR. EISUKE'S FIANCÉE, MISS MOTOKA, WAS KILLED IN THAT PHONE BOOTH...
...SHE WAS OUT ON A DATE WITH MR. EISUKE. HE CALLED THE HOUSE THAT NIGHT.
HE SAID, "MOTOKA MISSED THE LAST TRAIN, SO IS IT OKAY IF SHE STAYS OVER AT OUR HOUSE?"
BUT THE MASTER, WHO WAS WATCHING TV IN THE LIVING ROOM WITH MR. TSUGUTAKA AND MR. SHIGEHIDE, SUDDENLY GRABBED THE PHONE AND TOLD MR. EISUKE TO PUT MISS MOTOKA ON THE LINE...
I'LL NEVER ALLOW A HUSSY LIKE YOU TO MARRY INTO THE KARIYA FAMILY!! HOW DARE YOU BETRAY MY SON?
IF YOU SET ONE FOOT IN THIS HOUSE AGAIN, YOUR LIFE IS OVER!!
SO MOTOKA WAS HAVING AN AFFAIR TOO?
YES, PROBABLY. BUT I DON'T KNOW HOW THE MASTER FOUND OUT ABOUT IT.
AT ANY RATE, THEY WERE MURDERED WHILE WANDERING THE STREETS WITH NO PLACE TO GO.
DID YOU TELL THE POLICE ABOUT THIS?
WE DID TELL THEM ABOUT THE PHONE CALL, BUT WE DIDN'T SAY ANYTHING ABOUT THE AFFAIR.
MR. SHIGEHIDE SAID THERE WAS NO NEED TO TALK ABOUT THE SHAME IN THE FAMILY, SINCE IT HAD NOTHING TO DO WITH THE CASE.

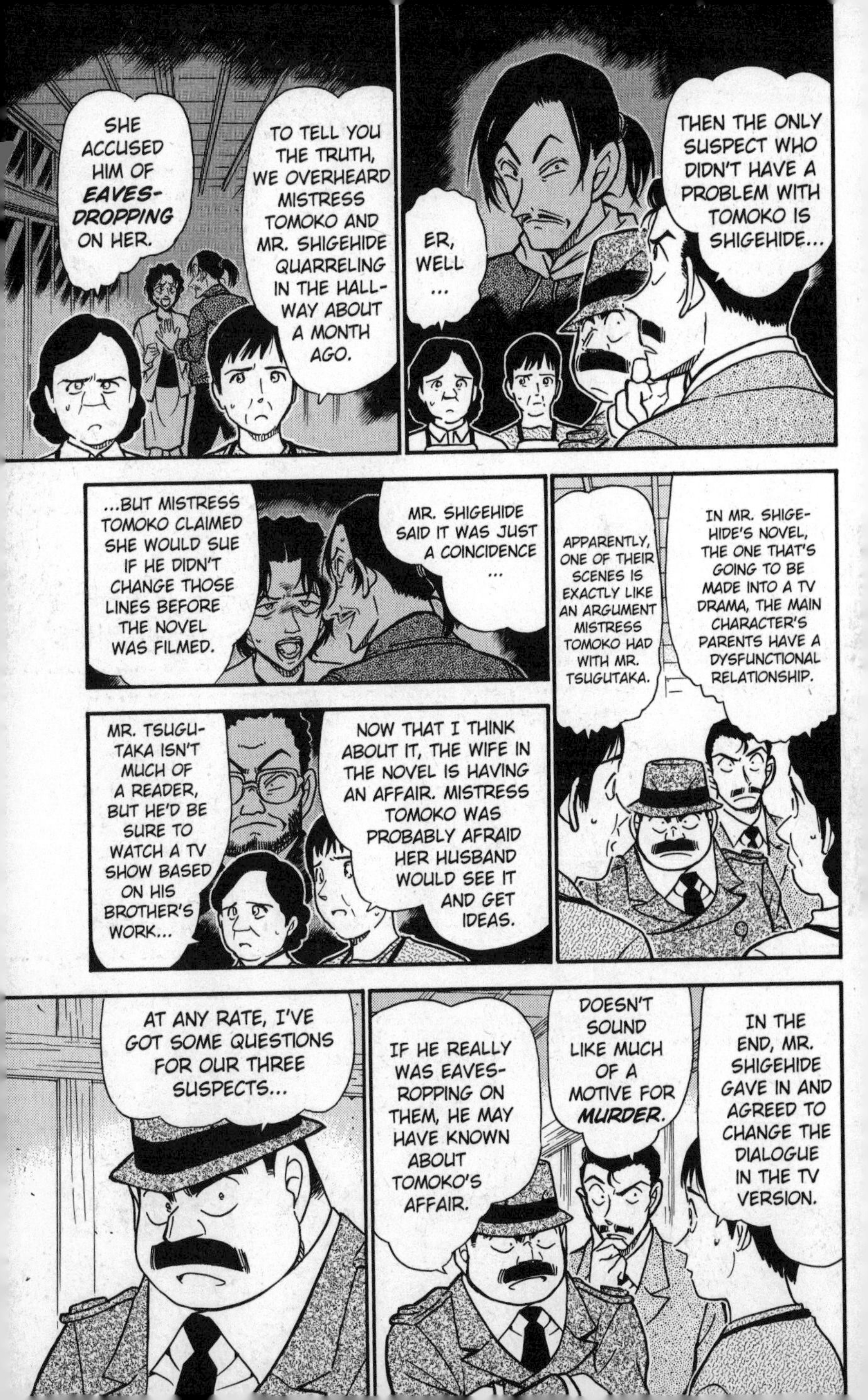
THEN THE ONLY SUSPECT WHO DIDN'T HAVE A PROBLEM WITH TOMOKO IS SHIGEHIDE...
ER, WELL ...
TO TELL YOU THE TRUTH, WE OVERHEARD MISTRESS TOMOKO AND MR. SHIGEHIDE QUARRELING IN THE HALLWAY ABOUT A MONTH AGO.
SHE ACCUSED HIM OF ***EAVES-DROPPING*** ON HER.
IN MR. SHIGEHIDE'S NOVEL, THE ONE THAT'S GOING TO BE MADE INTO A TV DRAMA, THE MAIN CHARACTER'S PARENTS HAVE A DYSFUNCTIONAL RELATIONSHIP.
APPARENTLY, ONE OF THEIR SCENES IS EXACTLY LIKE AN ARGUMENT MISTRESS TOMOKO HAD WITH MR. TSUGUTAKA.
MR. SHIGEHIDE SAID IT WAS JUST A COINCIDENCE ...
...BUT MISTRESS TOMOKO CLAIMED SHE WOULD SUE IF HE DIDN'T CHANGE THOSE LINES BEFORE THE NOVEL WAS FILMED.
NOW THAT I THINK ABOUT IT, THE WIFE IN THE NOVEL IS HAVING AN AFFAIR. MISTRESS TOMOKO WAS PROBABLY AFRAID HER HUSBAND WOULD SEE IT AND GET IDEAS.
MR. TSUGUTAKA ISN'T MUCH OF A READER, BUT HE'D BE SURE TO WATCH A TV SHOW BASED ON HIS BROTHER'S WORK...
IN THE END, MR. SHIGEHIDE GAVE IN AND AGREED TO CHANGE THE DIALOGUE IN THE TV VERSION.
DOESN'T SOUND LIKE MUCH OF A MOTIVE FOR ***MURDER***.
IF HE REALLY WAS EAVES-ROPPING ON THEM, HE MAY HAVE KNOWN ABOUT TOMOKO'S AFFAIR.
AT ANY RATE, I'VE GOT SOME QUESTIONS FOR OUR THREE SUSPECTS...

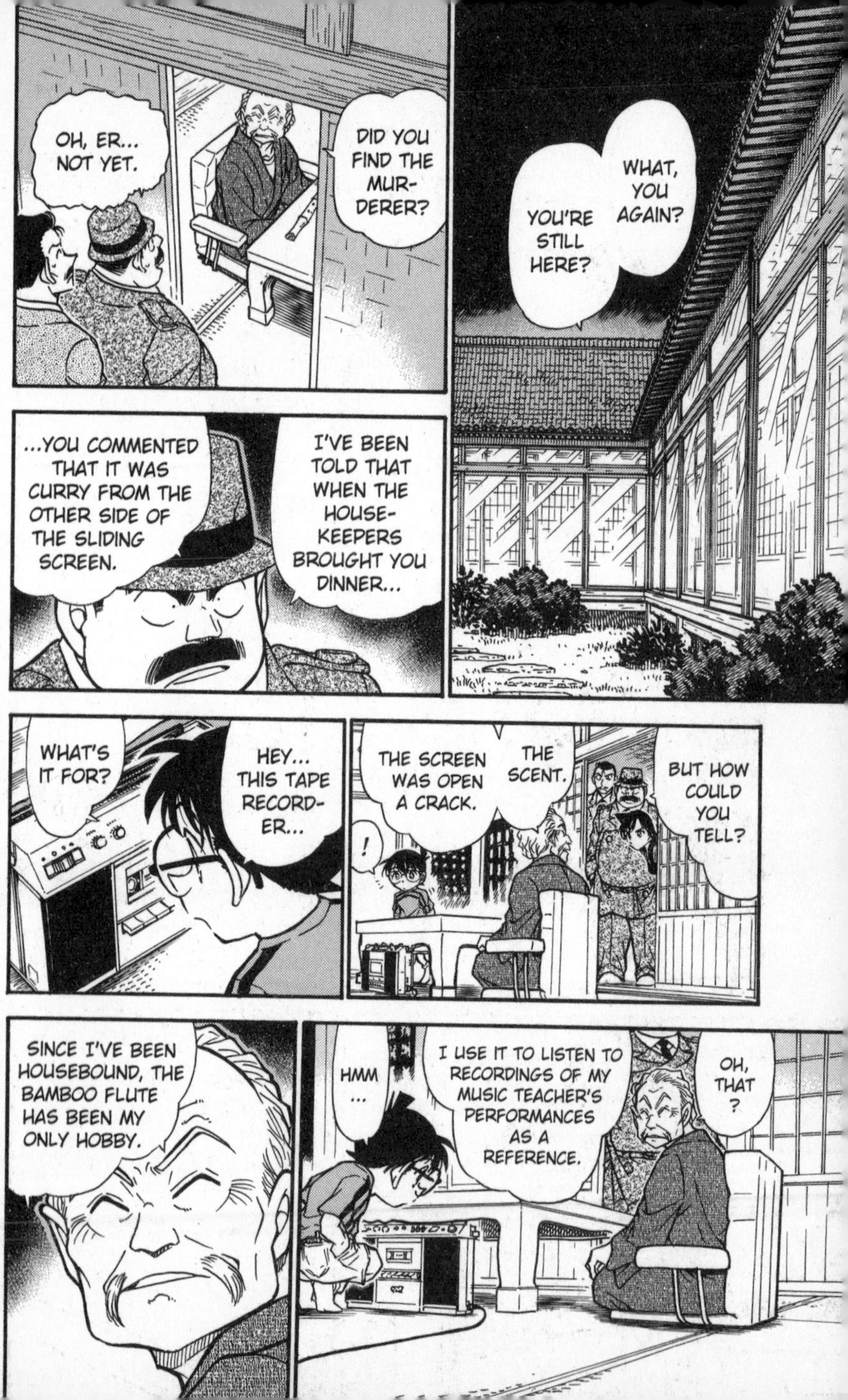
WHAT, YOU AGAIN?
YOU'RE STILL HERE?
DID YOU FIND THE MUR-DERER?
OH, ER... NOT YET.
I'VE BEEN TOLD THAT WHEN THE HOUSE-KEEPERS BROUGHT YOU DINNER...
...YOU COMMENTED THAT IT WAS CURRY FROM THE OTHER SIDE OF THE SLIDING SCREEN.
BUT HOW COULD YOU TELL?
THE SCENT.
THE SCREEN WAS OPEN A CRACK.
!
HEY... THIS TAPE RECORD-ER...
WHAT'S IT FOR?
OH, THAT?
I USE IT TO LISTEN TO RECORDINGS OF MY MUSIC TEACHER'S PERFORMANCES AS A REFERENCE.
HMM ...
SINCE I'VE BEEN HOUSEBOUND, THE BAMBOO FLUTE HAS BEEN MY ONLY HOBBY.

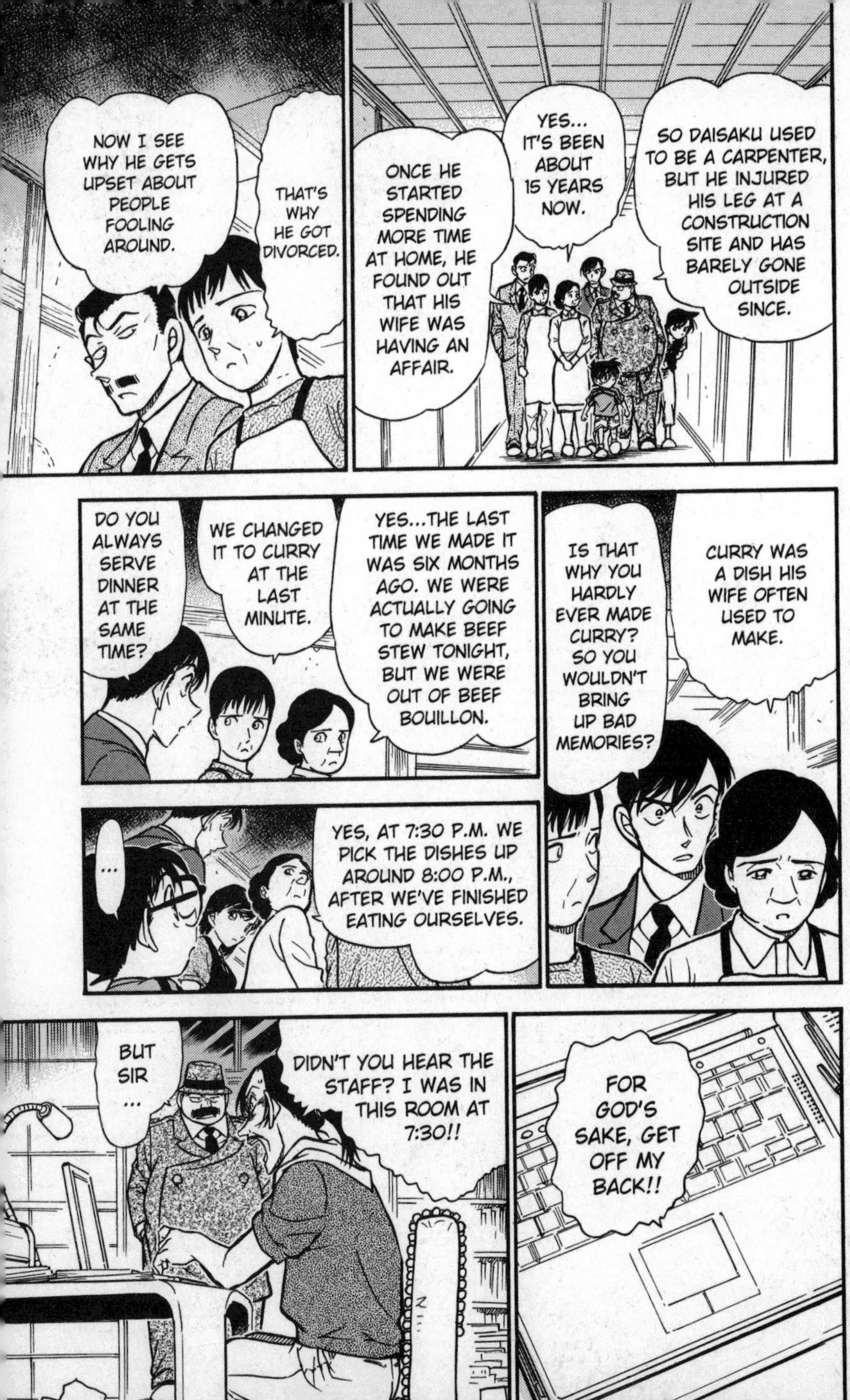
SO DAISAKU USED TO BE A CARPENTER, BUT HE INJURED HIS LEG AT A CONSTRUCTION SITE AND HAS BARELY GONE OUTSIDE SINCE.
YES... IT'S BEEN ABOUT 15 YEARS NOW.
ONCE HE STARTED SPENDING MORE TIME AT HOME, HE FOUND OUT THAT HIS WIFE WAS HAVING AN AFFAIR.
THAT'S WHY HE GOT DIVORCED.
NOW I SEE WHY HE GETS UPSET ABOUT PEOPLE FOOLING AROUND.
CURRY WAS A DISH HIS WIFE OFTEN USED TO MAKE.
IS THAT WHY YOU HARDLY EVER MADE CURRY? SO YOU WOULDN'T BRING UP BAD MEMORIES?
YES...THE LAST TIME WE MADE IT WAS SIX MONTHS AGO. WE WERE ACTUALLY GOING TO MAKE BEEF STEW TONIGHT, BUT WE WERE OUT OF BEEF BOUILLON.
WE CHANGED IT TO CURRY AT THE LAST MINUTE.
DO YOU ALWAYS SERVE DINNER AT THE SAME TIME?
YES, AT 7:30 P.M. WE PICK THE DISHES UP AROUND 8:00 P.M., AFTER WE'VE FINISHED EATING OURSELVES.
...
FOR GOD'S SAKE, GET OFF MY BACK!!
DIDN'T YOU HEAR THE STAFF? I WAS IN THIS ROOM AT 7:30!!
BUT SIR ...

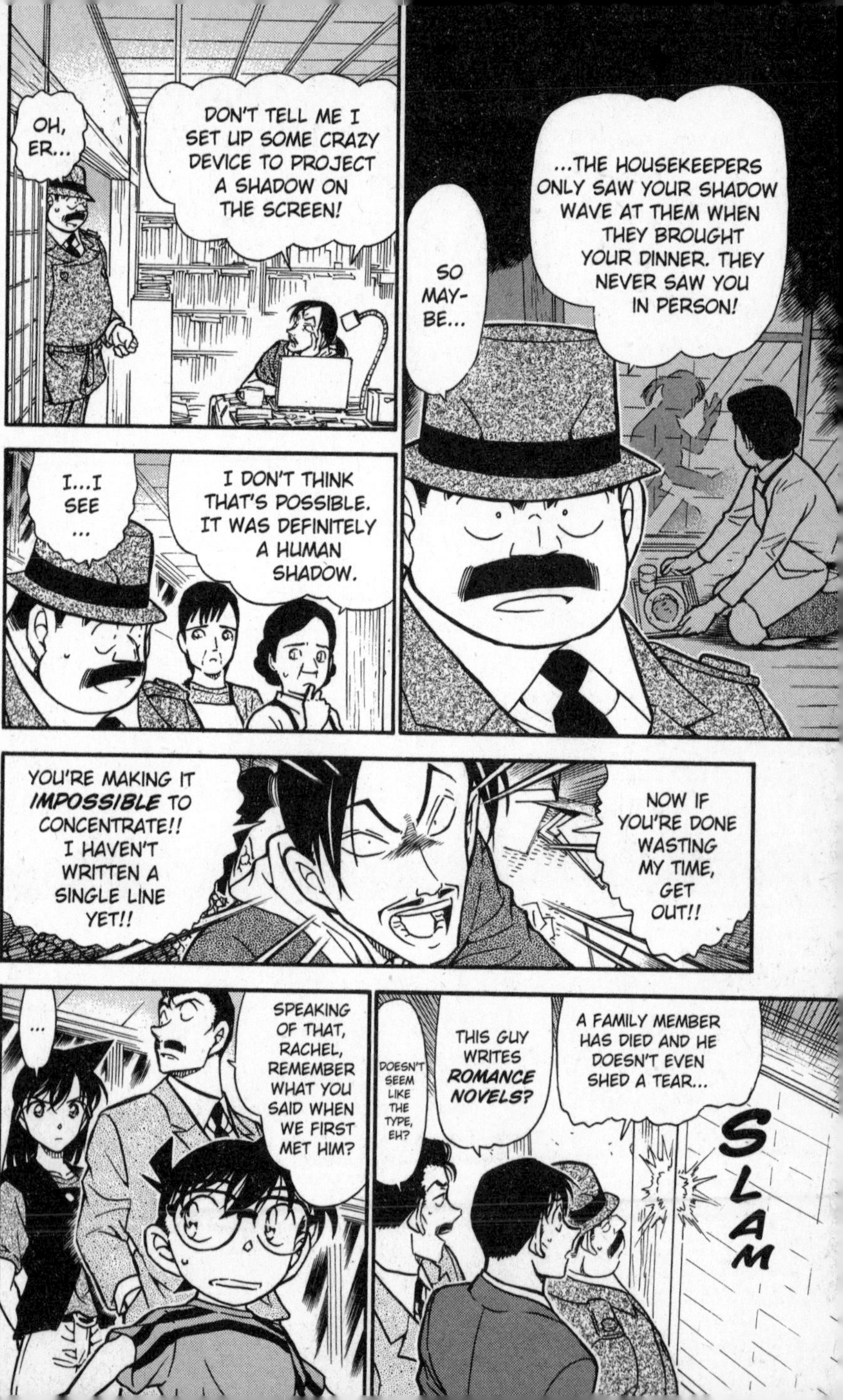
SO MAY-BE...
...THE HOUSEKEEPERS ONLY SAW YOUR SHADOW WAVE AT THEM WHEN THEY BROUGHT YOUR DINNER. THEY NEVER SAW YOU IN PERSON!
DON'T TELL ME I SET UP SOME CRAZY DEVICE TO PROJECT A SHADOW ON THE SCREEN!
OH, ER...
I DON'T THINK THAT'S POSSIBLE. IT WAS DEFINITELY A HUMAN SHADOW.
I...I SEE ...
NOW IF YOU'RE DONE WASTING MY TIME, GET OUT!!
YOU'RE MAKING IT *IMPOSSIBLE* TO CONCENTRATE!! I HAVEN'T WRITTEN A SINGLE LINE YET!!
SLAM
A FAMILY MEMBER HAS DIED AND HE DOESN'T EVEN SHED A TEAR...
THIS GUY WRITES *ROMANCE NOVELS*?
DOESN'T SEEM LIKE THE TYPE, EH?
SPEAKING OF THAT, RACHEL, REMEMBER WHAT YOU SAID WHEN WE FIRST MET HIM?
...

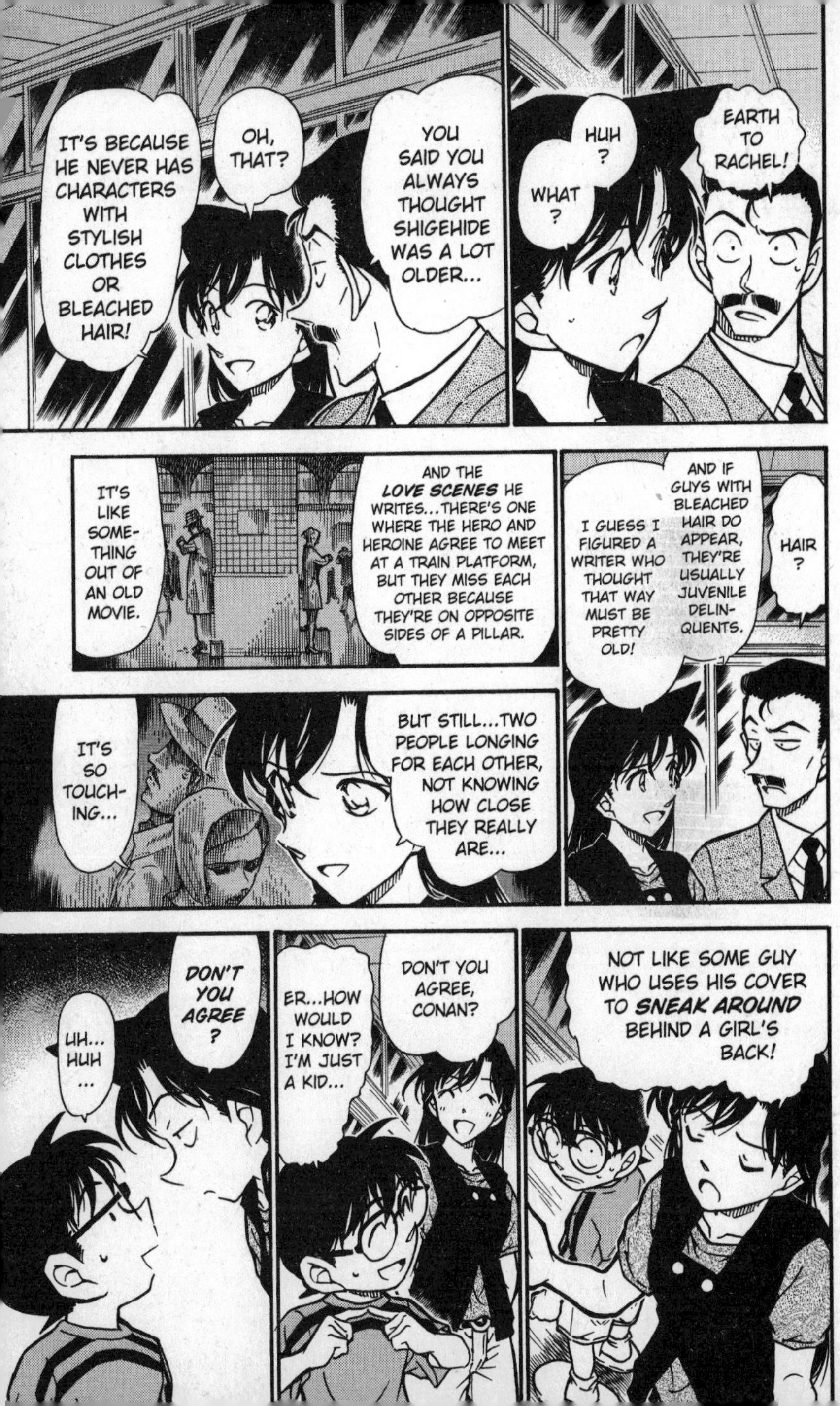
EARTH TO RACHEL!
HUH?
WHAT?
YOU SAID YOU ALWAYS THOUGHT SHIGEHIDE WAS A LOT OLDER...
OH, THAT?
IT'S BECAUSE HE NEVER HAS CHARACTERS WITH STYLISH CLOTHES OR BLEACHED HAIR!
HAIR?
AND IF GUYS WITH BLEACHED HAIR DO APPEAR, THEY'RE USUALLY JUVENILE DELINQUENTS.
I GUESS I FIGURED A WRITER WHO THOUGHT THAT WAY MUST BE PRETTY OLD!
AND THE LOVE SCENES HE WRITES...THERE'S ONE WHERE THE HERO AND HEROINE AGREE TO MEET AT A TRAIN PLATFORM, BUT THEY MISS EACH OTHER BECAUSE THEY'RE ON OPPOSITE SIDES OF A PILLAR.
IT'S LIKE SOMETHING OUT OF AN OLD MOVIE.
BUT STILL...TWO PEOPLE LONGING FOR EACH OTHER, NOT KNOWING HOW CLOSE THEY REALLY ARE...
IT'S SO TOUCHING...
NOT LIKE SOME GUY WHO USES HIS COVER TO SNEAK AROUND BEHIND A GIRL'S BACK!
DON'T YOU AGREE, CONAN?
ER...HOW WOULD I KNOW? I'M JUST A KID...
DON'T YOU AGREE?
UH...HUH...

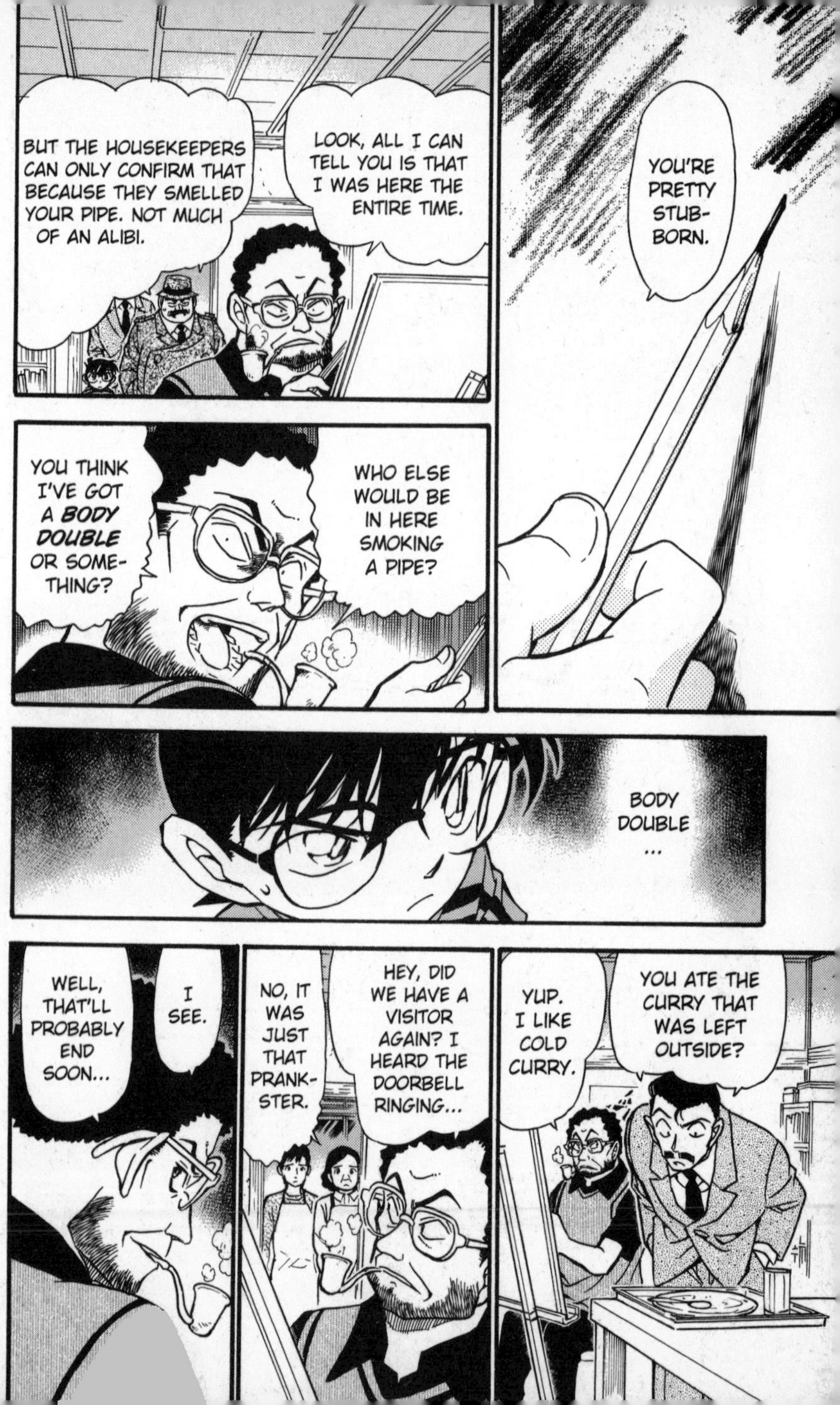
LOOK, ALL I CAN TELL YOU IS THAT I WAS HERE THE ENTIRE TIME.
BUT THE HOUSEKEEPERS CAN ONLY CONFIRM THAT BECAUSE THEY SMELLED YOUR PIPE. NOT MUCH OF AN ALIBI.
YOU'RE PRETTY STUB-BORN.
WHO ELSE WOULD BE IN HERE SMOKING A PIPE?
YOU THINK I'VE GOT A *BODY DOUBLE* OR SOME-THING?
BODY DOUBLE ...
YOU ATE THE CURRY THAT WAS LEFT OUTSIDE?
YUP. I LIKE COLD CURRY.
HEY, DID WE HAVE A VISITOR AGAIN? I HEARD THE DOORBELL RINGING...
NO, IT WAS JUST THAT PRANK-STER.
I SEE.
WELL, THAT'LL PROBABLY END SOON...

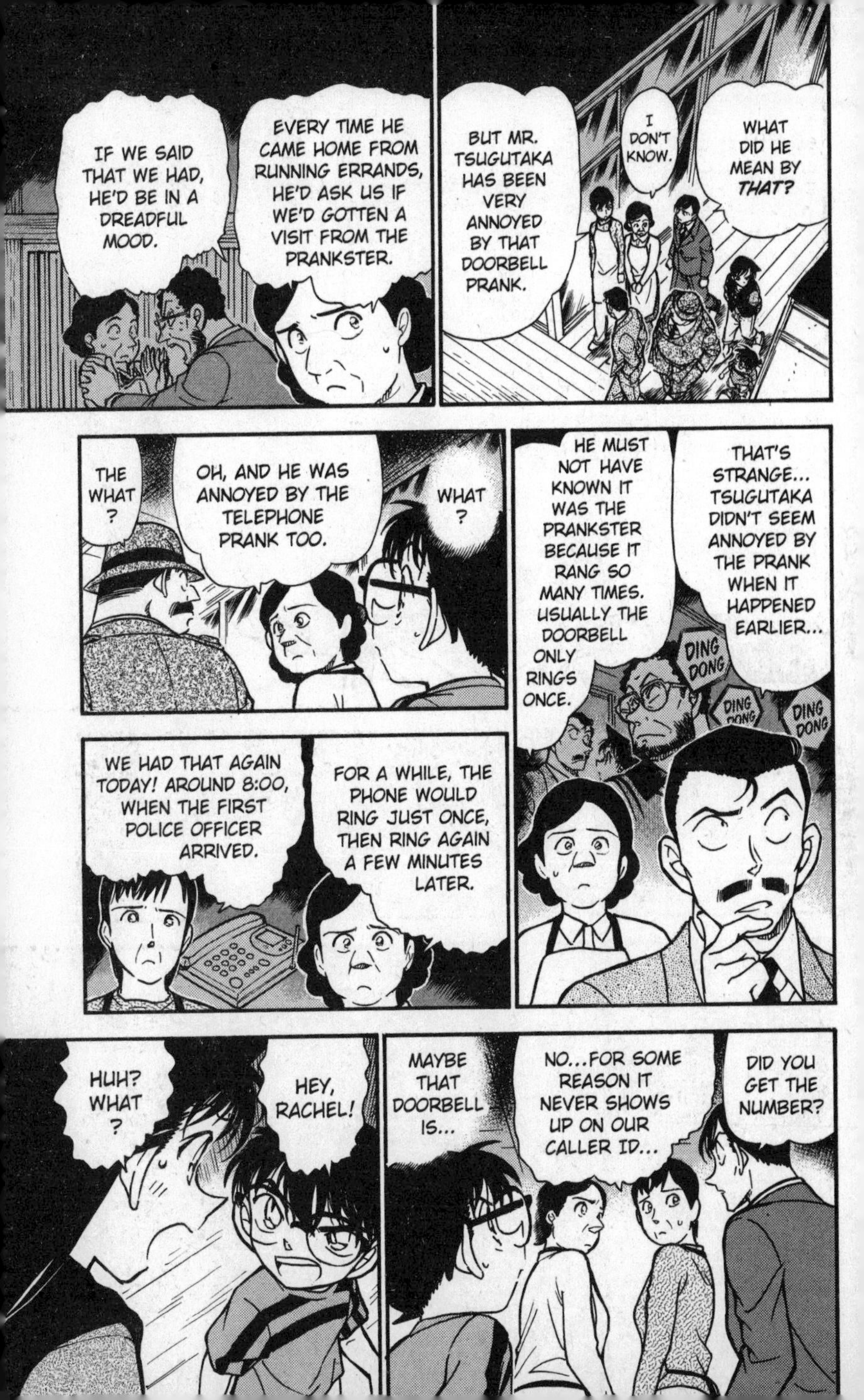
WHAT DID HE MEAN BY *THAT?*
I DON'T KNOW.
BUT MR. TSUGUTAKA HAS BEEN VERY ANNOYED BY THAT DOORBELL PRANK.
EVERY TIME HE CAME HOME FROM RUNNING ERRANDS, HE'D ASK US IF WE'D GOTTEN A VISIT FROM THE PRANKSTER.
IF WE SAID THAT WE HAD, HE'D BE IN A DREADFUL MOOD.
THAT'S STRANGE... TSUGUTAKA DIDN'T SEEM ANNOYED BY THE PRANK WHEN IT HAPPENED EARLIER...
HE MUST NOT HAVE KNOWN IT WAS THE PRANKSTER BECAUSE IT RANG SO MANY TIMES. USUALLY THE DOORBELL ONLY RINGS ONCE.
DING DONG
DING DONG
DING DONG
WHAT?
OH, AND HE WAS ANNOYED BY THE TELEPHONE PRANK TOO.
THE WHAT?
FOR A WHILE, THE PHONE WOULD RING JUST ONCE, THEN RING AGAIN A FEW MINUTES LATER.
WE HAD THAT AGAIN TODAY! AROUND 8:00, WHEN THE FIRST POLICE OFFICER ARRIVED.
DID YOU GET THE NUMBER?
NO...FOR SOME REASON IT NEVER SHOWS UP ON OUR CALLER ID...
MAYBE THAT DOORBELL IS...
HEY, RACHEL!
HUH? WHAT?

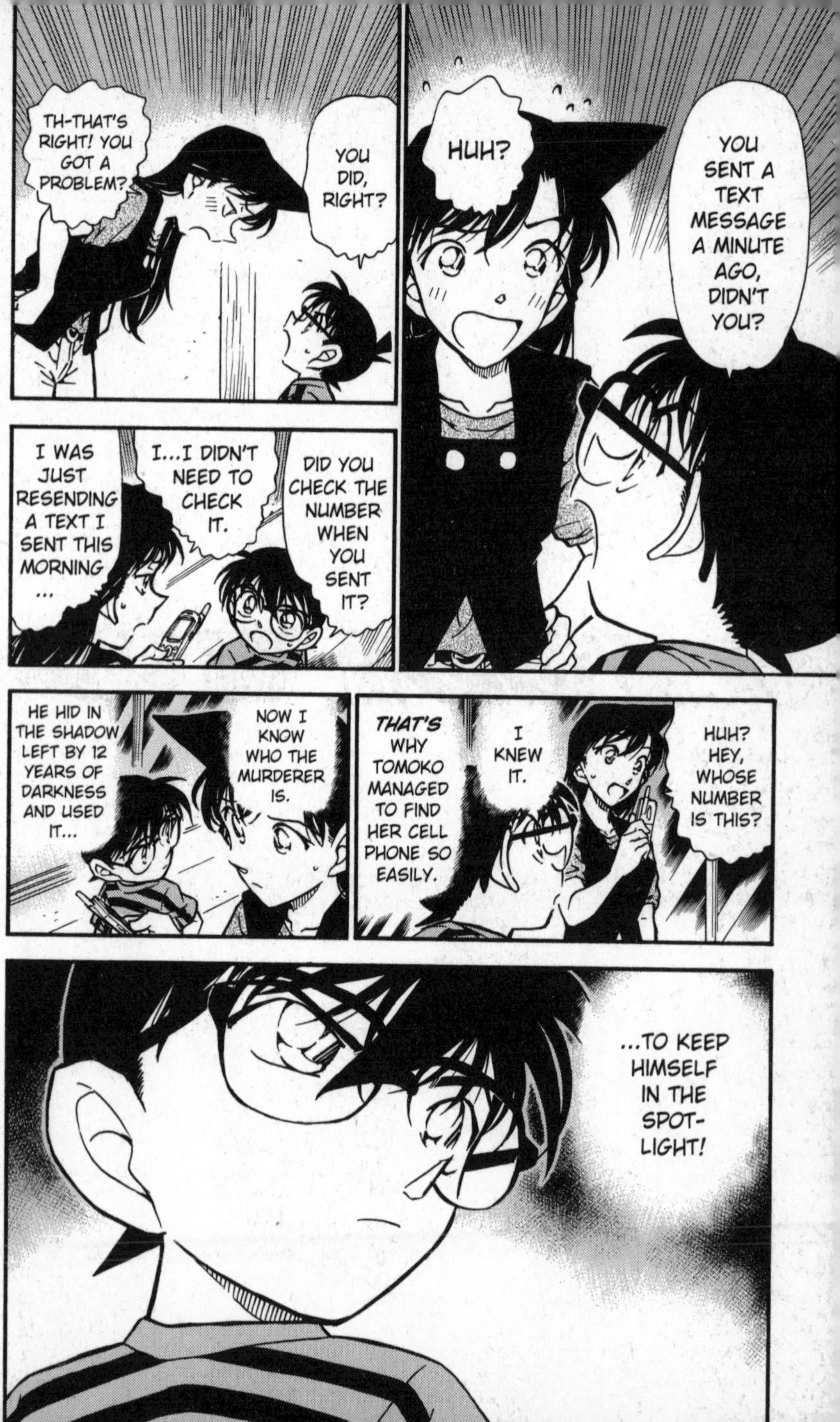
YOU SENT A TEXT MESSAGE A MINUTE AGO, DIDN'T YOU?
HUH?
YOU DID, RIGHT?
TH-THAT'S RIGHT! YOU GOT A PROBLEM?
DID YOU CHECK THE NUMBER WHEN YOU SENT IT?
I...I DIDN'T NEED TO CHECK IT.
I WAS JUST RESENDING A TEXT I SENT THIS MORNING...
HUH? HEY, WHOSE NUMBER IS THIS?
I KNEW IT.
THAT'S WHY TOMOKO MANAGED TO FIND HER CELL PHONE SO EASILY.
NOW I KNOW WHO THE MURDERER IS.
HE HID IN THE SHADOW LEFT BY 12 YEARS OF DARKNESS AND USED IT...
...TO KEEP HIMSELF IN THE SPOTLIGHT!

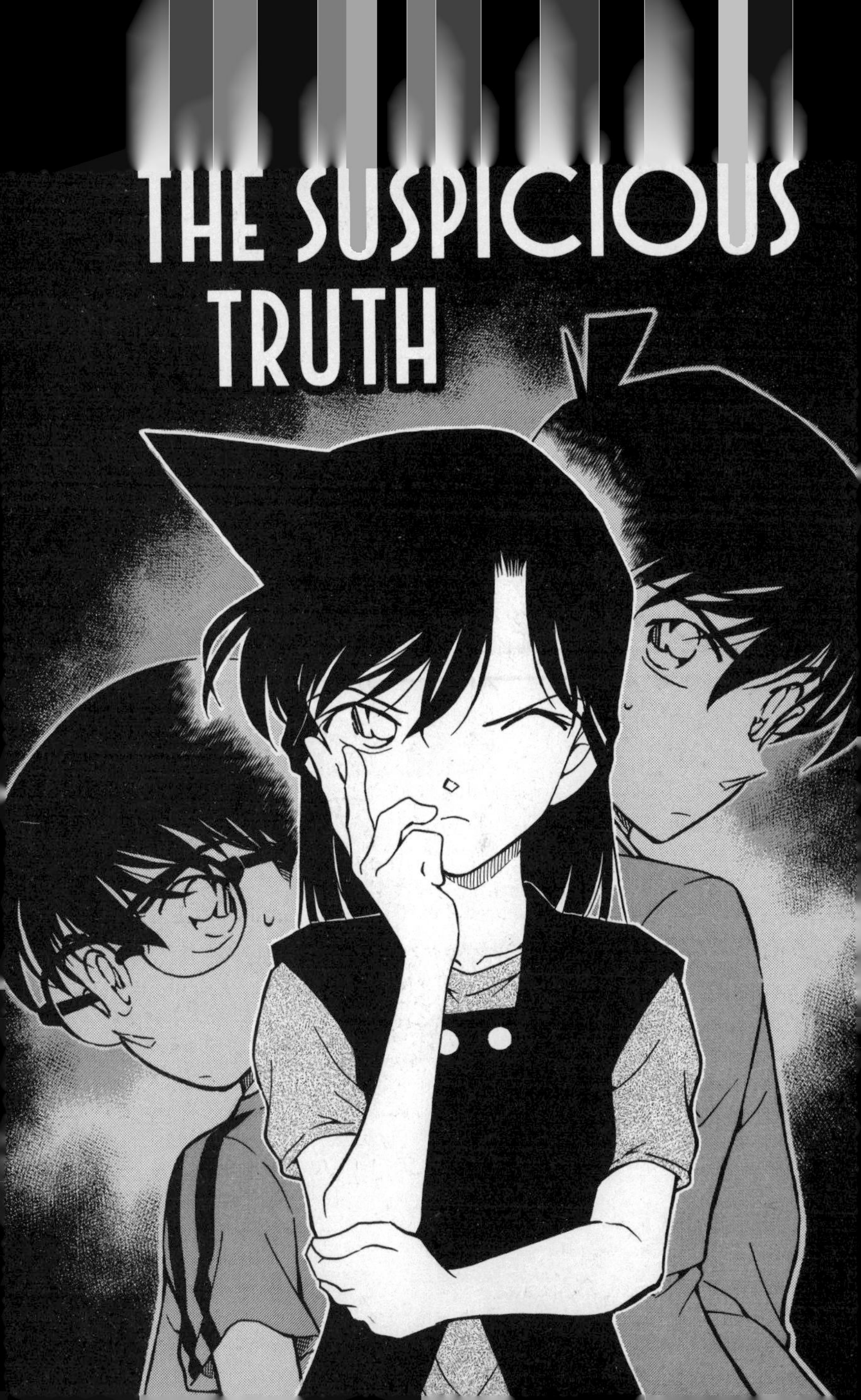
THE SUSPICIOUS TRUTH

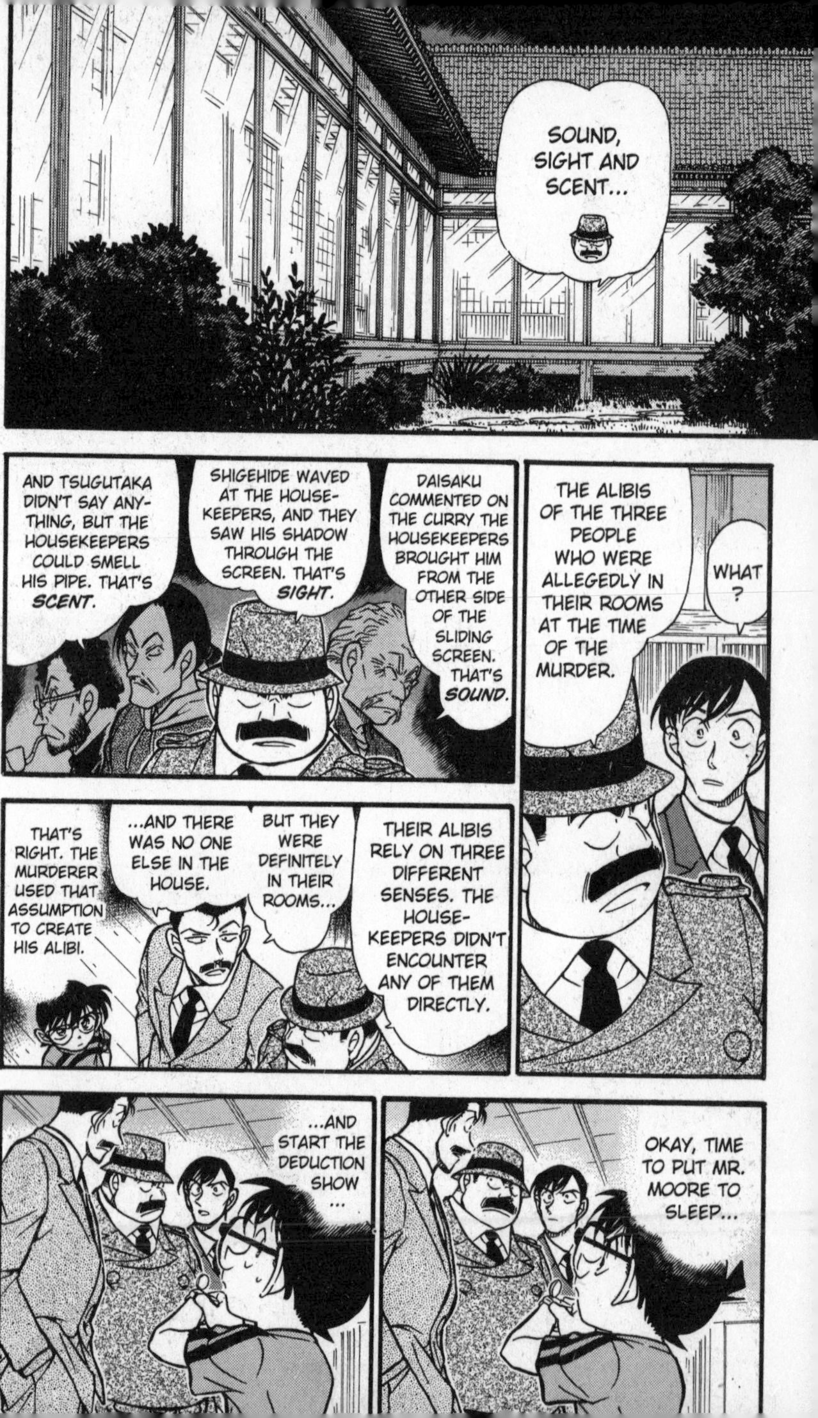
SOUND, SIGHT AND SCENT...
THE ALIBIS OF THE THREE PEOPLE WHO WERE ALLEGEDLY IN THEIR ROOMS AT THE TIME OF THE MURDER.
WHAT?
DAISAKU COMMENTED ON THE CURRY THE HOUSEKEEPERS BROUGHT HIM FROM THE OTHER SIDE OF THE SLIDING SCREEN. THAT'S *SOUND*.
SHIGEHIDE WAVED AT THE HOUSE-KEEPERS, AND THEY SAW HIS SHADOW THROUGH THE SCREEN. THAT'S *SIGHT*.
AND TSUGUTAKA DIDN'T SAY ANY-THING, BUT THE HOUSEKEEPERS COULD SMELL HIS PIPE. THAT'S *SCENT*.
THEIR ALIBIS RELY ON THREE DIFFERENT SENSES. THE HOUSE-KEEPERS DIDN'T ENCOUNTER ANY OF THEM DIRECTLY.
BUT THEY WERE DEFINITELY IN THEIR ROOMS...
...AND THERE WAS NO ONE ELSE IN THE HOUSE.
THAT'S RIGHT. THE MURDERER USED THAT ASSUMPTION TO CREATE HIS ALIBI.
OKAY, TIME TO PUT MR. MOORE TO SLEEP...
...AND START THE DEDUCTION SHOW...

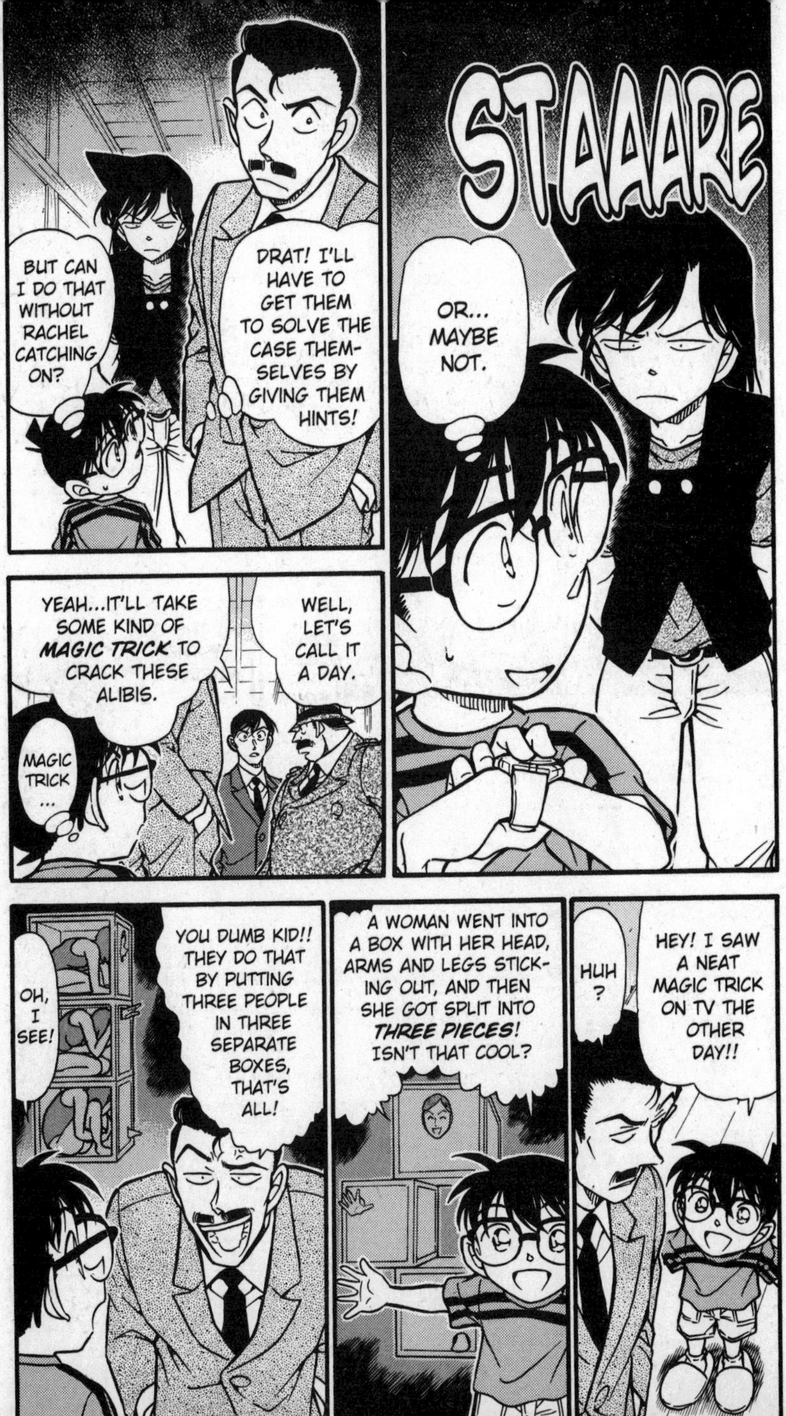
STAAARE
OR... MAYBE NOT.
DRAT! I'LL HAVE TO GET THEM TO SOLVE THE CASE THEM-SELVES BY GIVING THEM HINTS!
BUT CAN I DO THAT WITHOUT RACHEL CATCHING ON?
WELL, LET'S CALL IT A DAY.
YEAH...IT'LL TAKE SOME KIND OF MAGIC TRICK TO CRACK THESE ALIBIS.
MAGIC TRICK...
HEY! I SAW A NEAT MAGIC TRICK ON TV THE OTHER DAY!!
HUH?
A WOMAN WENT INTO A BOX WITH HER HEAD, ARMS AND LEGS STICK-ING OUT, AND THEN SHE GOT SPLIT INTO THREE PIECES! ISN'T THAT COOL?
YOU DUMB KID!! THEY DO THAT BY PUTTING THREE PEOPLE IN THREE SEPARATE BOXES, THAT'S ALL!
OH, I SEE!

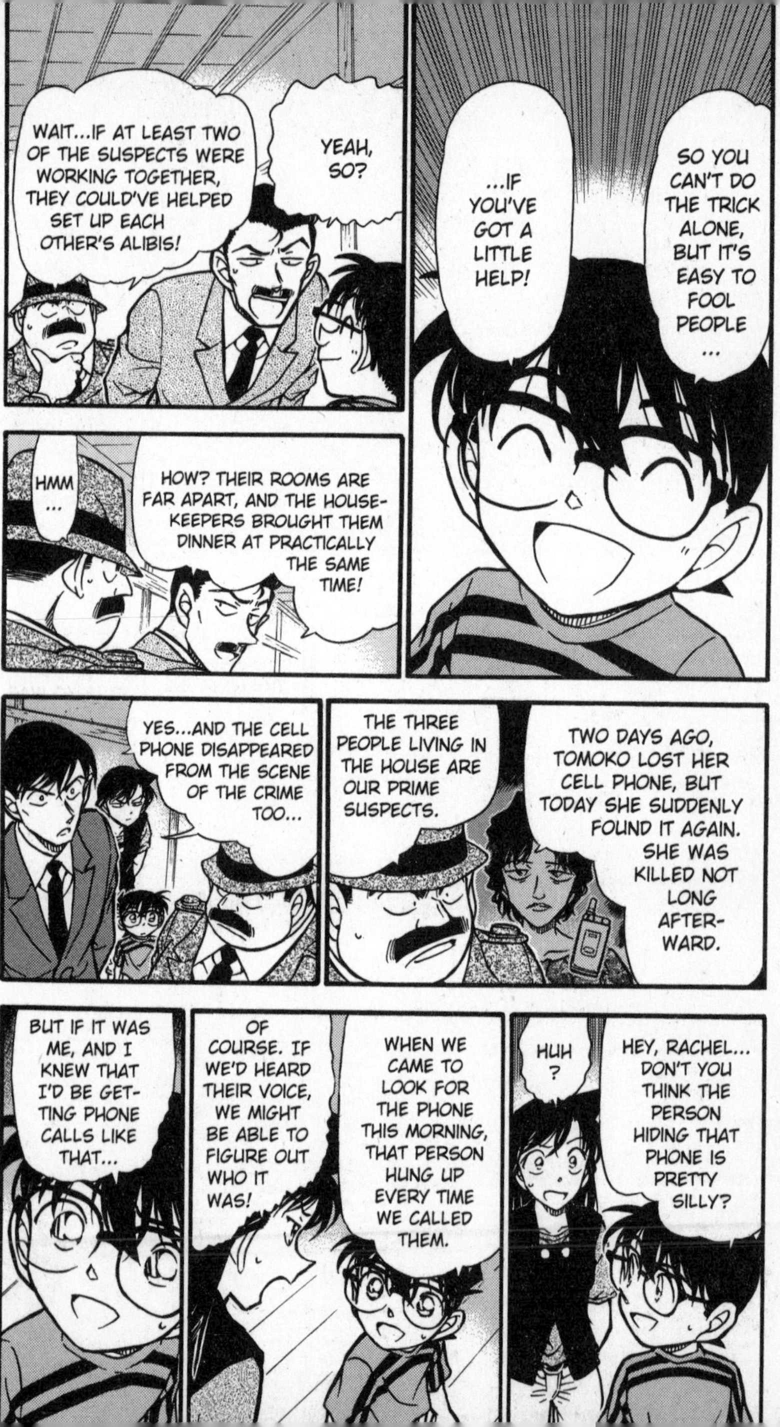
SO YOU CAN'T DO THE TRICK ALONE, BUT IT'S EASY TO FOOL PEOPLE ...
...IF YOU'VE GOT A LITTLE HELP!
WAIT...IF AT LEAST TWO OF THE SUSPECTS WERE WORKING TOGETHER, THEY COULD'VE HELPED SET UP EACH OTHER'S ALIBIS!
YEAH, SO?
HOW? THEIR ROOMS ARE FAR APART, AND THE HOUSE-KEEPERS BROUGHT THEM DINNER AT PRACTICALLY THE SAME TIME!
HMM ...
TWO DAYS AGO, TOMOKO LOST HER CELL PHONE, BUT TODAY SHE SUDDENLY FOUND IT AGAIN. SHE WAS KILLED NOT LONG AFTER-WARD.
THE THREE PEOPLE LIVING IN THE HOUSE ARE OUR PRIME SUSPECTS.
YES...AND THE CELL PHONE DISAPPEARED FROM THE SCENE OF THE CRIME TOO...
HEY, RACHEL... DON'T YOU THINK THE PERSON HIDING THAT PHONE IS PRETTY SILLY?
HUH ?
WHEN WE CAME TO LOOK FOR THE PHONE THIS MORNING, THAT PERSON HUNG UP EVERY TIME WE CALLED THEM.
OF COURSE. IF WE'D HEARD THEIR VOICE, WE MIGHT BE ABLE TO FIGURE OUT WHO IT WAS!
BUT IF IT WAS ME, AND I KNEW THAT I'D BE GET-TING PHONE CALLS LIKE THAT...

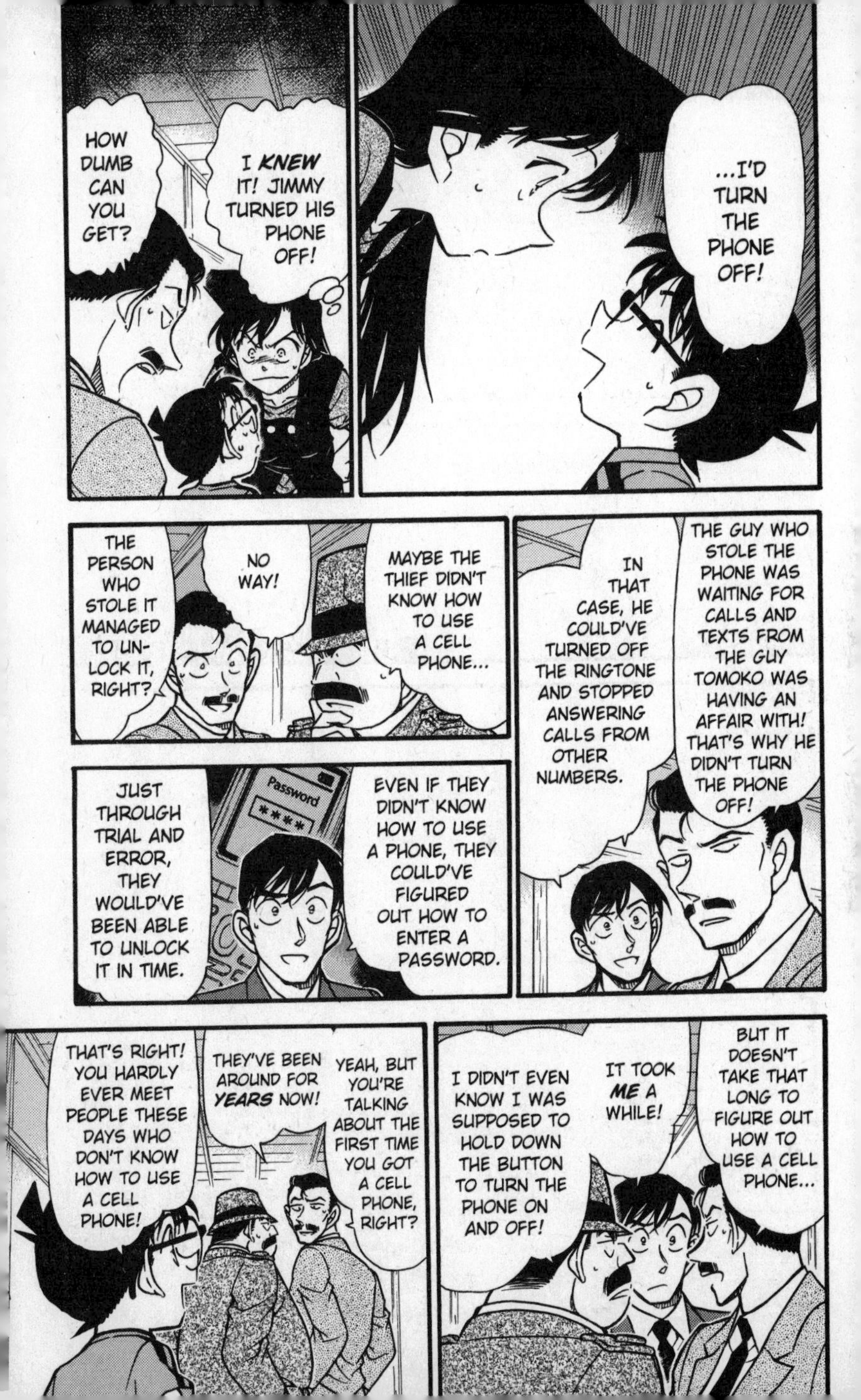
...I'D TURN THE PHONE OFF!
I *KNEW* IT! JIMMY TURNED HIS PHONE OFF!
HOW DUMB CAN YOU GET?
THE GUY WHO STOLE THE PHONE WAS WAITING FOR CALLS AND TEXTS FROM THE GUY TOMOKO WAS HAVING AN AFFAIR WITH! THAT'S WHY HE DIDN'T TURN THE PHONE OFF!
IN THAT CASE, HE COULD'VE TURNED OFF THE RINGTONE AND STOPPED ANSWERING CALLS FROM OTHER NUMBERS.
MAYBE THE THIEF DIDN'T KNOW HOW TO USE A CELL PHONE...
NO WAY!
THE PERSON WHO STOLE IT MANAGED TO UN-LOCK IT, RIGHT?
Password
****
EVEN IF THEY DIDN'T KNOW HOW TO USE A PHONE, THEY COULD'VE FIGURED OUT HOW TO ENTER A PASSWORD.
JUST THROUGH TRIAL AND ERROR, THEY WOULD'VE BEEN ABLE TO UNLOCK IT IN TIME.
BUT IT DOESN'T TAKE THAT LONG TO FIGURE OUT HOW TO USE A CELL PHONE...
IT TOOK *ME* A WHILE!
I DIDN'T EVEN KNOW I WAS SUPPOSED TO HOLD DOWN THE BUTTON TO TURN THE PHONE ON AND OFF!
YEAH, BUT YOU'RE TALKING ABOUT THE FIRST TIME YOU GOT A CELL PHONE, RIGHT?
THEY'VE BEEN AROUND FOR *YEARS* NOW!
THAT'S RIGHT! YOU HARDLY EVER MEET PEOPLE THESE DAYS WHO DON'T KNOW HOW TO USE A CELL PHONE!

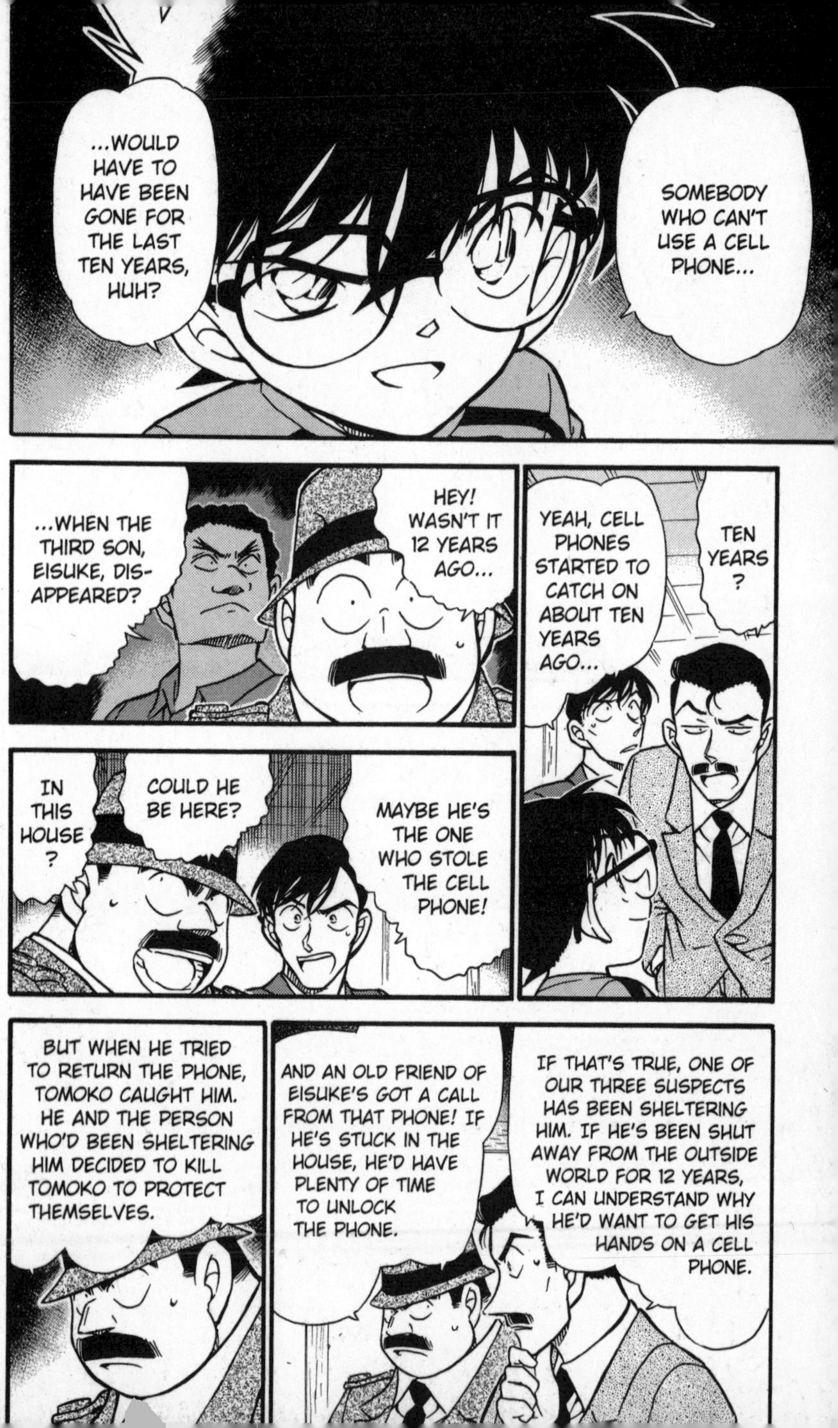

SOMEBODY WHO CAN'T USE A CELL PHONE...
...WOULD HAVE TO HAVE BEEN GONE FOR THE LAST TEN YEARS, HUH?
TEN YEARS ?
YEAH, CELL PHONES STARTED TO CATCH ON ABOUT TEN YEARS AGO...
HEY! WASN'T IT 12 YEARS AGO...
...WHEN THE THIRD SON, EISUKE, DIS-APPEARED?
MAYBE HE'S THE ONE WHO STOLE THE CELL PHONE!
COULD HE BE HERE?
IN THIS HOUSE ?
IF THAT'S TRUE, ONE OF OUR THREE SUSPECTS HAS BEEN SHELTERING HIM. IF HE'S BEEN SHUT AWAY FROM THE OUTSIDE WORLD FOR 12 YEARS, I CAN UNDERSTAND WHY HE'D WANT TO GET HIS HANDS ON A CELL PHONE.
AND AN OLD FRIEND OF EISUKE'S GOT A CALL FROM THAT PHONE! IF HE'S STUCK IN THE HOUSE, HE'D HAVE PLENTY OF TIME TO UNLOCK THE PHONE.
BUT WHEN HE TRIED TO RETURN THE PHONE, TOMOKO CAUGHT HIM. HE AND THE PERSON WHO'D BEEN SHELTERING HIM DECIDED TO KILL TOMOKO TO PROTECT THEMSELVES.

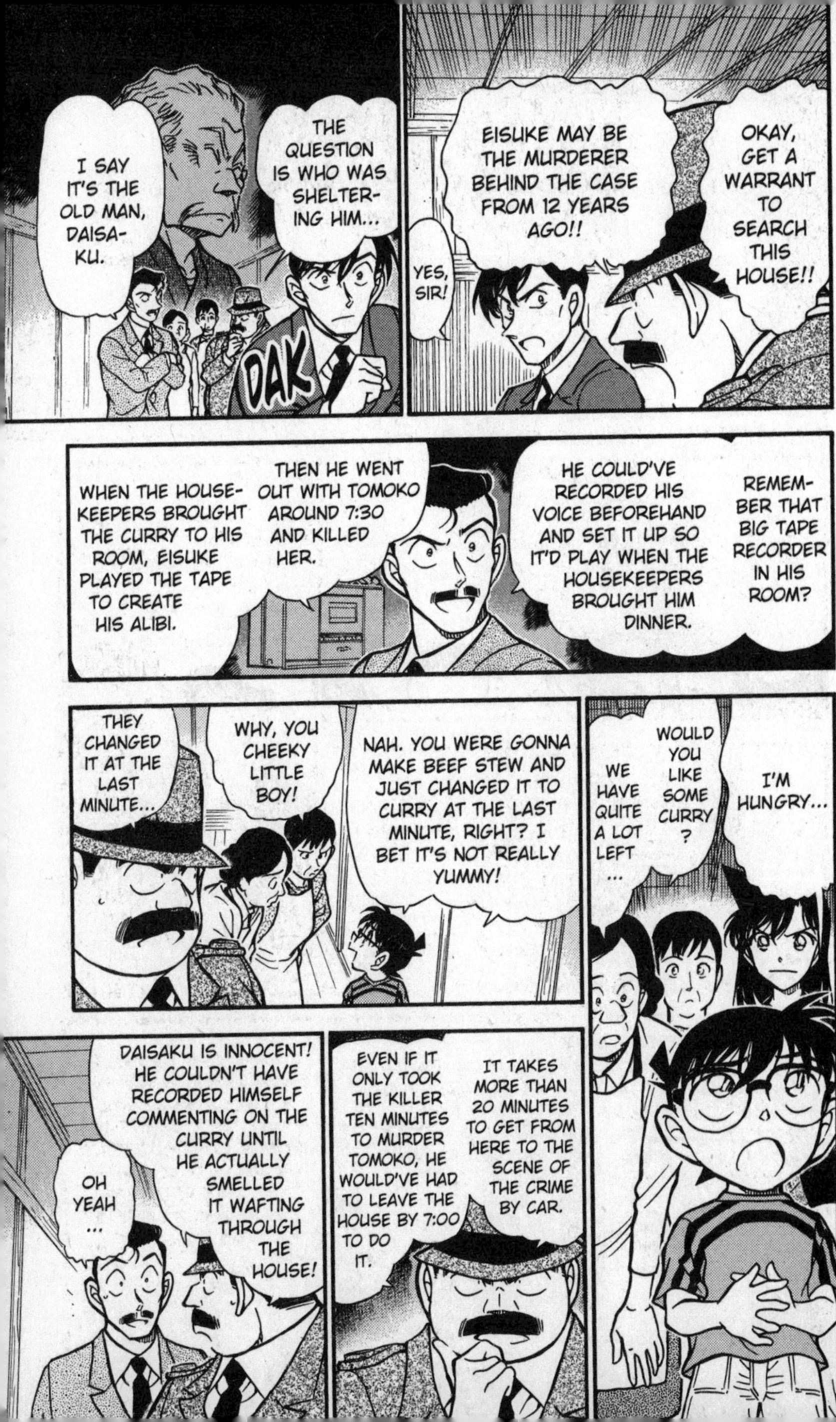
OKAY, GET A WARRANT TO SEARCH THIS HOUSE!!
EISUKE MAY BE THE MURDERER BEHIND THE CASE FROM 12 YEARS AGO!!
YES, SIR!
THE QUESTION IS WHO WAS SHELTER-ING HIM...
DAK
I SAY IT'S THE OLD MAN, DAISA-KU.
REMEM-BER THAT BIG TAPE RECORDER IN HIS ROOM?
HE COULD'VE RECORDED HIS VOICE BEFOREHAND AND SET IT UP SO IT'D PLAY WHEN THE HOUSEKEEPERS BROUGHT HIM DINNER.
THEN HE WENT OUT WITH TOMOKO AROUND 7:30 AND KILLED HER.
WHEN THE HOUSE-KEEPERS BROUGHT THE CURRY TO HIS ROOM, EISUKE PLAYED THE TAPE TO CREATE HIS ALIBI.
I'M HUNGRY...
WOULD YOU LIKE SOME CURRY?
WE HAVE QUITE A LOT LEFT...
NAH. YOU WERE GONNA MAKE BEEF STEW AND JUST CHANGED IT TO CURRY AT THE LAST MINUTE, RIGHT? I BET IT'S NOT REALLY YUMMY!
WHY, YOU CHEEKY LITTLE BOY!
THEY CHANGED IT AT THE LAST MINUTE...
IT TAKES MORE THAN 20 MINUTES TO GET FROM HERE TO THE SCENE OF THE CRIME BY CAR.
EVEN IF IT ONLY TOOK THE KILLER TEN MINUTES TO MURDER TOMOKO, HE WOULD'VE HAD TO LEAVE THE HOUSE BY 7:00 TO DO IT.
DAISAKU IS INNOCENT! HE COULDN'T HAVE RECORDED HIMSELF COMMENTING ON THE CURRY UNTIL HE ACTUALLY SMELLED IT WAFTING THROUGH THE HOUSE!
OH YEAH ...

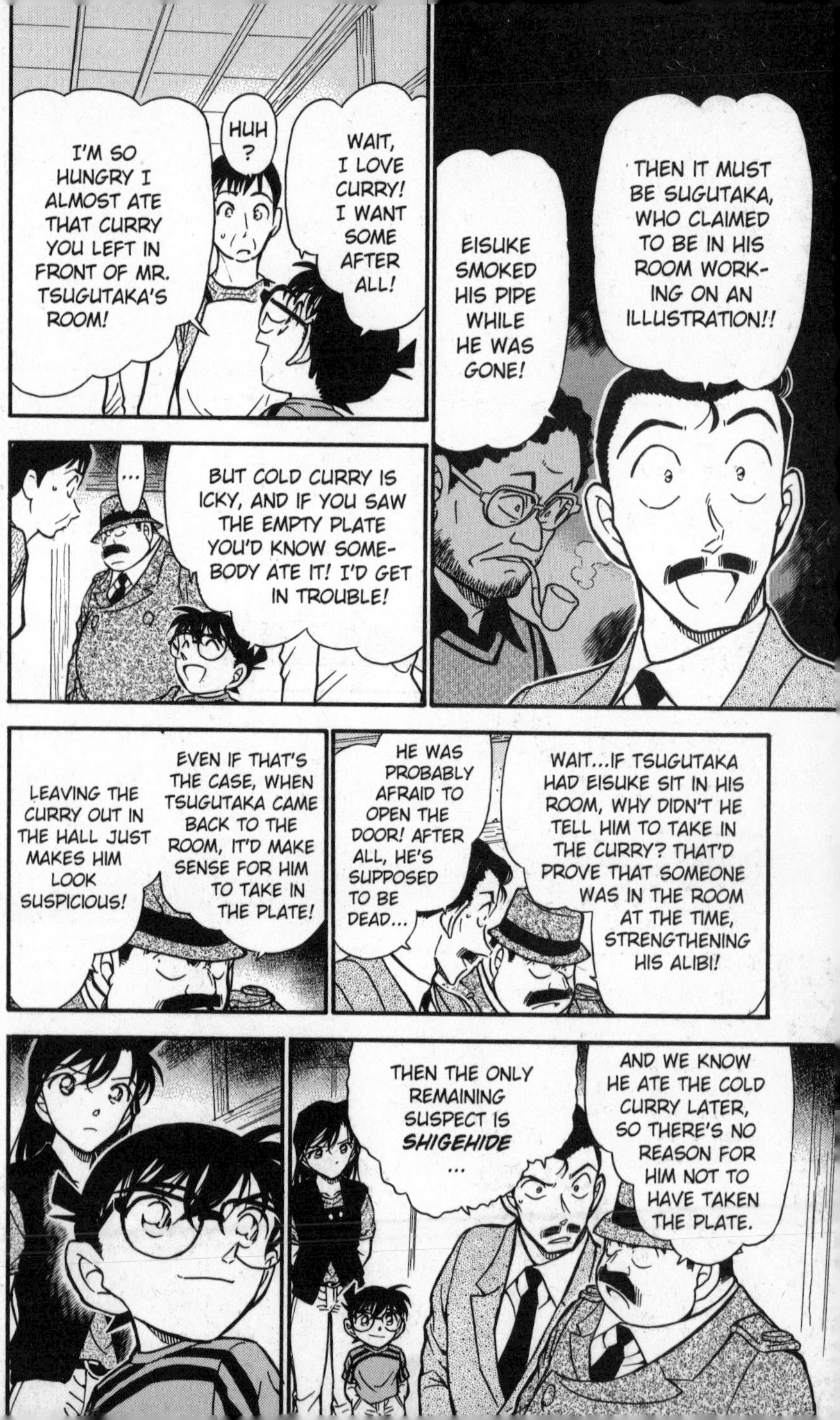

THEN IT MUST BE SUGUTAKA, WHO CLAIMED TO BE IN HIS ROOM WORKING ON AN ILLUSTRATION!!
EISUKE SMOKED HIS PIPE WHILE HE WAS GONE!
WAIT, I LOVE CURRY! I WANT SOME AFTER ALL!
HUH?
I'M SO HUNGRY I ALMOST ATE THAT CURRY YOU LEFT IN FRONT OF MR. TSUGUTAKA'S ROOM!
BUT COLD CURRY IS ICKY, AND IF YOU SAW THE EMPTY PLATE YOU'D KNOW SOMEBODY ATE IT! I'D GET IN TROUBLE!
...
WAIT...IF TSUGUTAKA HAD EISUKE SIT IN HIS ROOM, WHY DIDN'T HE TELL HIM TO TAKE IN THE CURRY? THAT'D PROVE THAT SOMEONE WAS IN THE ROOM AT THE TIME, STRENGTHENING HIS ALIBI!
HE WAS PROBABLY AFRAID TO OPEN THE DOOR! AFTER ALL, HE'S SUPPOSED TO BE DEAD...
EVEN IF THAT'S THE CASE, WHEN TSUGUTAKA CAME BACK TO THE ROOM, IT'D MAKE SENSE FOR HIM TO TAKE IN THE PLATE!
LEAVING THE CURRY OUT IN THE HALL JUST MAKES HIM LOOK SUSPICIOUS!
AND WE KNOW HE ATE THE COLD CURRY LATER, SO THERE'S NO REASON FOR HIM NOT TO HAVE TAKEN THE PLATE.
THEN THE ONLY REMAINING SUSPECT IS SHIGEHIDE...

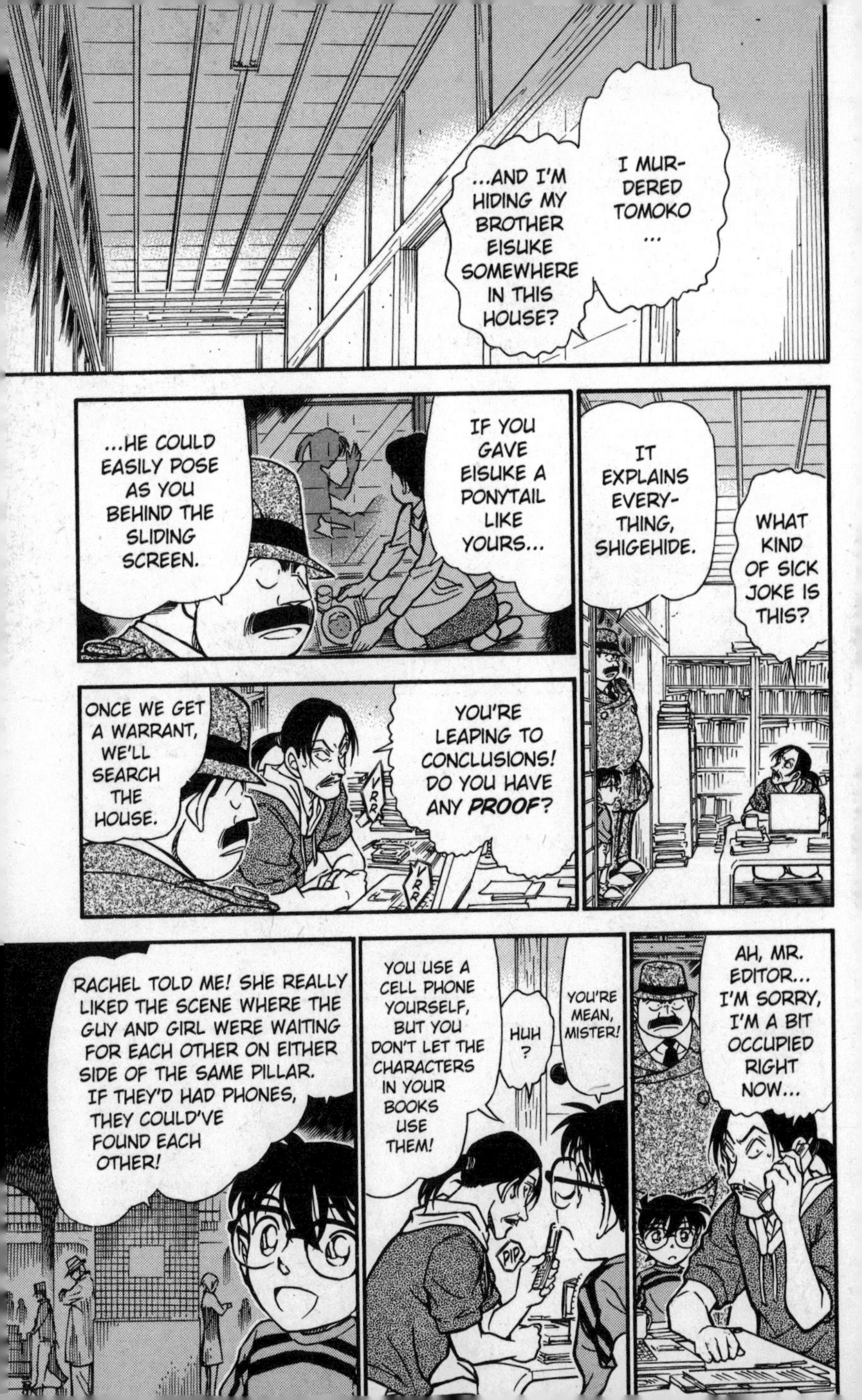
I MURDERED TOMOKO...
...AND I'M HIDING MY BROTHER EISUKE SOMEWHERE IN THIS HOUSE?
WHAT KIND OF SICK JOKE IS THIS?
IT EXPLAINS EVERYTHING, SHIGEHIDE.
IF YOU GAVE EISUKE A PONYTAIL LIKE YOURS...
...HE COULD EASILY POSE AS YOU BEHIND THE SLIDING SCREEN.
VRR
VRR
YOU'RE LEAPING TO CONCLUSIONS! DO YOU HAVE ANY *PROOF*?
ONCE WE GET A WARRANT, WE'LL SEARCH THE HOUSE.
AH, MR. EDITOR... I'M SORRY, I'M A BIT OCCUPIED RIGHT NOW...
YOU'RE MEAN, MISTER!
HUH?
PIP
YOU USE A CELL PHONE YOURSELF, BUT YOU DON'T LET THE CHARACTERS IN YOUR BOOKS USE THEM!
RACHEL TOLD ME! SHE REALLY LIKED THE SCENE WHERE THE GUY AND GIRL WERE WAITING FOR EACH OTHER ON EITHER SIDE OF THE SAME PILLAR. IF THEY'D HAD PHONES, THEY COULD'VE FOUND EACH OTHER!

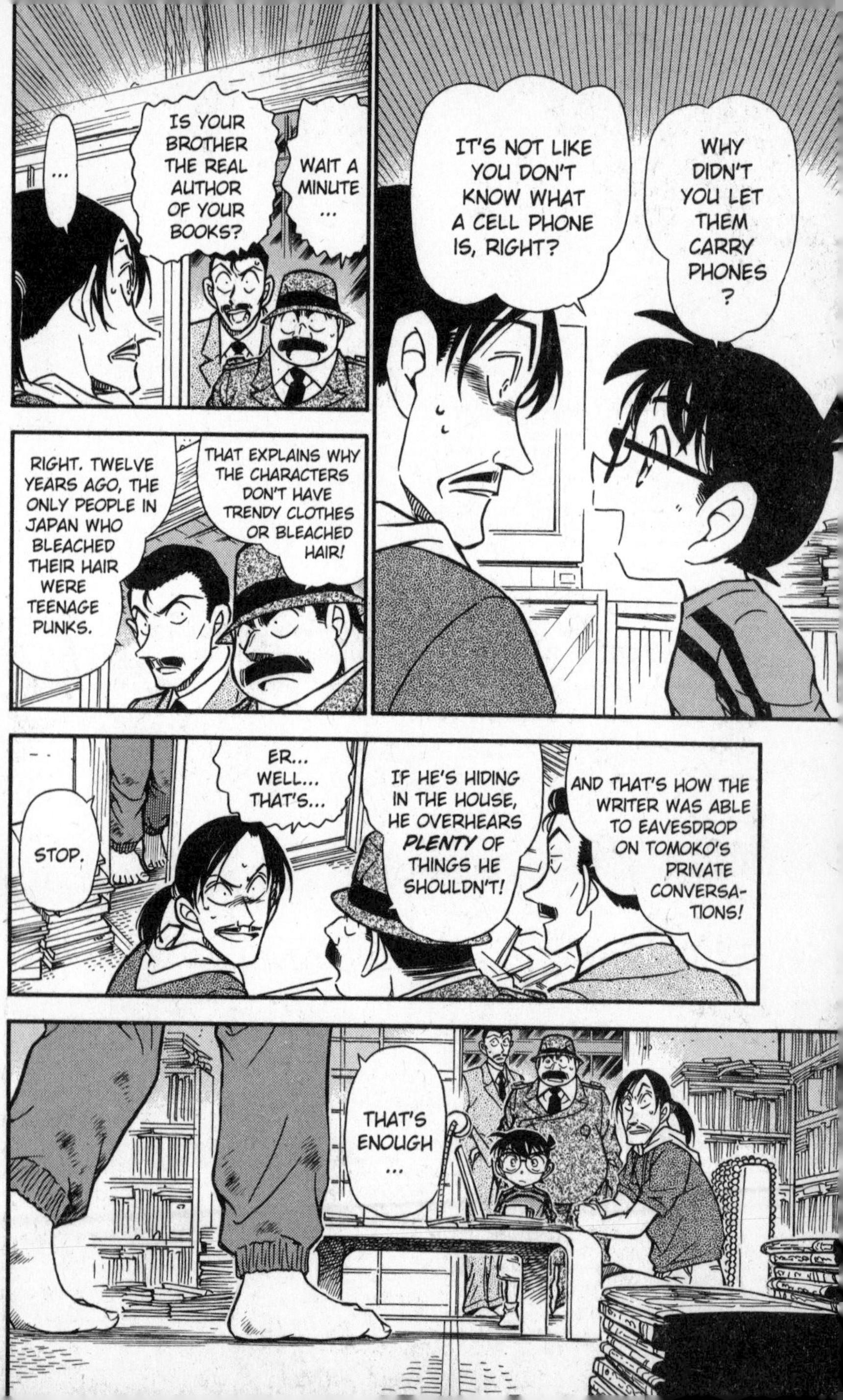
WHY DIDN'T YOU LET THEM CARRY PHONES?
IT'S NOT LIKE YOU DON'T KNOW WHAT A CELL PHONE IS, RIGHT?
WAIT A MINUTE...
IS YOUR BROTHER THE REAL AUTHOR OF YOUR BOOKS?
...
THAT EXPLAINS WHY THE CHARACTERS DON'T HAVE TRENDY CLOTHES OR BLEACHED HAIR!
RIGHT. TWELVE YEARS AGO, THE ONLY PEOPLE IN JAPAN WHO BLEACHED THEIR HAIR WERE TEENAGE PUNKS.
AND THAT'S HOW THE WRITER WAS ABLE TO EAVESDROP ON TOMOKO'S PRIVATE CONVERSATIONS!
IF HE'S HIDING IN THE HOUSE, HE OVERHEARS *PLENTY* OF THINGS HE SHOULDN'T!
ER... WELL... THAT'S...
STOP.
THAT'S ENOUGH...

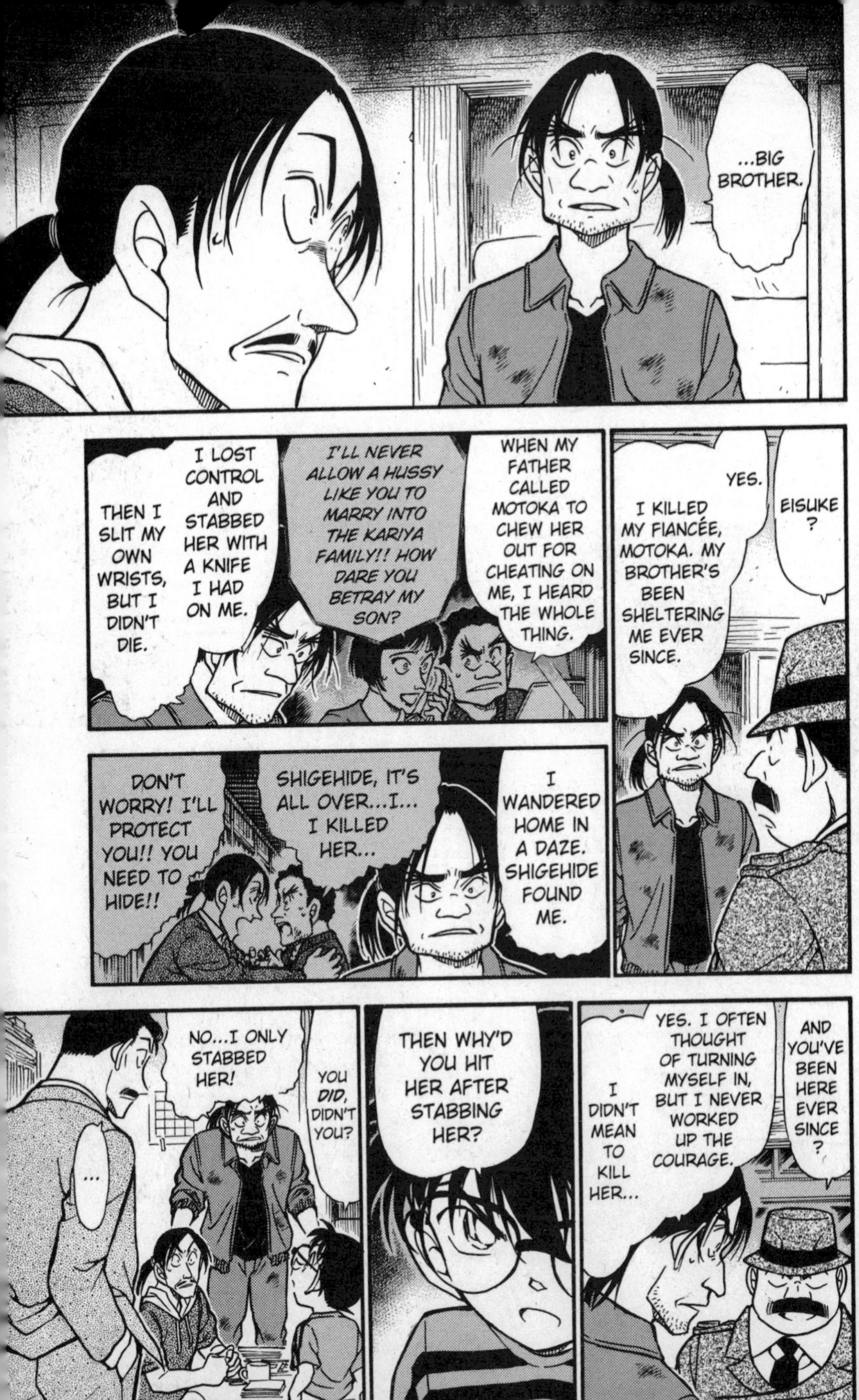
...BIG BROTHER.
EISUKE?
YES.
I KILLED MY FIANCÉE, MOTOKA. MY BROTHER'S BEEN SHELTERING ME EVER SINCE.
WHEN MY FATHER CALLED MOTOKA TO CHEW HER OUT FOR CHEATING ON ME, I HEARD THE WHOLE THING.
I'LL NEVER ALLOW A HUSSY LIKE YOU TO MARRY INTO THE KARIYA FAMILY!! HOW DARE YOU BETRAY MY SON?
I LOST CONTROL AND STABBED HER WITH A KNIFE I HAD ON ME.
THEN I SLIT MY OWN WRISTS, BUT I DIDN'T DIE.
I WANDERED HOME IN A DAZE. SHIGEHIDE FOUND ME.
SHIGEHIDE, IT'S ALL OVER...I... I KILLED HER...
DON'T WORRY! I'LL PROTECT YOU!! YOU NEED TO HIDE!!
AND YOU'VE BEEN HERE EVER SINCE?
YES. I OFTEN THOUGHT OF TURNING MYSELF IN, BUT I NEVER WORKED UP THE COURAGE.
I DIDN'T MEAN TO KILL HER...
THEN WHY'D YOU HIT HER AFTER STABBING HER?
NO...I ONLY STABBED HER!
YOU *DID*, DIDN'T YOU?
...

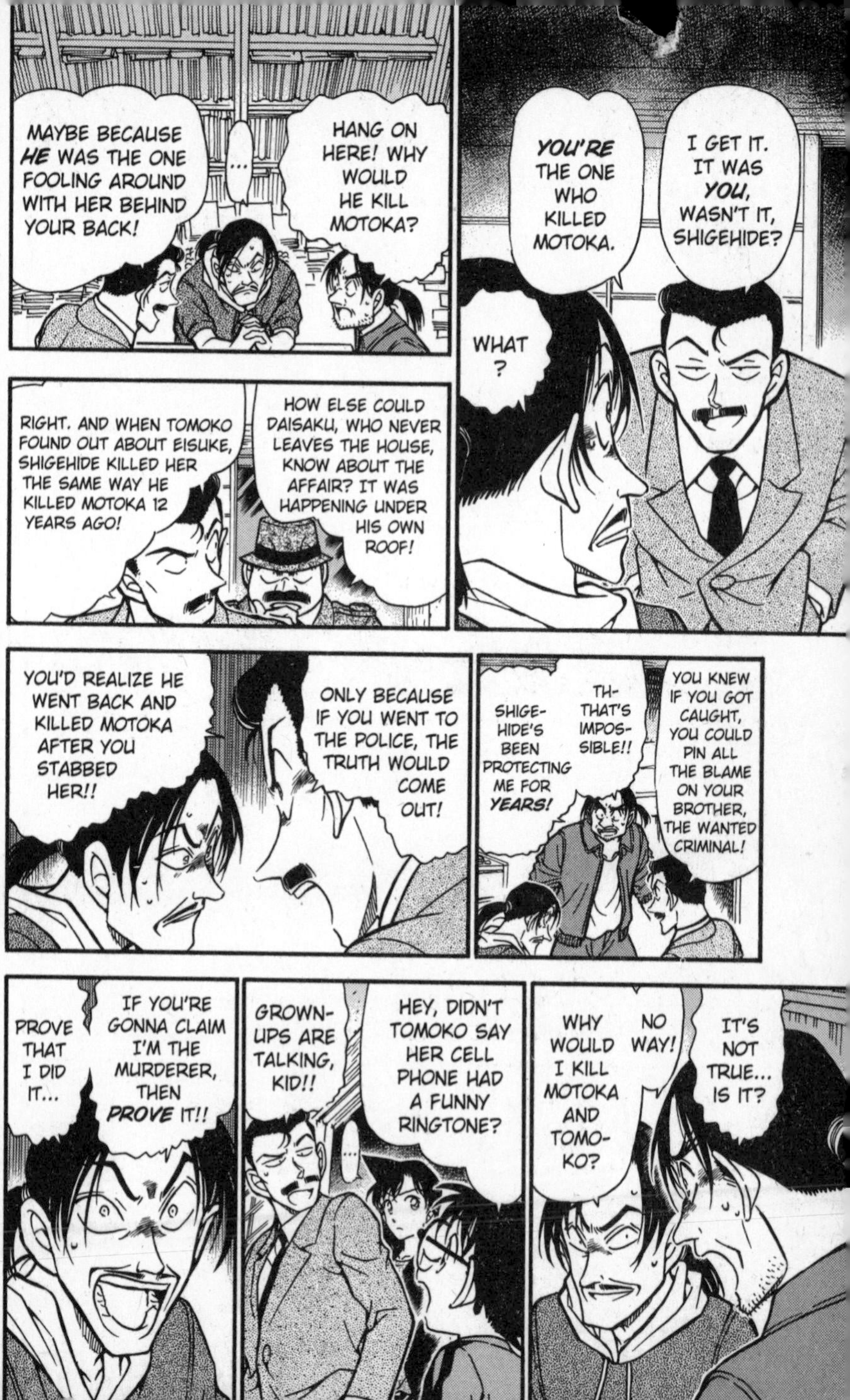
I GET IT. IT WAS YOU, WASN'T IT, SHIGEHIDE?
YOU'RE THE ONE WHO KILLED MOTOKA.
WHAT?
HANG ON HERE! WHY WOULD HE KILL MOTOKA?
...
MAYBE BECAUSE HE WAS THE ONE FOOLING AROUND WITH HER BEHIND YOUR BACK!
HOW ELSE COULD DAISAKU, WHO NEVER LEAVES THE HOUSE, KNOW ABOUT THE AFFAIR? IT WAS HAPPENING UNDER HIS OWN ROOF!
RIGHT. AND WHEN TOMOKO FOUND OUT ABOUT EISUKE, SHIGEHIDE KILLED HER THE SAME WAY HE KILLED MOTOKA 12 YEARS AGO!
YOU KNEW IF YOU GOT CAUGHT, YOU COULD PIN ALL THE BLAME ON YOUR BROTHER, THE WANTED CRIMINAL!
TH- THAT'S IMPOSSIBLE!!
SHIGEHIDE'S BEEN PROTECTING ME FOR YEARS!
ONLY BECAUSE IF YOU WENT TO THE POLICE, THE TRUTH WOULD COME OUT!
YOU'D REALIZE HE WENT BACK AND KILLED MOTOKA AFTER YOU STABBED HER!!
IT'S NOT TRUE... IS IT?
NO WAY!
WHY WOULD I KILL MOTOKA AND TOMOKO?
HEY, DIDN'T TOMOKO SAY HER CELL PHONE HAD A FUNNY RINGTONE?
...
GROWN-UPS ARE TALKING, KID!!
IF YOU'RE GONNA CLAIM I'M THE MURDERER, THEN PROVE IT!!
PROVE THAT I DID IT...

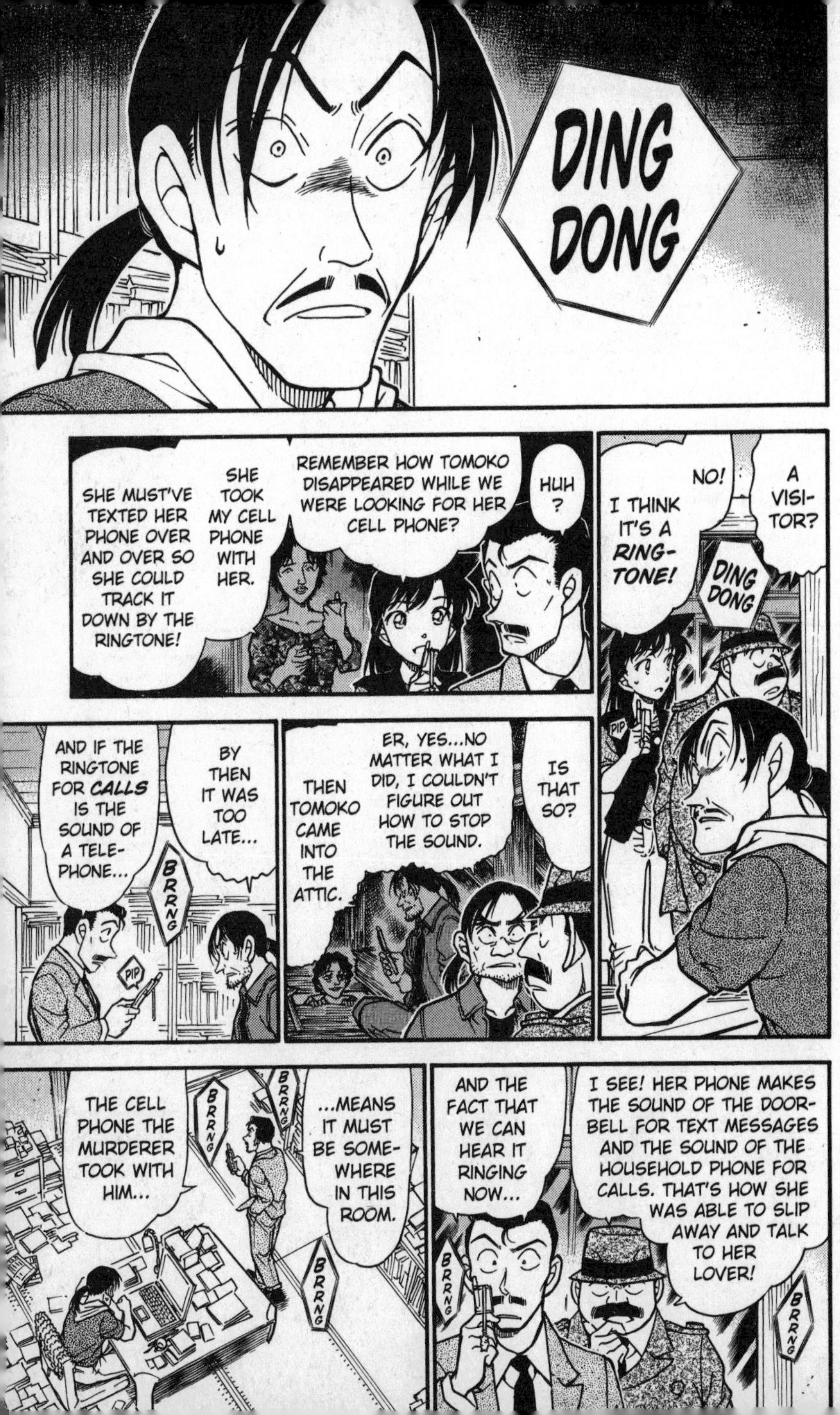
DING DONG
A VISI-TOR?
NO!
I THINK IT'S A *RINGTONE!*
DING DONG
PIP
HUH?
REMEMBER HOW TOMOKO DISAPPEARED WHILE WE WERE LOOKING FOR HER CELL PHONE?
SHE TOOK MY CELL PHONE WITH HER.
SHE MUST'VE TEXTED HER PHONE OVER AND OVER SO SHE COULD TRACK IT DOWN BY THE RINGTONE!
IS THAT SO?
ER, YES...NO MATTER WHAT I DID, I COULDN'T FIGURE OUT HOW TO STOP THE SOUND.
THEN TOMOKO CAME INTO THE ATTIC.
BY THEN IT WAS TOO LATE...
AND IF THE RINGTONE FOR *CALLS* IS THE SOUND OF A TELE-PHONE...
BRRNG
PIP
I SEE! HER PHONE MAKES THE SOUND OF THE DOOR-BELL FOR TEXT MESSAGES AND THE SOUND OF THE HOUSEHOLD PHONE FOR CALLS. THAT'S HOW SHE WAS ABLE TO SLIP AWAY AND TALK TO HER LOVER!
AND THE FACT THAT WE CAN HEAR IT RINGING NOW...
BRRNG
BRRNG
...MEANS IT MUST BE SOMEWHERE IN THIS ROOM.
BRRNG
THE CELL PHONE THE MURDERER TOOK WITH HIM...
BRRNG
BRRNG

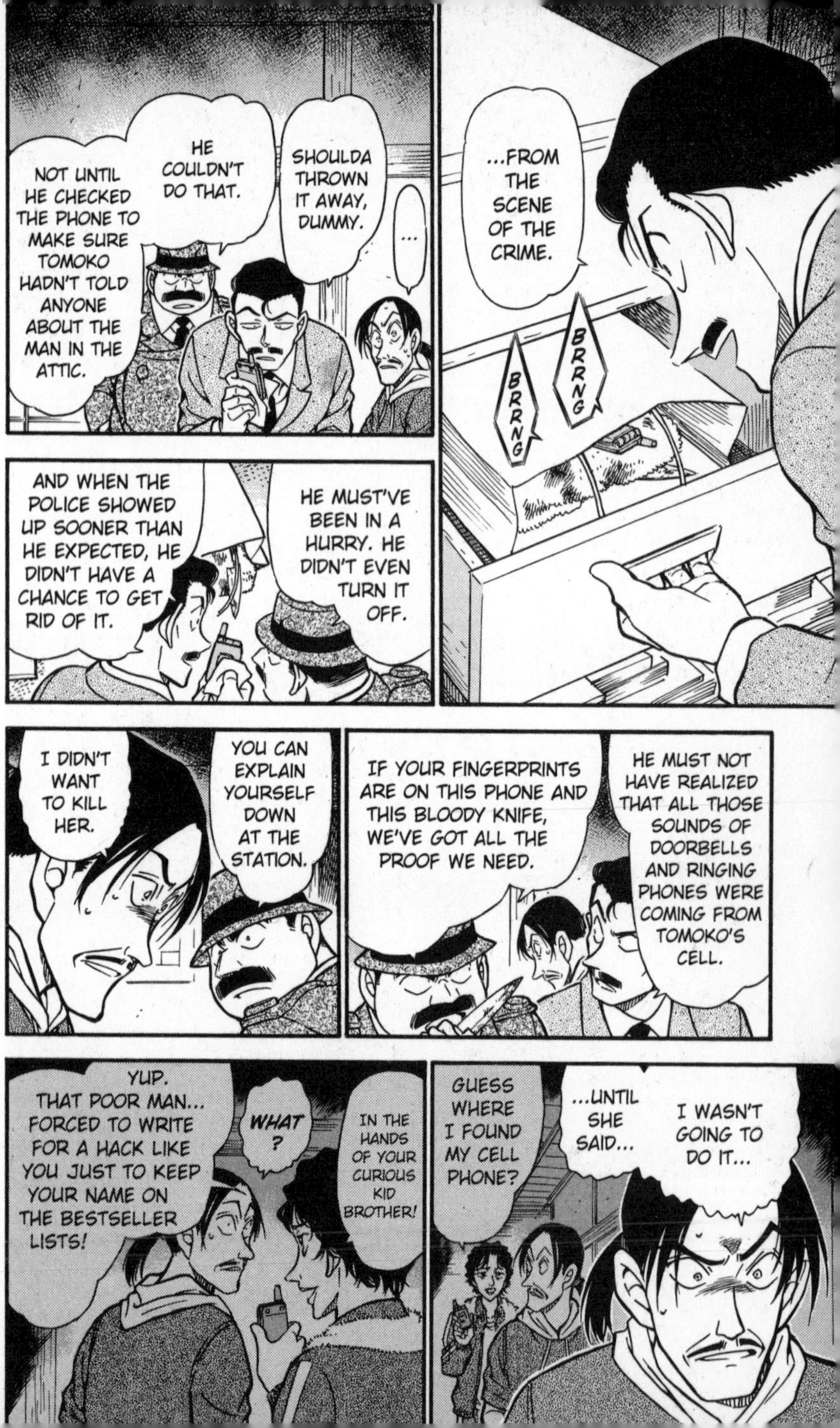
...FROM THE SCENE OF THE CRIME.
BRRNG
BRRNG
...
SHOULDA THROWN IT AWAY, DUMMY.
HE COULDN'T DO THAT.
NOT UNTIL HE CHECKED THE PHONE TO MAKE SURE TOMOKO HADN'T TOLD ANYONE ABOUT THE MAN IN THE ATTIC.
HE MUST'VE BEEN IN A HURRY. HE DIDN'T EVEN TURN IT OFF.
AND WHEN THE POLICE SHOWED UP SOONER THAN HE EXPECTED, HE DIDN'T HAVE A CHANCE TO GET RID OF IT.
HE MUST NOT HAVE REALIZED THAT ALL THOSE SOUNDS OF DOORBELLS AND RINGING PHONES WERE COMING FROM TOMOKO'S CELL.
IF YOUR FINGERPRINTS ARE ON THIS PHONE AND THIS BLOODY KNIFE, WE'VE GOT ALL THE PROOF WE NEED.
YOU CAN EXPLAIN YOURSELF DOWN AT THE STATION.
I DIDN'T WANT TO KILL HER.
I WASN'T GOING TO DO IT...
...UNTIL SHE SAID...
GUESS WHERE I FOUND MY CELL PHONE?
IN THE HANDS OF YOUR CURIOUS KID BROTHER!
WHAT?
YUP. THAT POOR MAN... FORCED TO WRITE FOR A HACK LIKE YOU JUST TO KEEP YOUR NAME ON THE BESTSELLER LISTS!

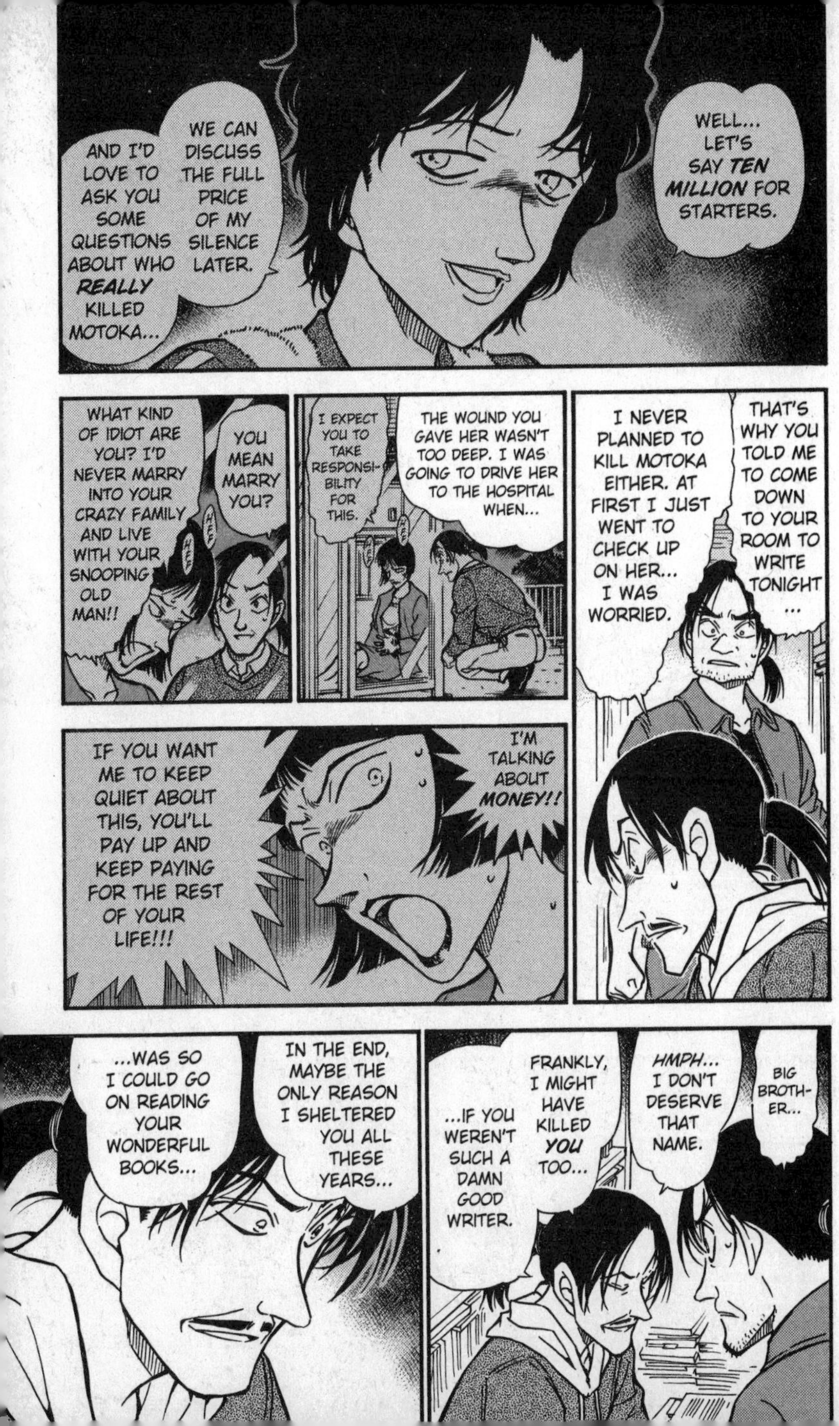
WELL... LET'S SAY *TEN MILLION* FOR STARTERS.
WE CAN DISCUSS THE FULL PRICE OF MY SILENCE LATER.
AND I'D LOVE TO ASK YOU SOME QUESTIONS ABOUT WHO *REALLY* KILLED MOTOKA...
THAT'S WHY YOU TOLD ME TO COME DOWN TO YOUR ROOM TO WRITE TONIGHT...
I NEVER PLANNED TO KILL MOTOKA EITHER. AT FIRST I JUST WENT TO CHECK UP ON HER... I WAS WORRIED.
THE WOUND YOU GAVE HER WASN'T TOO DEEP. I WAS GOING TO DRIVE HER TO THE HOSPITAL WHEN...
I EXPECT YOU TO TAKE RESPONSIBILITY FOR THIS.
YOU MEAN MARRY YOU?
WHAT KIND OF IDIOT ARE YOU? I'D NEVER MARRY INTO YOUR CRAZY FAMILY AND LIVE WITH YOUR SNOOPING OLD MAN!!
I'M TALKING ABOUT *MONEY!!*
IF YOU WANT ME TO KEEP QUIET ABOUT THIS, YOU'LL PAY UP AND KEEP PAYING FOR THE REST OF YOUR LIFE!!!
BIG BROTHER...
HMPH... I DON'T DESERVE THAT NAME.
FRANKLY, I MIGHT HAVE KILLED *YOU* TOO...
...IF YOU WEREN'T SUCH A DAMN GOOD WRITER.
IN THE END, MAYBE THE ONLY REASON I SHELTERED YOU ALL THESE YEARS...
...WAS SO I COULD GO ON READING YOUR WONDERFUL BOOKS...

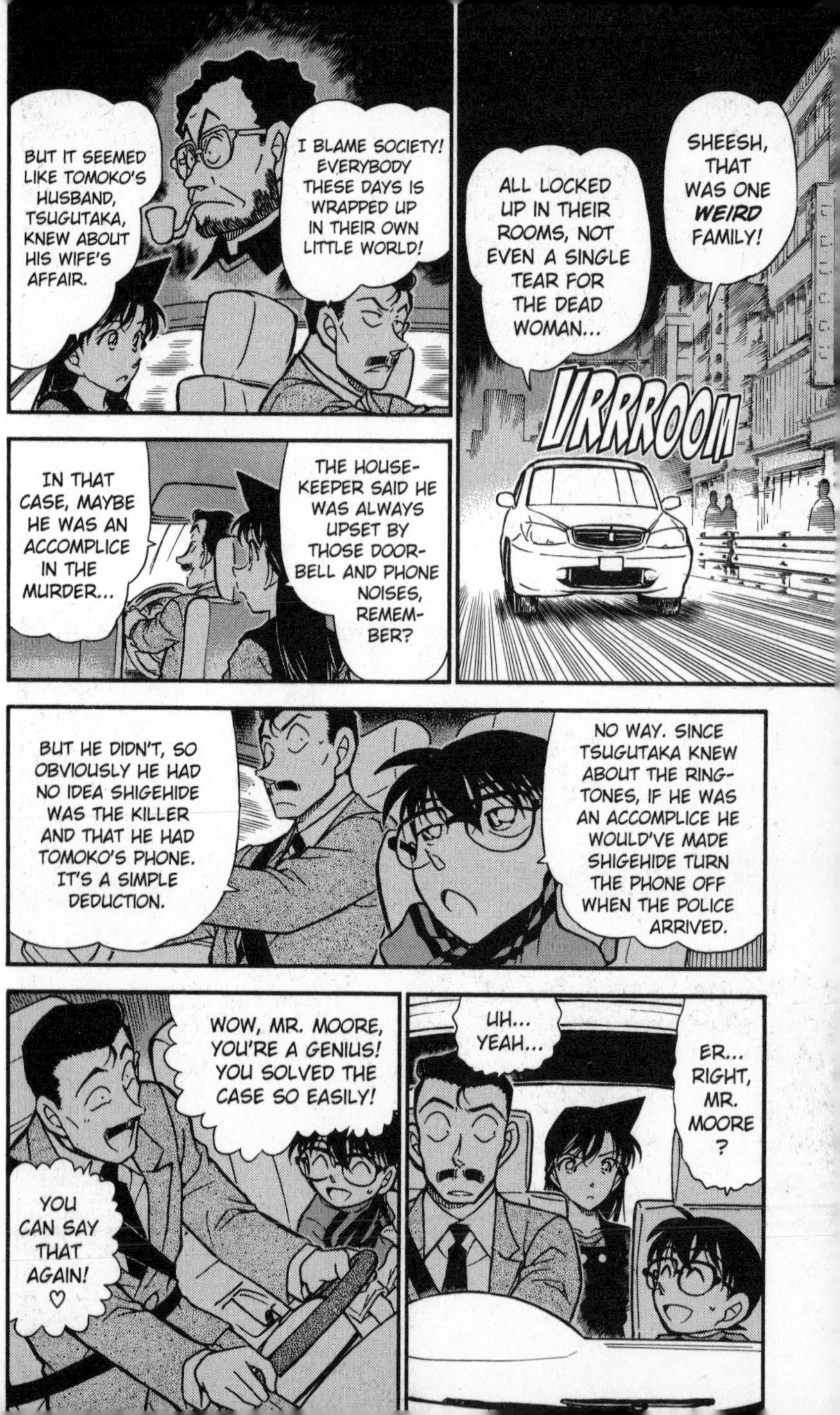
SHEESH, THAT WAS ONE *WEIRD* FAMILY!
ALL LOCKED UP IN THEIR ROOMS, NOT EVEN A SINGLE TEAR FOR THE DEAD WOMAN...
VRRROOM
I BLAME SOCIETY! EVERYBODY THESE DAYS IS WRAPPED UP IN THEIR OWN LITTLE WORLD!
BUT IT SEEMED LIKE TOMOKO'S HUSBAND, TSUGUTAKA, KNEW ABOUT HIS WIFE'S AFFAIR.
THE HOUSE-KEEPER SAID HE WAS ALWAYS UPSET BY THOSE DOOR-BELL AND PHONE NOISES, REMEMBER?
IN THAT CASE, MAYBE HE WAS AN ACCOMPLICE IN THE MURDER...
NO WAY. SINCE TSUGUTAKA KNEW ABOUT THE RING-TONES, IF HE WAS AN ACCOMPLICE HE WOULD'VE MADE SHIGEHIDE TURN THE PHONE OFF WHEN THE POLICE ARRIVED.
BUT HE DIDN'T, SO OBVIOUSLY HE HAD NO IDEA SHIGEHIDE WAS THE KILLER AND THAT HE HAD TOMOKO'S PHONE. IT'S A SIMPLE DEDUCTION.
ER... RIGHT, MR. MOORE?
UH... YEAH...
WOW, MR. MOORE, YOU'RE A GENIUS! YOU SOLVED THE CASE SO EASILY!
YOU CAN SAY THAT AGAIN! ♡

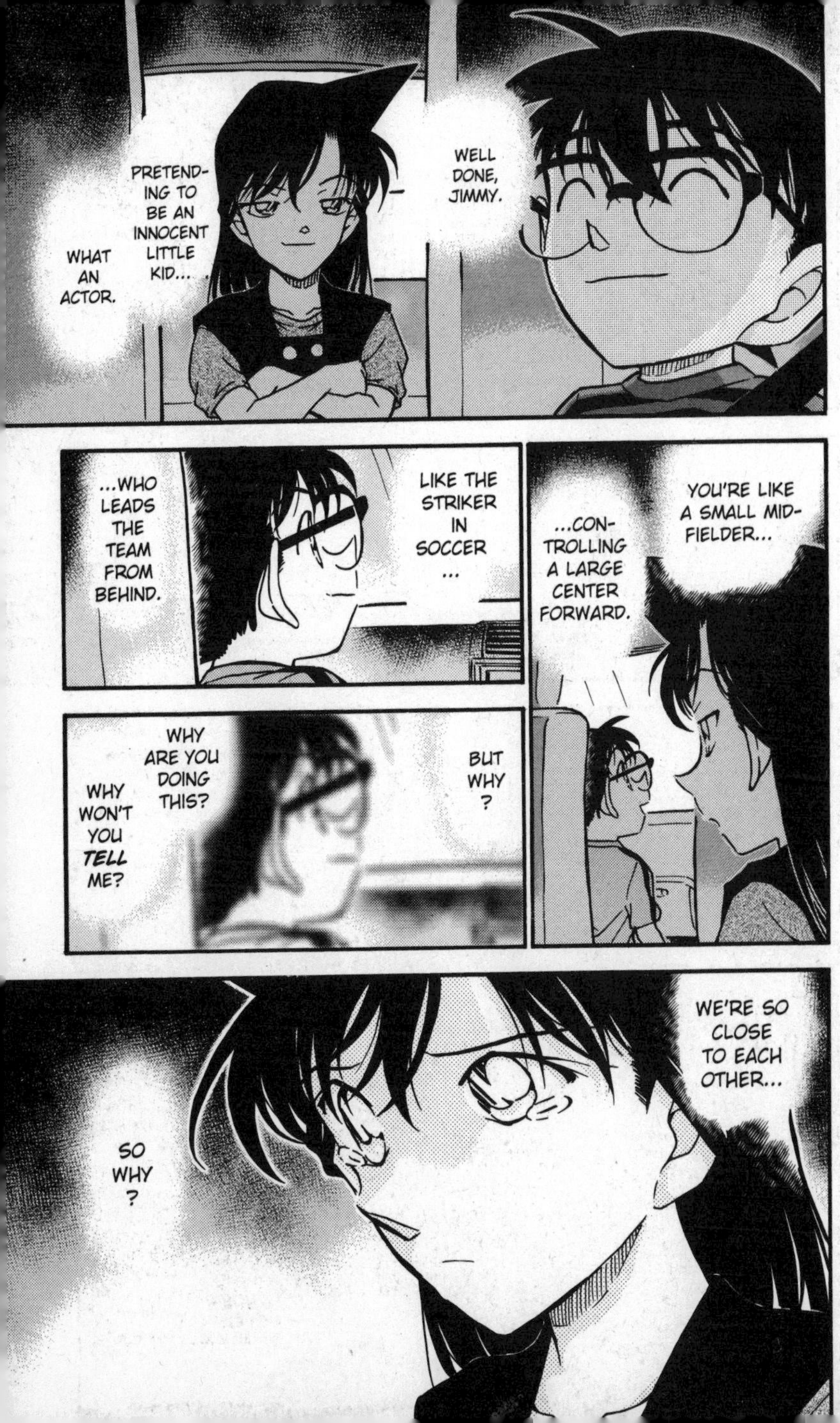
WELL DONE, JIMMY.
PRETENDING TO BE AN INNOCENT LITTLE KID...
WHAT AN ACTOR.
YOU'RE LIKE A SMALL MIDFIELDER...
...CONTROLLING A LARGE CENTER FORWARD.
LIKE THE STRIKER IN SOCCER...
...WHO LEADS THE TEAM FROM BEHIND.
BUT WHY?
WHY ARE YOU DOING THIS?
WHY WON'T YOU *TELL* ME?
WE'RE SO CLOSE TO EACH OTHER...
SO WHY?

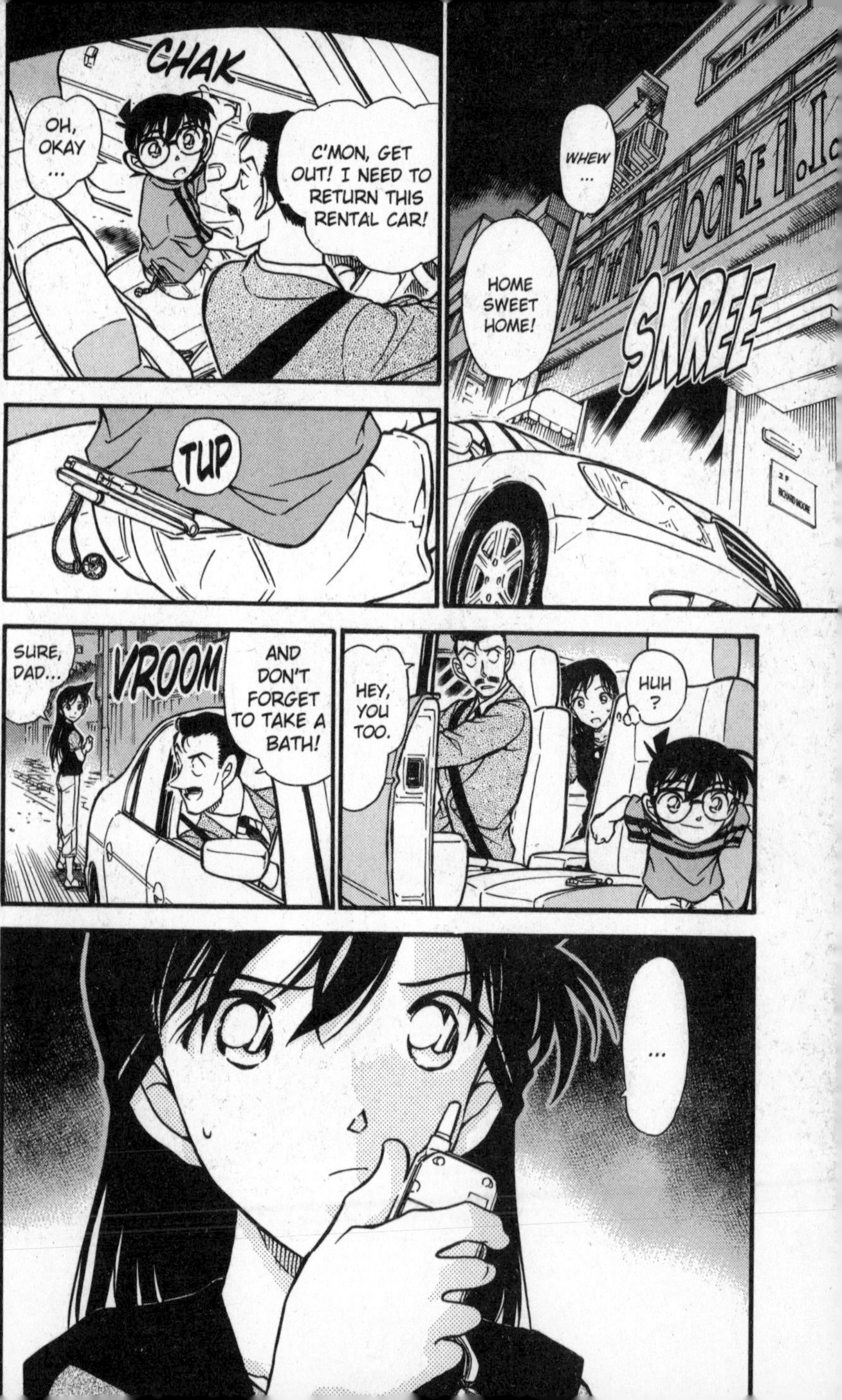
WHEW ...
HOME SWEET HOME!
SKREE
2F RICHARD MOORE
CHAK
C'MON, GET OUT! I NEED TO RETURN THIS RENTAL CAR!
OH, OKAY ...
TUP
HUH ?
HEY, YOU TOO.
AND DON'T FORGET TO TAKE A BATH!
VROOM
SURE, DAD...
...

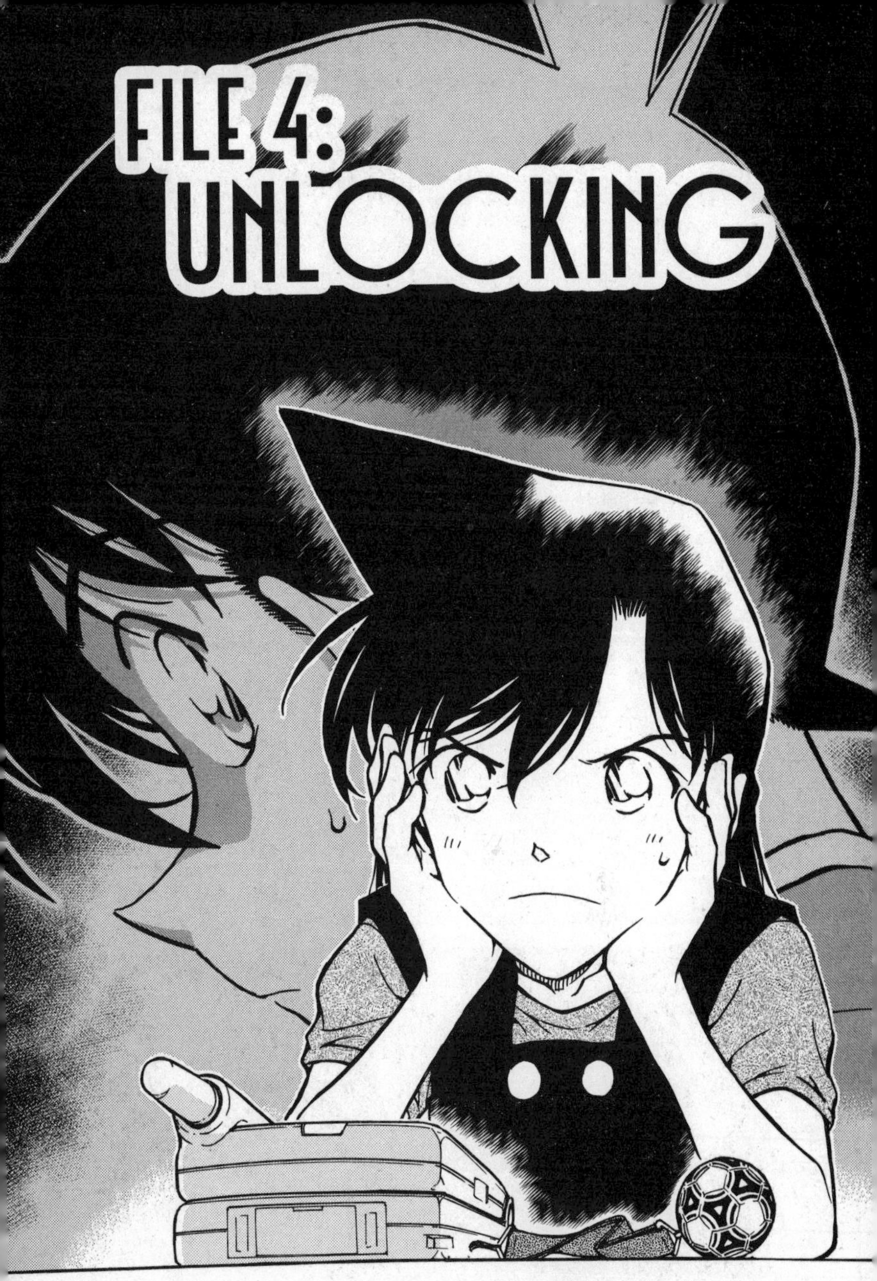
FILE 4:
UNLOCKING

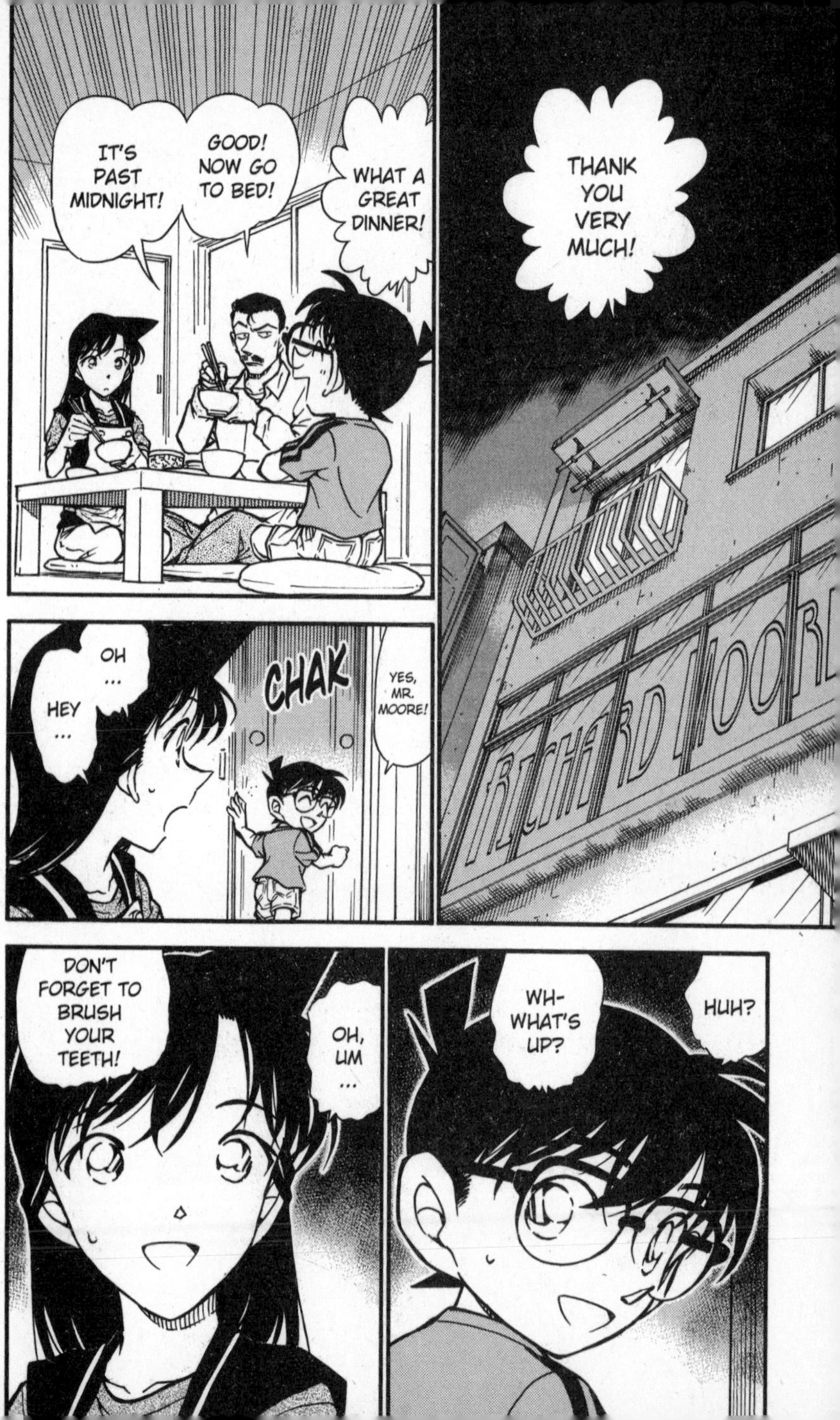
THANK YOU VERY MUCH!
WHAT A GREAT DINNER!
GOOD! NOW GO TO BED!
IT'S PAST MIDNIGHT!
YES, MR. MOORE!
CHAK
OH ...
HEY ...
HUH?
WH-WHAT'S UP?
OH, UM ...
DON'T FORGET TO BRUSH YOUR TEETH!

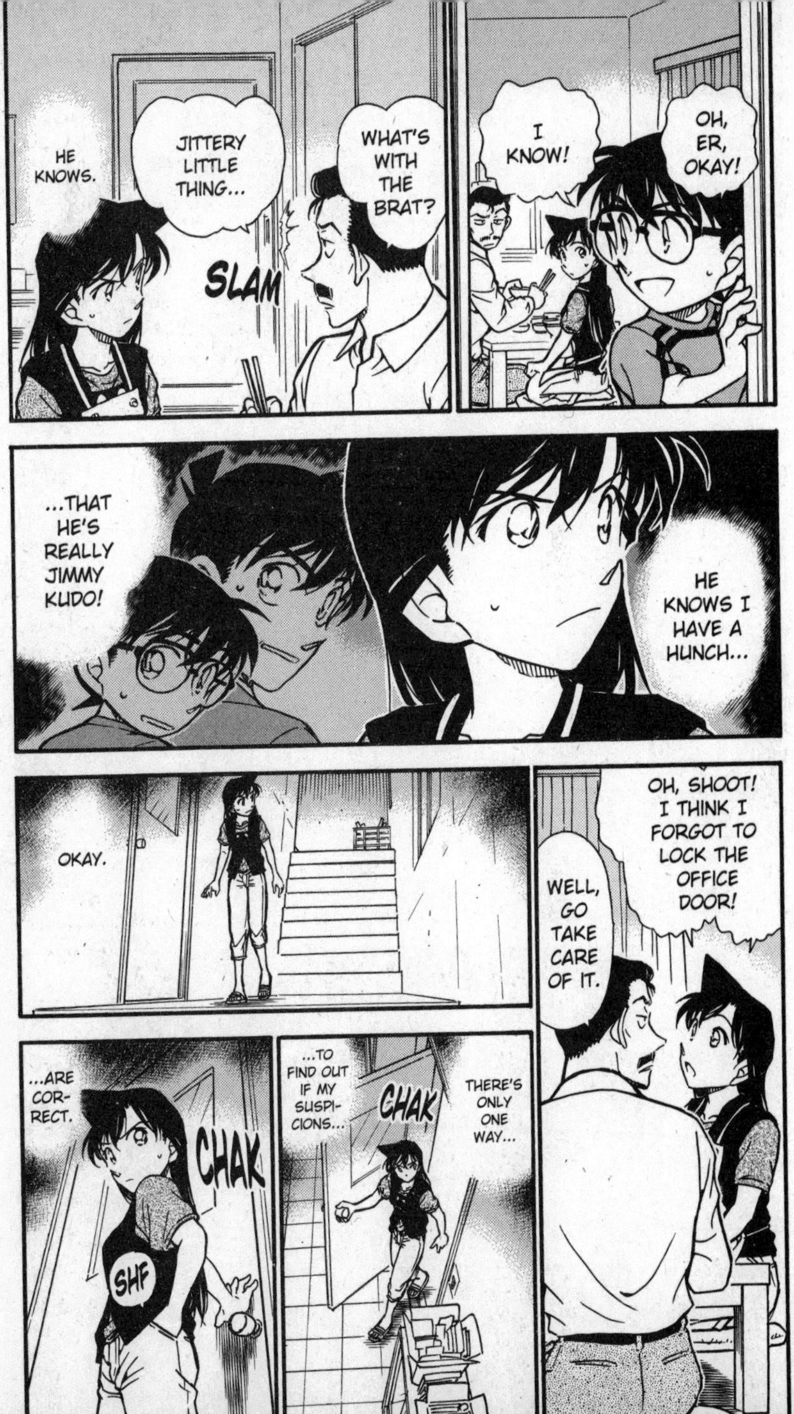
OH, ER, OKAY!
I KNOW!
WHAT'S WITH THE BRAT?
SLAM
JITTERY LITTLE THING...
HE KNOWS.
HE KNOWS I HAVE A HUNCH...
...THAT HE'S REALLY JIMMY KUDO!
OH, SHOOT! I THINK I FORGOT TO LOCK THE OFFICE DOOR!
WELL, GO TAKE CARE OF IT.
OKAY.
THERE'S ONLY ONE WAY...
CHAK
...TO FIND OUT IF MY SUSPI-CIONS...
CHAK
...ARE COR-RECT.
SHF

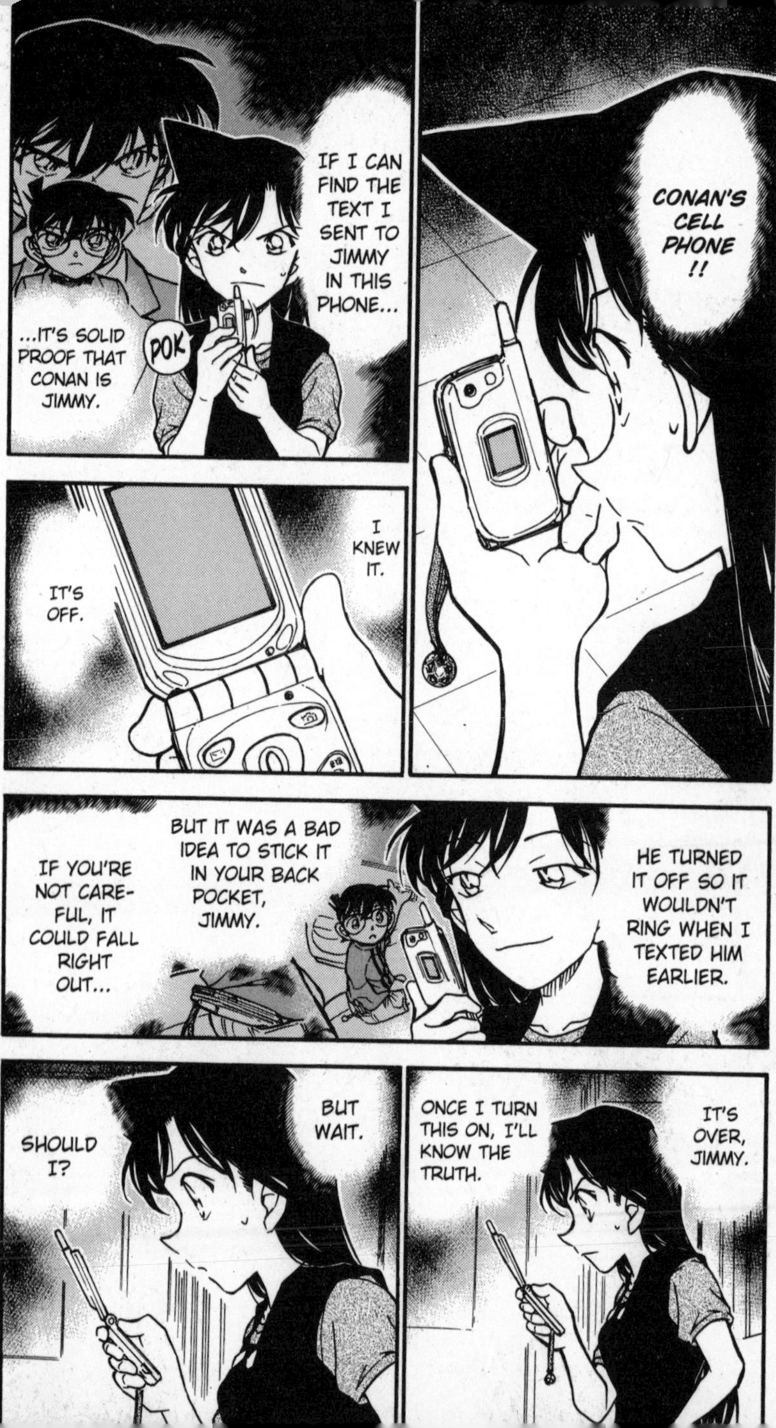
CONAN'S CELL PHONE !!
IF I CAN FIND THE TEXT I SENT TO JIMMY IN THIS PHONE...
POK
...IT'S SOLID PROOF THAT CONAN IS JIMMY.
I KNEW IT.
IT'S OFF.
HE TURNED IT OFF SO IT WOULDN'T RING WHEN I TEXTED HIM EARLIER.
BUT IT WAS A BAD IDEA TO STICK IT IN YOUR BACK POCKET, JIMMY.
IF YOU'RE NOT CARE-FUL, IT COULD FALL RIGHT OUT...
IT'S OVER, JIMMY.
ONCE I TURN THIS ON, I'LL KNOW THE TRUTH.
BUT WAIT.
SHOULD I?

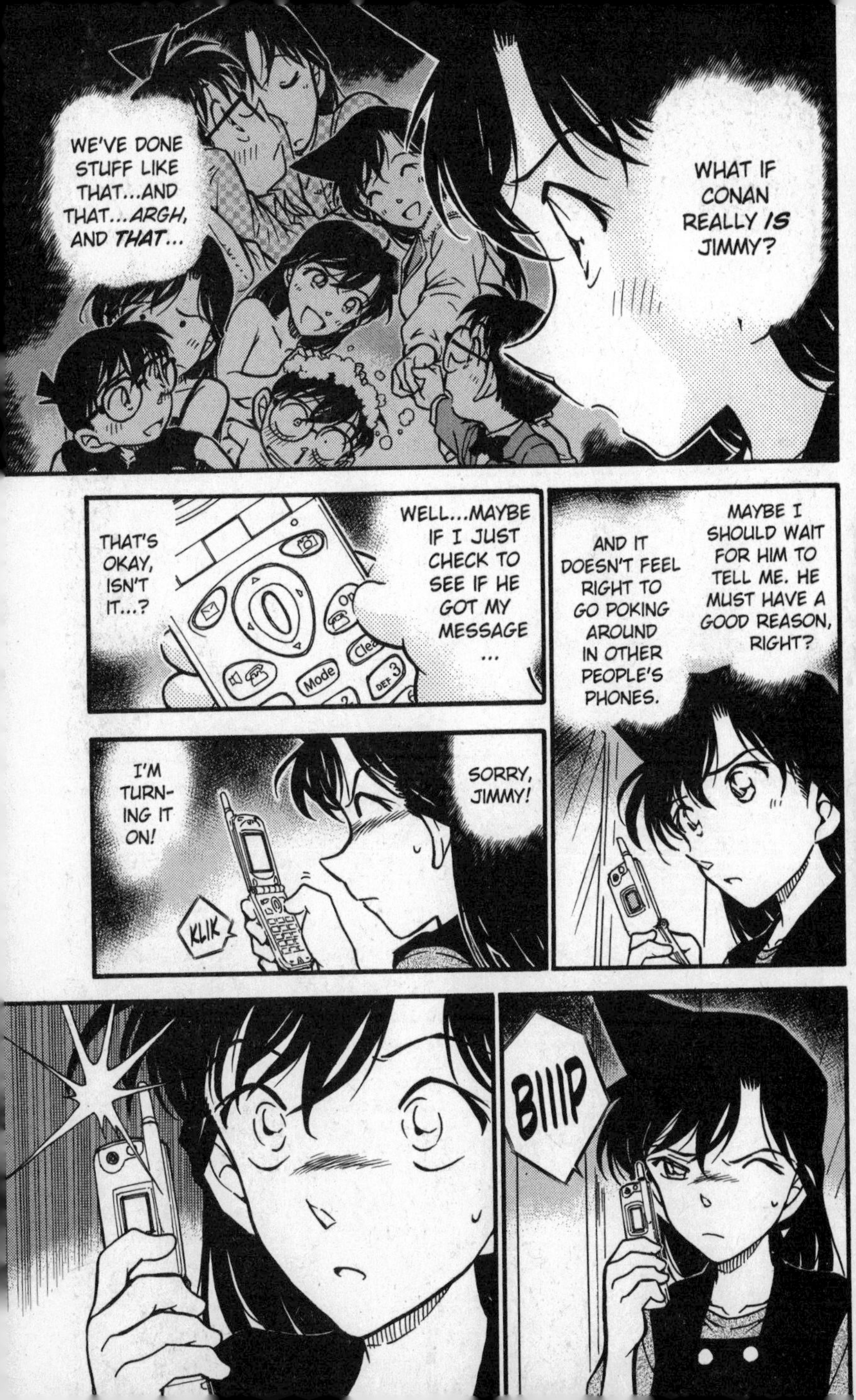
WHAT IF CONAN REALLY *IS* JIMMY?
WE'VE DONE STUFF LIKE THAT...AND THAT...*ARGH*, AND *THAT*...
MAYBE I SHOULD WAIT FOR HIM TO TELL ME. HE MUST HAVE A GOOD REASON, RIGHT?
AND IT DOESN'T FEEL RIGHT TO GO POKING AROUND IN OTHER PEOPLE'S PHONES.
WELL...MAYBE IF I JUST CHECK TO SEE IF HE GOT MY MESSAGE...
THAT'S OKAY, ISN'T IT...?
SORRY, JIMMY!
I'M TURNING IT ON!
KLIK
BIIIP

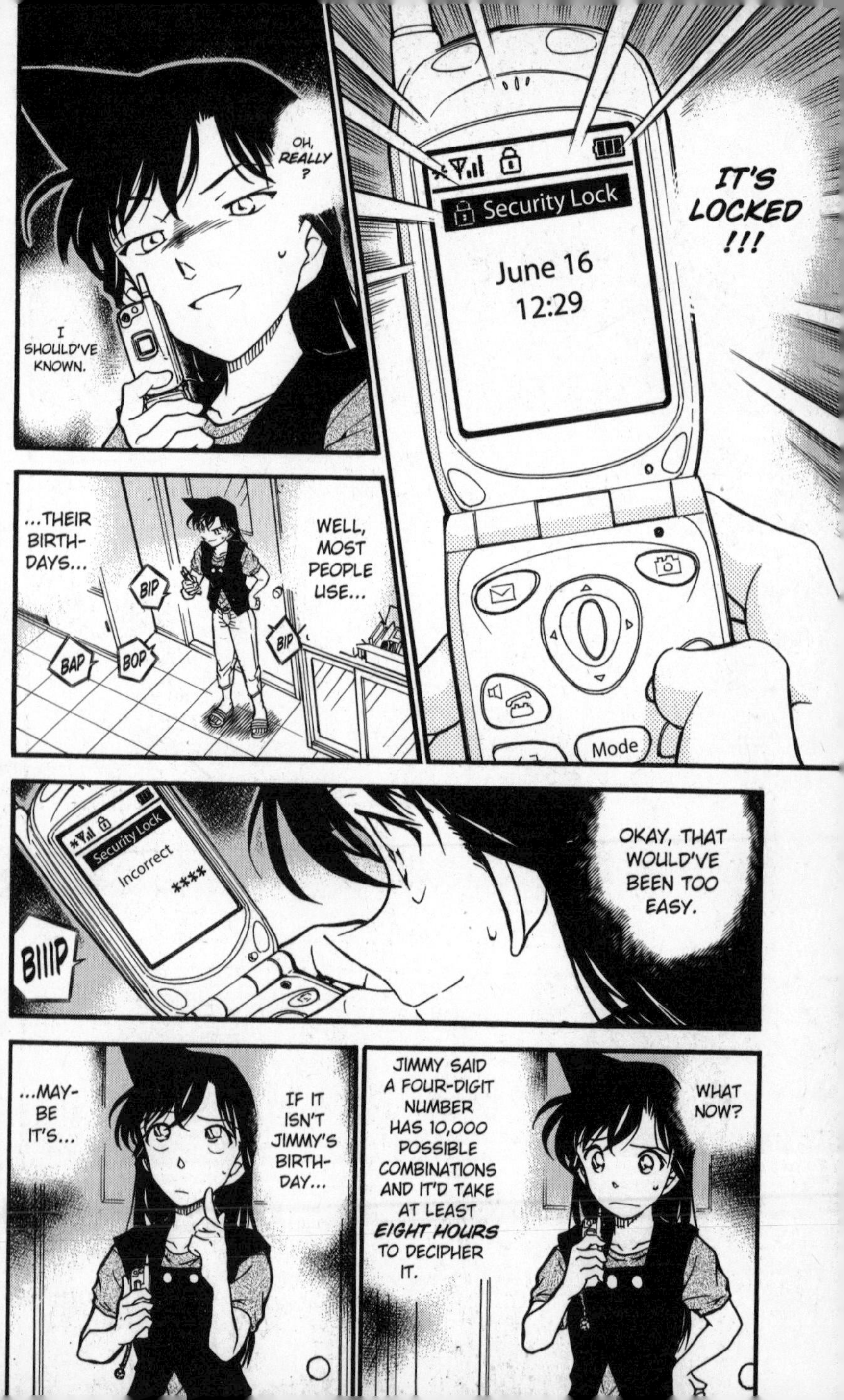
Security Lock
June 16
12:29
Mode
IT'S LOCKED!!!
OH, REALLY?
I SHOULD'VE KNOWN.
WELL, MOST PEOPLE USE...
...THEIR BIRTH-DAYS...
BIP
BIP
BOP
BAP
Security Lock
Incorrect
****
BIIIP
OKAY, THAT WOULD'VE BEEN TOO EASY.
WHAT NOW?
JIMMY SAID A FOUR-DIGIT NUMBER HAS 10,000 POSSIBLE COMBINATIONS AND IT'D TAKE AT LEAST EIGHT HOURS TO DECIPHER IT.
IF IT ISN'T JIMMY'S BIRTH-DAY...
...MAY-BE IT'S...

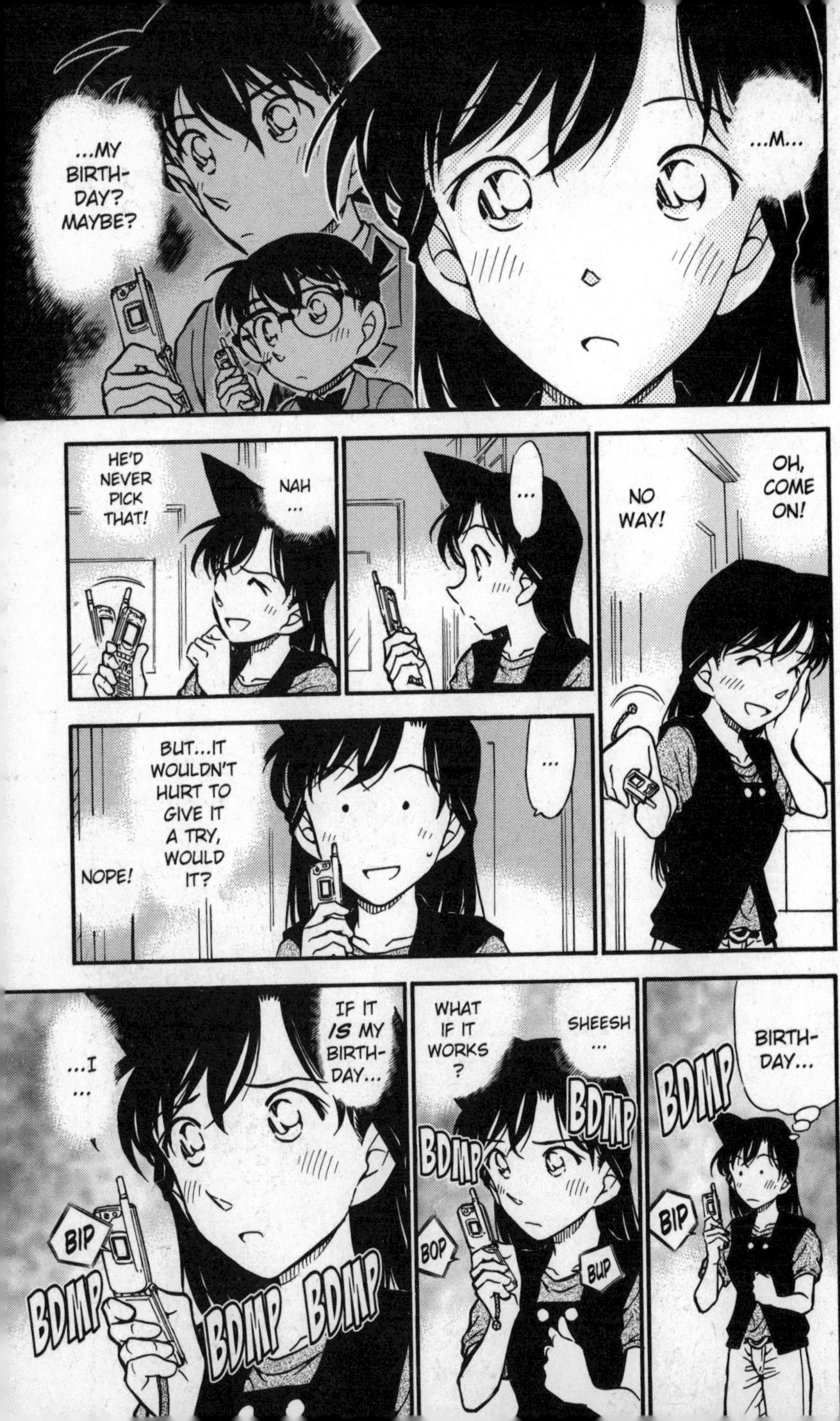
...M...
...MY BIRTH-DAY? MAYBE?
OH, COME ON!
NO WAY!
...
NAH ...
HE'D NEVER PICK THAT!
...
BUT...IT WOULDN'T HURT TO GIVE IT A TRY, WOULD IT?
NOPE!
BIRTH-DAY...
BDMP
BIP
SHEESH ...
WHAT IF IT WORKS ?
BDMP
BDMP
BOP
BUP
IF IT *IS* MY BIRTH-DAY...
...I ...
BIP
BDMP
BDMP
BDMP

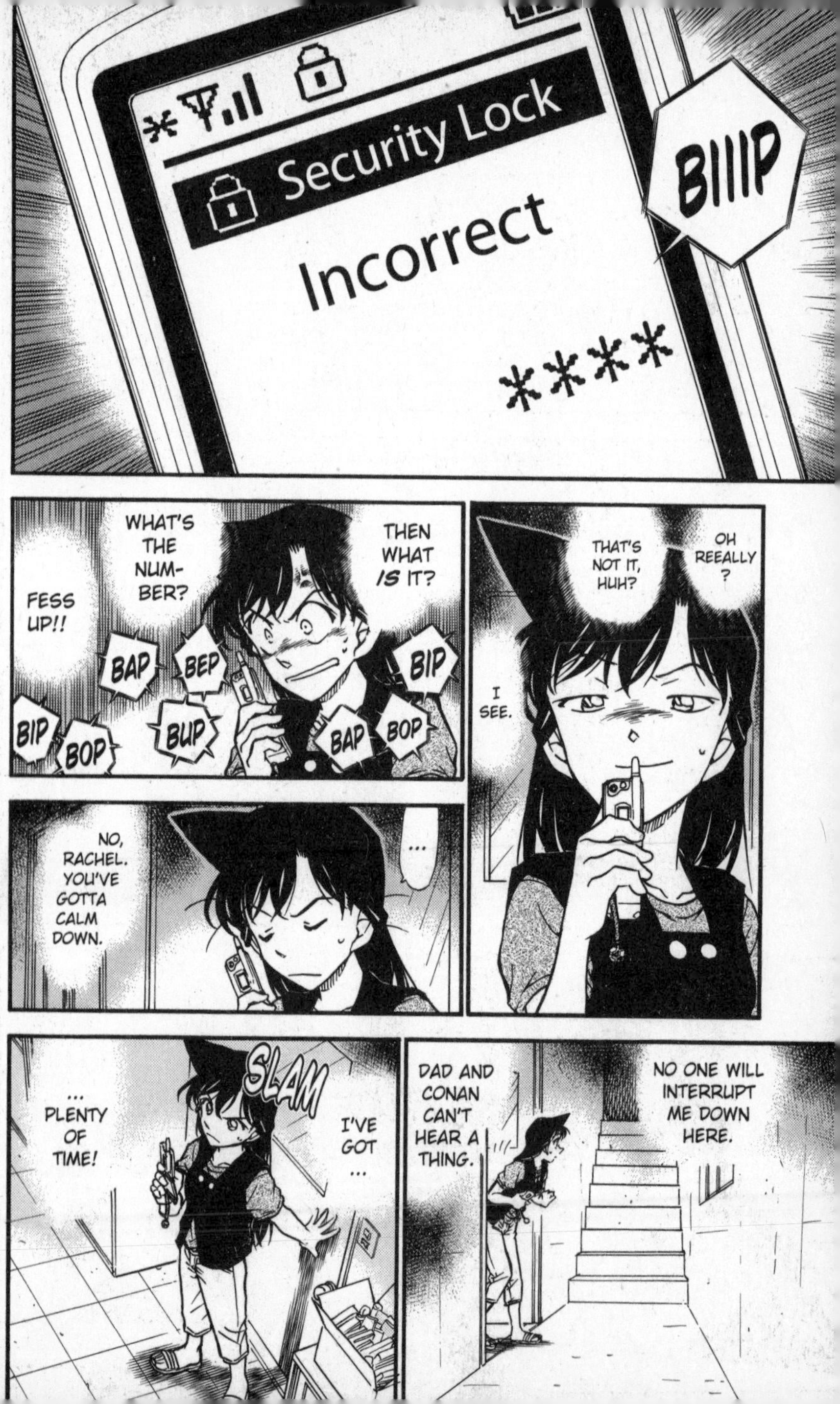
Security Lock
Incorrect
****
BIIIP
OH REEALLY?
THAT'S NOT IT, HUH?
I SEE.
THEN WHAT *IS* IT?
WHAT'S THE NUM-BER?
FESS UP!!
BIP
BOP
BAP
BUP
BEP
BAP
BIP
BOP
...
NO, RACHEL. YOU'VE GOTTA CALM DOWN.
NO ONE WILL INTERRUPT ME DOWN HERE.
DAD AND CONAN CAN'T HEAR A THING.
SLAM
I'VE GOT ...
... PLENTY OF TIME!

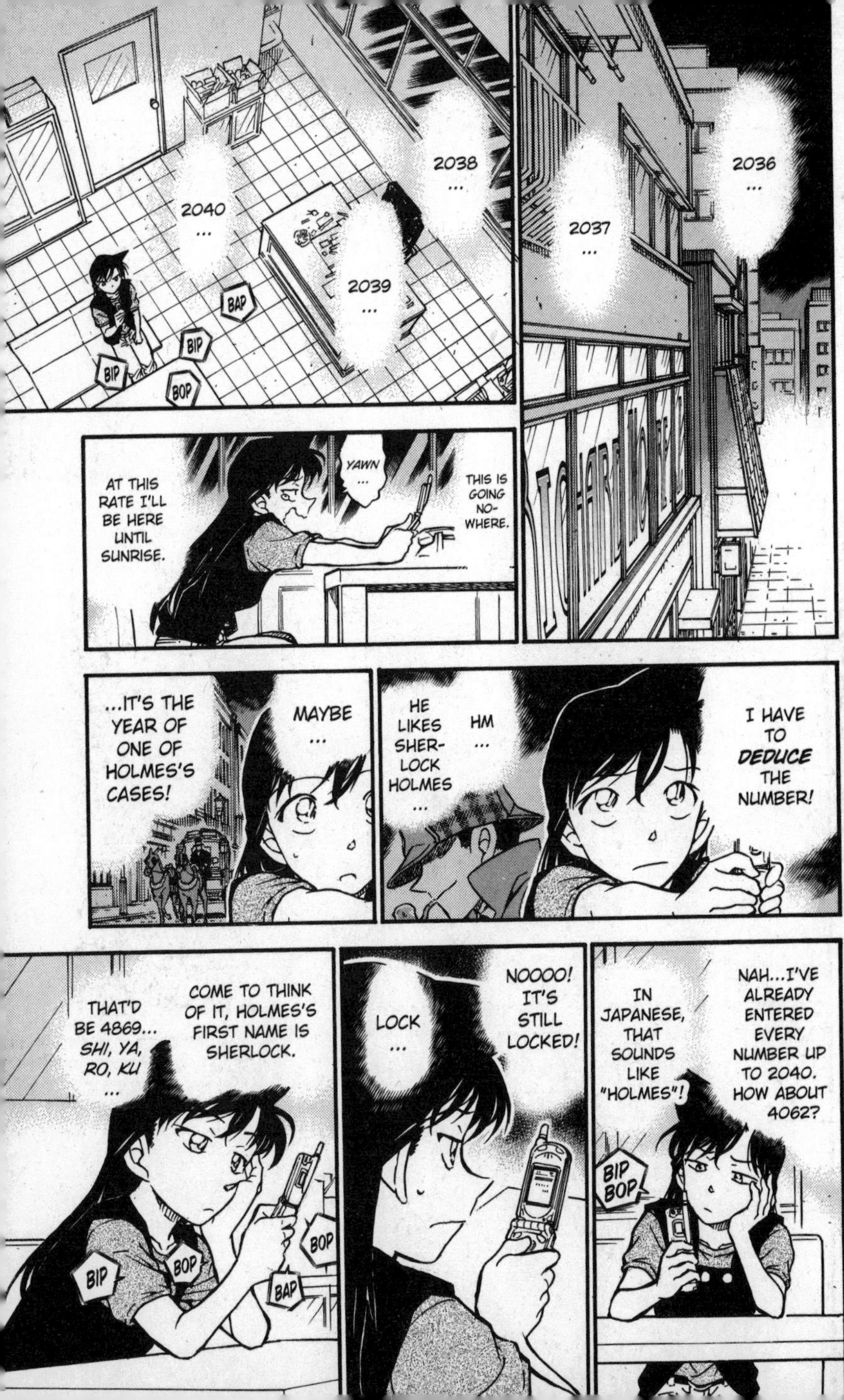
2036
...
2037
...
2038
...
2039
...
2040
...
BAP
BIP
BIP
BOP
THIS IS GOING NOWHERE.
YAWN ...
AT THIS RATE I'LL BE HERE UNTIL SUNRISE.
I HAVE TO **DEDUCE** THE NUMBER!
HM ...
HE LIKES SHERLOCK HOLMES ...
MAYBE ...
...IT'S THE YEAR OF ONE OF HOLMES'S CASES!
NAH...I'VE ALREADY ENTERED EVERY NUMBER UP TO 2040. HOW ABOUT 4062?
IN JAPANESE, THAT SOUNDS LIKE "HOLMES"!
BIP BOP
NOOOO! IT'S STILL LOCKED!
LOCK ...
COME TO THINK OF IT, HOLMES'S FIRST NAME IS SHERLOCK.
THAT'D BE 4869... *SHI, YA, RO, KU* ...
BOP
BOP
BIP
BAP

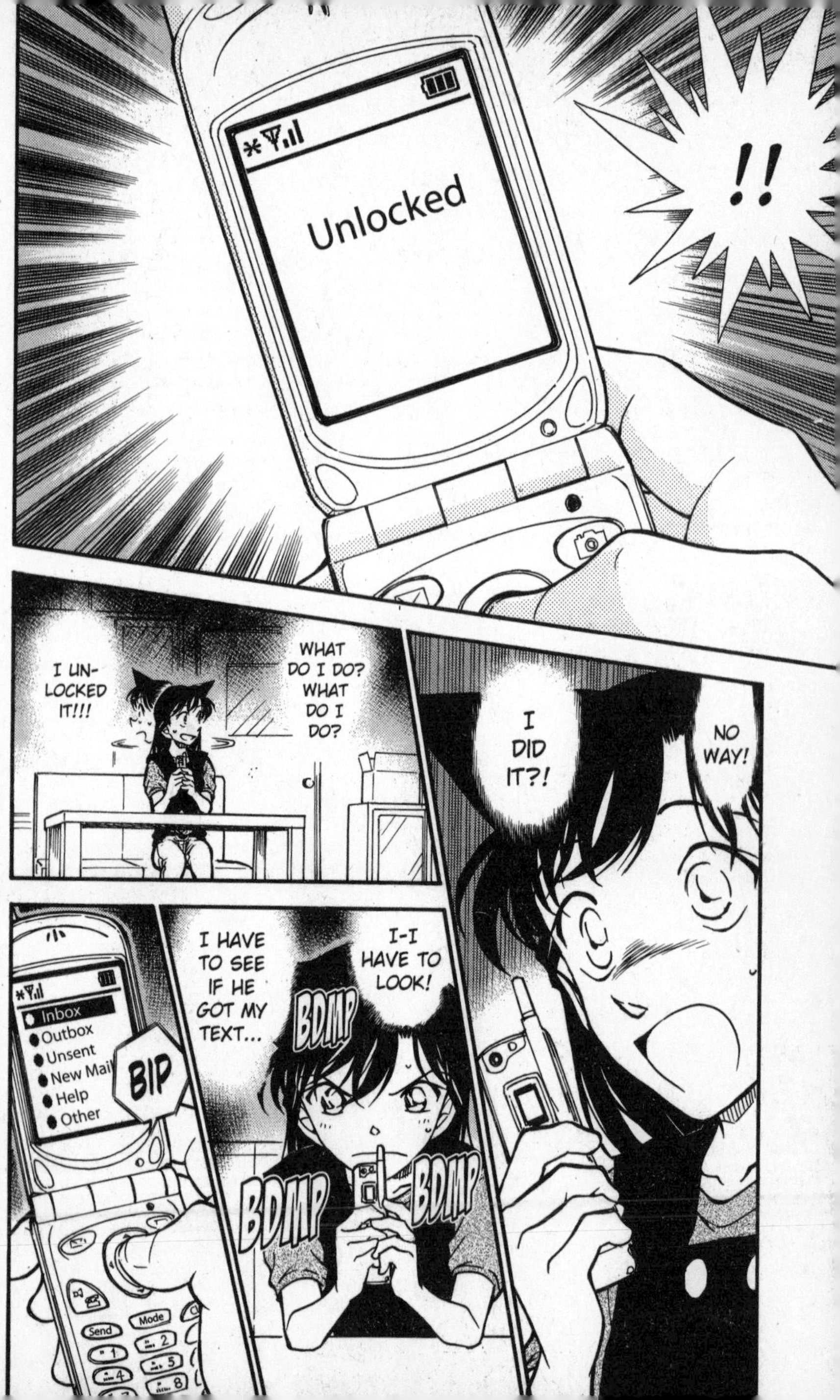
Unlocked
!!
NO WAY!
I DID IT?!
WHAT DO I DO? WHAT DO I DO?
I UN-LOCKED IT!!!
I-I HAVE TO LOOK!
I HAVE TO SEE IF HE GOT MY TEXT...
BDMP
BDMP
BDMP
Inbox
Outbox
Unsent
New Mail
Help
Other
BIP
Mode
Send

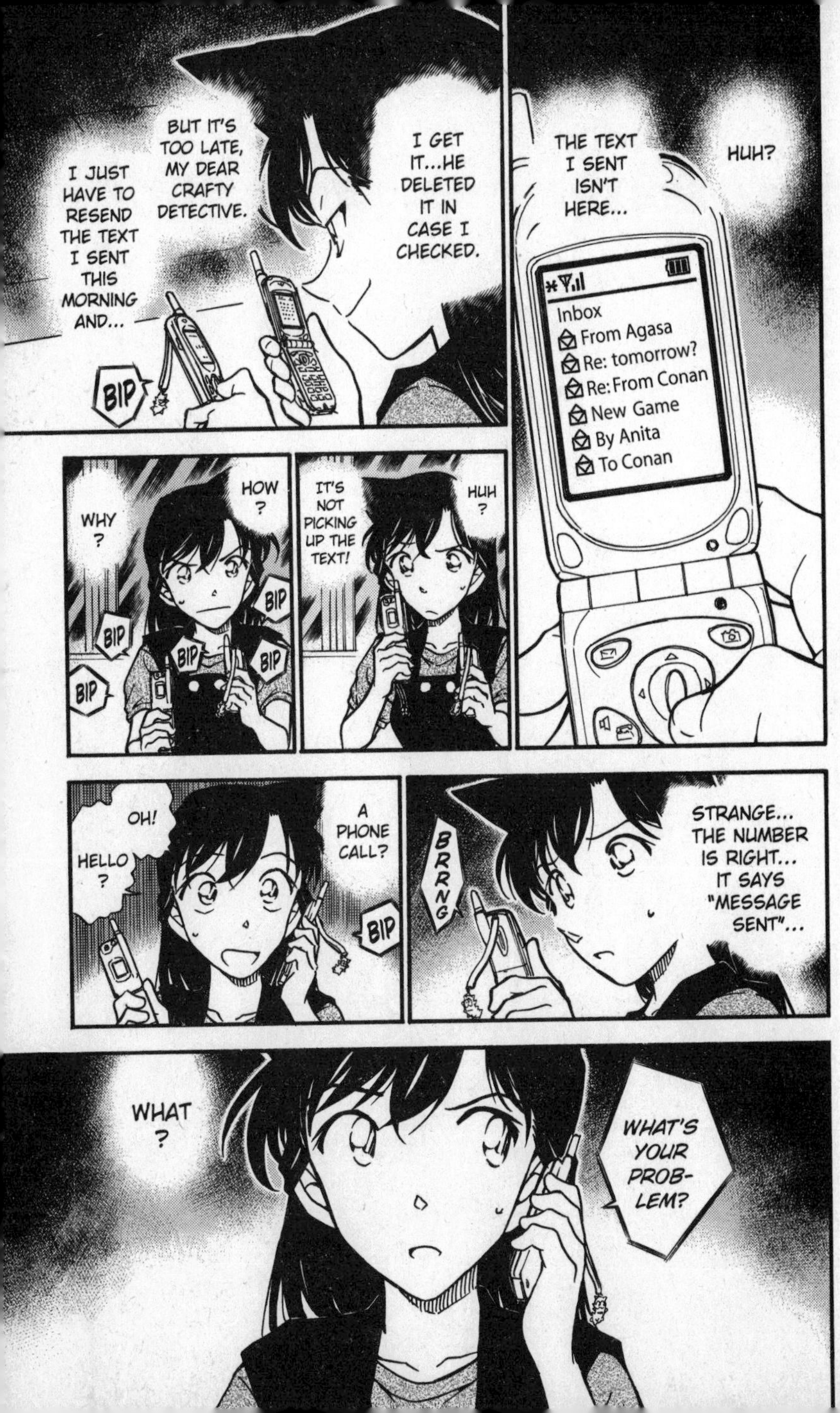
HUH?
THE TEXT I SENT ISN'T HERE...
Inbox
From Agasa
Re: tomorrow?
Re: From Conan
New Game
By Anita
To Conan
I GET IT...HE DELETED IT IN CASE I CHECKED.
BUT IT'S TOO LATE, MY DEAR CRAFTY DETECTIVE.
I JUST HAVE TO RESEND THE TEXT I SENT THIS MORNING AND...
BIP
HUH?
IT'S NOT PICKING UP THE TEXT!
HOW?
WHY?
BIP
BIP
BIP
BIP
BIP
STRANGE... THE NUMBER IS RIGHT... IT SAYS "MESSAGE SENT"...
BRRRNG
A PHONE CALL?
BIP
OH!
HELLO?
WHAT'S YOUR PROBLEM?
WHAT?

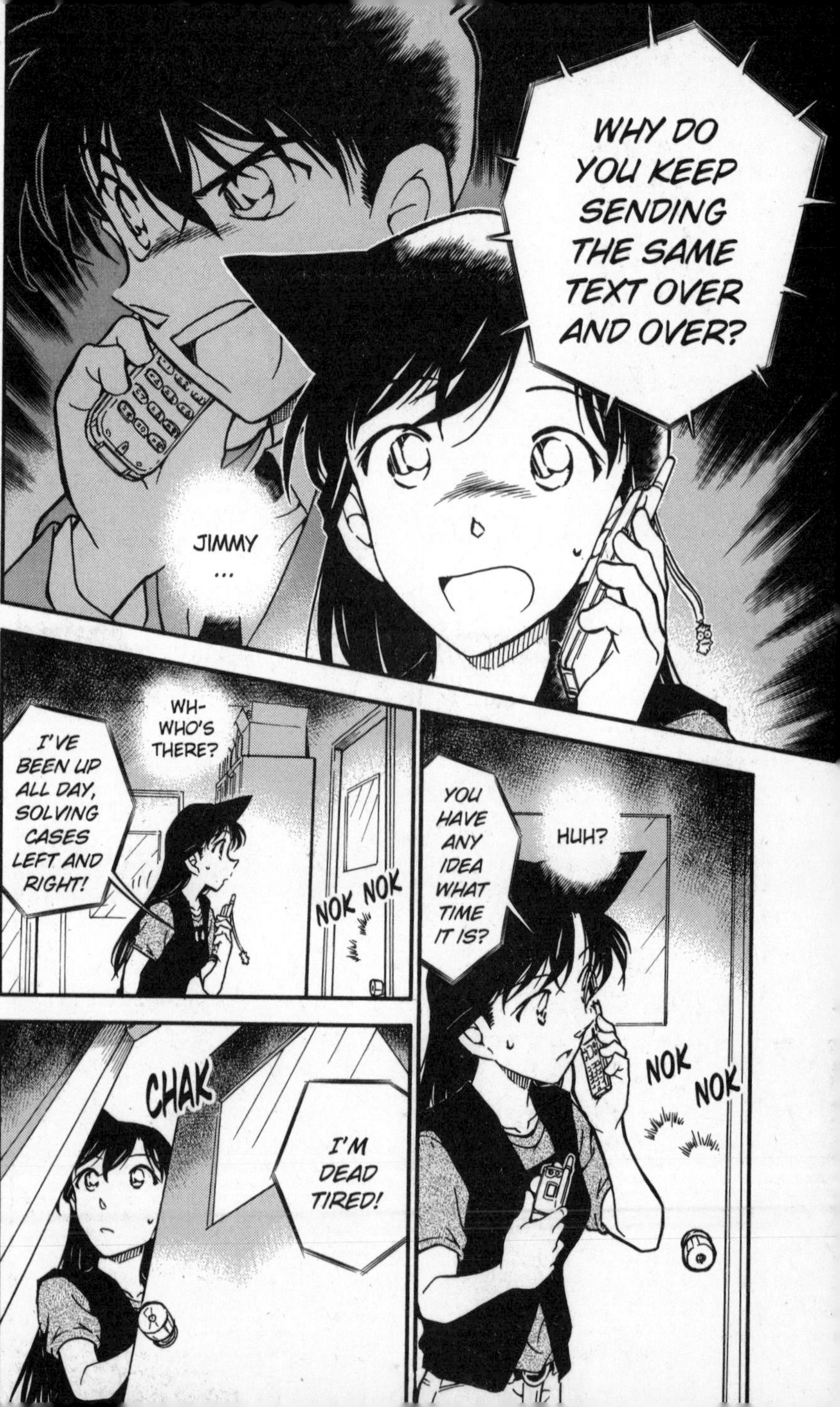
WHY DO YOU KEEP SENDING THE SAME TEXT OVER AND OVER?
JIMMY ...
YOU HAVE ANY IDEA WHAT TIME IT IS?
HUH?
NOK NOK
I'VE BEEN UP ALL DAY, SOLVING CASES LEFT AND RIGHT!
WH- WHO'S THERE?
NOK NOK
I'M DEAD TIRED!
CHAK

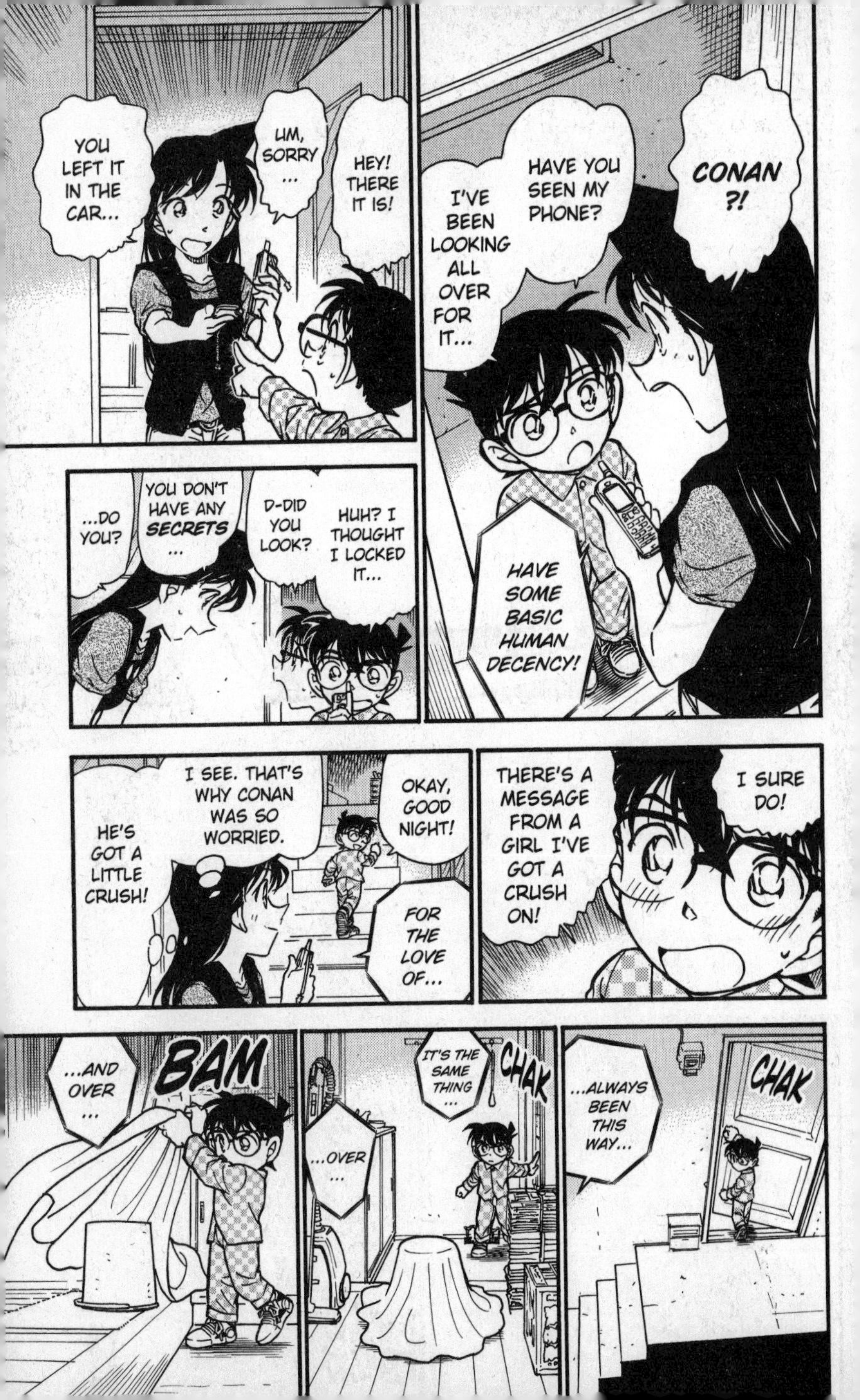
CONAN ?!
HAVE YOU SEEN MY PHONE?
I'VE BEEN LOOKING ALL OVER FOR IT...
HAVE SOME BASIC HUMAN DECENCY!
HEY! THERE IT IS!
UM, SORRY ...
YOU LEFT IT IN THE CAR...
HUH? I THOUGHT I LOCKED IT...
D-DID YOU LOOK?
YOU DON'T HAVE ANY SECRETS ...
...DO YOU?
I SURE DO!
THERE'S A MESSAGE FROM A GIRL I'VE GOT A CRUSH ON!
OKAY, GOOD NIGHT!
FOR THE LOVE OF...
I SEE. THAT'S WHY CONAN WAS SO WORRIED.
HE'S GOT A LITTLE CRUSH!
CHAK
...ALWAYS BEEN THIS WAY...
CHAK
IT'S THE SAME THING ...
...OVER ...
BAM
...AND OVER ...

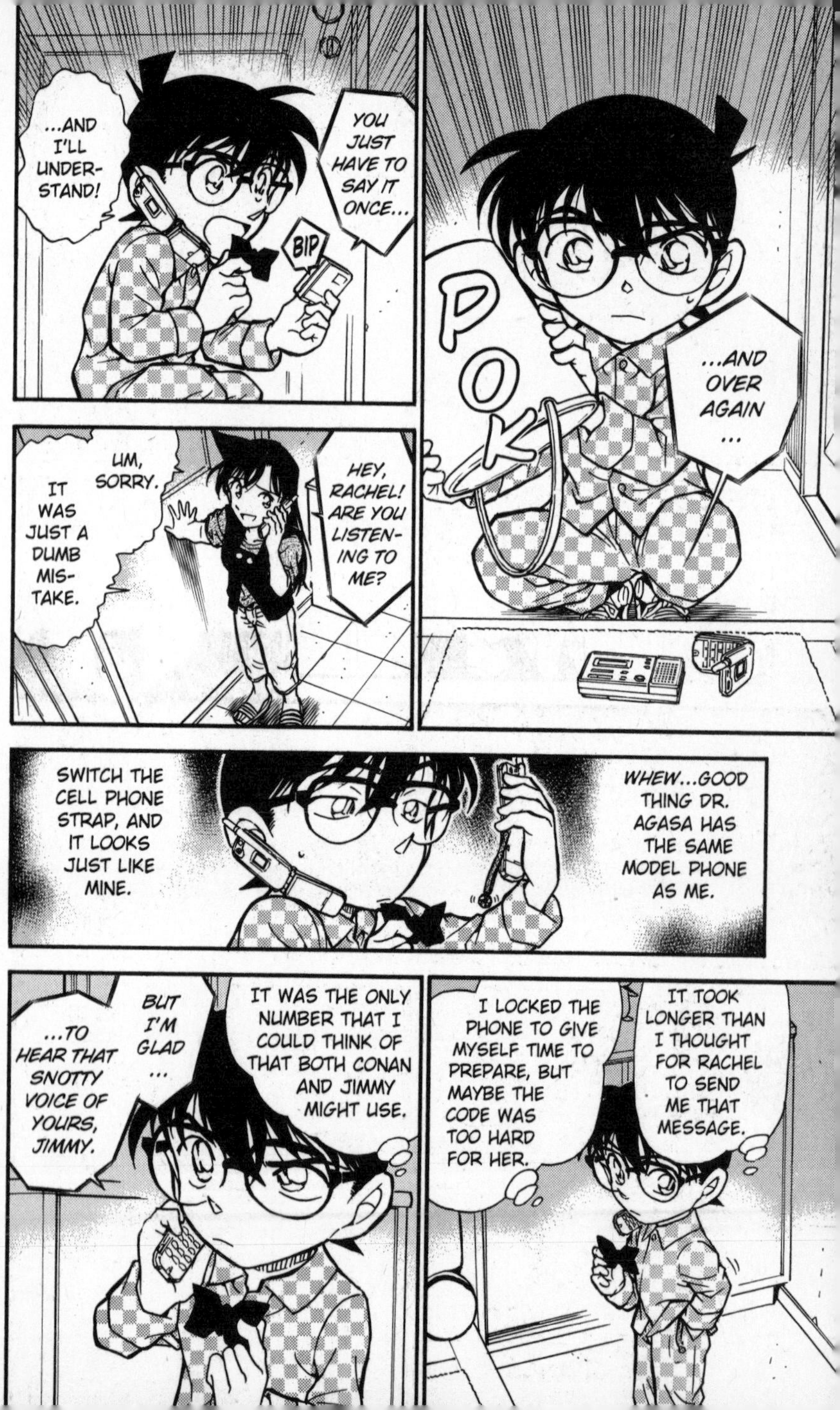
POK
...AND OVER AGAIN ...
YOU JUST HAVE TO SAY IT ONCE...
BIP
...AND I'LL UNDER-STAND!
HEY, RACHEL! ARE YOU LISTEN-ING TO ME?
UM, SORRY.
IT WAS JUST A DUMB MIS-TAKE.
WHEW...GOOD THING DR. AGASA HAS THE SAME MODEL PHONE AS ME.
SWITCH THE CELL PHONE STRAP, AND IT LOOKS JUST LIKE MINE.
IT TOOK LONGER THAN I THOUGHT FOR RACHEL TO SEND ME THAT MESSAGE.
I LOCKED THE PHONE TO GIVE MYSELF TIME TO PREPARE, BUT MAYBE THE CODE WAS TOO HARD FOR HER.
IT WAS THE ONLY NUMBER THAT I COULD THINK OF THAT BOTH CONAN AND JIMMY MIGHT USE.
BUT I'M GLAD ...
...TO HEAR THAT SNOTTY VOICE OF YOURS, JIMMY.

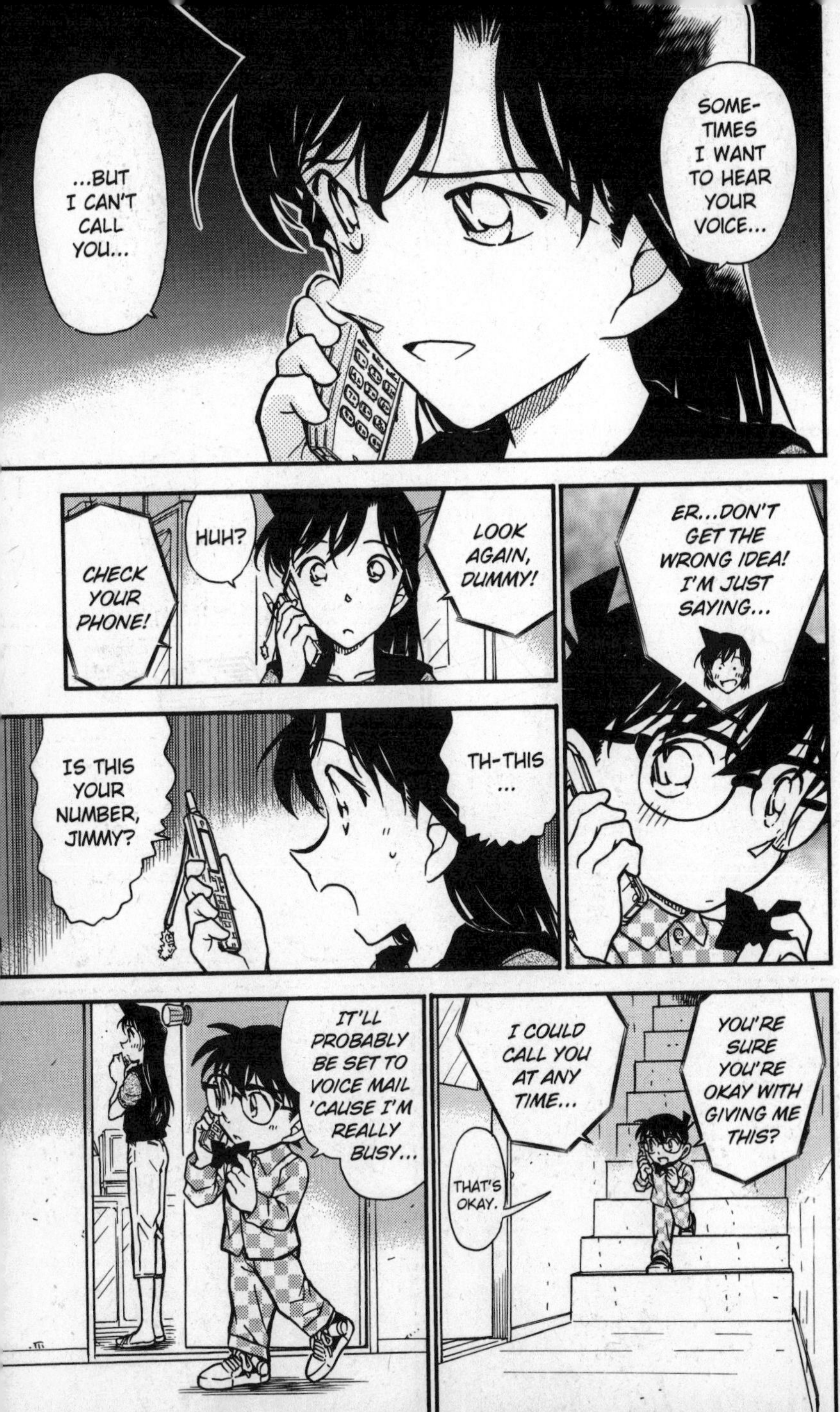
SOME-TIMES I WANT TO HEAR YOUR VOICE...
...BUT I CAN'T CALL YOU...
ER...DON'T GET THE WRONG IDEA! I'M JUST SAYING...
LOOK AGAIN, DUMMY!
HUH?
CHECK YOUR PHONE!
TH-THIS ...
IS THIS YOUR NUMBER, JIMMY?
YOU'RE SURE YOU'RE OKAY WITH GIVING ME THIS?
I COULD CALL YOU AT ANY TIME...
THAT'S OKAY.
IT'LL PROBABLY BE SET TO VOICE MAIL 'CAUSE I'M REALLY BUSY...

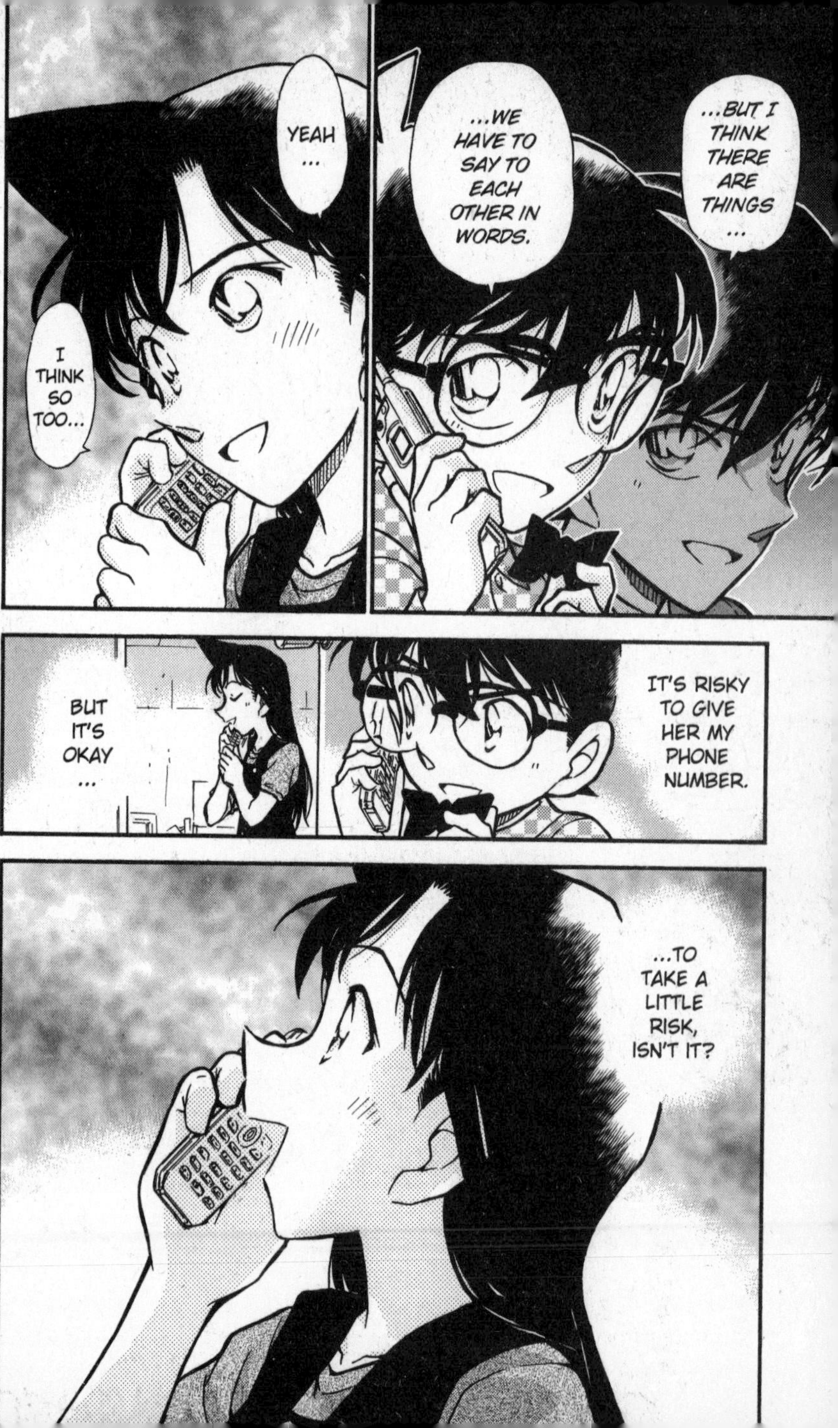
...BUT I THINK THERE ARE THINGS...
...WE HAVE TO SAY TO EACH OTHER IN WORDS.
YEAH...
I THINK SO TOO...
IT'S RISKY TO GIVE HER MY PHONE NUMBER.
BUT IT'S OKAY...
...TO TAKE A LITTLE RISK, ISN'T IT?

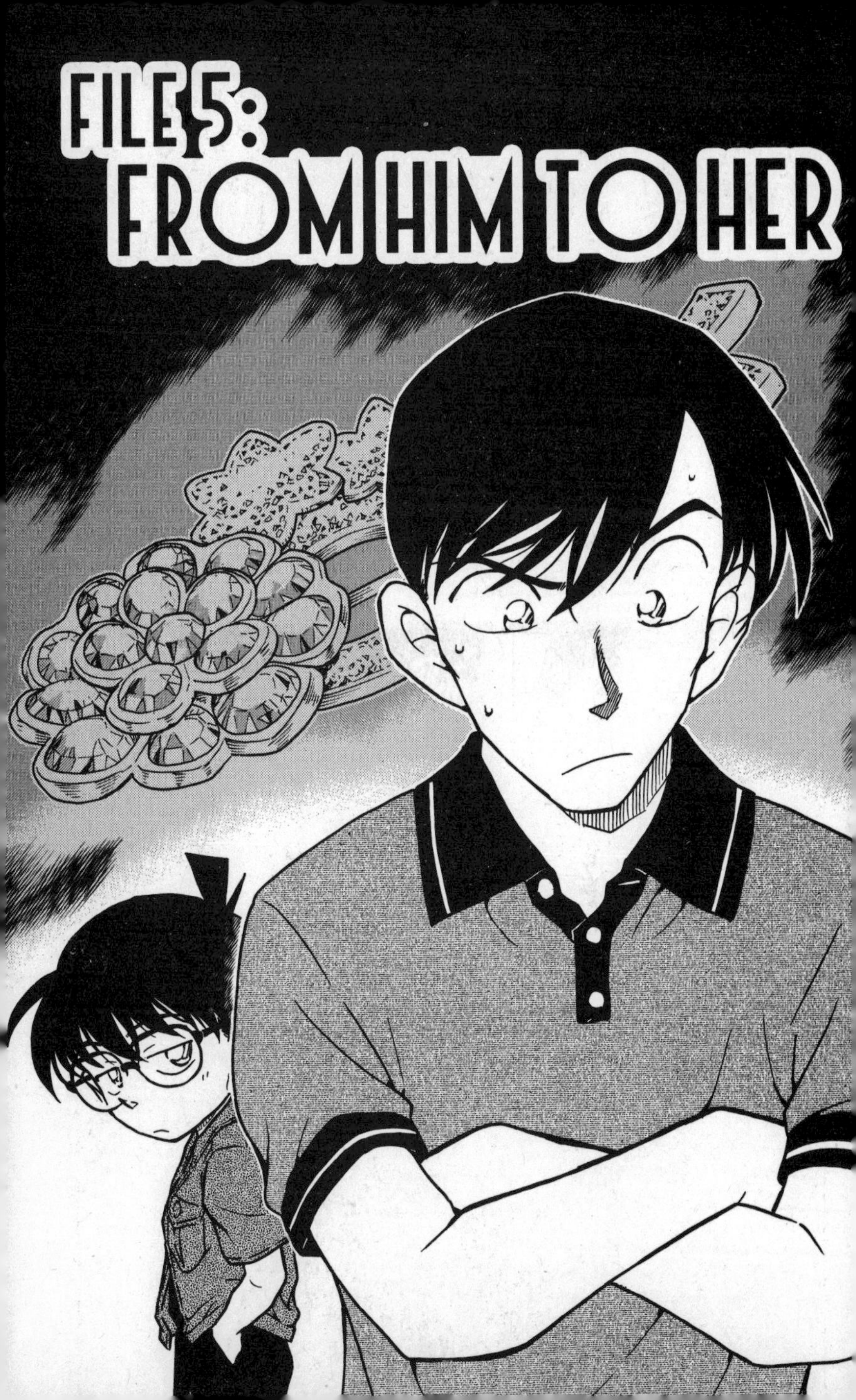
FILE 5:
FROM HIM TO HER

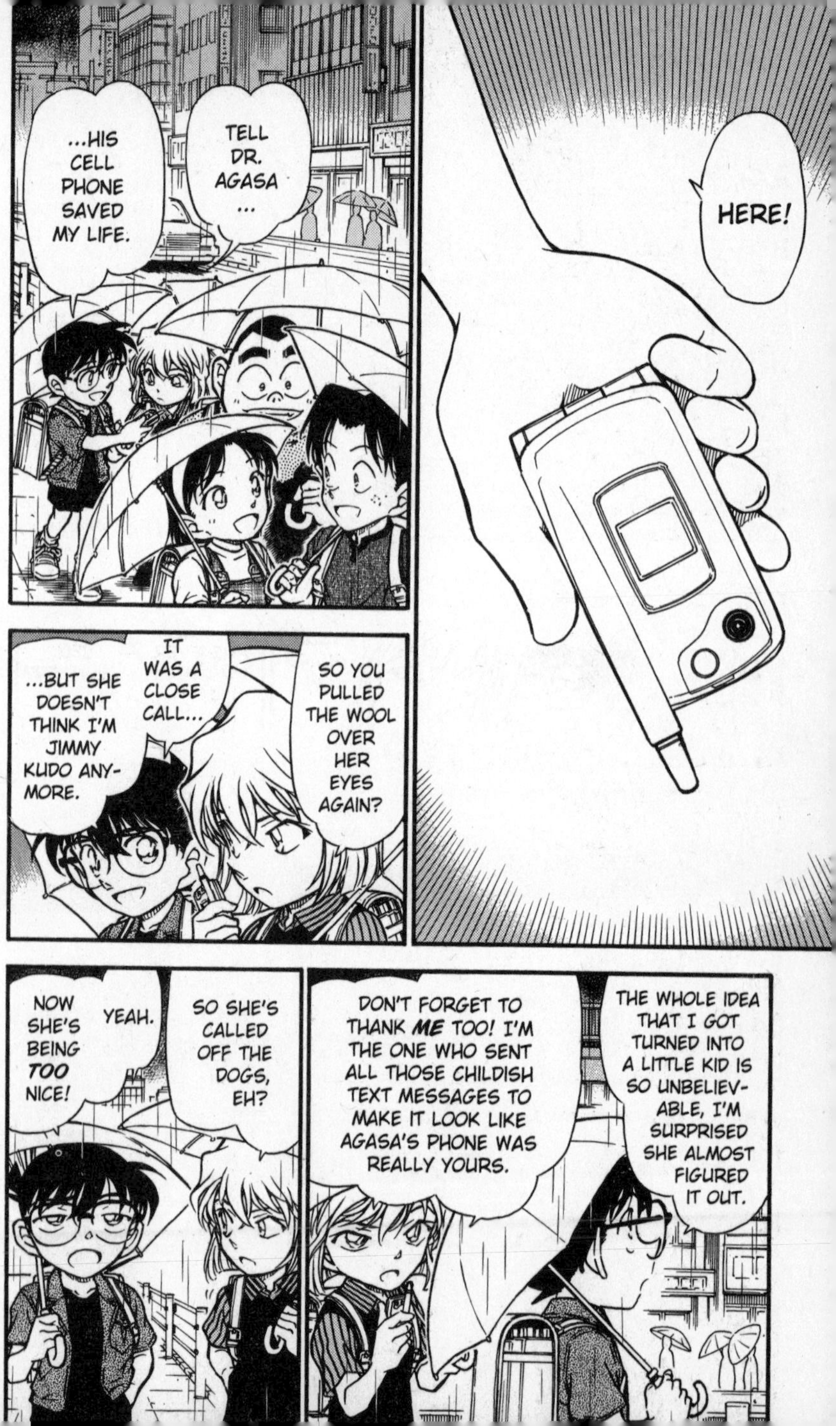
HERE!
TELL DR. AGASA ...
...HIS CELL PHONE SAVED MY LIFE.
SO YOU PULLED THE WOOL OVER HER EYES AGAIN?
IT WAS A CLOSE CALL...
...BUT SHE DOESN'T THINK I'M JIMMY KUDO ANYMORE.
THE WHOLE IDEA THAT I GOT TURNED INTO A LITTLE KID IS SO UNBELIEVABLE, I'M SURPRISED SHE ALMOST FIGURED IT OUT.
DON'T FORGET TO THANK *ME* TOO! I'M THE ONE WHO SENT ALL THOSE CHILDISH TEXT MESSAGES TO MAKE IT LOOK LIKE AGASA'S PHONE WAS REALLY YOURS.
SO SHE'S CALLED OFF THE DOGS, EH?
YEAH.
NOW SHE'S BEING *TOO* NICE!

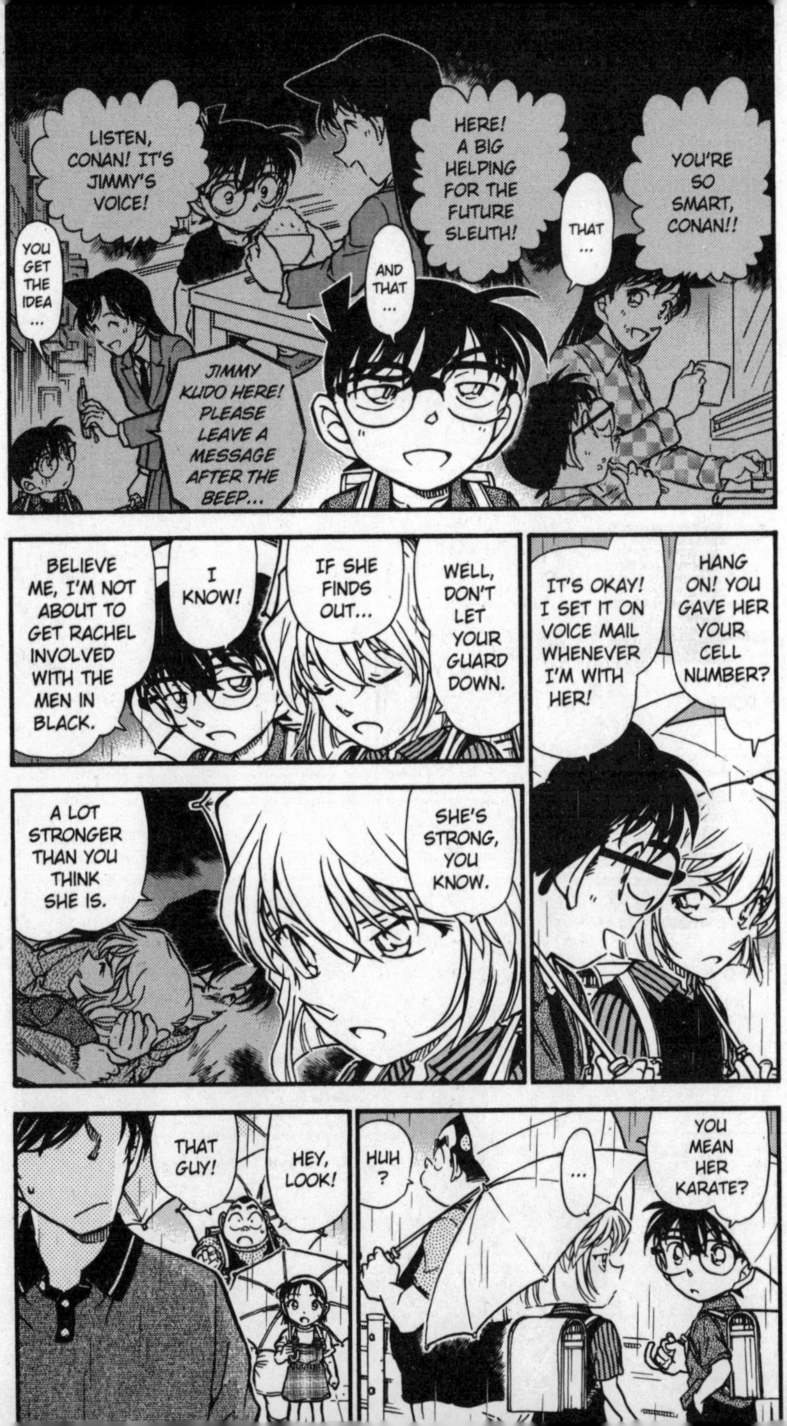
YOU'RE SO SMART, CONAN!!
THAT ...
HERE! A BIG HELPING FOR THE FUTURE SLEUTH!
AND THAT ...
LISTEN, CONAN! IT'S JIMMY'S VOICE!
JIMMY KUDO HERE! PLEASE LEAVE A MESSAGE AFTER THE BEEP...
YOU GET THE IDEA ...
HANG ON! YOU GAVE HER YOUR CELL NUMBER?
IT'S OKAY! I SET IT ON VOICE MAIL WHENEVER I'M WITH HER!
WELL, DON'T LET YOUR GUARD DOWN.
IF SHE FINDS OUT...
I KNOW!
BELIEVE ME, I'M NOT ABOUT TO GET RACHEL INVOLVED WITH THE MEN IN BLACK.
SHE'S STRONG, YOU KNOW.
A LOT STRONGER THAN YOU THINK SHE IS.
YOU MEAN HER KARATE?
...
HUH ?
HEY, LOOK!
THAT GUY!

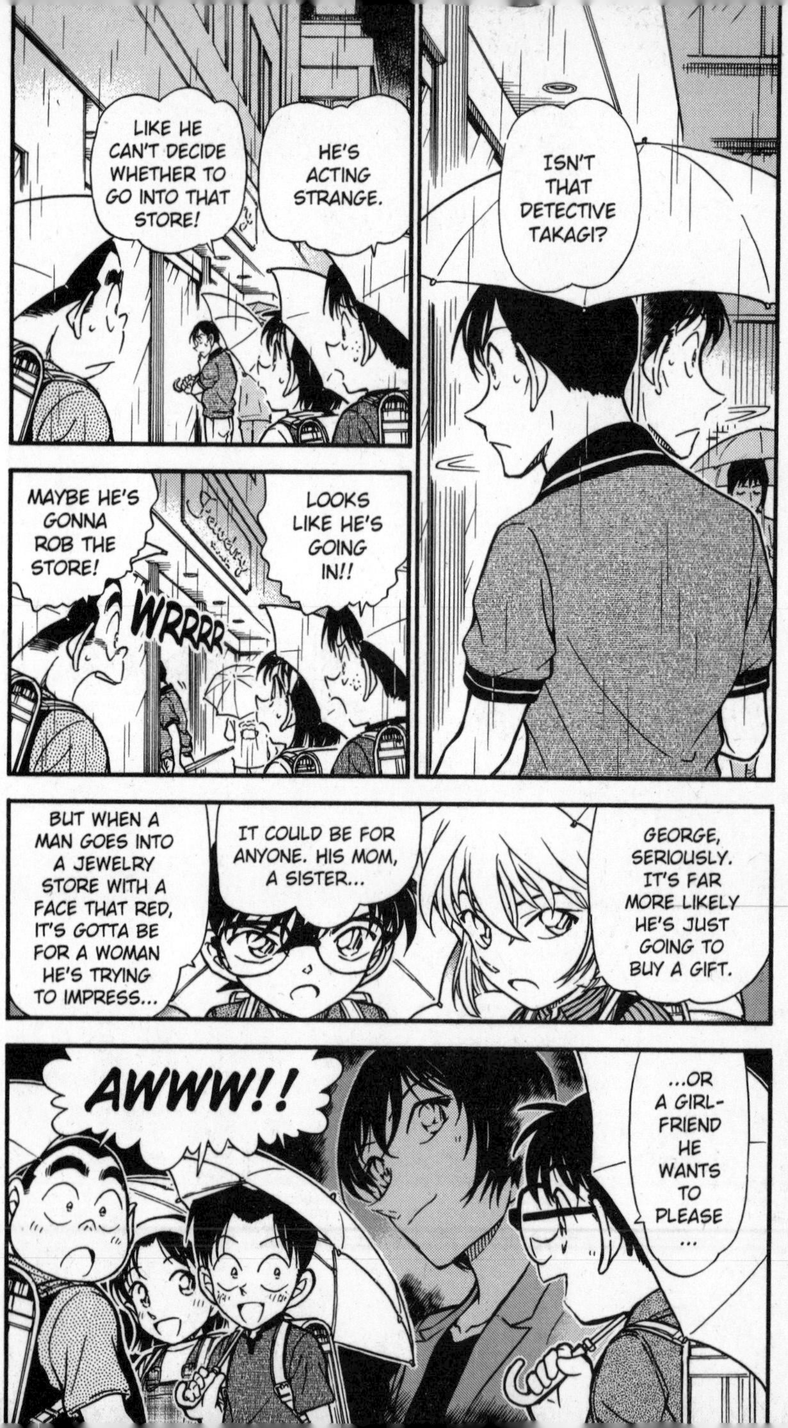
ISN'T THAT DETECTIVE TAKAGI?
HE'S ACTING STRANGE.
LIKE HE CAN'T DECIDE WHETHER TO GO INTO THAT STORE!
LOOKS LIKE HE'S GOING IN!!
Jewelry
MAYBE HE'S GONNA ROB THE STORE!
WRRRR
GEORGE, SERIOUSLY. IT'S FAR MORE LIKELY HE'S JUST GOING TO BUY A GIFT.
IT COULD BE FOR ANYONE. HIS MOM, A SISTER...
BUT WHEN A MAN GOES INTO A JEWELRY STORE WITH A FACE THAT RED, IT'S GOTTA BE FOR A WOMAN HE'S TRYING TO IMPRESS...
...OR A GIRL-FRIEND HE WANTS TO PLEASE...
AWWW!!

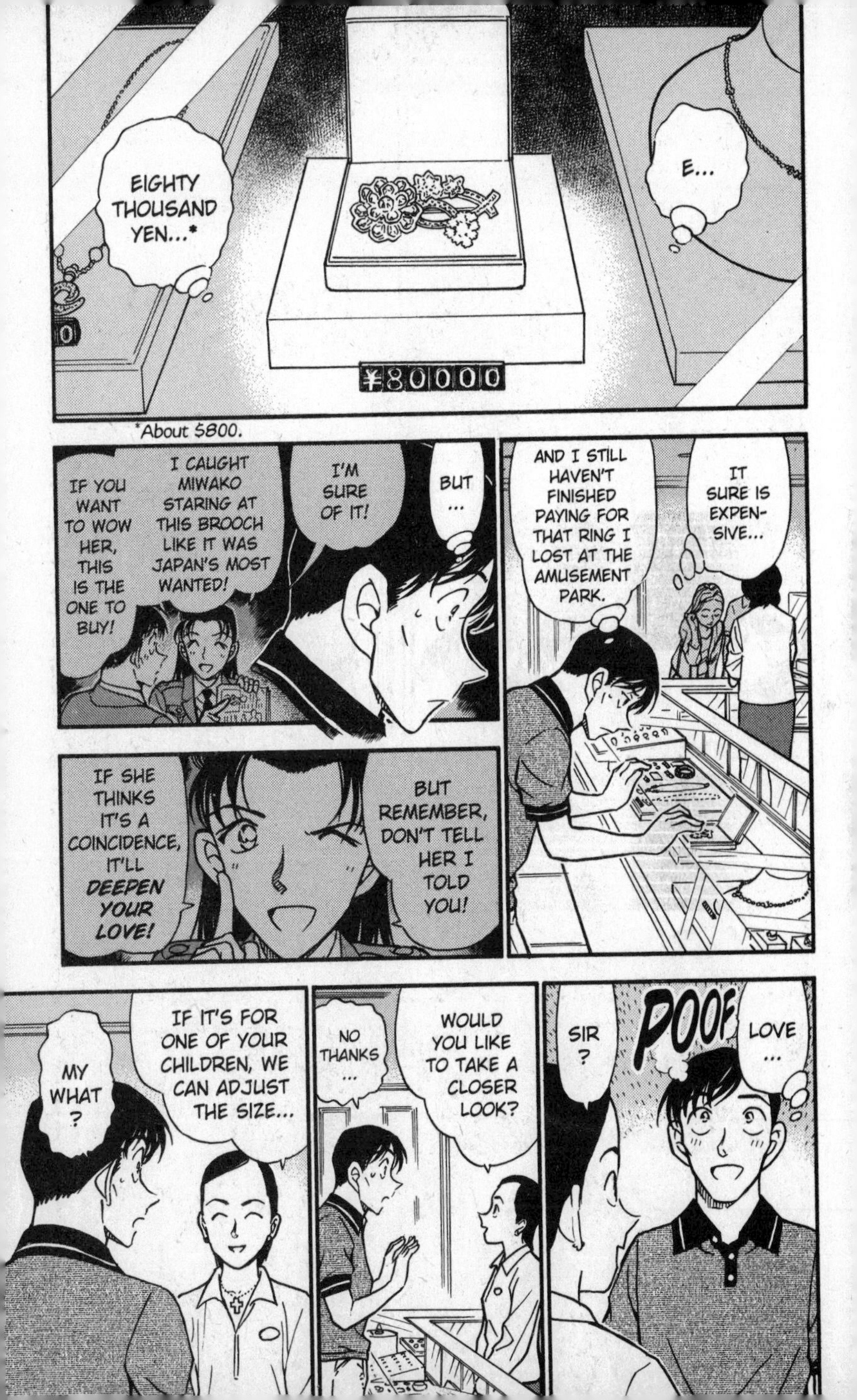
E...
EIGHTY THOUSAND YEN...*
¥80000
IT SURE IS EXPENSIVE...
AND I STILL HAVEN'T FINISHED PAYING FOR THAT RING I LOST AT THE AMUSEMENT PARK.
BUT...
I'M SURE OF IT!
I CAUGHT MIWAKO STARING AT THIS BROOCH LIKE IT WAS JAPAN'S MOST WANTED!
IF YOU WANT TO WOW HER, THIS IS THE ONE TO BUY!
BUT REMEMBER, DON'T TELL HER I TOLD YOU!
IF SHE THINKS IT'S A COINCIDENCE, IT'LL ***DEEPEN YOUR LOVE!***
LOVE...
POOF
SIR?
WOULD YOU LIKE TO TAKE A CLOSER LOOK?
NO THANKS...
IF IT'S FOR ONE OF YOUR CHILDREN, WE CAN ADJUST THE SIZE...
MY WHAT?

*About $800.

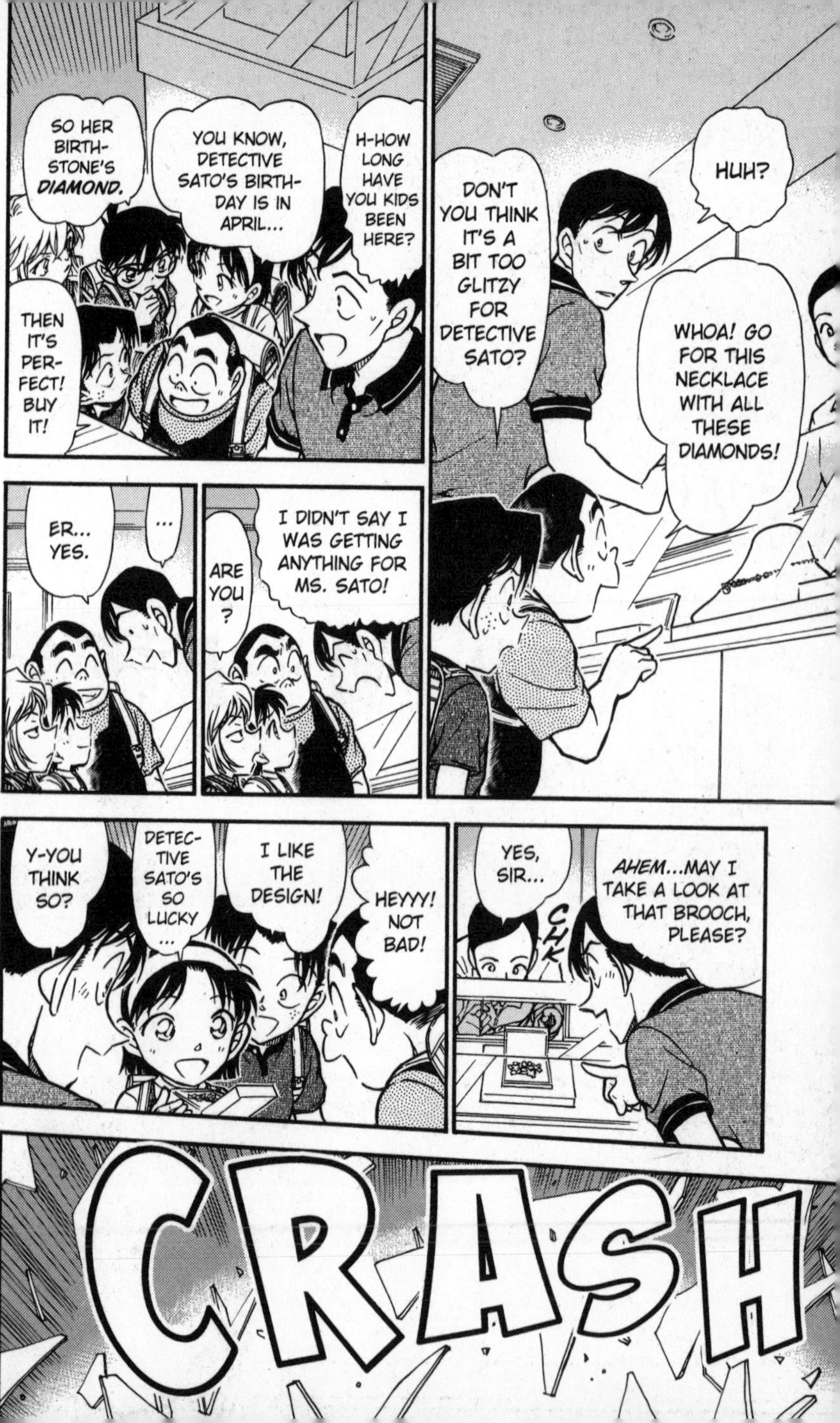
HUH?
DON'T YOU THINK IT'S A BIT TOO GLITZY FOR DETECTIVE SATO?
WHOA! GO FOR THIS NECKLACE WITH ALL THESE DIAMONDS!
H-HOW LONG HAVE YOU KIDS BEEN HERE?
YOU KNOW, DETECTIVE SATO'S BIRTH-DAY IS IN APRIL...
SO HER BIRTH-STONE'S *DIAMOND.*
THEN IT'S PER-FECT! BUY IT!
I DIDN'T SAY I WAS GETTING ANYTHING FOR MS. SATO!
ARE YOU?
...
ER... YES.
AHEM...MAY I TAKE A LOOK AT THAT BROOCH, PLEASE?
CHK
YES, SIR...
HEYYY! NOT BAD!
I LIKE THE DESIGN!
DETEC-TIVE SATO'S SO LUCKY...
Y-YOU THINK SO?
CRASH

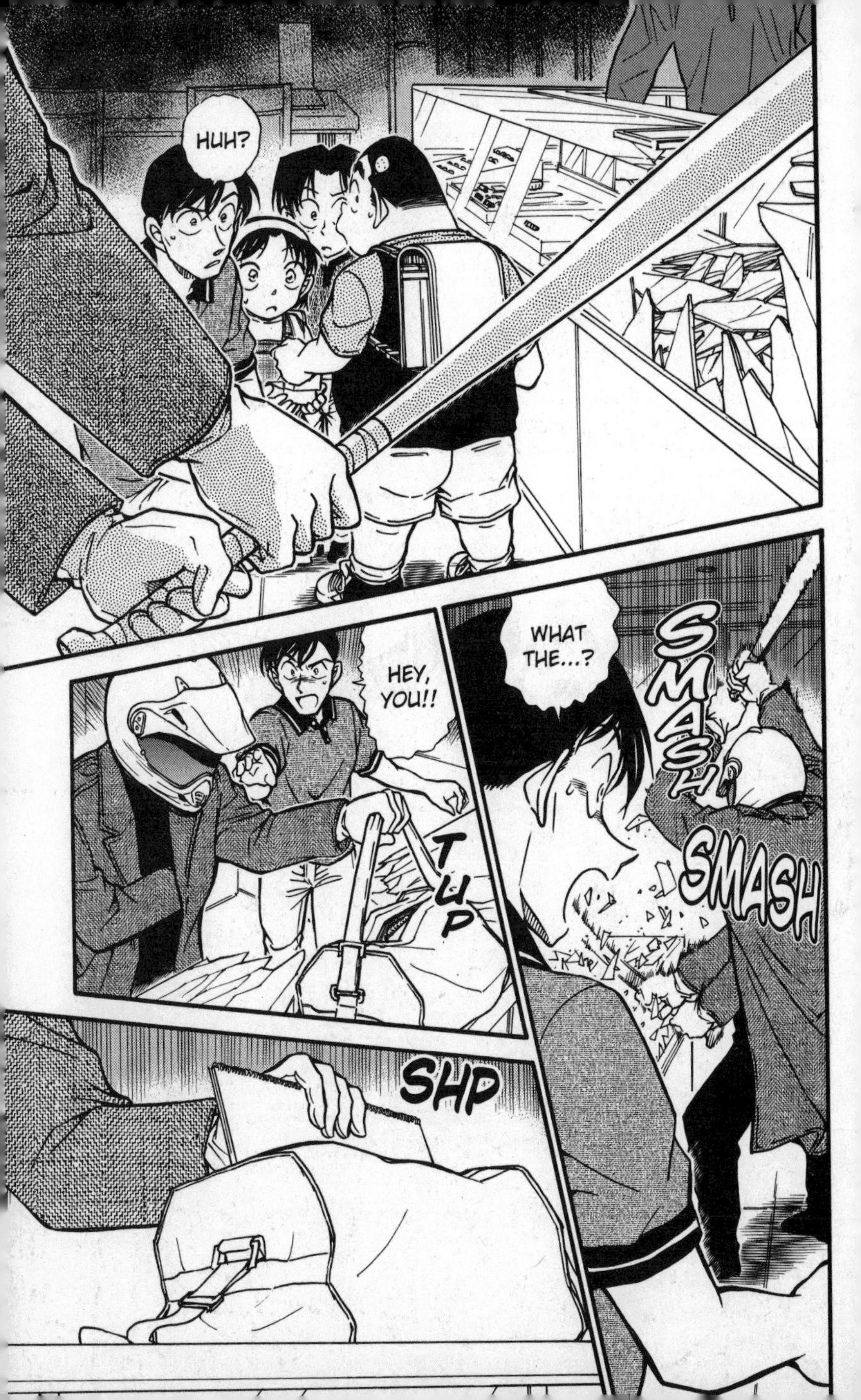
HUH?
WHAT THE...?
SMASH
SMASH
HEY, YOU!!
TUP
SHP

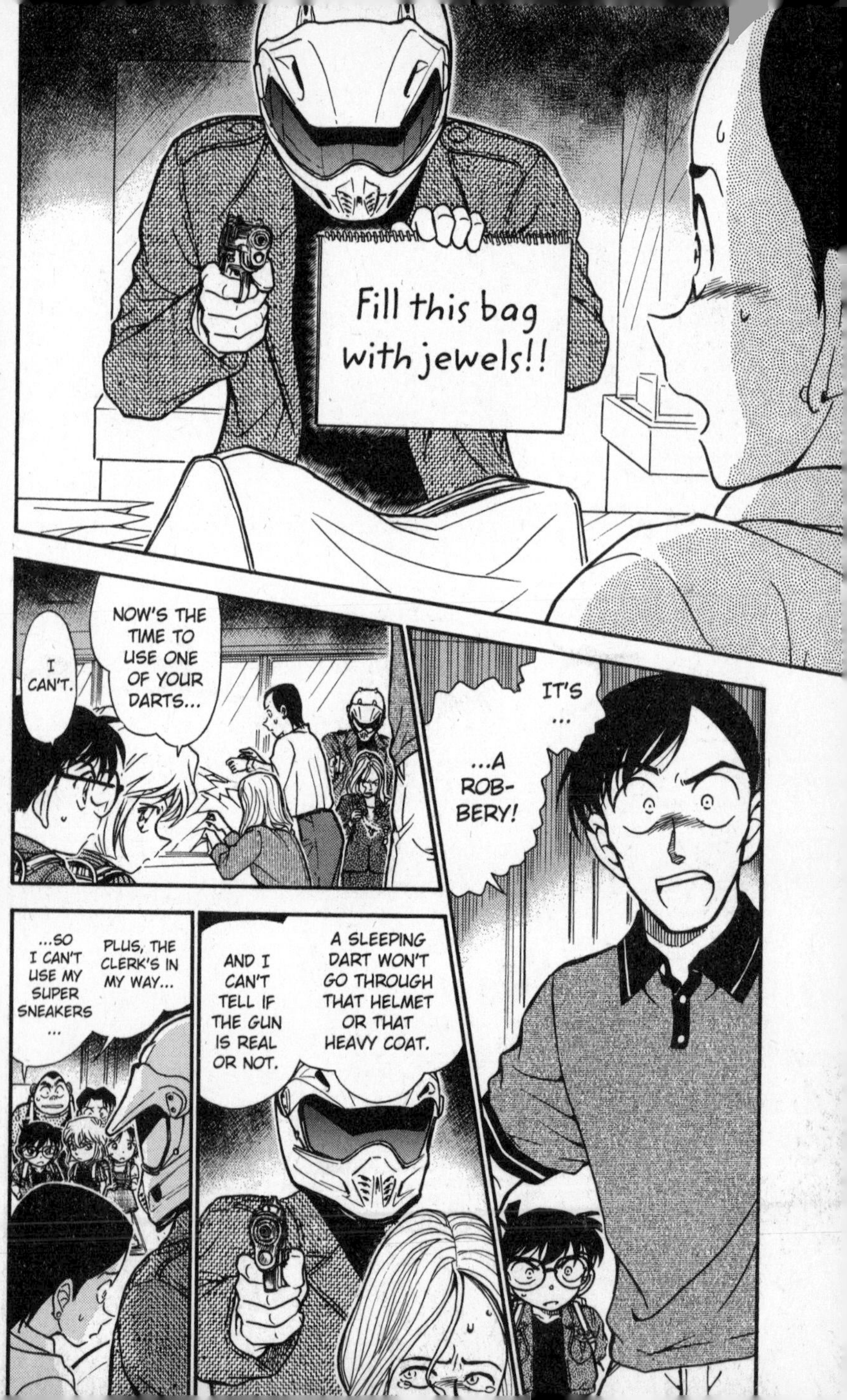
Fill this bag with jewels!!
IT'S ...
...A ROBBERY!
NOW'S THE TIME TO USE ONE OF YOUR DARTS...
I CAN'T.
A SLEEPING DART WON'T GO THROUGH THAT HELMET OR THAT HEAVY COAT.
AND I CAN'T TELL IF THE GUN IS REAL OR NOT.
PLUS, THE CLERK'S IN MY WAY...
...SO I CAN'T USE MY SUPER SNEAKERS ...

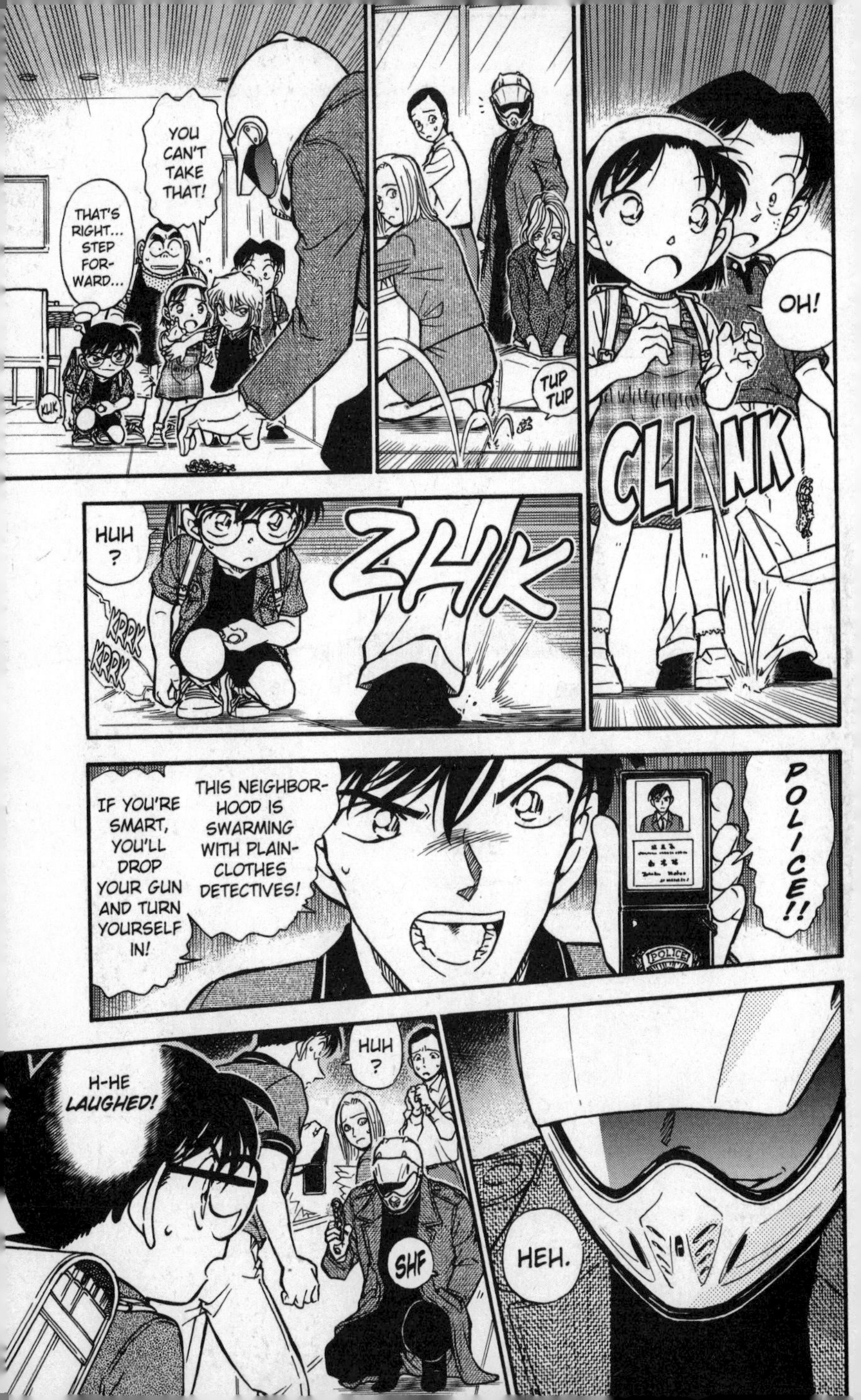
OH!
CLINK
TUP TUP
YOU CAN'T TAKE THAT!
THAT'S RIGHT... STEP FOR-WARD...
KUK
ZHK
HUH?
KRRK KRRK
POLICE!!
THIS NEIGHBOR-HOOD IS SWARMING WITH PLAIN-CLOTHES DETECTIVES!
IF YOU'RE SMART, YOU'LL DROP YOUR GUN AND TURN YOURSELF IN!
POLICE
HEH.
HUH?
SHF
H-HE *LAUGHED!*

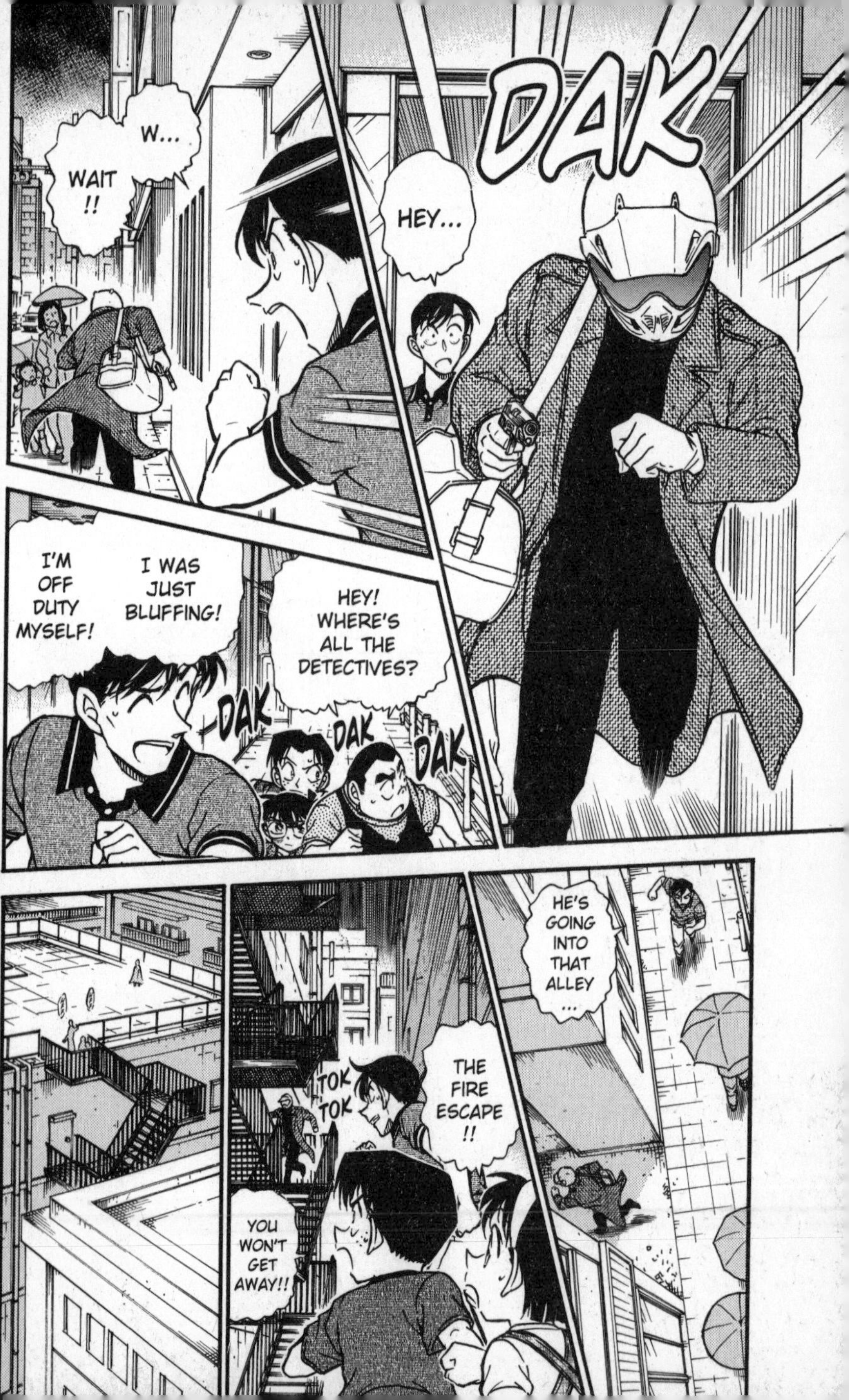
DAK
HEY...
W...
WAIT!!
HEY! WHERE'S ALL THE DETECTIVES?
I WAS JUST BLUFFING!
I'M OFF DUTY MYSELF!
DAK
DAK
DAK
HE'S GOING INTO THAT ALLEY...
THE FIRE ESCAPE!!
TOK TOK
YOU WON'T GET AWAY!!

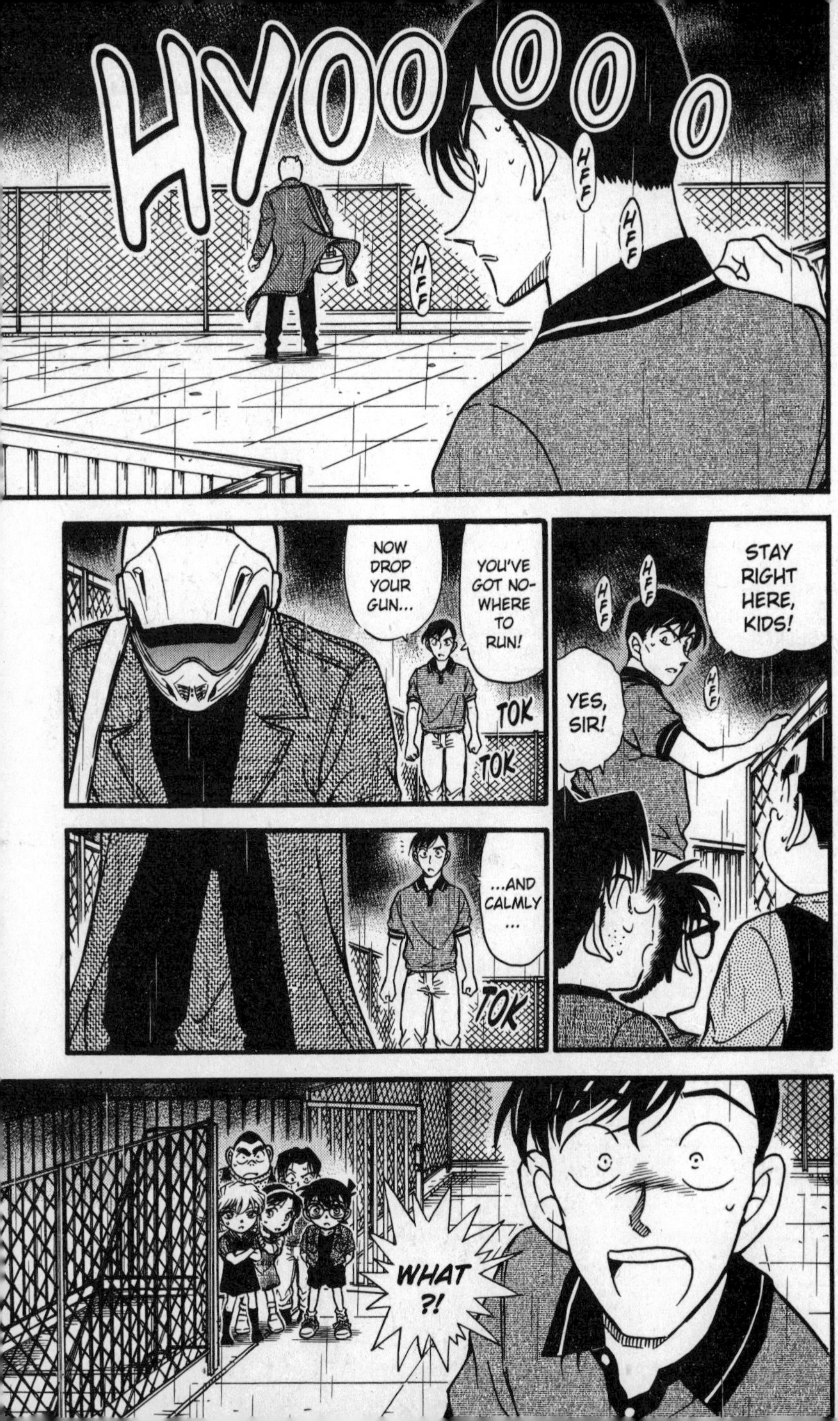
HYOOOOO
HFF
HFF
HFF
HFF
HFF
STAY RIGHT HERE, KIDS!
HFF
YES, SIR!
YOU'VE GOT NO-WHERE TO RUN!
NOW DROP YOUR GUN...
TOK
TOK
...AND CALMLY ...
TOK
WHAT ?!

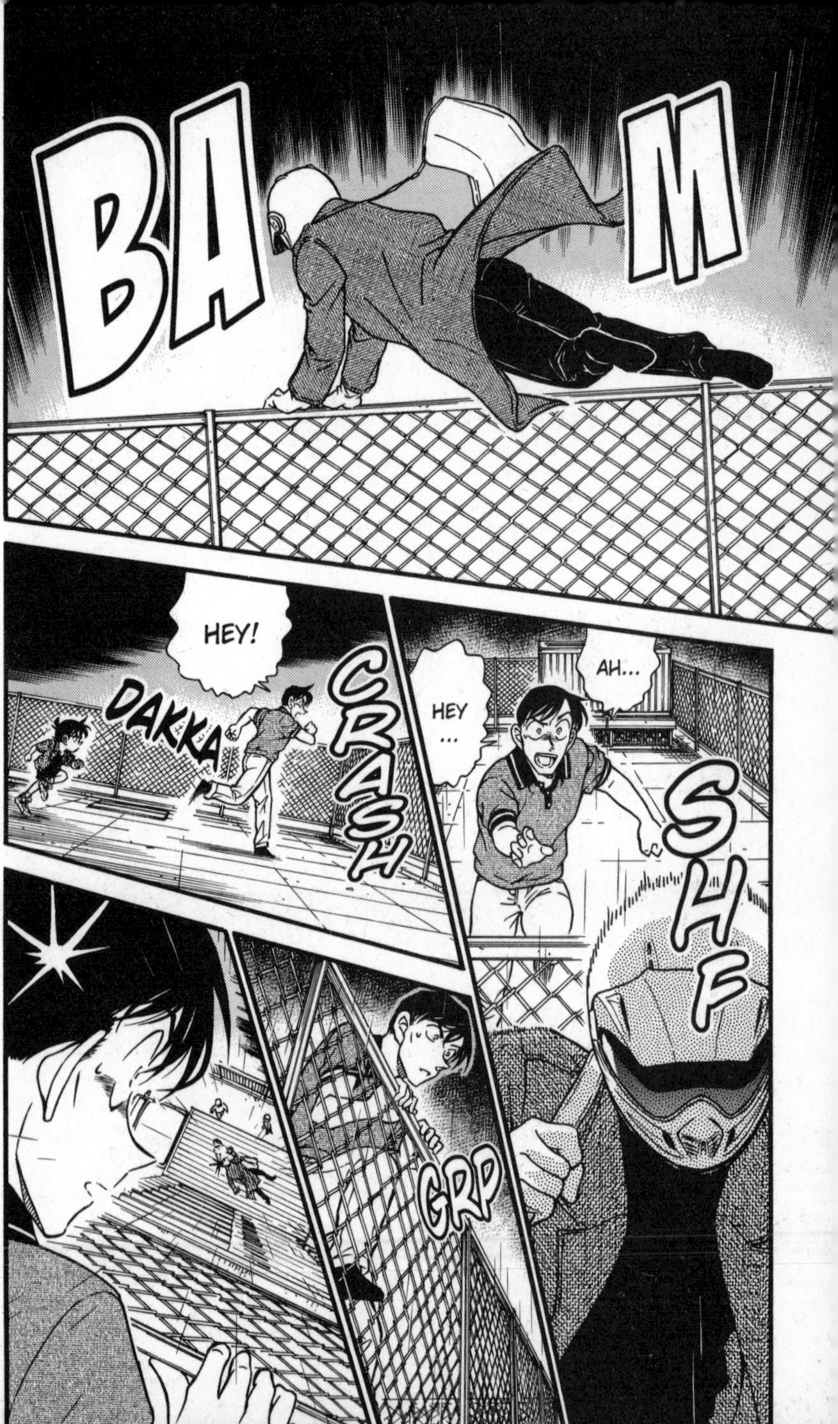
BAM
AH...
HEY ...
SHF
HEY!
CRASH
DAKKA
GRP

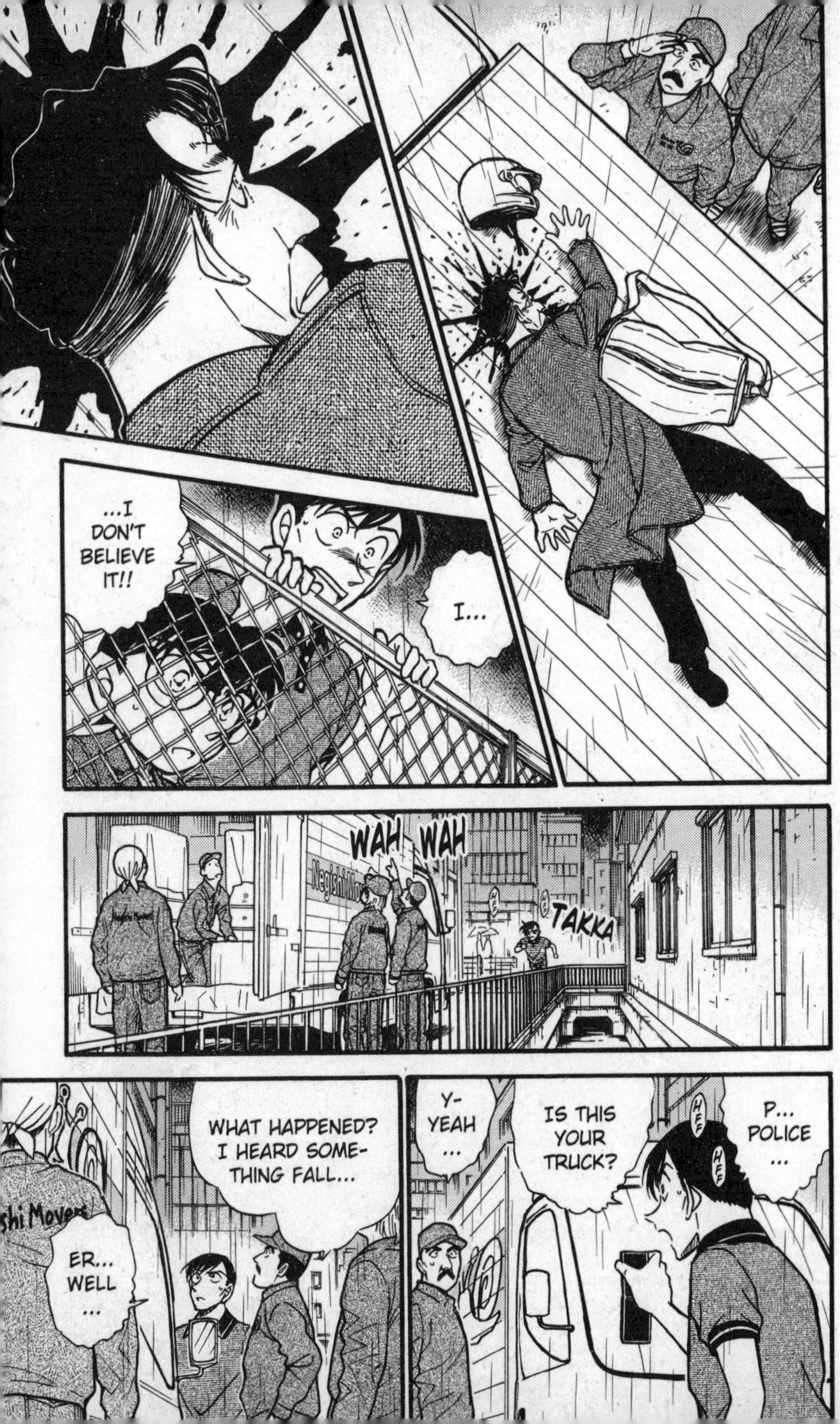
I...
...I DON'T BELIEVE IT!!
WAH WAH
HEF HEF
TAKKA
P... POLICE ...
HEF HEF
IS THIS YOUR TRUCK?
Y-YEAH ...
WHAT HAPPENED? I HEARD SOME-THING FALL...
ER... WELL ...

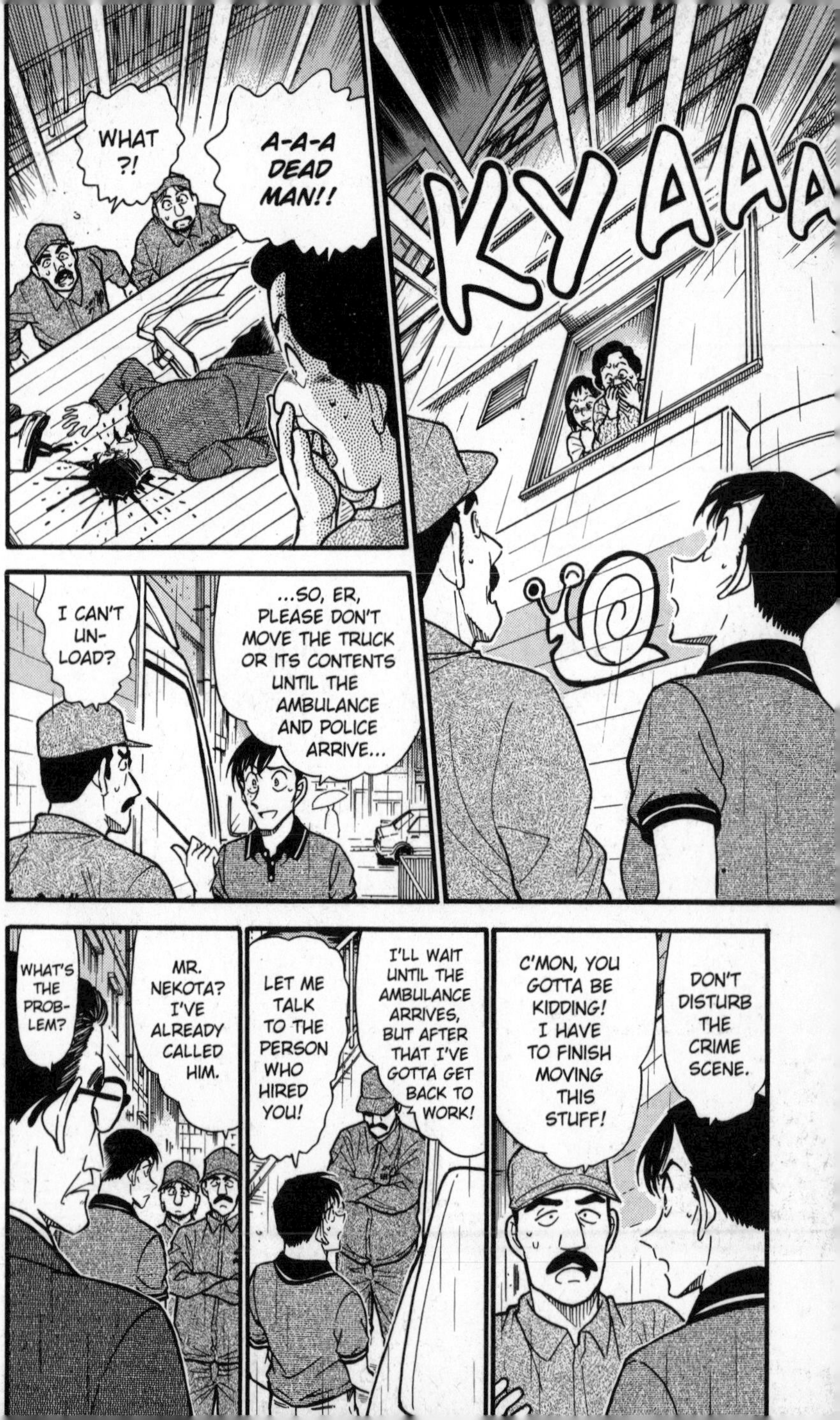
KYAAA
WHAT?!
A-A-A DEAD MAN!!
...SO, ER, PLEASE DON'T MOVE THE TRUCK OR ITS CONTENTS UNTIL THE AMBULANCE AND POLICE ARRIVE...
I CAN'T UN-LOAD?
DON'T DISTURB THE CRIME SCENE.
C'MON, YOU GOTTA BE KIDDING! I HAVE TO FINISH MOVING THIS STUFF!
I'LL WAIT UNTIL THE AMBULANCE ARRIVES, BUT AFTER THAT I'VE GOTTA GET BACK TO WORK!
LET ME TALK TO THE PERSON WHO HIRED YOU!
MR. NEKOTA? I'VE ALREADY CALLED HIM.
WHAT'S THE PROB-LEM?

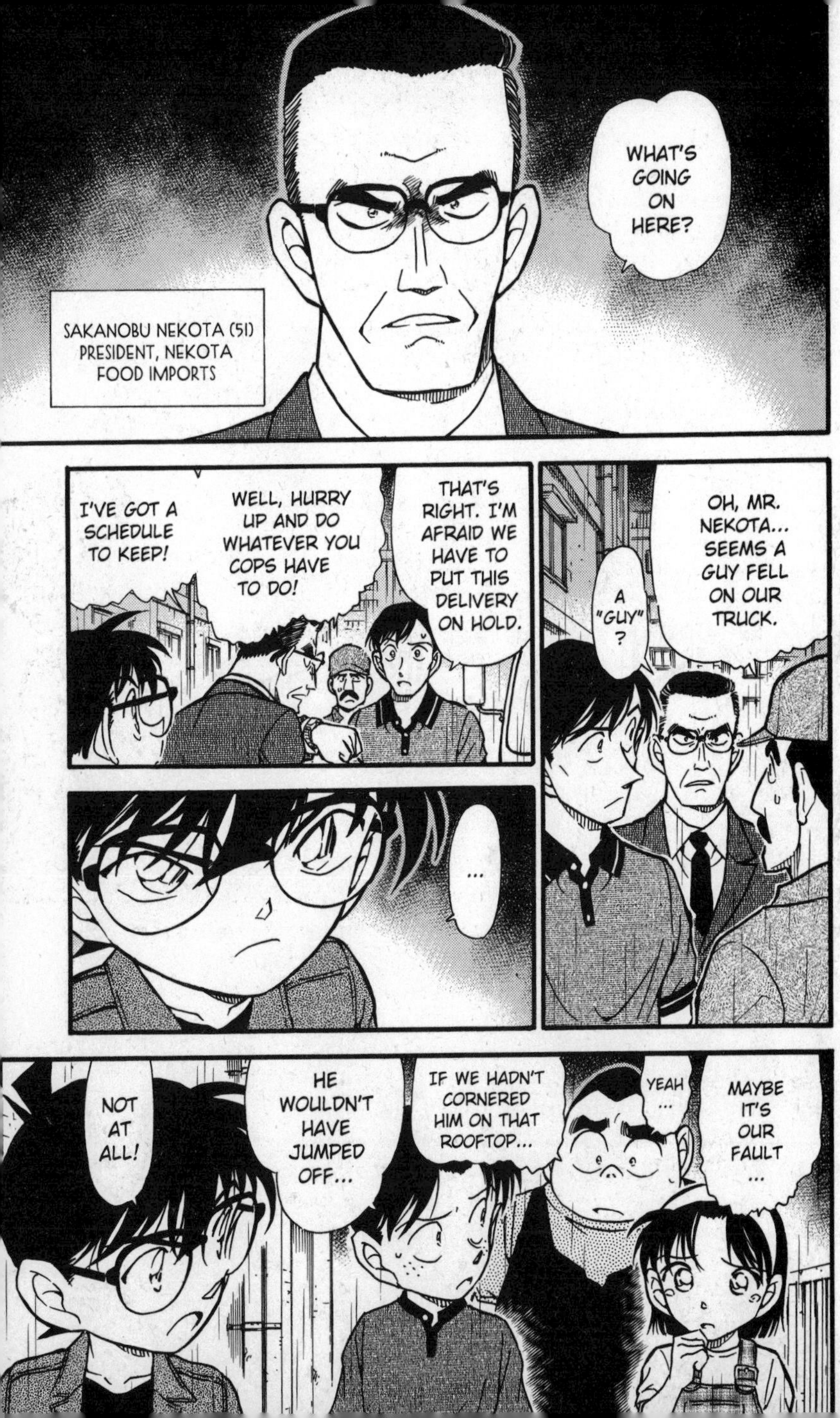
WHAT'S GOING ON HERE?
SAKANOBU NEKOTA (51) PRESIDENT, NEKOTA FOOD IMPORTS
OH, MR. NEKOTA... SEEMS A GUY FELL ON OUR TRUCK.
A "GUY"?
THAT'S RIGHT. I'M AFRAID WE HAVE TO PUT THIS DELIVERY ON HOLD.
WELL, HURRY UP AND DO WHATEVER YOU COPS HAVE TO DO!
I'VE GOT A SCHEDULE TO KEEP!
...
MAYBE IT'S OUR FAULT...
YEAH...
IF WE HADN'T CORNERED HIM ON THAT ROOFTOP...
HE WOULDN'T HAVE JUMPED OFF...
NOT AT ALL!

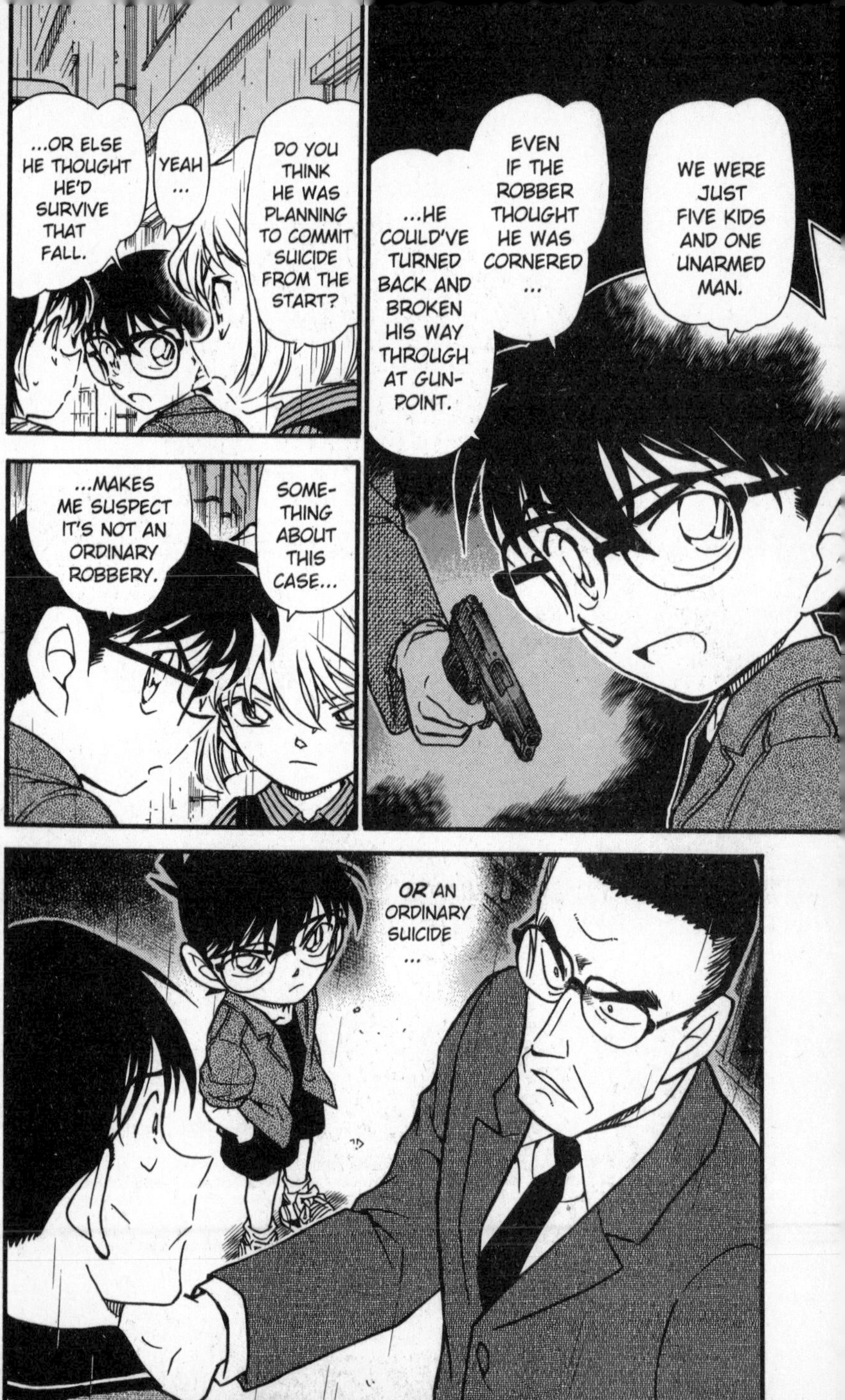
WE WERE JUST FIVE KIDS AND ONE UNARMED MAN.
EVEN IF THE ROBBER THOUGHT HE WAS CORNERED ...
...HE COULD'VE TURNED BACK AND BROKEN HIS WAY THROUGH AT GUN-POINT.
DO YOU THINK HE WAS PLANNING TO COMMIT SUICIDE FROM THE START?
YEAH ...
...OR ELSE HE THOUGHT HE'D SURVIVE THAT FALL.
SOME-THING ABOUT THIS CASE...
...MAKES ME SUSPECT IT'S NOT AN ORDINARY ROBBERY.
OR AN ORDINARY SUICIDE ...

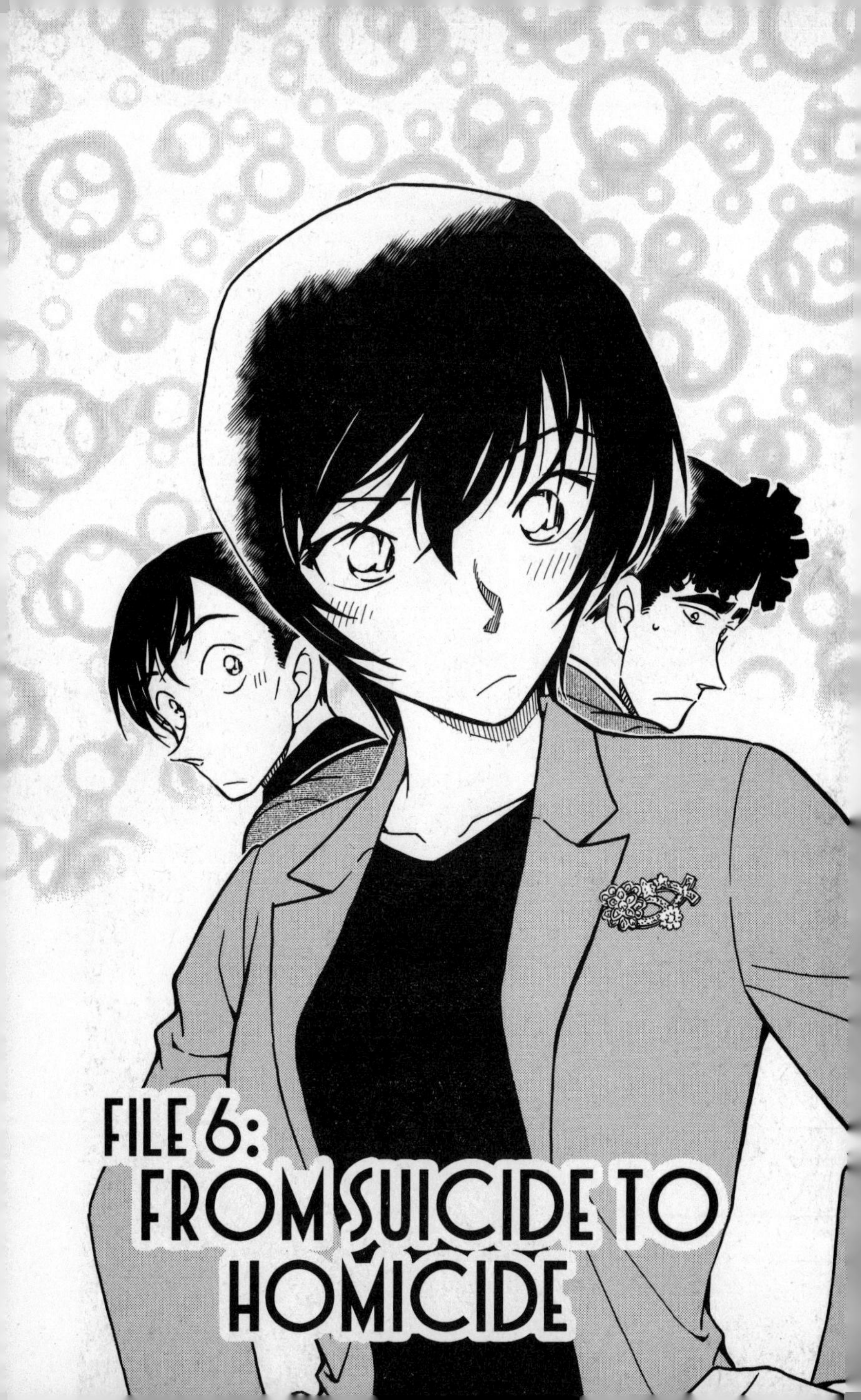
FILE 6:
FROM SUICIDE TO HOMICIDE

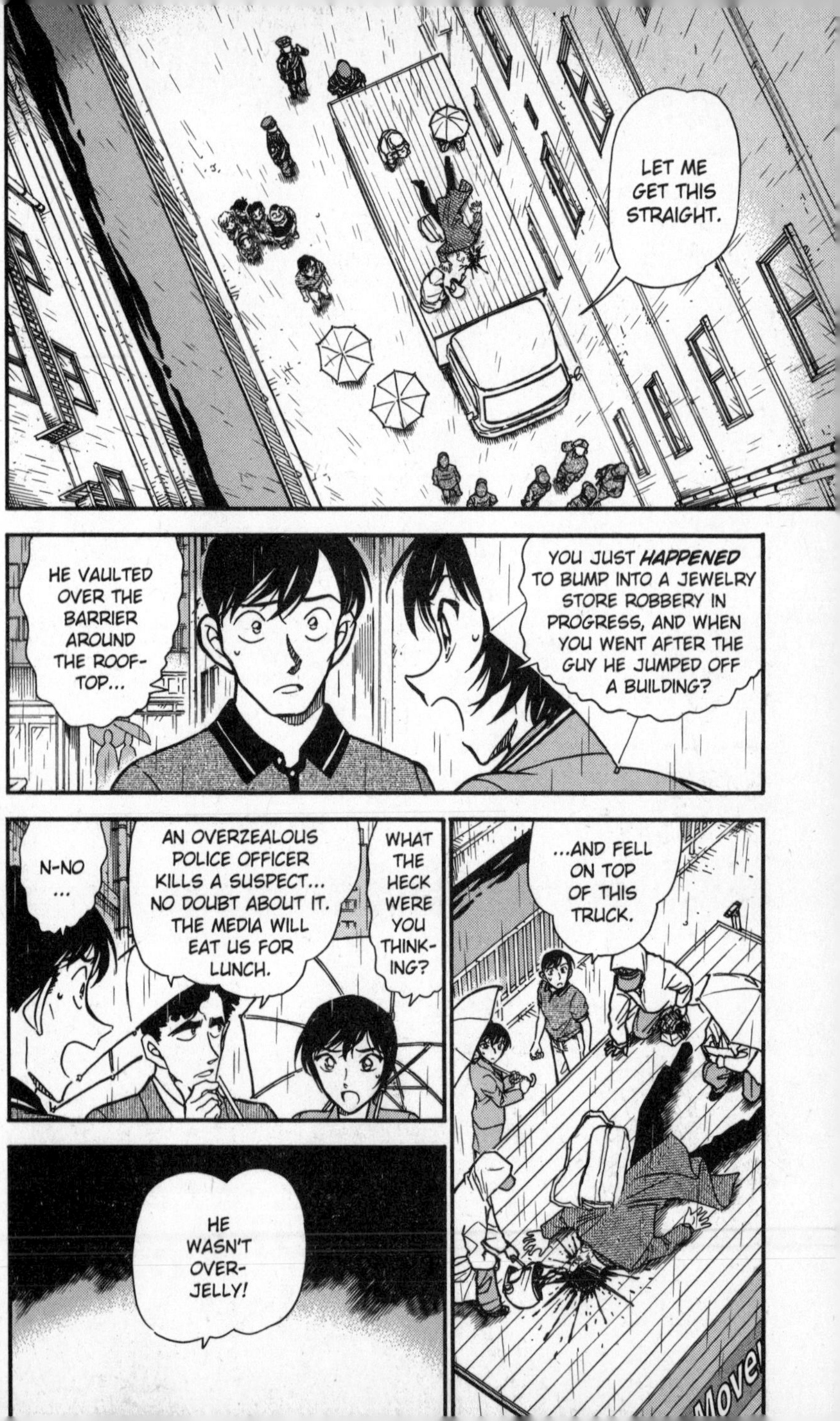
LET ME GET THIS STRAIGHT.
YOU JUST *HAPPENED* TO BUMP INTO A JEWELRY STORE ROBBERY IN PROGRESS, AND WHEN YOU WENT AFTER THE GUY HE JUMPED OFF A BUILDING?
HE VAULTED OVER THE BARRIER AROUND THE ROOF-TOP...
...AND FELL ON TOP OF THIS TRUCK.
WHAT THE HECK WERE YOU THINKING?
AN OVERZEALOUS POLICE OFFICER KILLS A SUSPECT... NO DOUBT ABOUT IT. THE MEDIA WILL EAT US FOR LUNCH.
N-NO ...
HE WASN'T OVER-JELLY!
Mover

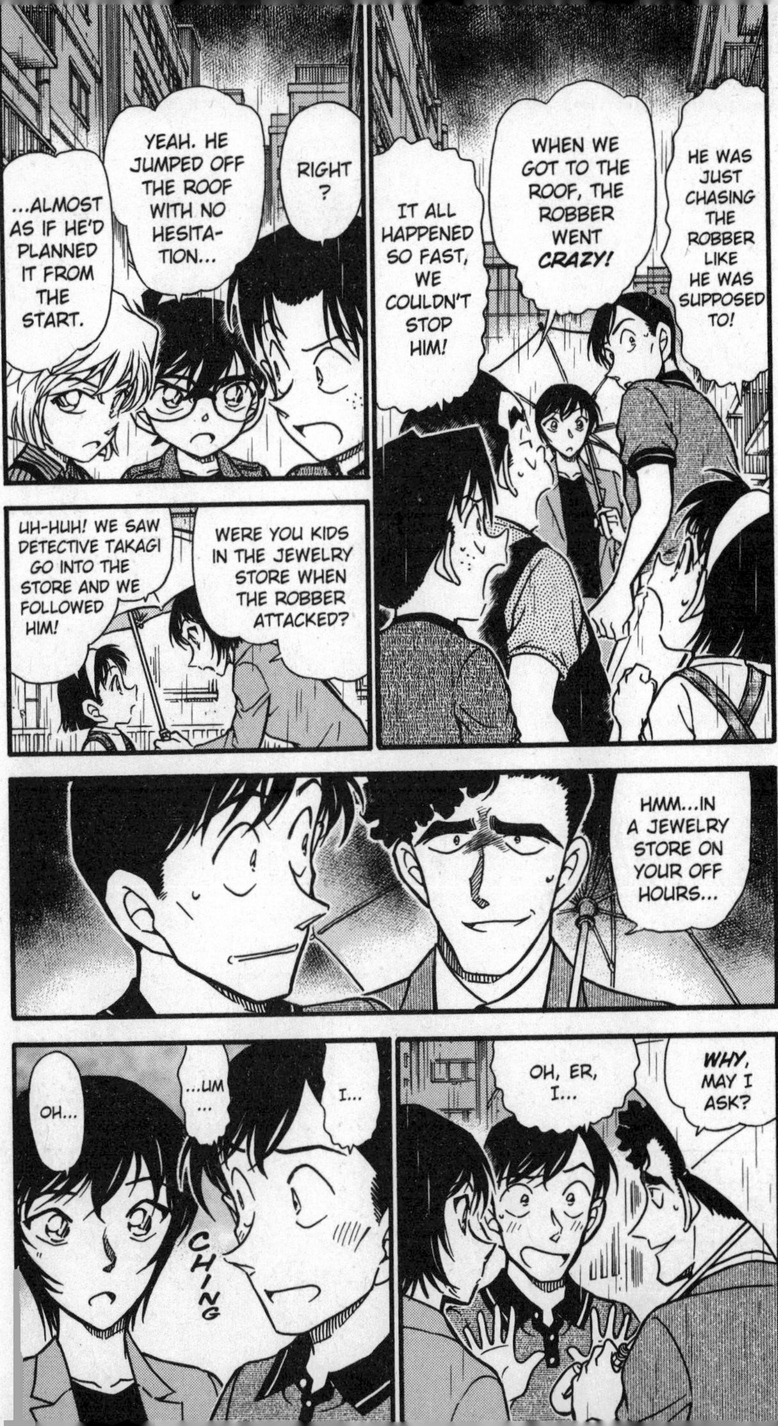
HE WAS JUST CHASING THE ROBBER LIKE HE WAS SUPPOSED TO!
WHEN WE GOT TO THE ROOF, THE ROBBER WENT *CRAZY!*
IT ALL HAPPENED SO FAST, WE COULDN'T STOP HIM!
RIGHT?
YEAH. HE JUMPED OFF THE ROOF WITH NO HESITA-TION...
...ALMOST AS IF HE'D PLANNED IT FROM THE START.
WERE YOU KIDS IN THE JEWELRY STORE WHEN THE ROBBER ATTACKED?
UH-HUH! WE SAW DETECTIVE TAKAGI GO INTO THE STORE AND WE FOLLOWED HIM!
HMM...IN A JEWELRY STORE ON YOUR OFF HOURS...
WHY, MAY I ASK?
OH, ER, I...
I...
...UM ...
OH...
CHING

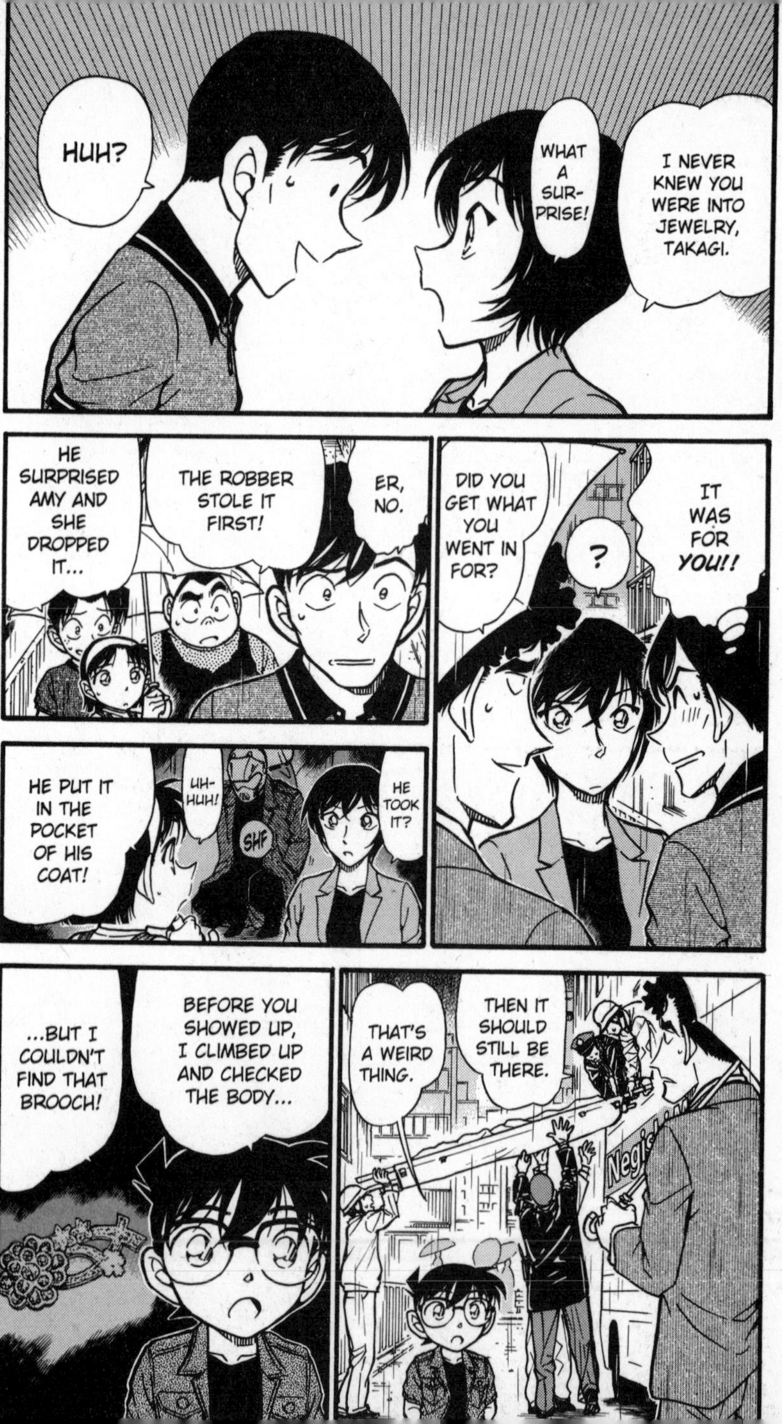
I NEVER KNEW YOU WERE INTO JEWELRY, TAKAGI.
WHAT A SUR-PRISE!
HUH?
IT WAS FOR *YOU!!*
?
DID YOU GET WHAT YOU WENT IN FOR?
ER, NO.
THE ROBBER STOLE IT FIRST!
HE SURPRISED AMY AND SHE DROPPED IT...
HE TOOK IT?
UH-HUH!
SHF
HE PUT IT IN THE POCKET OF HIS COAT!
THEN IT SHOULD STILL BE THERE.
THAT'S A WEIRD THING.
BEFORE YOU SHOWED UP, I CLIMBED UP AND CHECKED THE BODY...
...BUT I COULDN'T FIND THAT BROOCH!

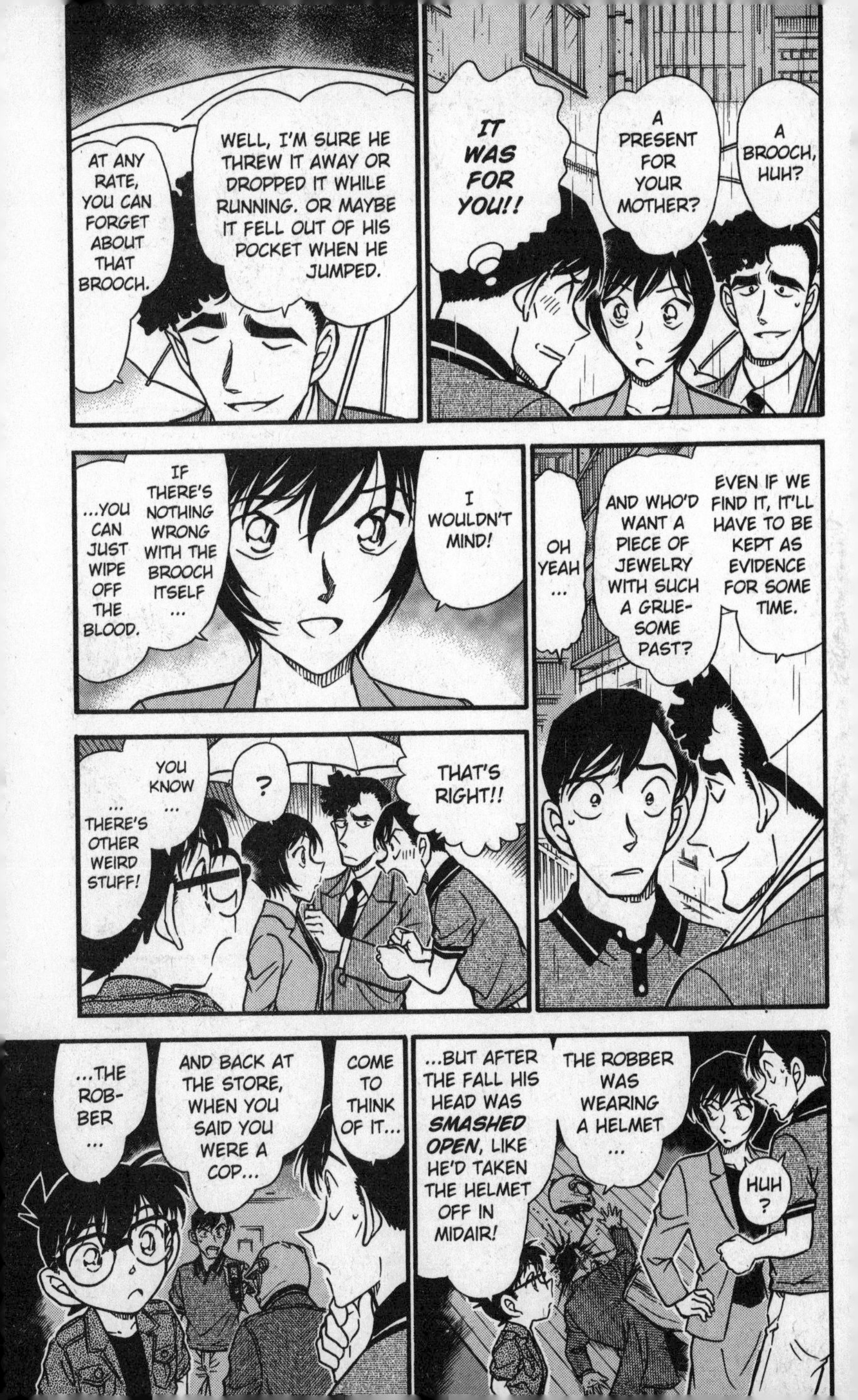
A BROOCH, HUH?
A PRESENT FOR YOUR MOTHER?
IT WAS FOR YOU!!
WELL, I'M SURE HE THREW IT AWAY OR DROPPED IT WHILE RUNNING. OR MAYBE IT FELL OUT OF HIS POCKET WHEN HE JUMPED.
AT ANY RATE, YOU CAN FORGET ABOUT THAT BROOCH.
EVEN IF WE FIND IT, IT'LL HAVE TO BE KEPT AS EVIDENCE FOR SOME TIME.
AND WHO'D WANT A PIECE OF JEWELRY WITH SUCH A GRUE-SOME PAST?
OH YEAH...
I WOULDN'T MIND!
IF THERE'S NOTHING WRONG WITH THE BROOCH ITSELF...
...YOU CAN JUST WIPE OFF THE BLOOD.
THAT'S RIGHT!!
?
YOU KNOW...
...THERE'S OTHER WEIRD STUFF!
HUH?
THE ROBBER WAS WEARING A HELMET...
...BUT AFTER THE FALL HIS HEAD WAS SMASHED OPEN, LIKE HE'D TAKEN THE HELMET OFF IN MIDAIR!
COME TO THINK OF IT...
AND BACK AT THE STORE, WHEN YOU SAID YOU WERE A COP...
...THE ROBBER...

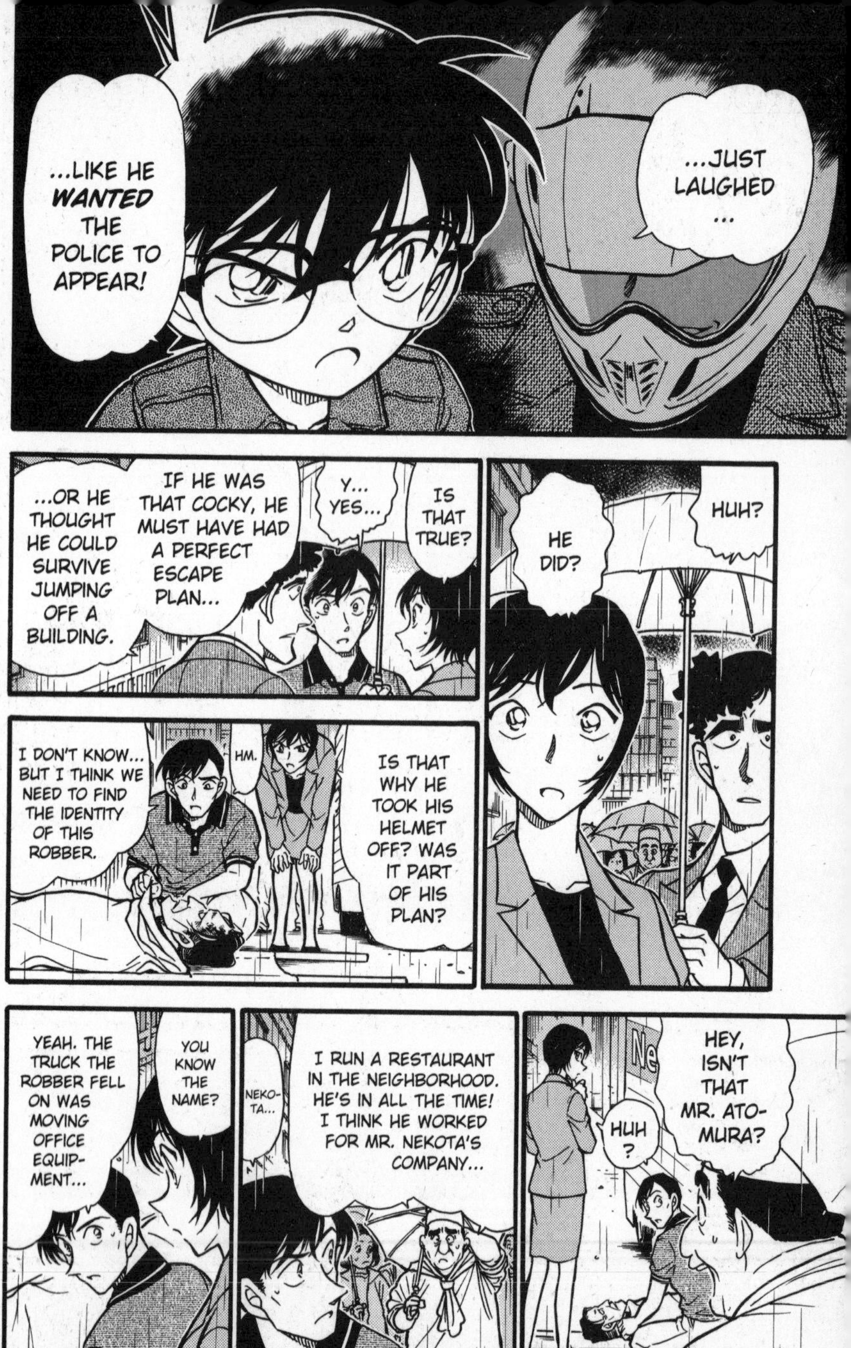
...JUST LAUGHED ...
...LIKE HE WANTED THE POLICE TO APPEAR!
HUH?
HE DID?
IS THAT TRUE?
Y... YES...
IF HE WAS THAT COCKY, HE MUST HAVE HAD A PERFECT ESCAPE PLAN...
...OR HE THOUGHT HE COULD SURVIVE JUMPING OFF A BUILDING.
IS THAT WHY HE TOOK HIS HELMET OFF? WAS IT PART OF HIS PLAN?
HM.
I DON'T KNOW... BUT I THINK WE NEED TO FIND THE IDENTITY OF THIS ROBBER.
HEY, ISN'T THAT MR. ATO-MURA?
HUH ?
I RUN A RESTAURANT IN THE NEIGHBORHOOD. HE'S IN ALL THE TIME! I THINK HE WORKED FOR MR. NEKOTA'S COMPANY...
NEKO-TA...
YOU KNOW THE NAME?
YEAH. THE TRUCK THE ROBBER FELL ON WAS MOVING OFFICE EQUIP-MENT...

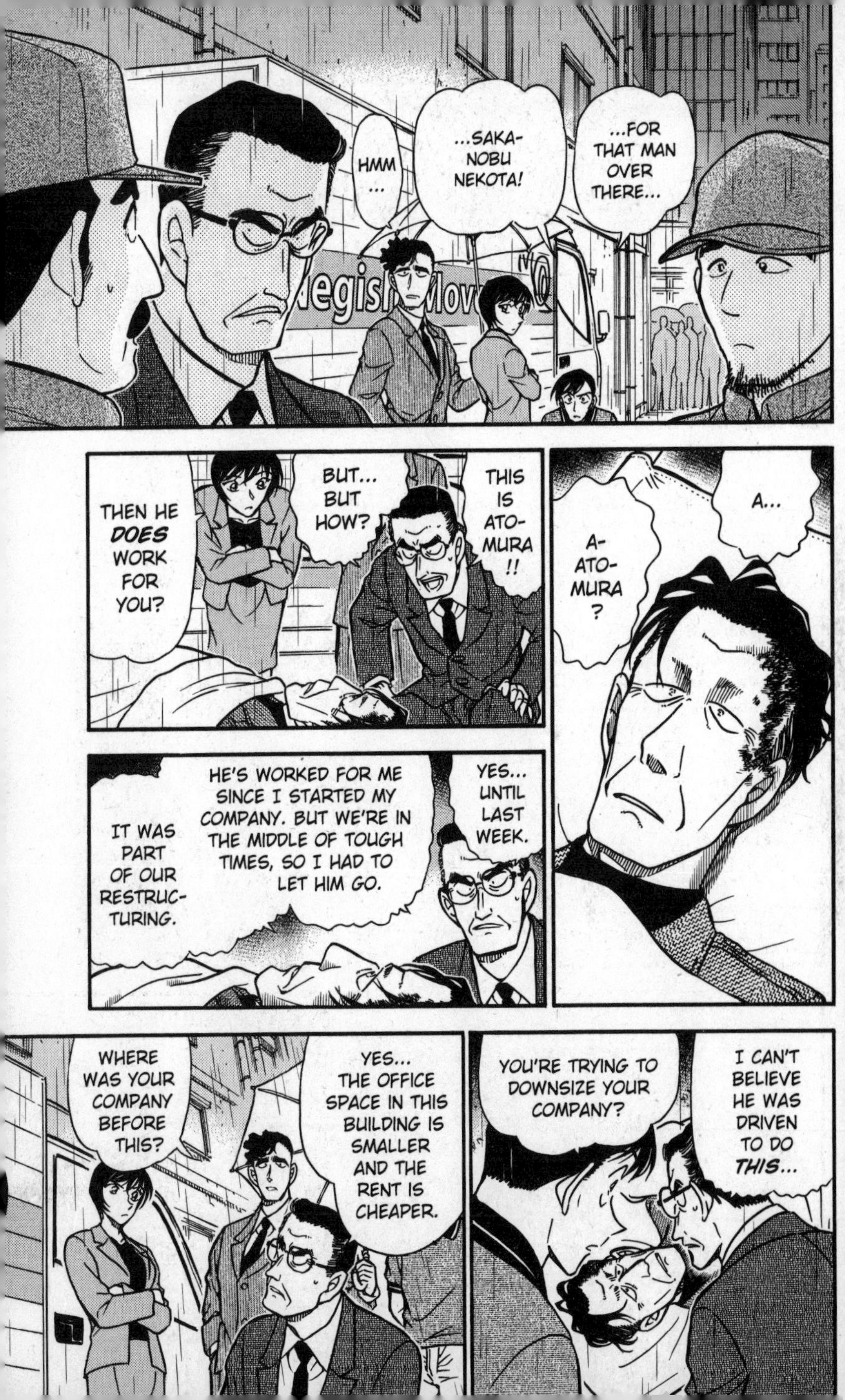
...FOR THAT MAN OVER THERE...
...SAKA-NOBU NEKOTA!
HMM ...
A...
A-ATO-MURA?
THIS IS ATO-MURA!!
BUT... BUT HOW?
THEN HE **DOES** WORK FOR YOU?
YES... UNTIL LAST WEEK.
HE'S WORKED FOR ME SINCE I STARTED MY COMPANY. BUT WE'RE IN THE MIDDLE OF TOUGH TIMES, SO I HAD TO LET HIM GO.
IT WAS PART OF OUR RESTRUC-TURING.
I CAN'T BELIEVE HE WAS DRIVEN TO DO ***THIS***...
YOU'RE TRYING TO DOWNSIZE YOUR COMPANY?
YES... THE OFFICE SPACE IN THIS BUILDING IS SMALLER AND THE RENT IS CHEAPER.
WHERE WAS YOUR COMPANY BEFORE THIS?

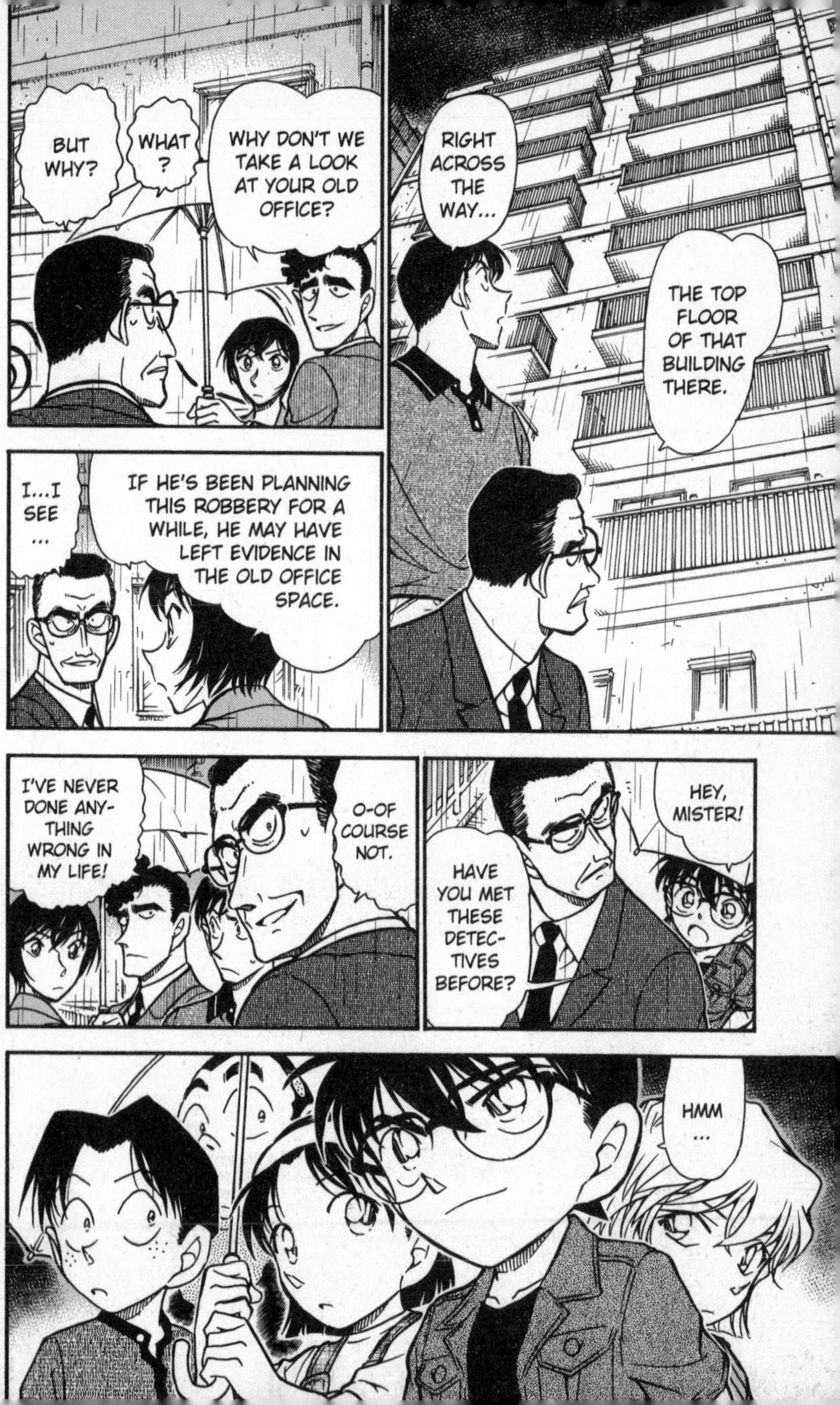
RIGHT ACROSS THE WAY...
THE TOP FLOOR OF THAT BUILDING THERE.
WHY DON'T WE TAKE A LOOK AT YOUR OLD OFFICE?
WHAT?
BUT WHY?
IF HE'S BEEN PLANNING THIS ROBBERY FOR A WHILE, HE MAY HAVE LEFT EVIDENCE IN THE OLD OFFICE SPACE.
I...I SEE...
HEY, MISTER!
HAVE YOU MET THESE DETECTIVES BEFORE?
O-OF COURSE NOT.
I'VE NEVER DONE ANYTHING WRONG IN MY LIFE!
HMM...

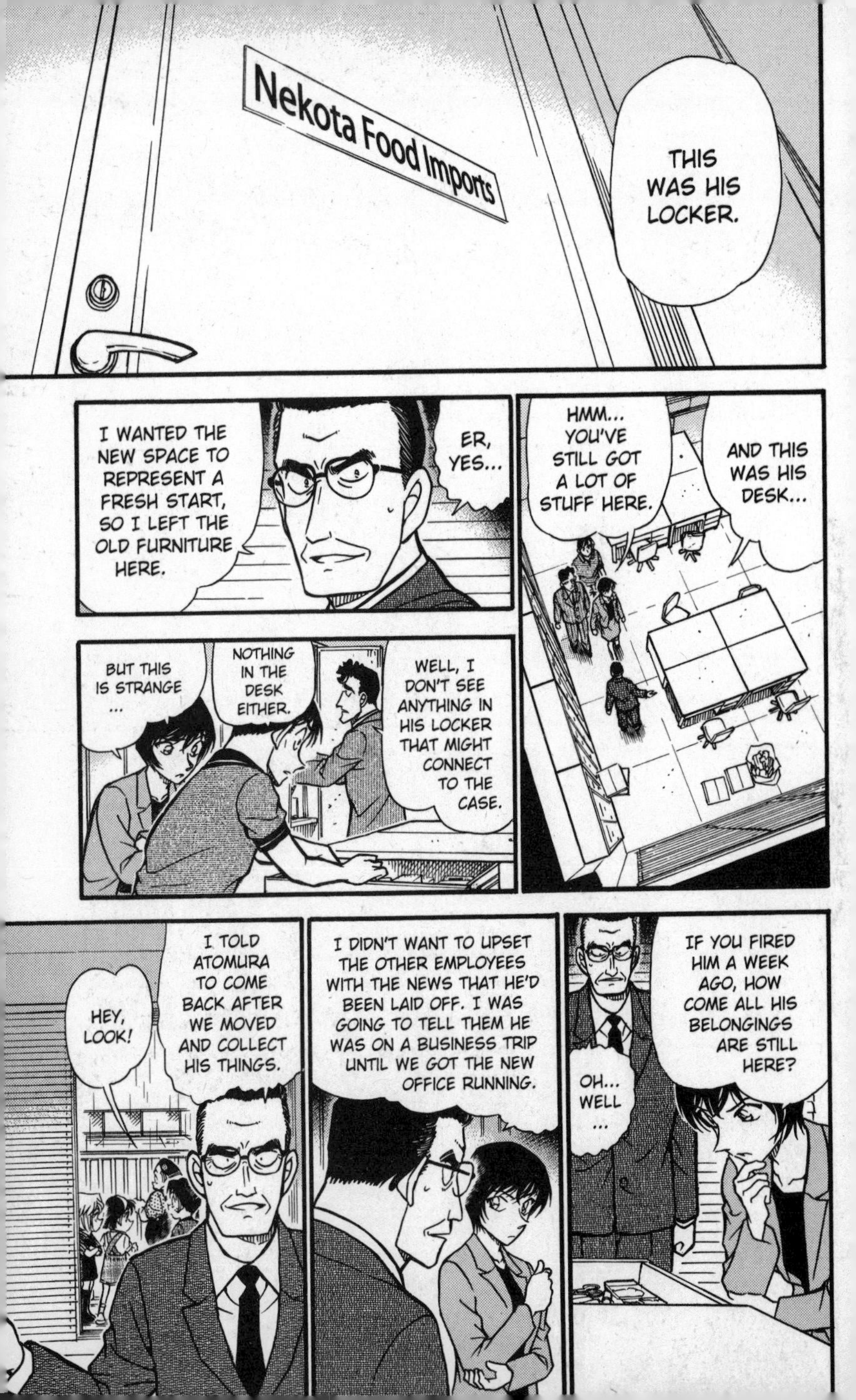
Nekota Food Imports
THIS WAS HIS LOCKER.
AND THIS WAS HIS DESK...
HMM... YOU'VE STILL GOT A LOT OF STUFF HERE.
ER, YES...
I WANTED THE NEW SPACE TO REPRESENT A FRESH START, SO I LEFT THE OLD FURNITURE HERE.
WELL, I DON'T SEE ANYTHING IN HIS LOCKER THAT MIGHT CONNECT TO THE CASE.
NOTHING IN THE DESK EITHER.
BUT THIS IS STRANGE ...
IF YOU FIRED HIM A WEEK AGO, HOW COME ALL HIS BELONGINGS ARE STILL HERE?
OH... WELL ...
I DIDN'T WANT TO UPSET THE OTHER EMPLOYEES WITH THE NEWS THAT HE'D BEEN LAID OFF. I WAS GOING TO TELL THEM HE WAS ON A BUSINESS TRIP UNTIL WE GOT THE NEW OFFICE RUNNING.
I TOLD ATOMURA TO COME BACK AFTER WE MOVED AND COLLECT HIS THINGS.
HEY, LOOK!

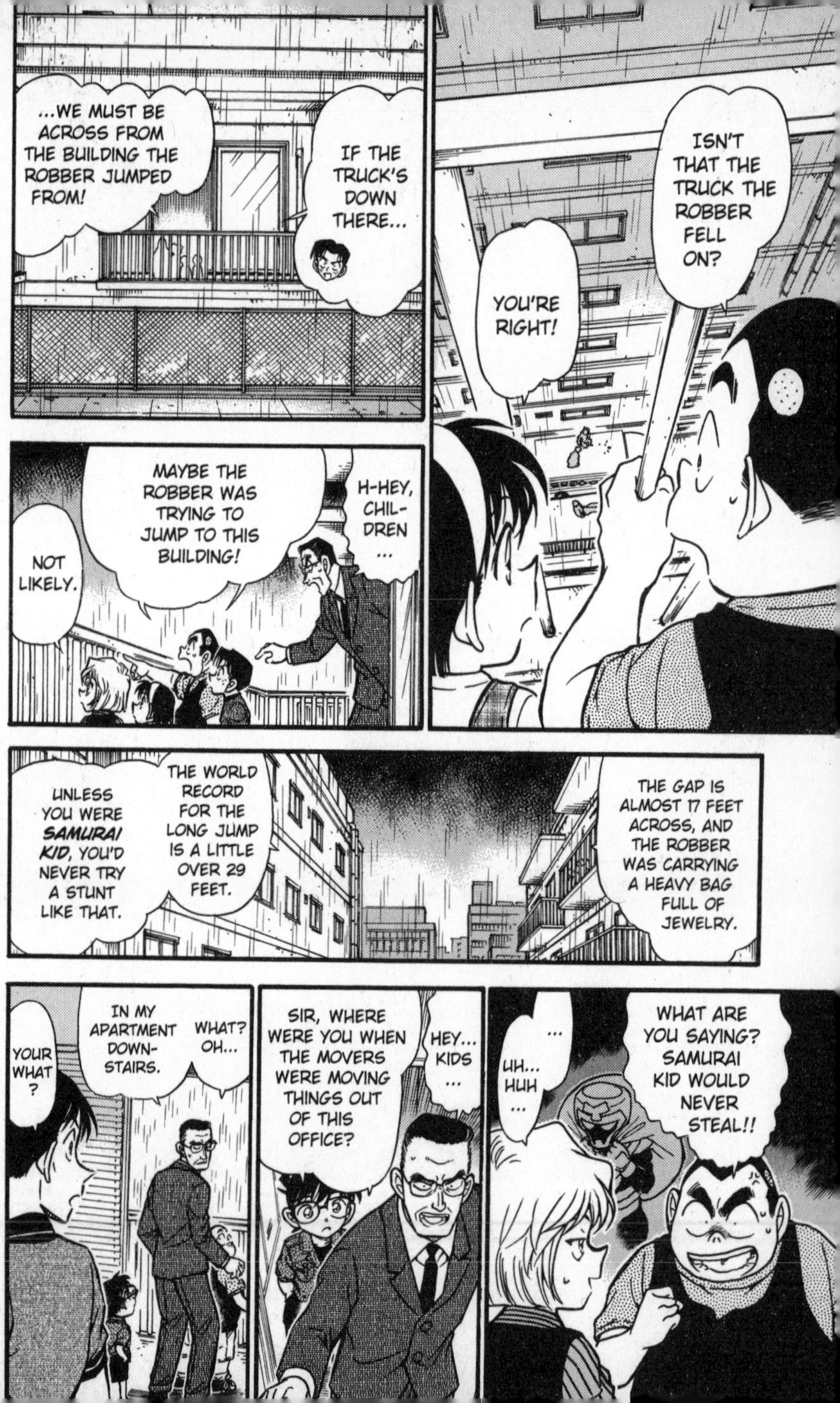
ISN'T THAT THE TRUCK THE ROBBER FELL ON?
YOU'RE RIGHT!
IF THE TRUCK'S DOWN THERE...
...WE MUST BE ACROSS FROM THE BUILDING THE ROBBER JUMPED FROM!
H-HEY, CHIL-DREN...
MAYBE THE ROBBER WAS TRYING TO JUMP TO THIS BUILDING!
NOT LIKELY.
THE GAP IS ALMOST 17 FEET ACROSS, AND THE ROBBER WAS CARRYING A HEAVY BAG FULL OF JEWELRY.
THE WORLD RECORD FOR THE LONG JUMP IS A LITTLE OVER 29 FEET.
UNLESS YOU WERE *SAMURAI KID*, YOU'D NEVER TRY A STUNT LIKE THAT.
WHAT ARE YOU SAYING? SAMURAI KID WOULD NEVER STEAL!!
...
UH... HUH...
HEY... KIDS...
SIR, WHERE WERE YOU WHEN THE MOVERS WERE MOVING THINGS OUT OF THIS OFFICE?
WHAT? OH...
IN MY APARTMENT DOWN-STAIRS.
YOUR WHAT?

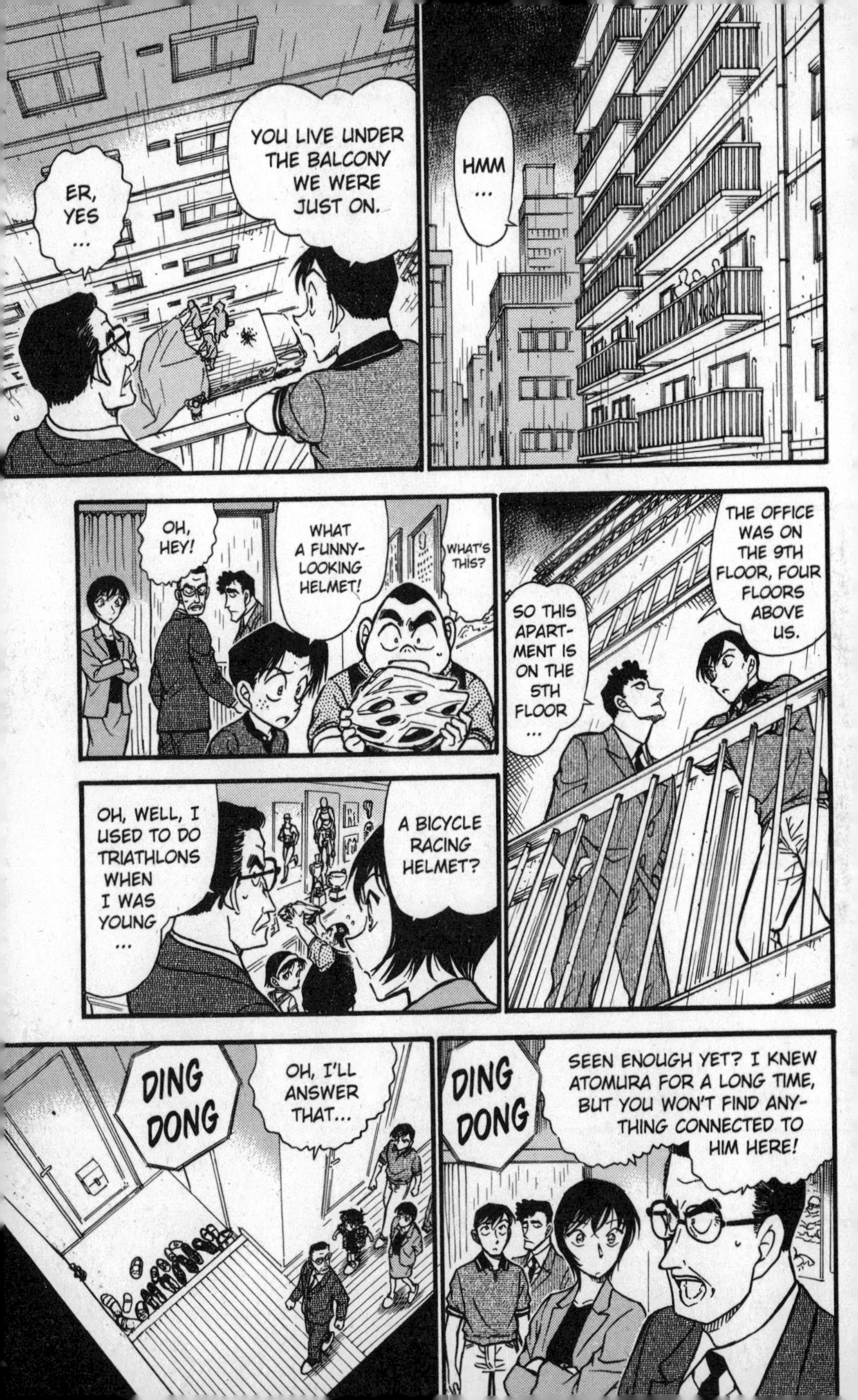
HMM ...
YOU LIVE UNDER THE BALCONY WE WERE JUST ON.
ER, YES ...
THE OFFICE WAS ON THE 9TH FLOOR, FOUR FLOORS ABOVE US.
SO THIS APARTMENT IS ON THE 5TH FLOOR ...
WHAT'S THIS?
WHAT A FUNNY-LOOKING HELMET!
OH, HEY!
A BICYCLE RACING HELMET?
OH, WELL, I USED TO DO TRIATHLONS WHEN I WAS YOUNG ...
DING DONG
SEEN ENOUGH YET? I KNEW ATOMURA FOR A LONG TIME, BUT YOU WON'T FIND ANY-THING CONNECTED TO HIM HERE!
DING DONG
OH, I'LL ANSWER THAT...

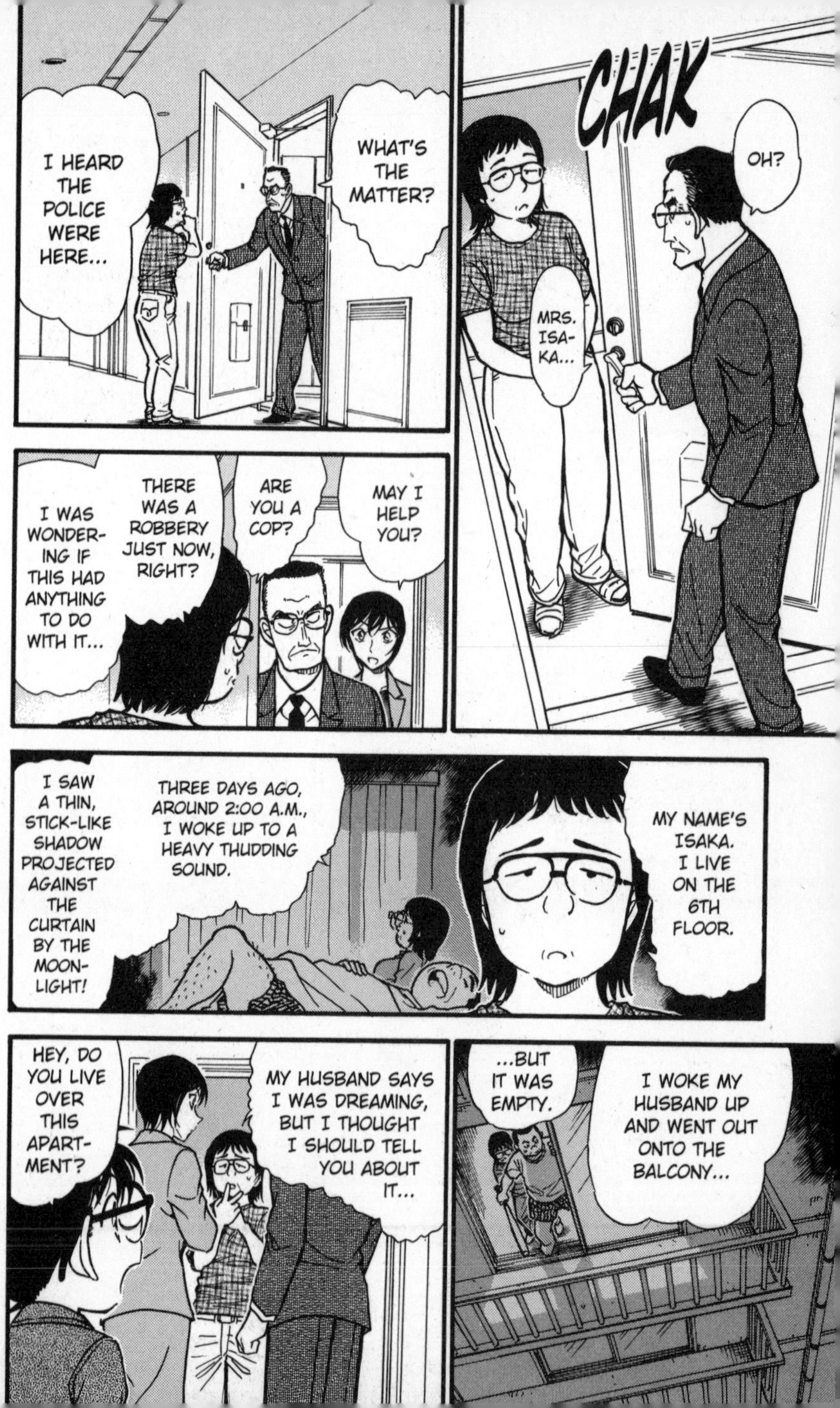
CHAK
OH?
MRS. ISAKA...
WHAT'S THE MATTER?
I HEARD THE POLICE WERE HERE...
MAY I HELP YOU?
ARE YOU A COP?
THERE WAS A ROBBERY JUST NOW, RIGHT?
I WAS WONDERING IF THIS HAD ANYTHING TO DO WITH IT...
MY NAME'S ISAKA. I LIVE ON THE 6TH FLOOR.
THREE DAYS AGO, AROUND 2:00 A.M., I WOKE UP TO A HEAVY THUDDING SOUND.
I SAW A THIN, STICK-LIKE SHADOW PROJECTED AGAINST THE CURTAIN BY THE MOON-LIGHT!
I WOKE MY HUSBAND UP AND WENT OUT ONTO THE BALCONY...
...BUT IT WAS EMPTY.
MY HUSBAND SAYS I WAS DREAMING, BUT I THOUGHT I SHOULD TELL YOU ABOUT IT...
HEY, DO YOU LIVE OVER THIS APART-MENT?

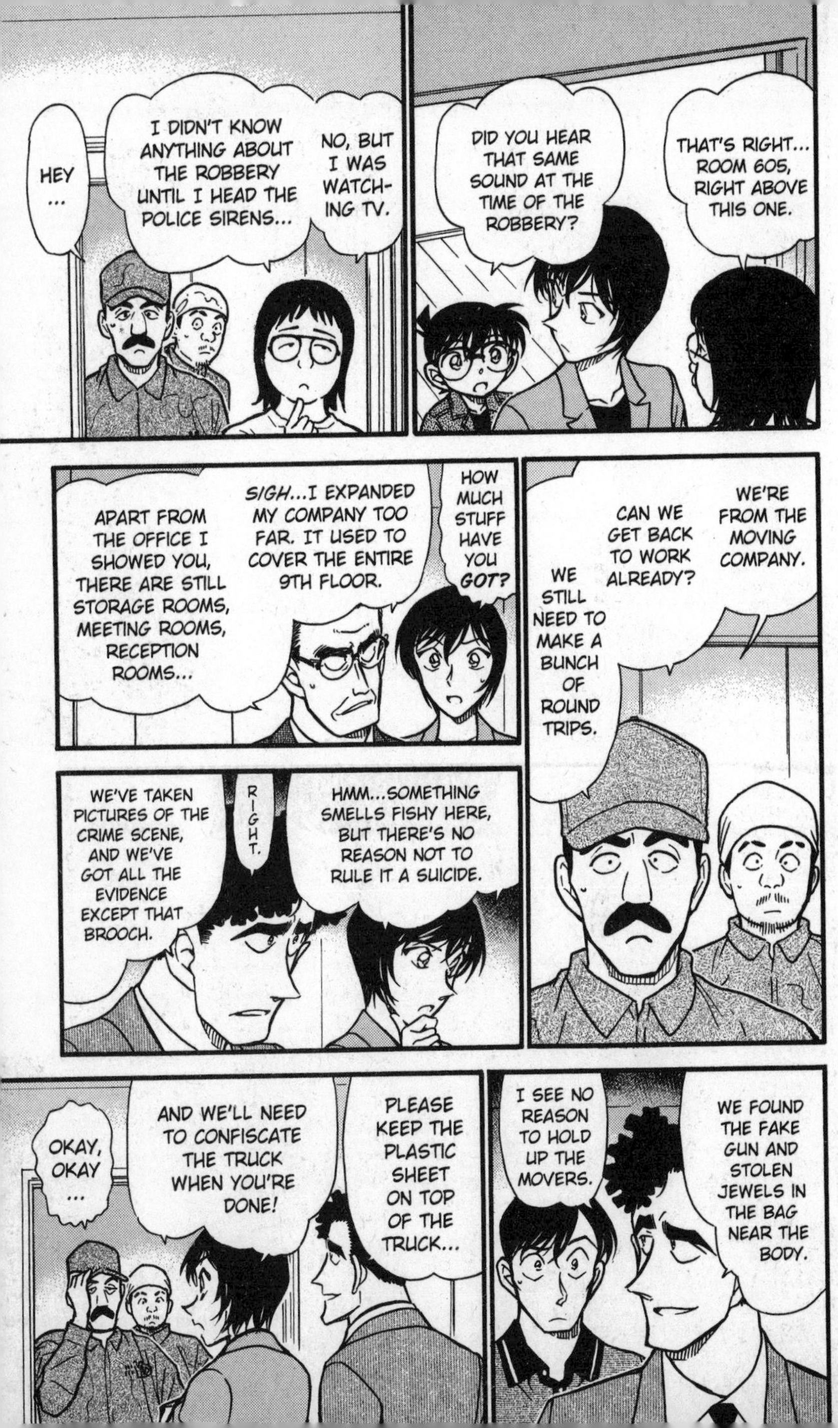
THAT'S RIGHT... ROOM 605, RIGHT ABOVE THIS ONE.
DID YOU HEAR THAT SAME SOUND AT THE TIME OF THE ROBBERY?
NO, BUT I WAS WATCHING TV.
I DIDN'T KNOW ANYTHING ABOUT THE ROBBERY UNTIL I HEAD THE POLICE SIRENS...
HEY ...
WE'RE FROM THE MOVING COMPANY.
CAN WE GET BACK TO WORK ALREADY?
WE STILL NEED TO MAKE A BUNCH OF ROUND TRIPS.
HOW MUCH STUFF HAVE YOU *GOT?*
SIGH...I EXPANDED MY COMPANY TOO FAR. IT USED TO COVER THE ENTIRE 9TH FLOOR.
APART FROM THE OFFICE I SHOWED YOU, THERE ARE STILL STORAGE ROOMS, MEETING ROOMS, RECEPTION ROOMS...
HMM...SOMETHING SMELLS FISHY HERE, BUT THERE'S NO REASON NOT TO RULE IT A SUICIDE.
RIGHT.
WE'VE TAKEN PICTURES OF THE CRIME SCENE, AND WE'VE GOT ALL THE EVIDENCE EXCEPT THAT BROOCH.
WE FOUND THE FAKE GUN AND STOLEN JEWELS IN THE BAG NEAR THE BODY.
I SEE NO REASON TO HOLD UP THE MOVERS.
PLEASE KEEP THE PLASTIC SHEET ON TOP OF THE TRUCK...
AND WE'LL NEED TO CONFISCATE THE TRUCK WHEN YOU'RE DONE!
OKAY, OKAY ...

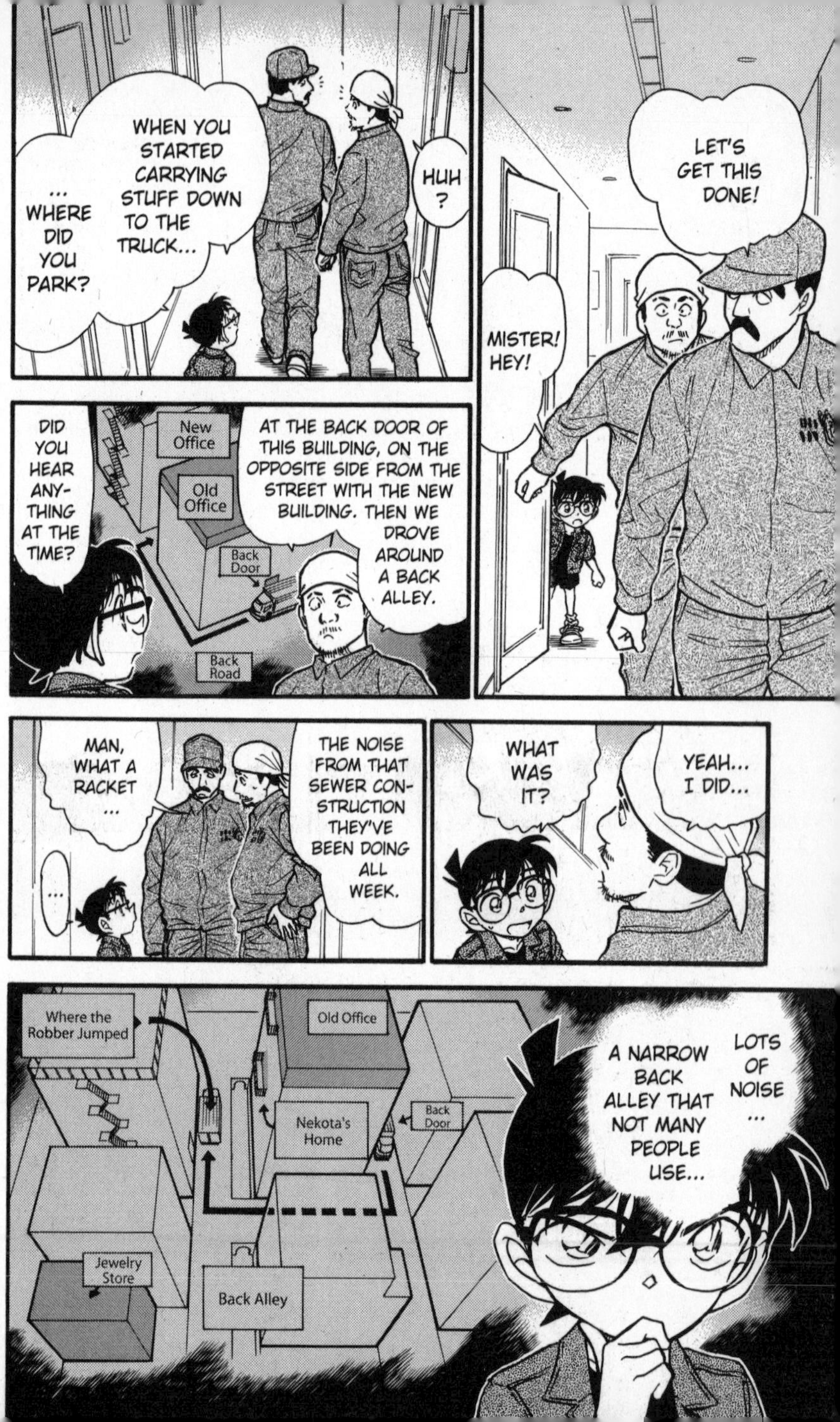
LET'S GET THIS DONE!
MISTER! HEY!
WHEN YOU STARTED CARRYING STUFF DOWN TO THE TRUCK...
... WHERE DID YOU PARK?
HUH?
AT THE BACK DOOR OF THIS BUILDING, ON THE OPPOSITE SIDE FROM THE STREET WITH THE NEW BUILDING. THEN WE DROVE AROUND A BACK ALLEY.
New Office
Old Office
Back Door
Back Road
DID YOU HEAR ANY-THING AT THE TIME?
YEAH... I DID...
WHAT WAS IT?
THE NOISE FROM THAT SEWER CON-STRUCTION THEY'VE BEEN DOING ALL WEEK.
MAN, WHAT A RACKET ...
...
LOTS OF NOISE ...
A NARROW BACK ALLEY THAT NOT MANY PEOPLE USE...
Where the Robber Jumped
Old Office
Nekota's Home
Back Door
Jewelry Store
Back Alley

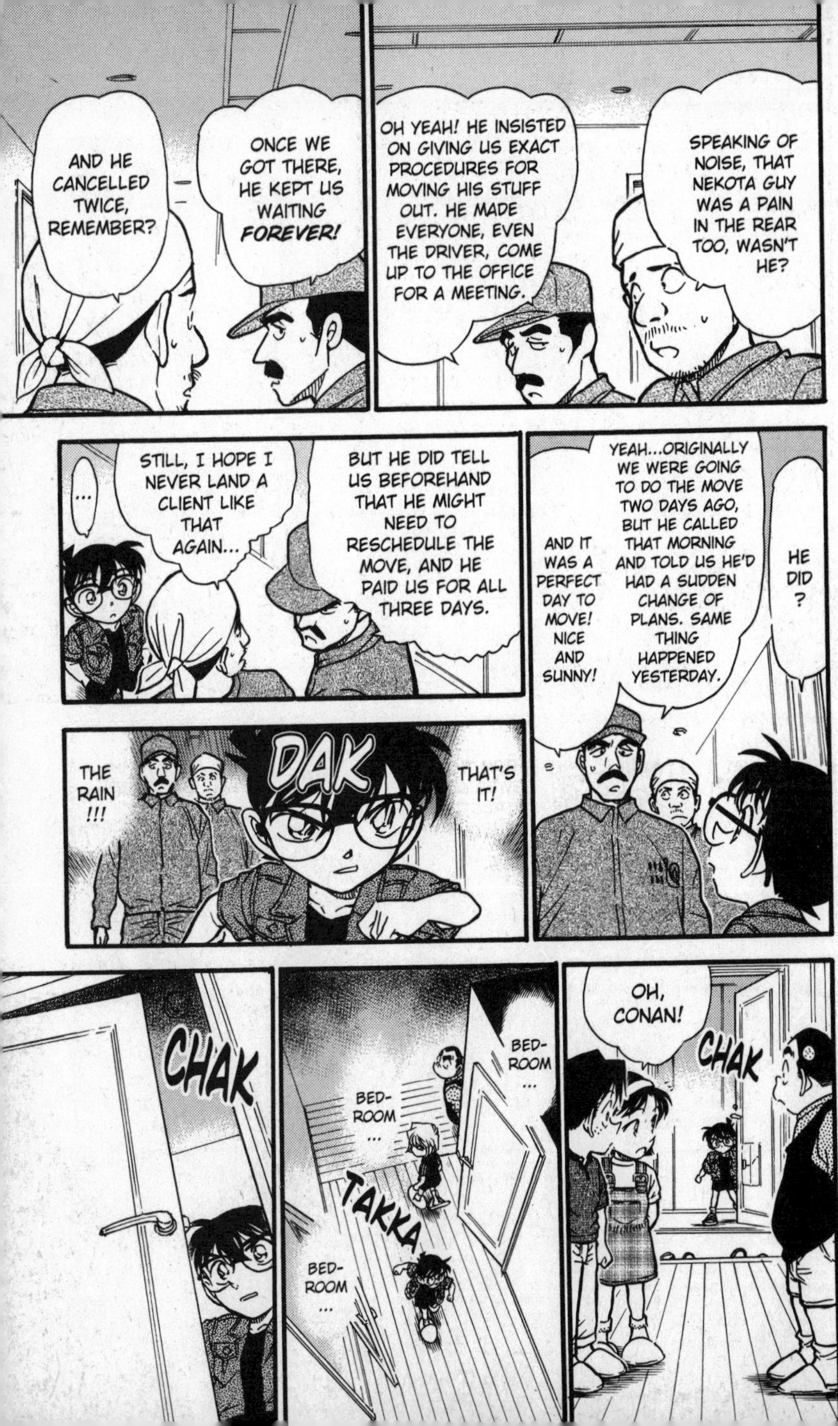
SPEAKING OF NOISE, THAT NEKOTA GUY WAS A PAIN IN THE REAR TOO, WASN'T HE?
OH YEAH! HE INSISTED ON GIVING US EXACT PROCEDURES FOR MOVING HIS STUFF OUT. HE MADE EVERYONE, EVEN THE DRIVER, COME UP TO THE OFFICE FOR A MEETING.
ONCE WE GOT THERE, HE KEPT US WAITING ***FOREVER!***
AND HE CANCELLED TWICE, REMEMBER?
HE DID?
YEAH...ORIGINALLY WE WERE GOING TO DO THE MOVE TWO DAYS AGO, BUT HE CALLED THAT MORNING AND TOLD US HE'D HAD A SUDDEN CHANGE OF PLANS. SAME THING HAPPENED YESTERDAY.
AND IT WAS A PERFECT DAY TO MOVE! NICE AND SUNNY!
BUT HE DID TELL US BEFOREHAND THAT HE MIGHT NEED TO RESCHEDULE THE MOVE, AND HE PAID US FOR ALL THREE DAYS.
STILL, I HOPE I NEVER LAND A CLIENT LIKE THAT AGAIN...
...
THAT'S IT!
DAK
THE RAIN!!!
OH, CONAN!
CHAK
BED-ROOM...
BED-ROOM...
TAKKA
BED-ROOM...
CHAK

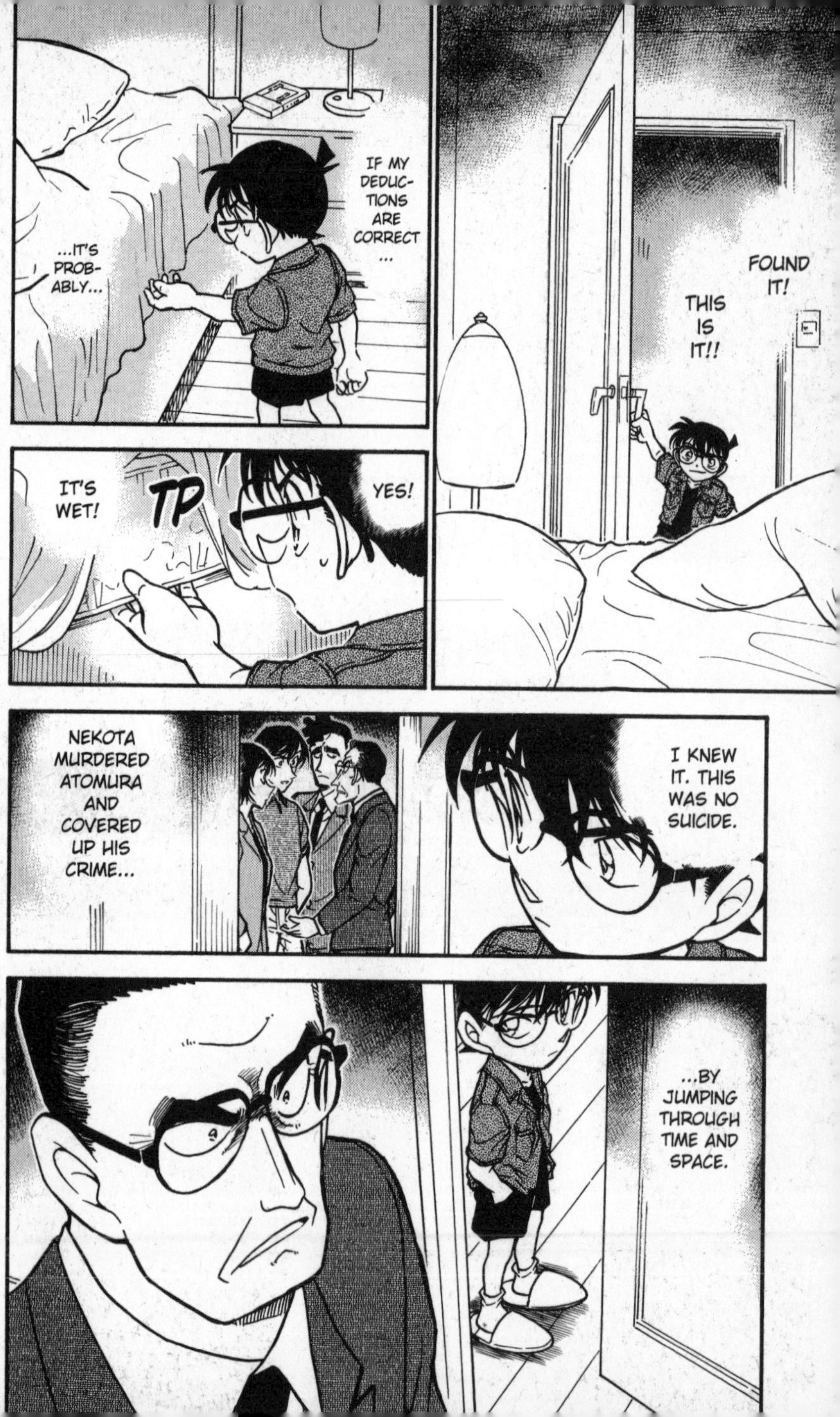
FOUND IT!
THIS IS IT!!
IF MY DEDUCTIONS ARE CORRECT ...
...IT'S PROBABLY...
YES!
TP
IT'S WET!
I KNEW IT. THIS WAS NO SUICIDE.
NEKOTA MURDERED ATOMURA AND COVERED UP HIS CRIME...
...BY JUMPING THROUGH TIME AND SPACE.

FROM HEAVEN TO EARTH

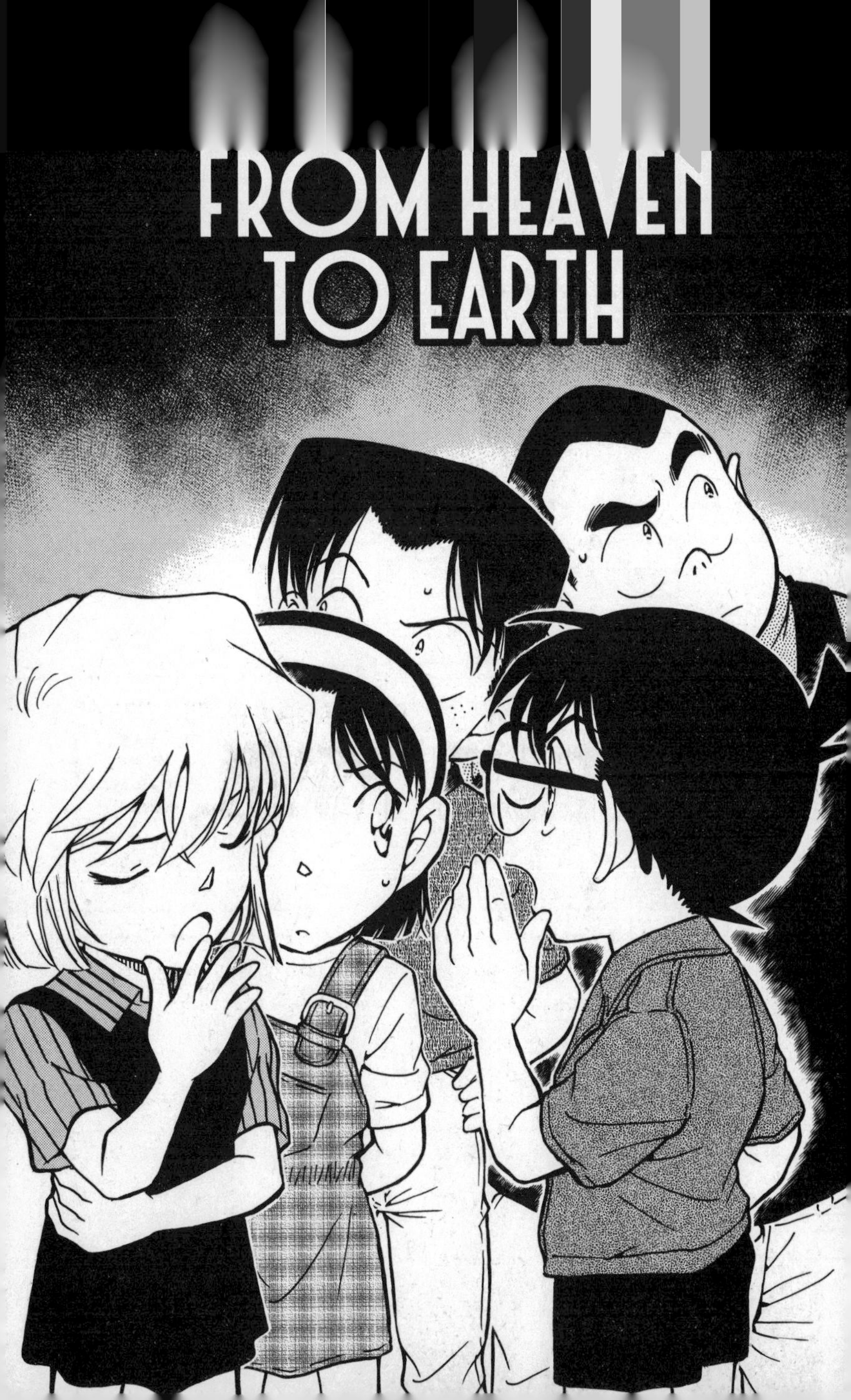

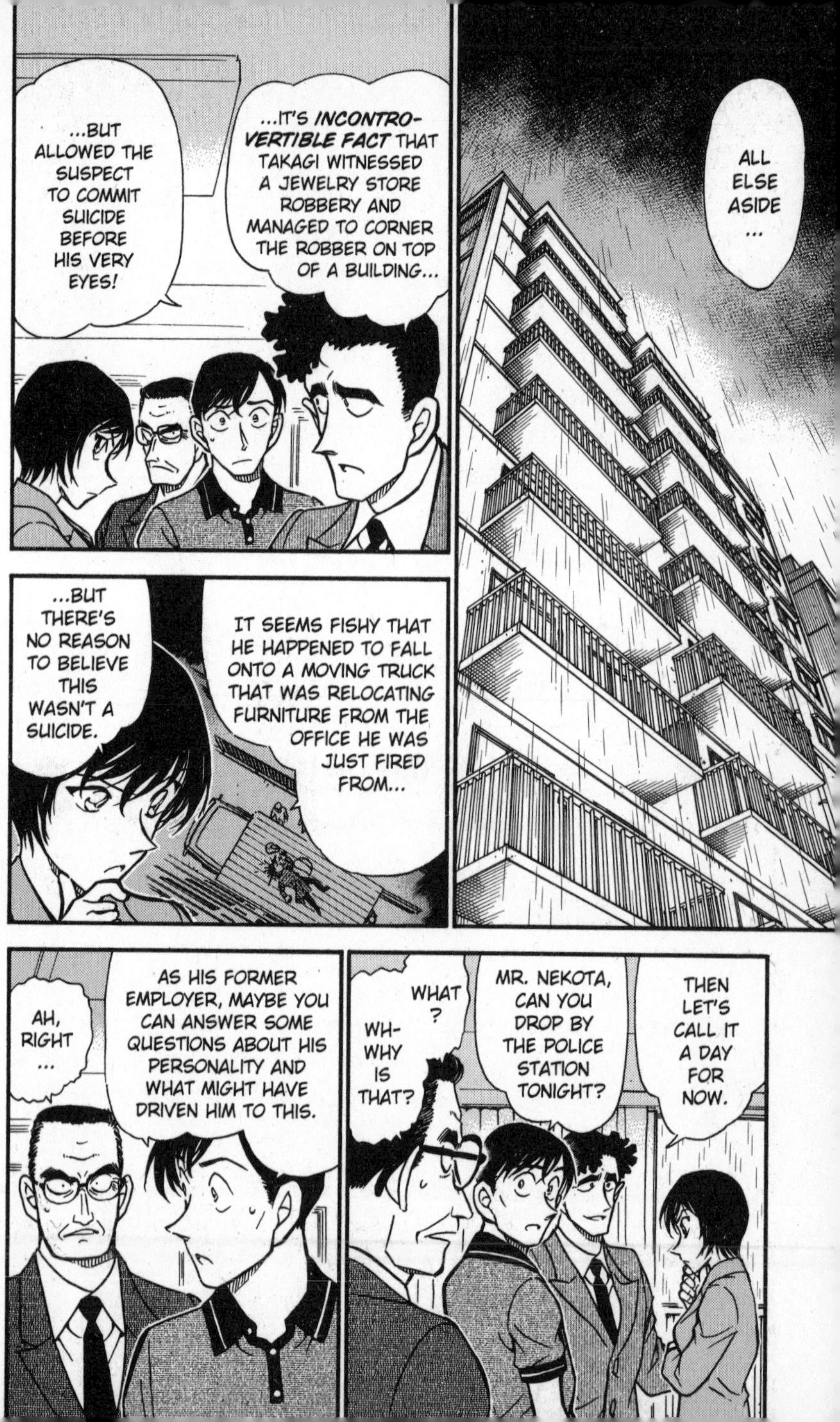
ALL ELSE ASIDE ...
...IT'S *INCONTROVERTIBLE FACT* THAT TAKAGI WITNESSED A JEWELRY STORE ROBBERY AND MANAGED TO CORNER THE ROBBER ON TOP OF A BUILDING...
...BUT ALLOWED THE SUSPECT TO COMMIT SUICIDE BEFORE HIS VERY EYES!
IT SEEMS FISHY THAT HE HAPPENED TO FALL ONTO A MOVING TRUCK THAT WAS RELOCATING FURNITURE FROM THE OFFICE HE WAS JUST FIRED FROM...
...BUT THERE'S NO REASON TO BELIEVE THIS WASN'T A SUICIDE.
THEN LET'S CALL IT A DAY FOR NOW.
MR. NEKOTA, CAN YOU DROP BY THE POLICE STATION TONIGHT?
WHAT?
WH-WHY IS THAT?
AS HIS FORMER EMPLOYER, MAYBE YOU CAN ANSWER SOME QUESTIONS ABOUT HIS PERSONALITY AND WHAT MIGHT HAVE DRIVEN HIM TO THIS.
AH, RIGHT ...

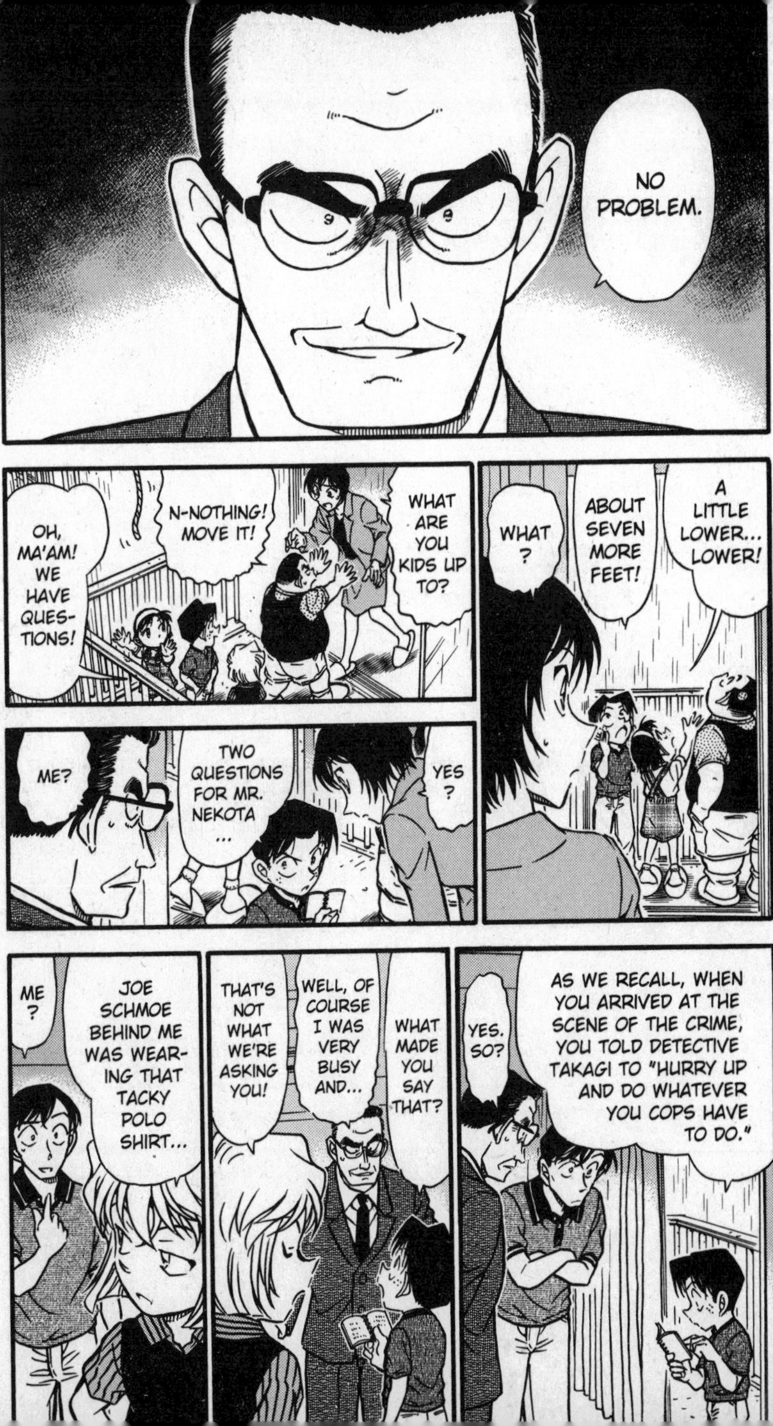
NO PROBLEM.
A LITTLE LOWER... LOWER!
ABOUT SEVEN MORE FEET!
WHAT?
WHAT ARE YOU KIDS UP TO?
N-NOTHING! MOVE IT!
OH, MA'AM! WE HAVE QUES-TIONS!
YES?
TWO QUESTIONS FOR MR. NEKOTA...
ME?
AS WE RECALL, WHEN YOU ARRIVED AT THE SCENE OF THE CRIME, YOU TOLD DETECTIVE TAKAGI TO "HURRY UP AND DO WHATEVER YOU COPS HAVE TO DO."
YES. SO?
WHAT MADE YOU SAY THAT?
WELL, OF COURSE I WAS VERY BUSY AND...
THAT'S NOT WHAT WE'RE ASKING YOU!
JOE SCHMOE BEHIND ME WAS WEAR-ING THAT TACKY POLO SHIRT...
ME?

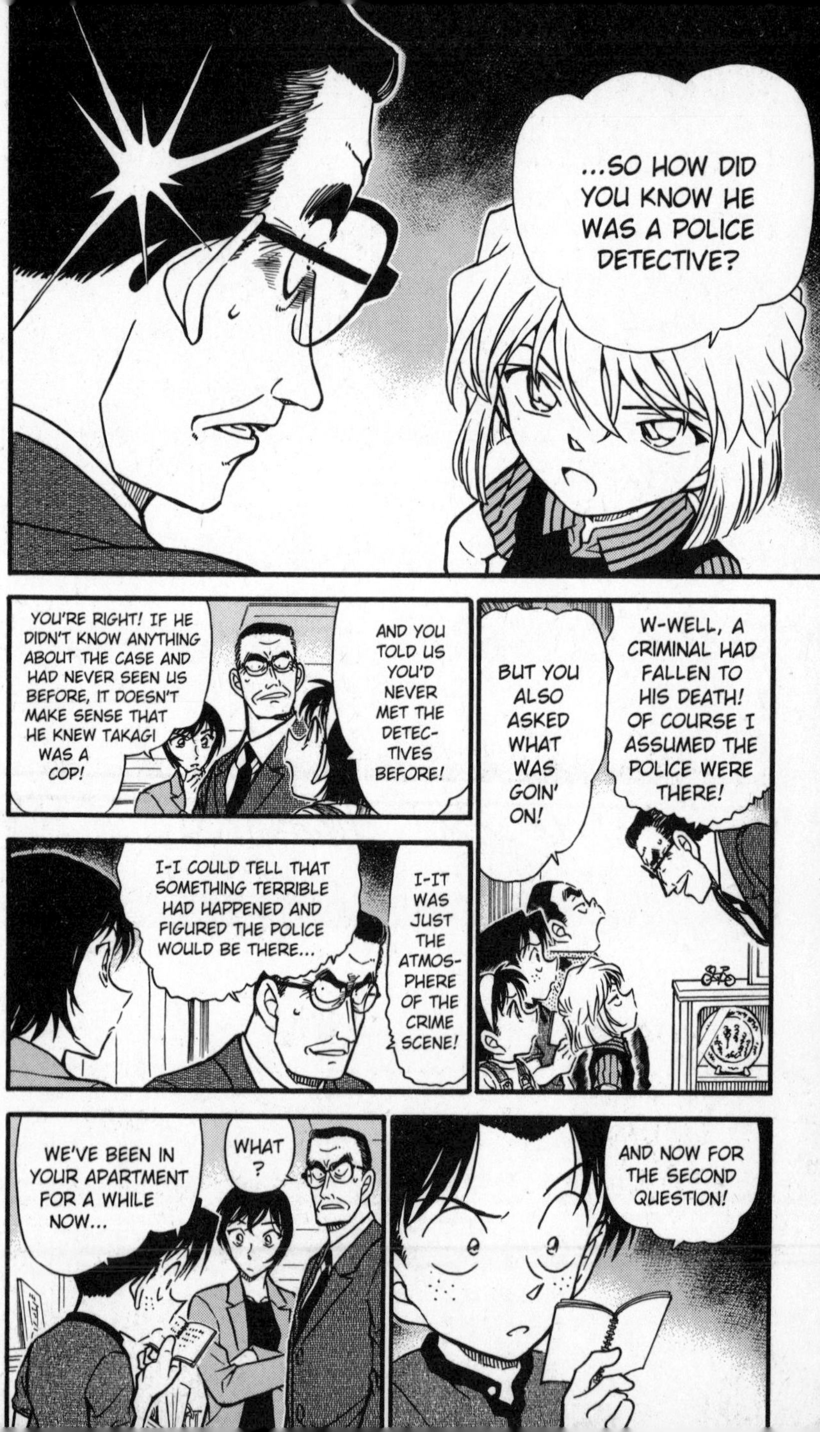
...SO HOW DID YOU KNOW HE WAS A POLICE DETECTIVE?
YOU'RE RIGHT! IF HE DIDN'T KNOW ANYTHING ABOUT THE CASE AND HAD NEVER SEEN US BEFORE, IT DOESN'T MAKE SENSE THAT HE KNEW TAKAGI WAS A COP!
AND YOU TOLD US YOU'D NEVER MET THE DETEC-TIVES BEFORE!
I-I COULD TELL THAT SOMETHING TERRIBLE HAD HAPPENED AND FIGURED THE POLICE WOULD BE THERE...
I-IT WAS JUST THE ATMOS-PHERE OF THE CRIME SCENE!
BUT YOU ALSO ASKED WHAT WAS GOIN' ON!
W-WELL, A CRIMINAL HAD FALLEN TO HIS DEATH! OF COURSE I ASSUMED THE POLICE WERE THERE!
AND NOW FOR THE SECOND QUESTION!
WE'VE BEEN IN YOUR APARTMENT FOR A WHILE NOW...
WHAT?

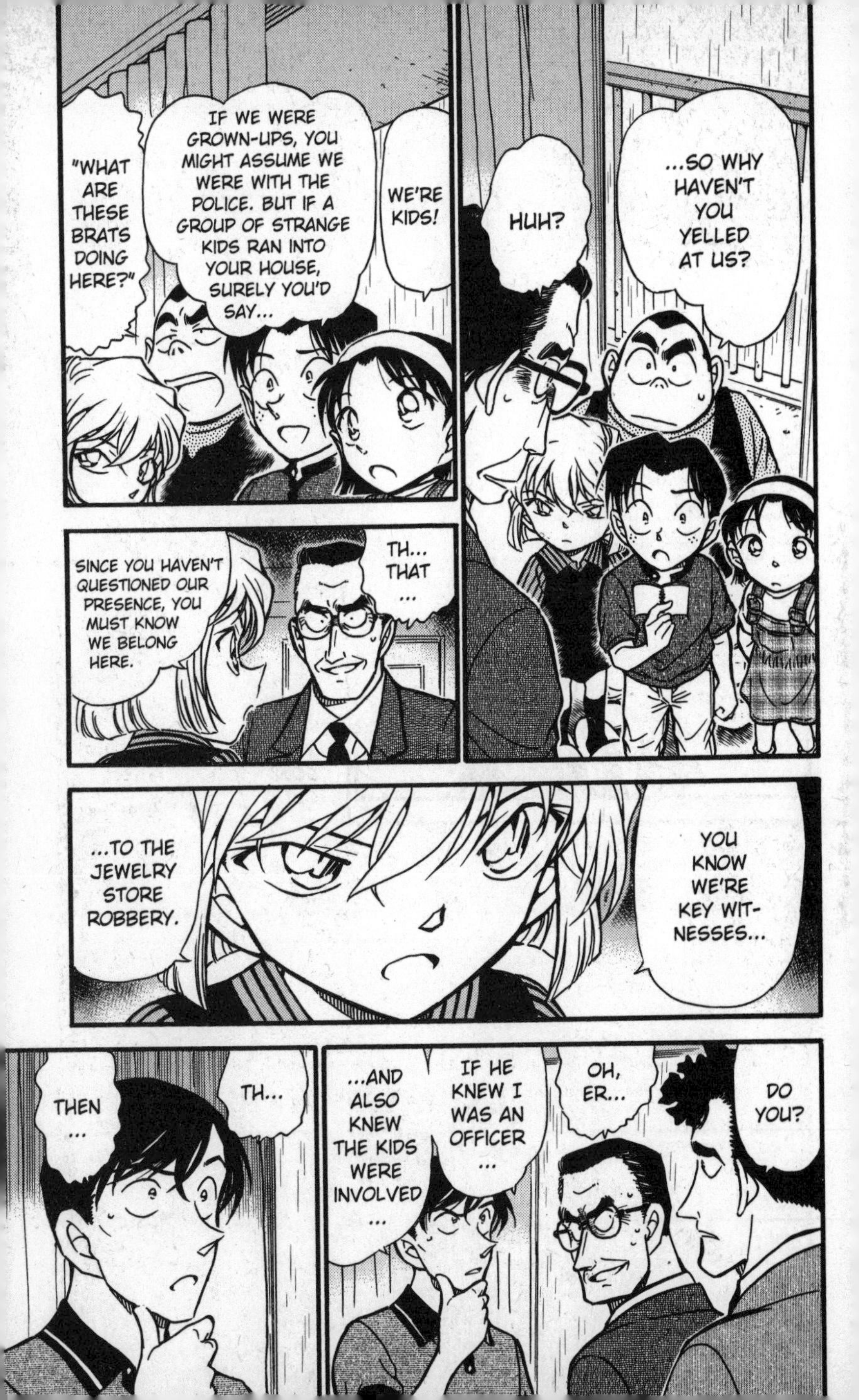
...SO WHY HAVEN'T YOU YELLED AT US?
HUH?
WE'RE KIDS!
IF WE WERE GROWN-UPS, YOU MIGHT ASSUME WE WERE WITH THE POLICE. BUT IF A GROUP OF STRANGE KIDS RAN INTO YOUR HOUSE, SURELY YOU'D SAY...
"WHAT ARE THESE BRATS DOING HERE?"
SINCE YOU HAVEN'T QUESTIONED OUR PRESENCE, YOU MUST KNOW WE BELONG HERE.
TH... THAT ...
YOU KNOW WE'RE KEY WIT-NESSES...
...TO THE JEWELRY STORE ROBBERY.
DO YOU?
OH, ER...
IF HE KNEW I WAS AN OFFICER ...
...AND ALSO KNEW THE KIDS WERE INVOLVED ...
TH...
THEN ...

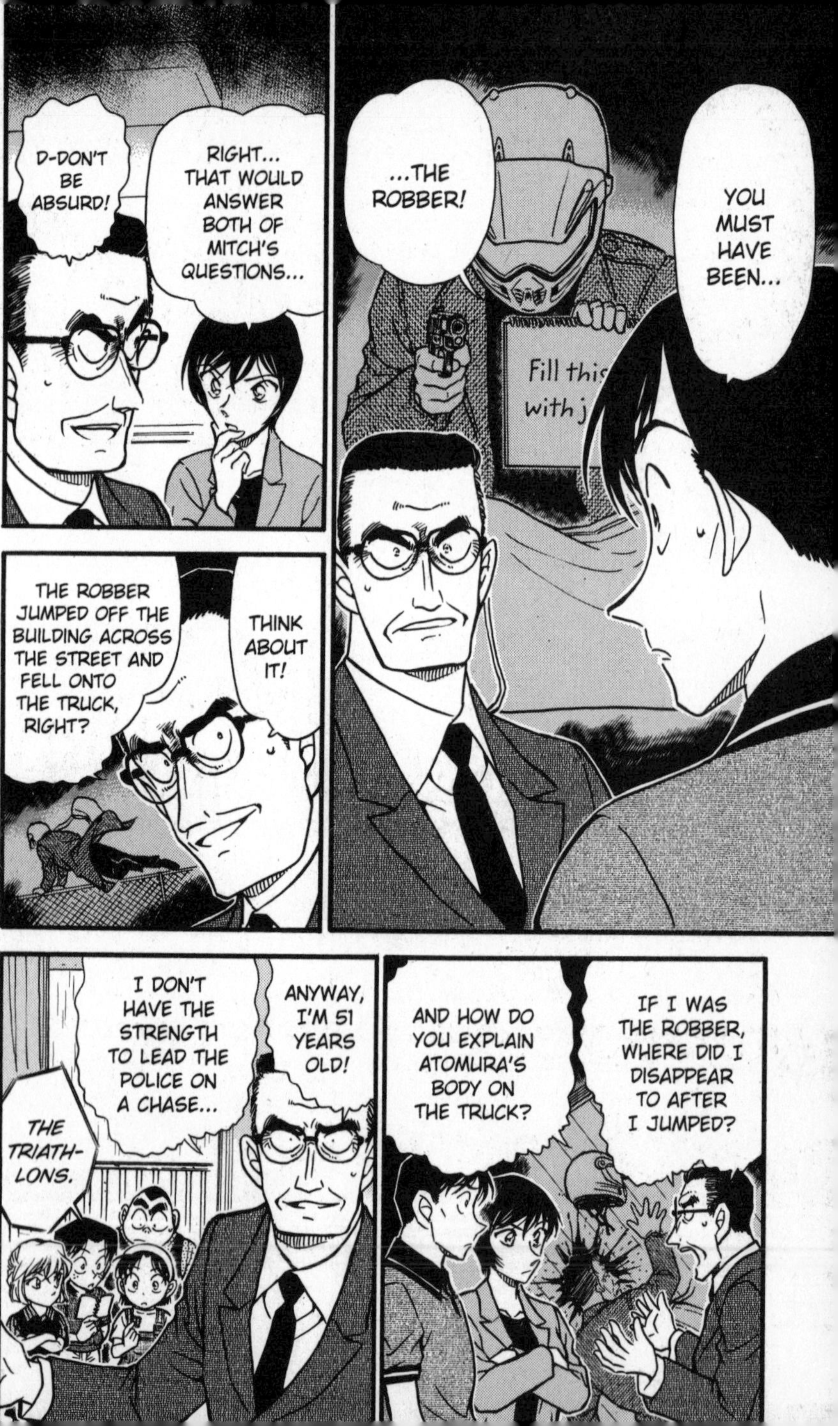
YOU MUST HAVE BEEN...
...THE ROBBER!
RIGHT... THAT WOULD ANSWER BOTH OF MITCH'S QUESTIONS...
D-DON'T BE ABSURD!
THINK ABOUT IT!
THE ROBBER JUMPED OFF THE BUILDING ACROSS THE STREET AND FELL ONTO THE TRUCK, RIGHT?
IF I WAS THE ROBBER, WHERE DID I DISAPPEAR TO AFTER I JUMPED?
AND HOW DO YOU EXPLAIN ATOMURA'S BODY ON THE TRUCK?
ANYWAY, I'M 51 YEARS OLD!
I DON'T HAVE THE STRENGTH TO LEAD THE POLICE ON A CHASE...
THE TRIATHLONS.

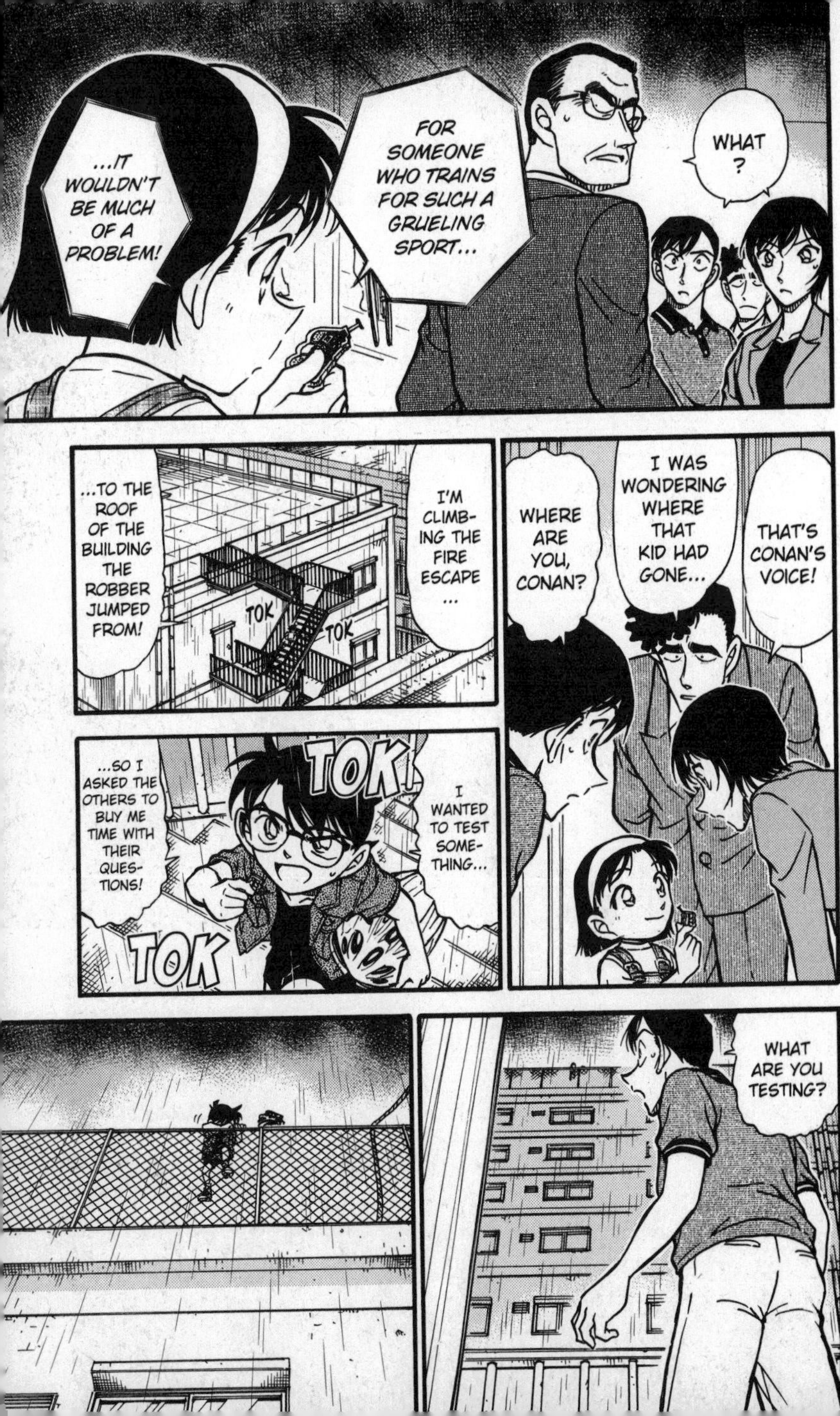
FOR SOMEONE WHO TRAINS FOR SUCH A GRUELING SPORT...
...IT WOULDN'T BE MUCH OF A PROBLEM!
WHAT ?
THAT'S CONAN'S VOICE!
I WAS WONDERING WHERE THAT KID HAD GONE...
WHERE ARE YOU, CONAN?
I'M CLIMBING THE FIRE ESCAPE...
...TO THE ROOF OF THE BUILDING THE ROBBER JUMPED FROM!
TOK
TOK
TOK
I WANTED TO TEST SOMETHING...
...SO I ASKED THE OTHERS TO BUY ME TIME WITH THEIR QUESTIONS!
TOK
WHAT ARE YOU TESTING?

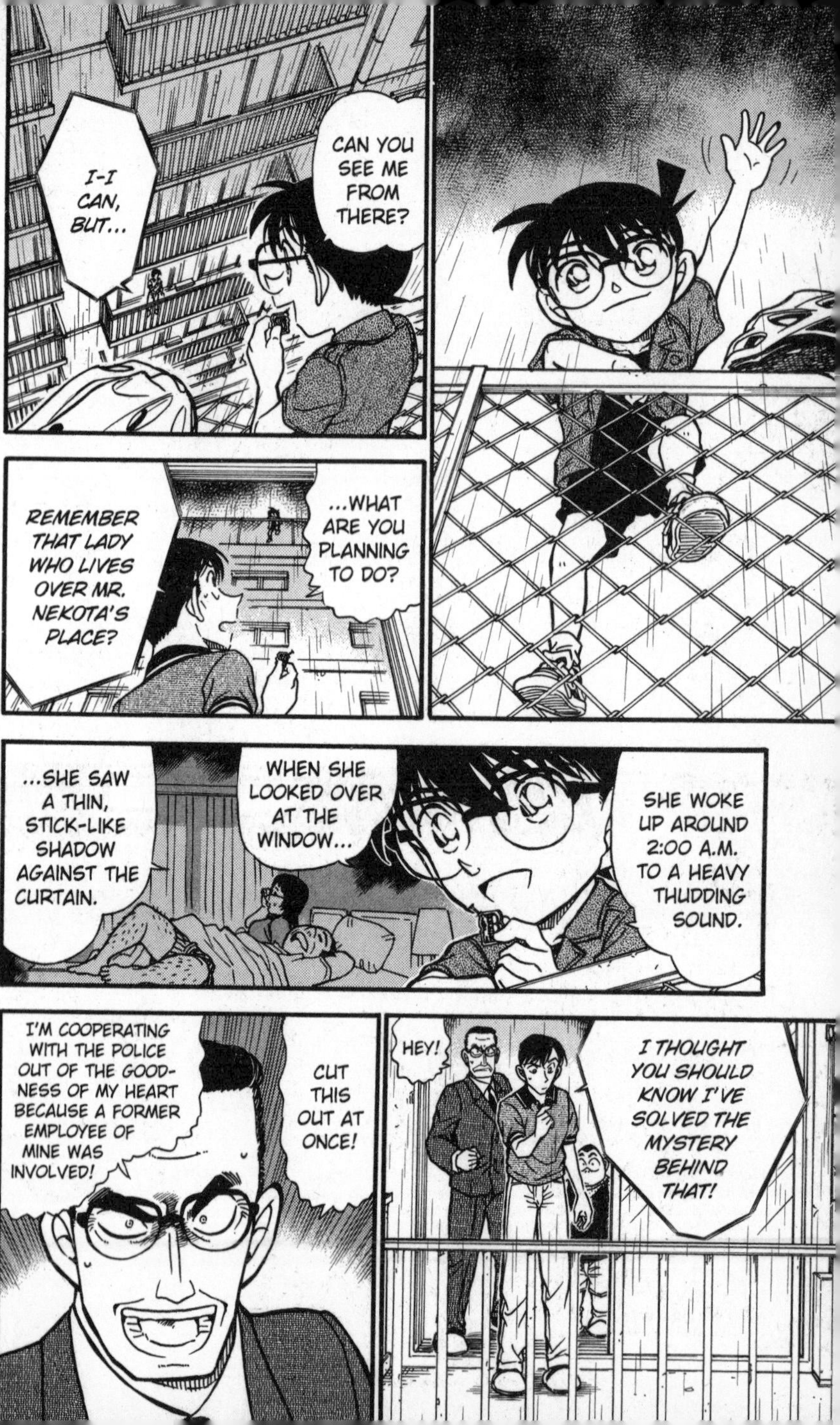
CAN YOU SEE ME FROM THERE?
I-I CAN, BUT...
...WHAT ARE YOU PLANNING TO DO?
REMEMBER THAT LADY WHO LIVES OVER MR. NEKOTA'S PLACE?
SHE WOKE UP AROUND 2:00 A.M. TO A HEAVY THUDDING SOUND.
WHEN SHE LOOKED OVER AT THE WINDOW...
...SHE SAW A THIN, STICK-LIKE SHADOW AGAINST THE CURTAIN.
I THOUGHT YOU SHOULD KNOW I'VE SOLVED THE MYSTERY BEHIND THAT!
HEY!
CUT THIS OUT AT ONCE!
I'M COOPERATING WITH THE POLICE OUT OF THE GOODNESS OF MY HEART BECAUSE A FORMER EMPLOYEE OF MINE WAS INVOLVED!

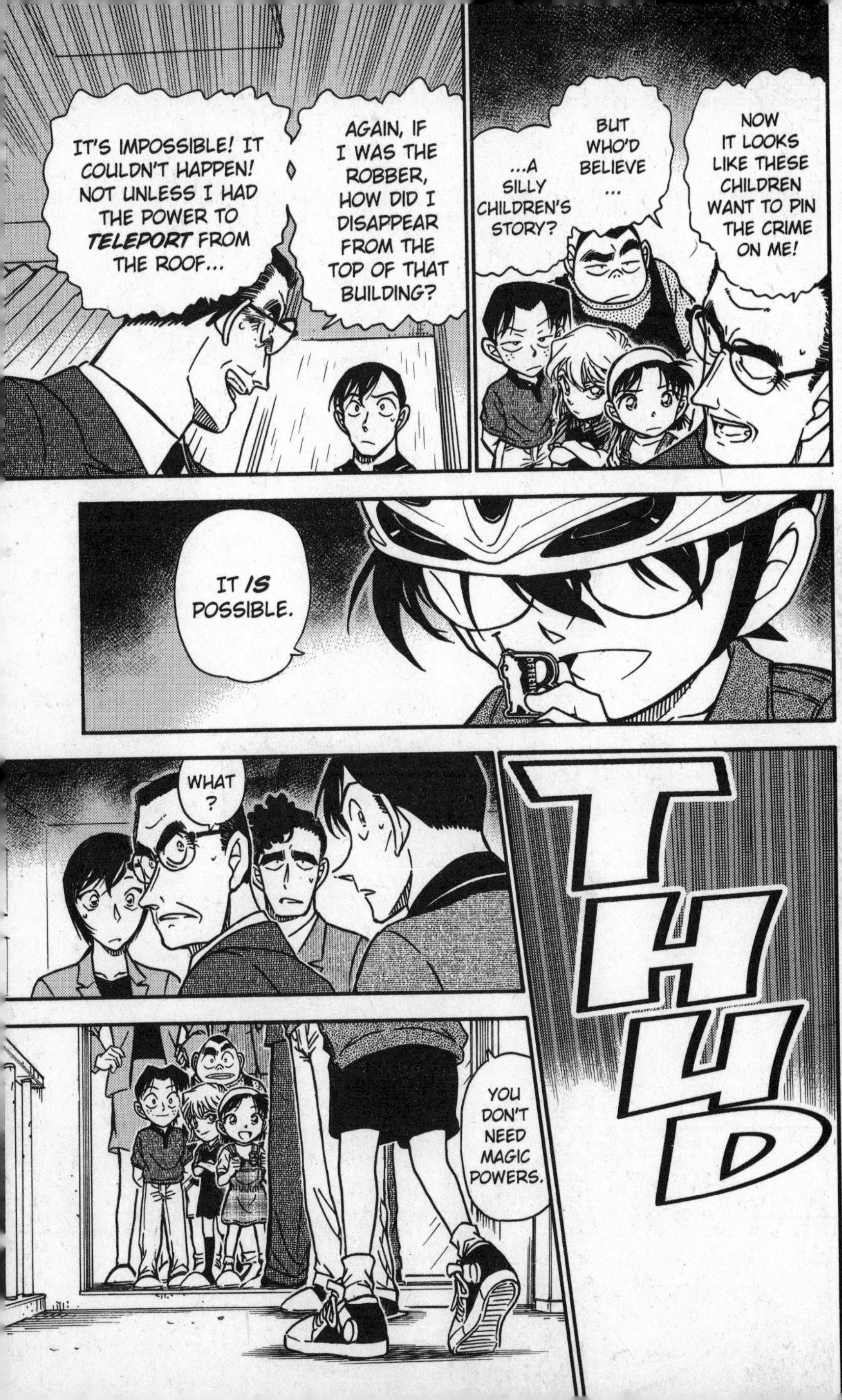
IT'S IMPOSSIBLE! IT COULDN'T HAPPEN! NOT UNLESS I HAD THE POWER TO *TELEPORT* FROM THE ROOF...
AGAIN, IF I WAS THE ROBBER, HOW DID I DISAPPEAR FROM THE TOP OF THAT BUILDING?
BUT WHO'D BELIEVE ...
...A SILLY CHILDREN'S STORY?
NOW IT LOOKS LIKE THESE CHILDREN WANT TO PIN THE CRIME ON ME!
IT *IS* POSSIBLE.
WHAT?
YOU DON'T NEED MAGIC POWERS.
THUD

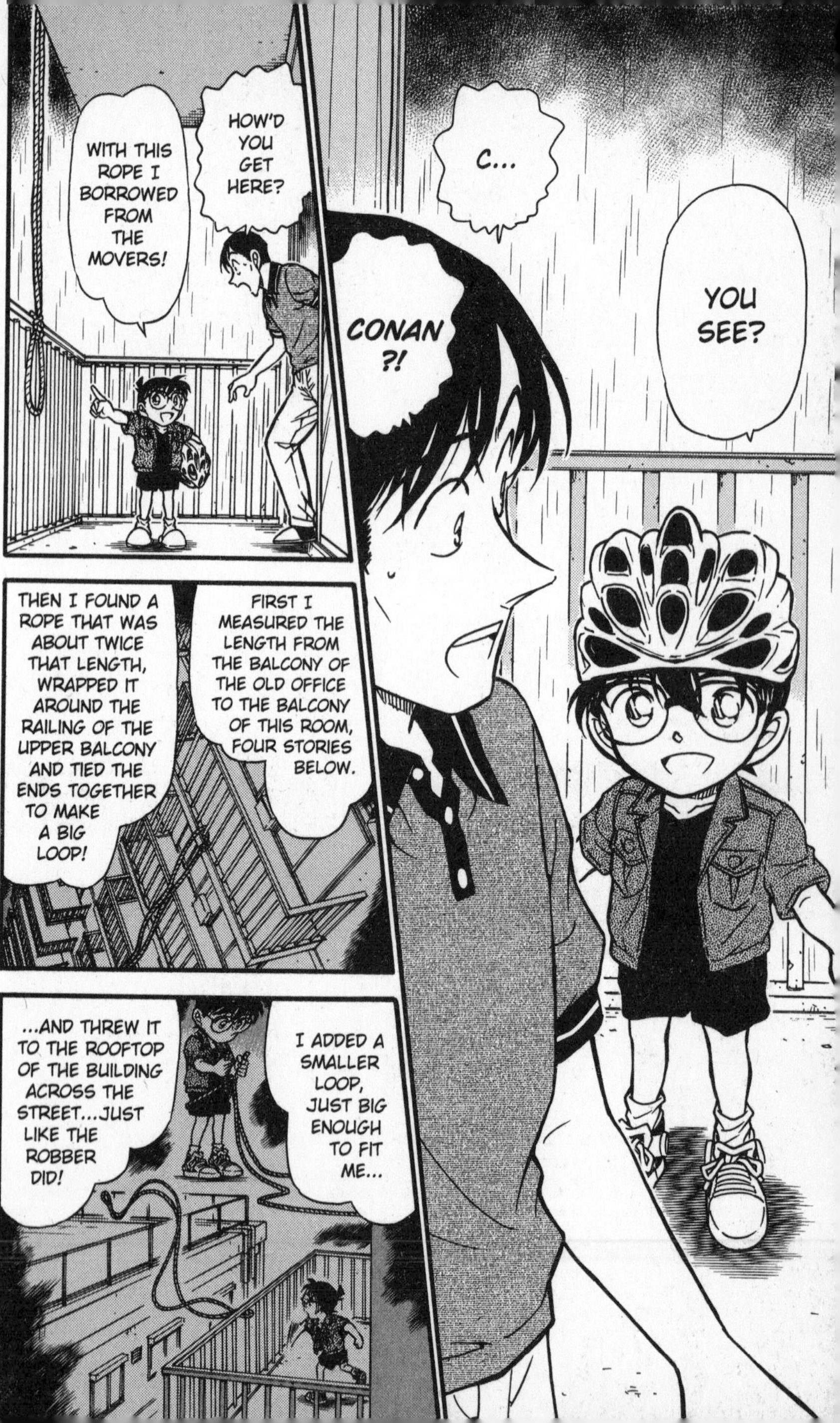
YOU SEE?
C...
CONAN ?!
HOW'D YOU GET HERE?
WITH THIS ROPE I BORROWED FROM THE MOVERS!
FIRST I MEASURED THE LENGTH FROM THE BALCONY OF THE OLD OFFICE TO THE BALCONY OF THIS ROOM, FOUR STORIES BELOW.
THEN I FOUND A ROPE THAT WAS ABOUT TWICE THAT LENGTH, WRAPPED IT AROUND THE RAILING OF THE UPPER BALCONY AND TIED THE ENDS TOGETHER TO MAKE A BIG LOOP!
I ADDED A SMALLER LOOP, JUST BIG ENOUGH TO FIT ME...
...AND THREW IT TO THE ROOFTOP OF THE BUILDING ACROSS THE STREET...JUST LIKE THE ROBBER DID!

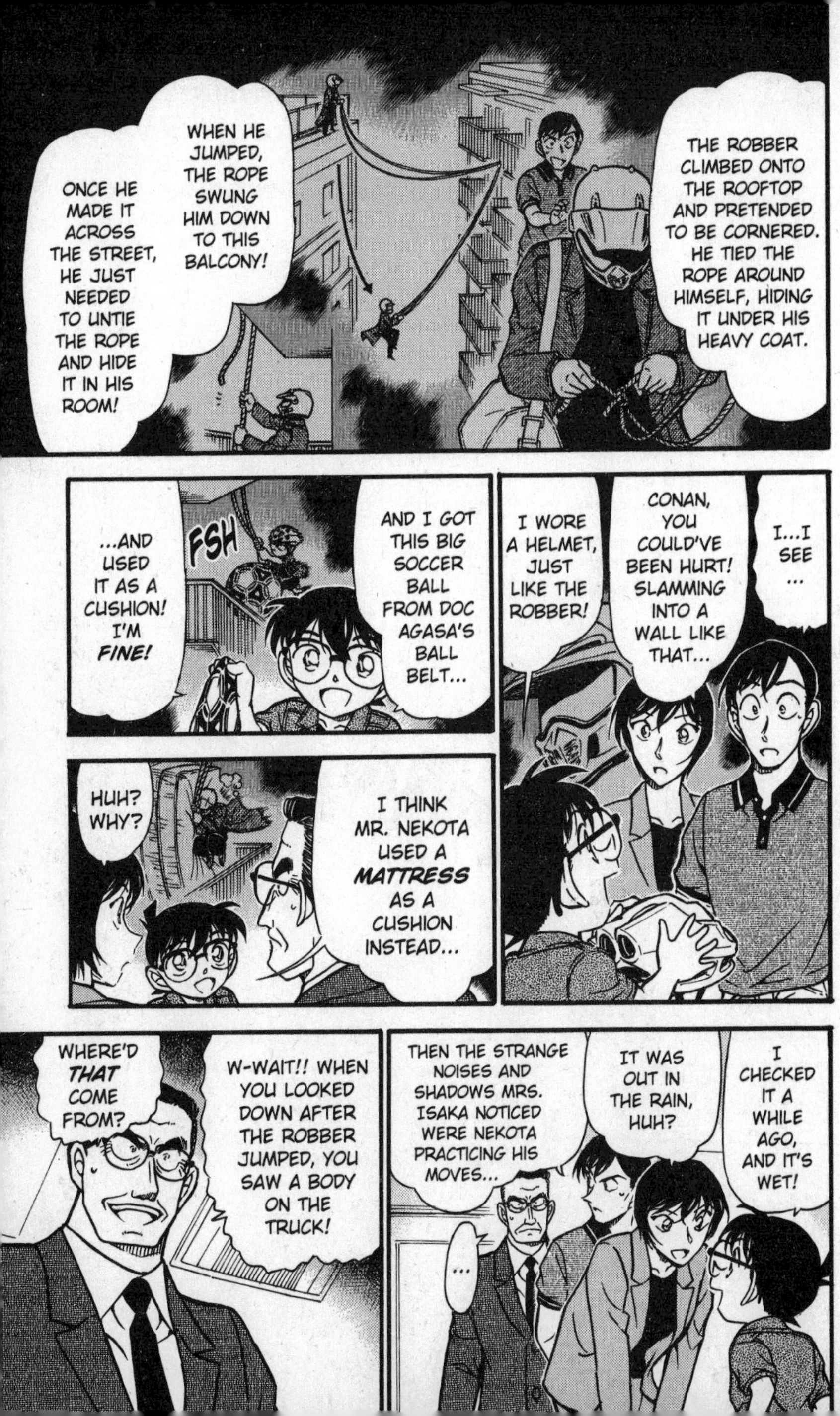
THE ROBBER CLIMBED ONTO THE ROOFTOP AND PRETENDED TO BE CORNERED. HE TIED THE ROPE AROUND HIMSELF, HIDING IT UNDER HIS HEAVY COAT.
WHEN HE JUMPED, THE ROPE SWUNG HIM DOWN TO THIS BALCONY!
ONCE HE MADE IT ACROSS THE STREET, HE JUST NEEDED TO UNTIE THE ROPE AND HIDE IT IN HIS ROOM!
I...I SEE...
CONAN, YOU COULD'VE BEEN HURT! SLAMMING INTO A WALL LIKE THAT...
I WORE A HELMET, JUST LIKE THE ROBBER!
AND I GOT THIS BIG SOCCER BALL FROM DOC AGASA'S BALL BELT...
FSH
...AND USED IT AS A CUSHION! I'M *FINE!*
I THINK MR. NEKOTA USED A ***MATTRESS*** AS A CUSHION INSTEAD...
HUH? WHY?
I CHECKED IT A WHILE AGO, AND IT'S WET!
IT WAS OUT IN THE RAIN, HUH?
THEN THE STRANGE NOISES AND SHADOWS MRS. ISAKA NOTICED WERE NEKOTA PRACTICING HIS MOVES...
...
W-WAIT!! WHEN YOU LOOKED DOWN AFTER THE ROBBER JUMPED, YOU SAW A BODY ON THE TRUCK!
WHERE'D ***THAT*** COME FROM?

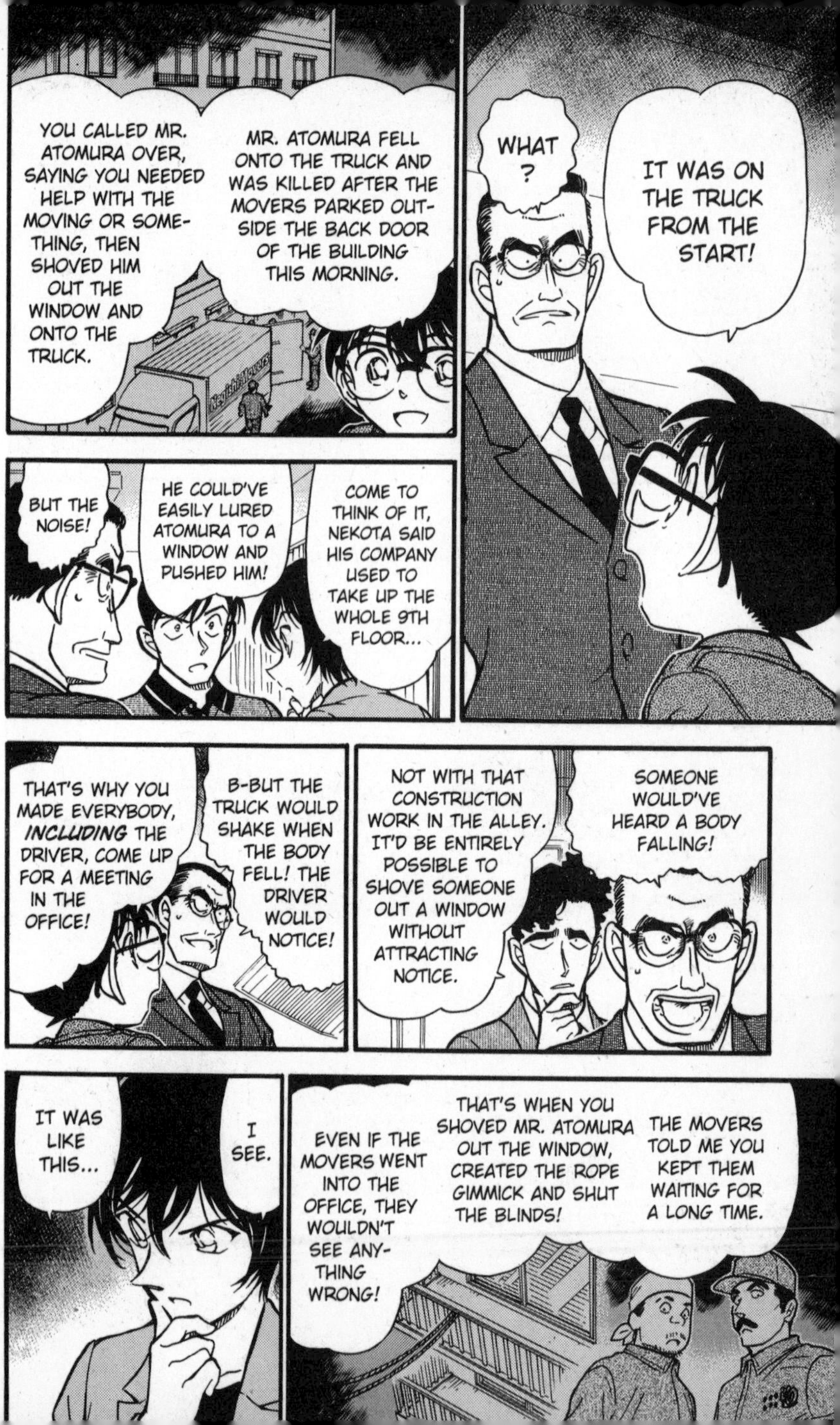
IT WAS ON THE TRUCK FROM THE START!
WHAT ?
MR. ATOMURA FELL ONTO THE TRUCK AND WAS KILLED AFTER THE MOVERS PARKED OUTSIDE THE BACK DOOR OF THE BUILDING THIS MORNING.
YOU CALLED MR. ATOMURA OVER, SAYING YOU NEEDED HELP WITH THE MOVING OR SOMETHING, THEN SHOVED HIM OUT THE WINDOW AND ONTO THE TRUCK.
COME TO THINK OF IT, NEKOTA SAID HIS COMPANY USED TO TAKE UP THE WHOLE 9TH FLOOR...
HE COULD'VE EASILY LURED ATOMURA TO A WINDOW AND PUSHED HIM!
BUT THE NOISE!
SOMEONE WOULD'VE HEARD A BODY FALLING!
NOT WITH THAT CONSTRUCTION WORK IN THE ALLEY. IT'D BE ENTIRELY POSSIBLE TO SHOVE SOMEONE OUT A WINDOW WITHOUT ATTRACTING NOTICE.
B-BUT THE TRUCK WOULD SHAKE WHEN THE BODY FELL! THE DRIVER WOULD NOTICE!
THAT'S WHY YOU MADE EVERYBODY, *INCLUDING* THE DRIVER, COME UP FOR A MEETING IN THE OFFICE!
THE MOVERS TOLD ME YOU KEPT THEM WAITING FOR A LONG TIME.
THAT'S WHEN YOU SHOVED MR. ATOMURA OUT THE WINDOW, CREATED THE ROPE GIMMICK AND SHUT THE BLINDS!
EVEN IF THE MOVERS WENT INTO THE OFFICE, THEY WOULDN'T SEE ANYTHING WRONG!
I SEE.
IT WAS LIKE THIS...

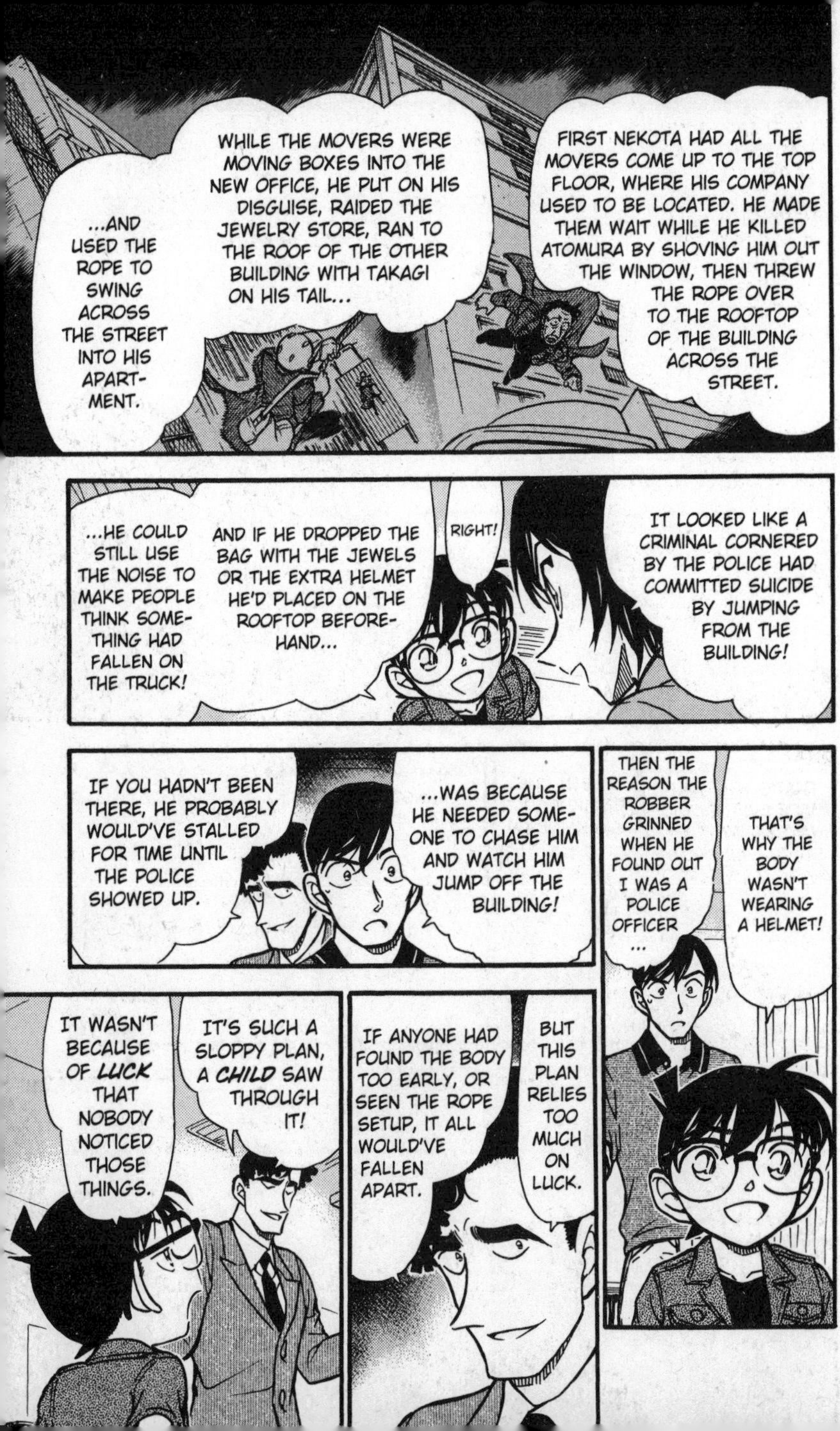
FIRST NEKOTA HAD ALL THE MOVERS COME UP TO THE TOP FLOOR, WHERE HIS COMPANY USED TO BE LOCATED. HE MADE THEM WAIT WHILE HE KILLED ATOMURA BY SHOVING HIM OUT THE WINDOW, THEN THREW THE ROPE OVER TO THE ROOFTOP OF THE BUILDING ACROSS THE STREET.
WHILE THE MOVERS WERE MOVING BOXES INTO THE NEW OFFICE, HE PUT ON HIS DISGUISE, RAIDED THE JEWELRY STORE, RAN TO THE ROOF OF THE OTHER BUILDING WITH TAKAGI ON HIS TAIL...
...AND USED THE ROPE TO SWING ACROSS THE STREET INTO HIS APART-MENT.
IT LOOKED LIKE A CRIMINAL CORNERED BY THE POLICE HAD COMMITTED SUICIDE BY JUMPING FROM THE BUILDING!
RIGHT!
AND IF HE DROPPED THE BAG WITH THE JEWELS OR THE EXTRA HELMET HE'D PLACED ON THE ROOFTOP BEFORE-HAND...
...HE COULD STILL USE THE NOISE TO MAKE PEOPLE THINK SOME-THING HAD FALLEN ON THE TRUCK!
THAT'S WHY THE BODY WASN'T WEARING A HELMET!
THEN THE REASON THE ROBBER GRINNED WHEN HE FOUND OUT I WAS A POLICE OFFICER...
...WAS BECAUSE HE NEEDED SOME-ONE TO CHASE HIM AND WATCH HIM JUMP OFF THE BUILDING!
IF YOU HADN'T BEEN THERE, HE PROBABLY WOULD'VE STALLED FOR TIME UNTIL THE POLICE SHOWED UP.
BUT THIS PLAN RELIES TOO MUCH ON LUCK.
IF ANYONE HAD FOUND THE BODY TOO EARLY, OR SEEN THE ROPE SETUP, IT ALL WOULD'VE FALLEN APART.
IT'S SUCH A SLOPPY PLAN, A CHILD SAW THROUGH IT!
IT WASN'T BECAUSE OF LUCK THAT NOBODY NOTICED THOSE THINGS.

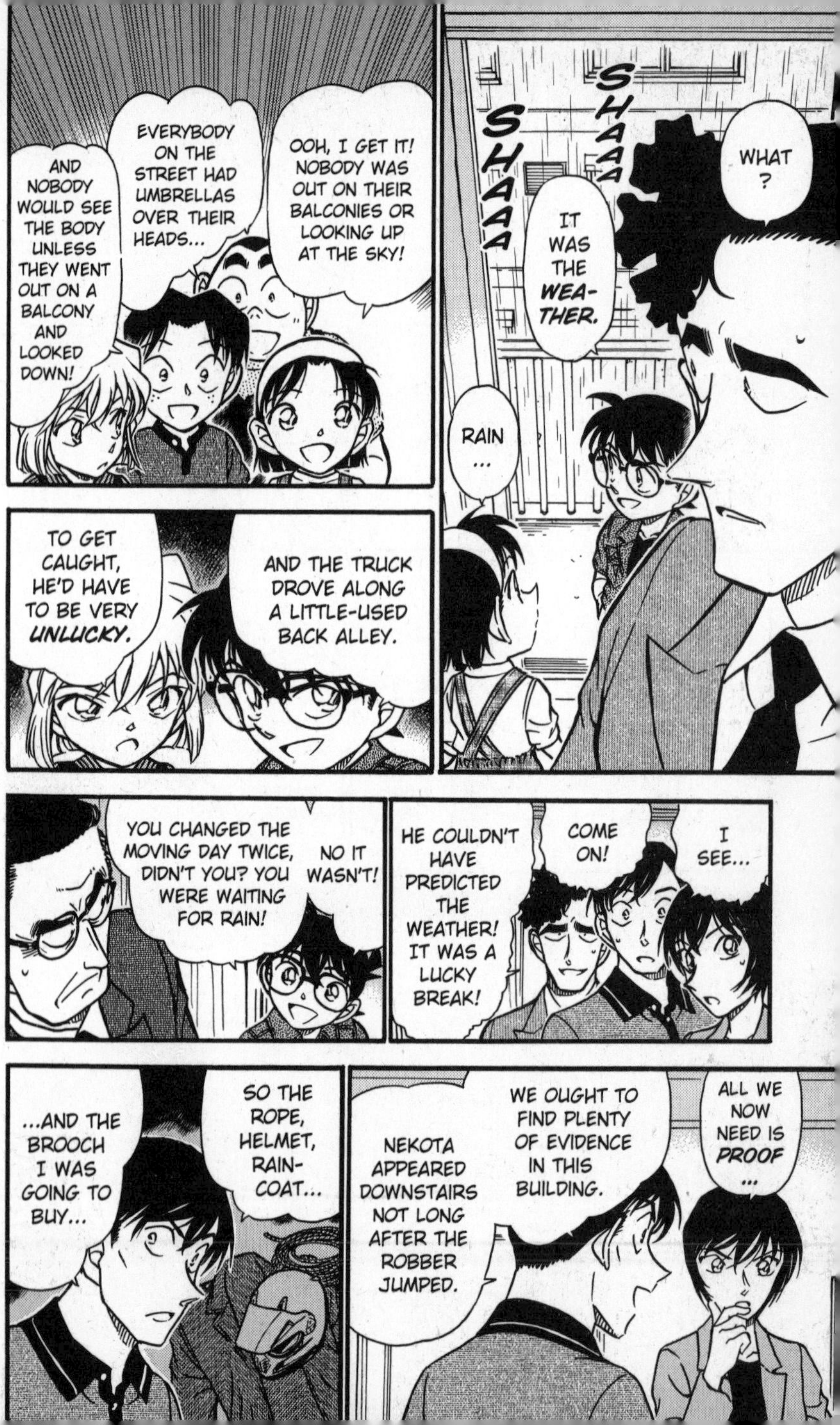
WHAT?
SHAAAA
SHAAAA
IT WAS THE *WEATHER.*
RAIN...
OOH, I GET IT! NOBODY WAS OUT ON THEIR BALCONIES OR LOOKING UP AT THE SKY!
EVERYBODY ON THE STREET HAD UMBRELLAS OVER THEIR HEADS...
AND NOBODY WOULD SEE THE BODY UNLESS THEY WENT OUT ON A BALCONY AND LOOKED DOWN!
AND THE TRUCK DROVE ALONG A LITTLE-USED BACK ALLEY.
TO GET CAUGHT, HE'D HAVE TO BE VERY *UNLUCKY.*
I SEE...
COME ON!
HE COULDN'T HAVE PREDICTED THE WEATHER! IT WAS A LUCKY BREAK!
YOU CHANGED THE MOVING DAY TWICE, DIDN'T YOU? YOU WERE WAITING FOR RAIN!
NO IT WASN'T!
ALL WE NOW NEED IS *PROOF*...
WE OUGHT TO FIND PLENTY OF EVIDENCE IN THIS BUILDING.
NEKOTA APPEARED DOWNSTAIRS NOT LONG AFTER THE ROBBER JUMPED.
SO THE ROPE, HELMET, RAIN-COAT...
...AND THE BROOCH I WAS GOING TO BUY...

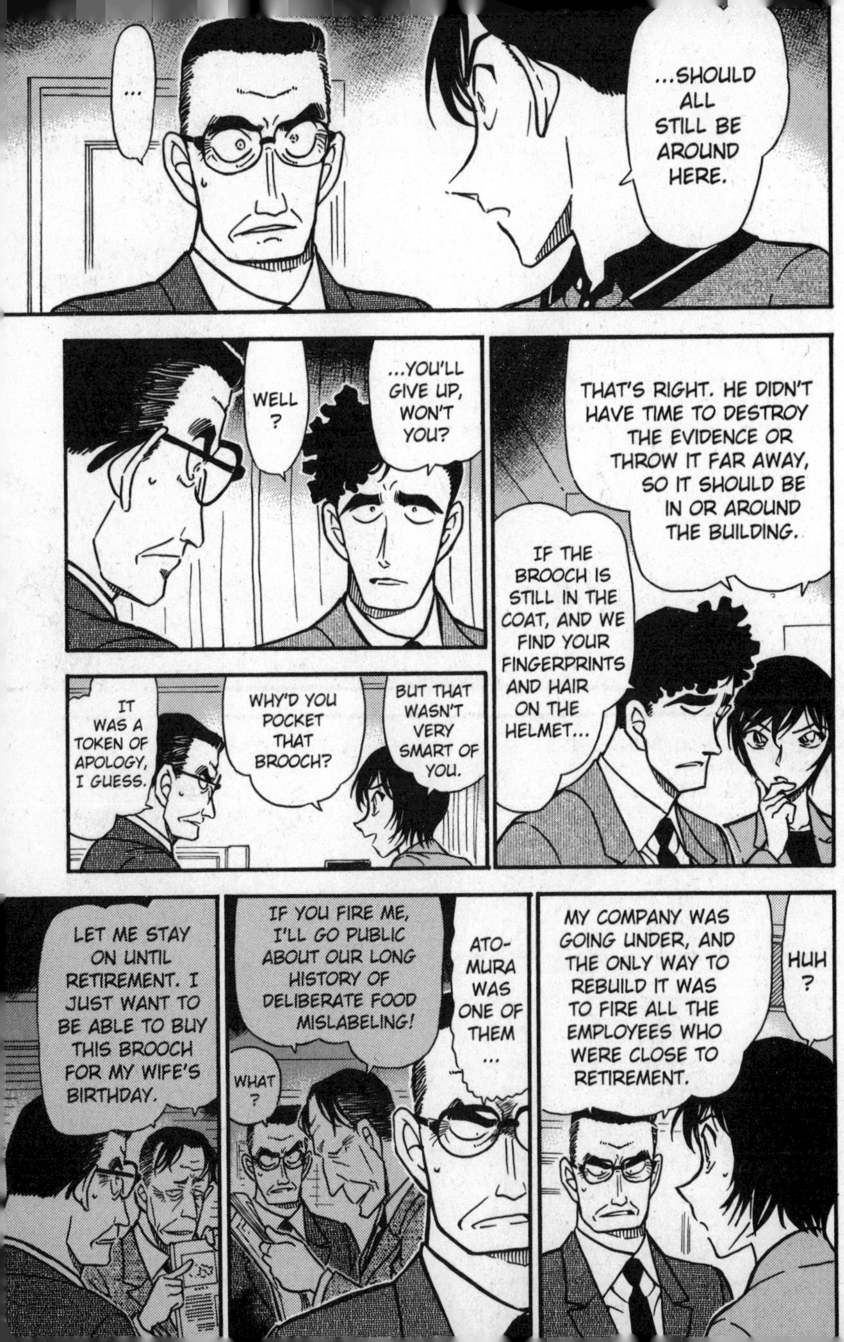
...SHOULD ALL STILL BE AROUND HERE.
...
THAT'S RIGHT. HE DIDN'T HAVE TIME TO DESTROY THE EVIDENCE OR THROW IT FAR AWAY, SO IT SHOULD BE IN OR AROUND THE BUILDING.
IF THE BROOCH IS STILL IN THE COAT, AND WE FIND YOUR FINGERPRINTS AND HAIR ON THE HELMET...
...YOU'LL GIVE UP, WON'T YOU?
WELL?
BUT THAT WASN'T VERY SMART OF YOU.
WHY'D YOU POCKET THAT BROOCH?
IT WAS A TOKEN OF APOLOGY, I GUESS.
HUH?
MY COMPANY WAS GOING UNDER, AND THE ONLY WAY TO REBUILD IT WAS TO FIRE ALL THE EMPLOYEES WHO WERE CLOSE TO RETIREMENT.
ATO-MURA WAS ONE OF THEM...
IF YOU FIRE ME, I'LL GO PUBLIC ABOUT OUR LONG HISTORY OF DELIBERATE FOOD MISLABELING!
WHAT?
LET ME STAY ON UNTIL RETIREMENT. I JUST WANT TO BE ABLE TO BUY THIS BROOCH FOR MY WIFE'S BIRTHDAY.

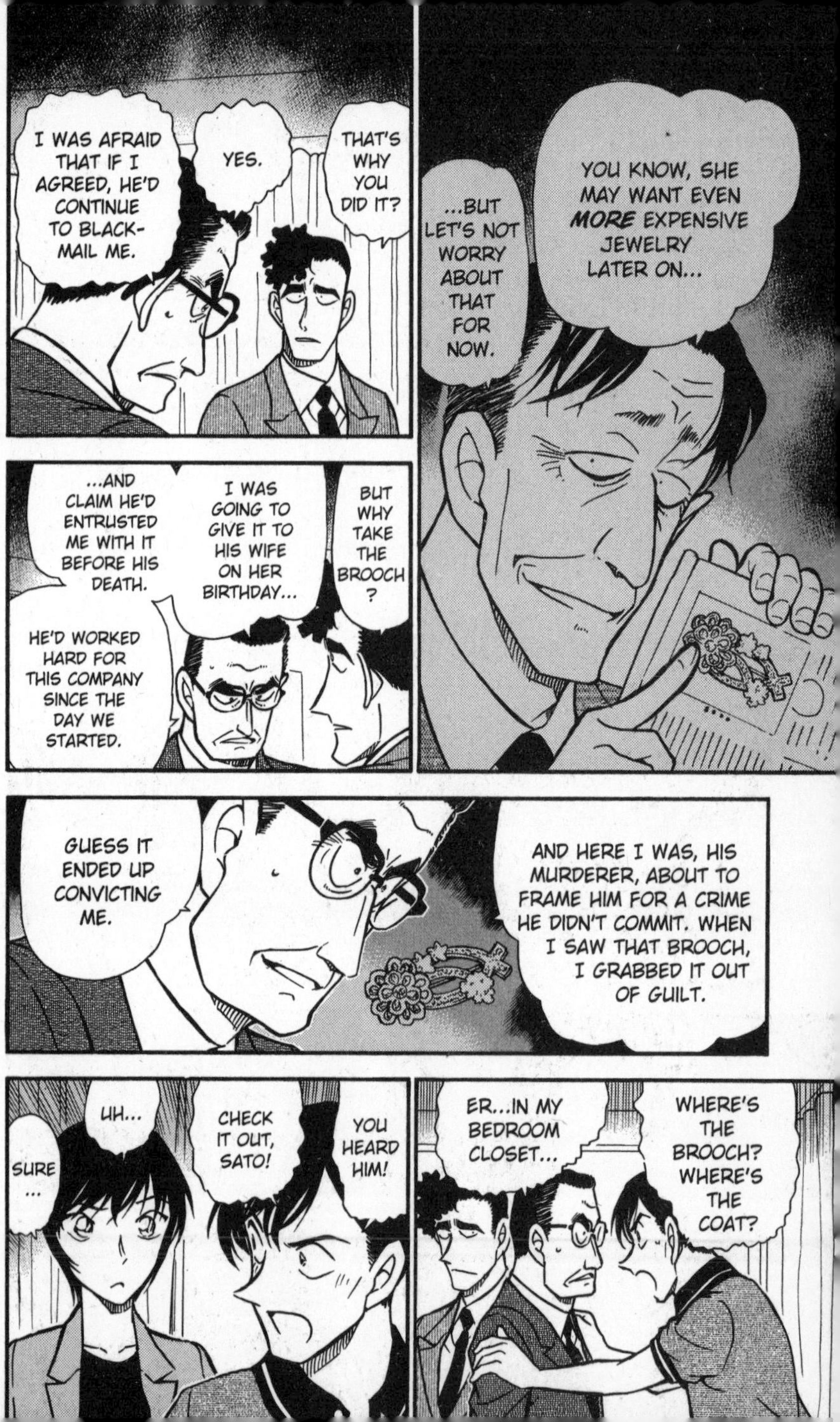

YOU KNOW, SHE MAY WANT EVEN *MORE* EXPENSIVE JEWELRY LATER ON...
...BUT LET'S NOT WORRY ABOUT THAT FOR NOW.
THAT'S WHY YOU DID IT?
YES.
I WAS AFRAID THAT IF I AGREED, HE'D CONTINUE TO BLACK-MAIL ME.
BUT WHY TAKE THE BROOCH?
I WAS GOING TO GIVE IT TO HIS WIFE ON HER BIRTHDAY...
...AND CLAIM HE'D ENTRUSTED ME WITH IT BEFORE HIS DEATH.
HE'D WORKED HARD FOR THIS COMPANY SINCE THE DAY WE STARTED.
AND HERE I WAS, HIS MURDERER, ABOUT TO FRAME HIM FOR A CRIME HE DIDN'T COMMIT. WHEN I SAW THAT BROOCH, I GRABBED IT OUT OF GUILT.
GUESS IT ENDED UP CONVICTING ME.
WHERE'S THE BROOCH? WHERE'S THE COAT?
ER...IN MY BEDROOM CLOSET...
YOU HEARD HIM!
CHECK IT OUT, SATO!
UH...
SURE...

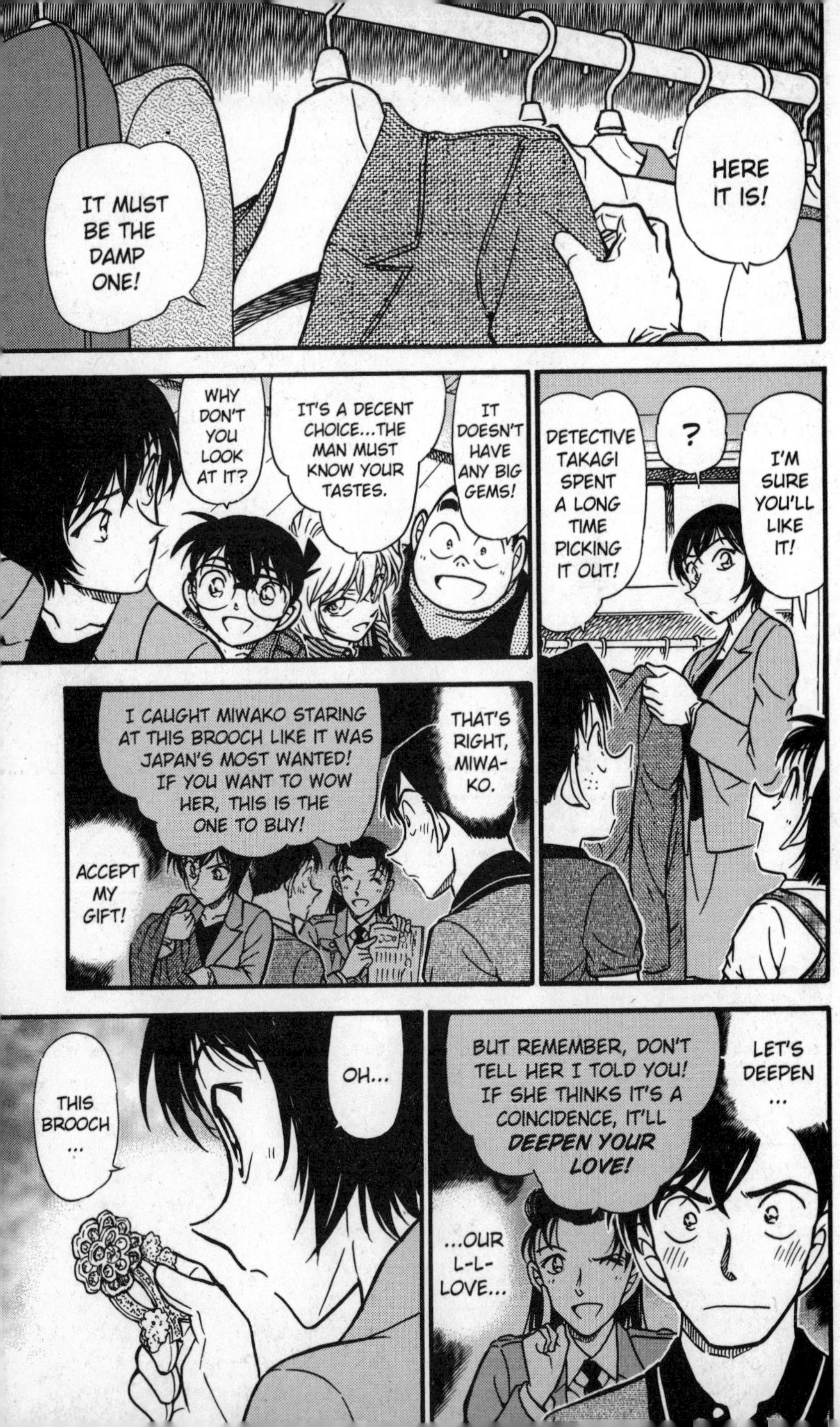
HERE IT IS!
IT MUST BE THE DAMP ONE!
I'M SURE YOU'LL LIKE IT!
?
DETECTIVE TAKAGI SPENT A LONG TIME PICKING IT OUT!
IT DOESN'T HAVE ANY BIG GEMS!
IT'S A DECENT CHOICE...THE MAN MUST KNOW YOUR TASTES.
WHY DON'T YOU LOOK AT IT?
THAT'S RIGHT, MIWA-KO.
I CAUGHT MIWAKO STARING AT THIS BROOCH LIKE IT WAS JAPAN'S MOST WANTED! IF YOU WANT TO WOW HER, THIS IS THE ONE TO BUY!
ACCEPT MY GIFT!
LET'S DEEPEN ...
BUT REMEMBER, DON'T TELL HER I TOLD YOU! IF SHE THINKS IT'S A COINCIDENCE, IT'LL *DEEPEN YOUR LOVE!*
...OUR L-L-LOVE...
OH...
THIS BROOCH ...

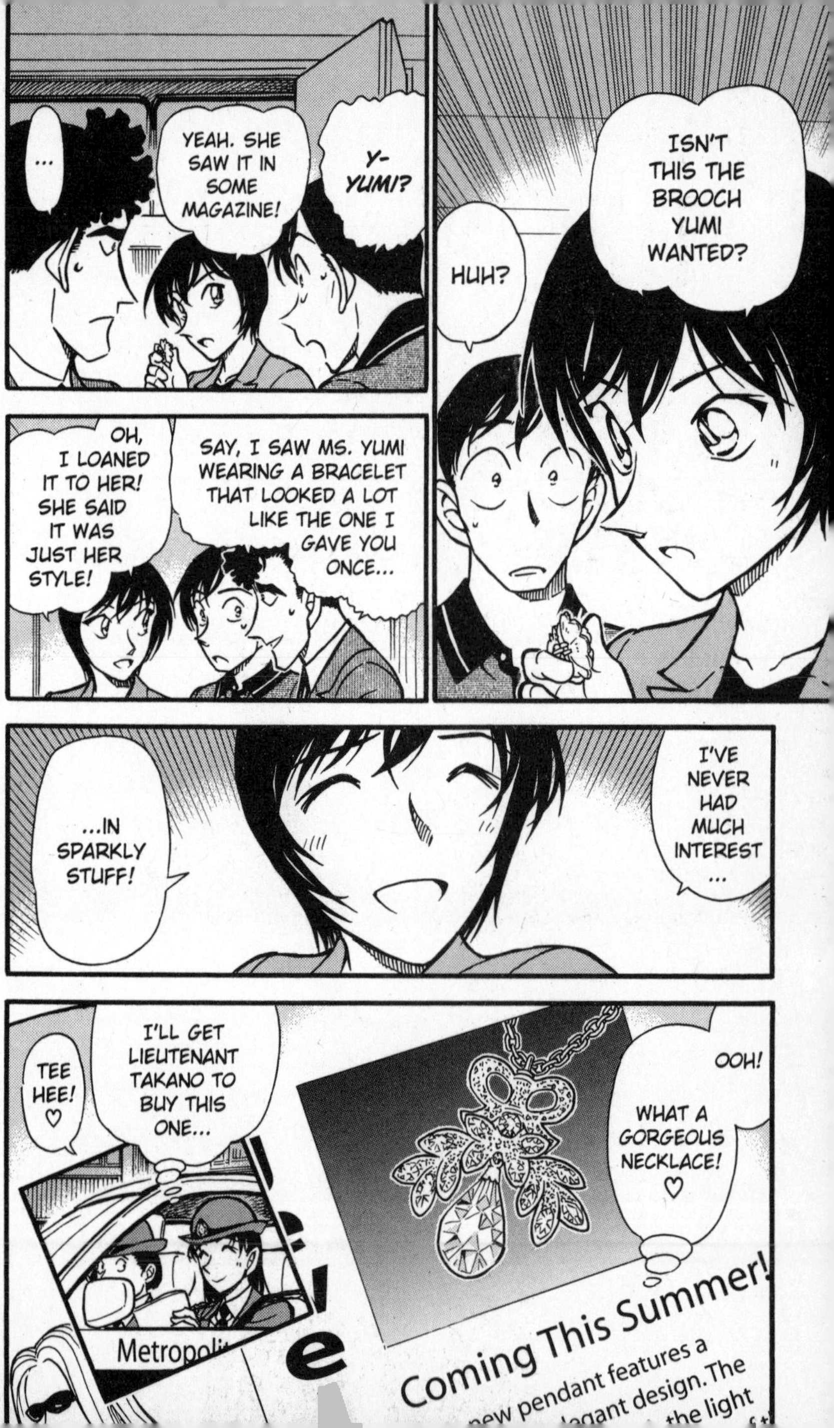
ISN'T THIS THE BROOCH YUMI WANTED?
HUH?
Y-YUMI?
YEAH. SHE SAW IT IN SOME MAGAZINE!
...
SAY, I SAW MS. YUMI WEARING A BRACELET THAT LOOKED A LOT LIKE THE ONE I GAVE YOU ONCE...
OH, I LOANED IT TO HER! SHE SAID IT WAS JUST HER STYLE!
I'VE NEVER HAD MUCH INTEREST...
...IN SPARKLY STUFF!
OOH! WHAT A GORGEOUS NECKLACE! ♡
I'LL GET LIEUTENANT TAKANO TO BUY THIS ONE...
TEE HEE! ♡
Coming This Summer!
new pendant features a

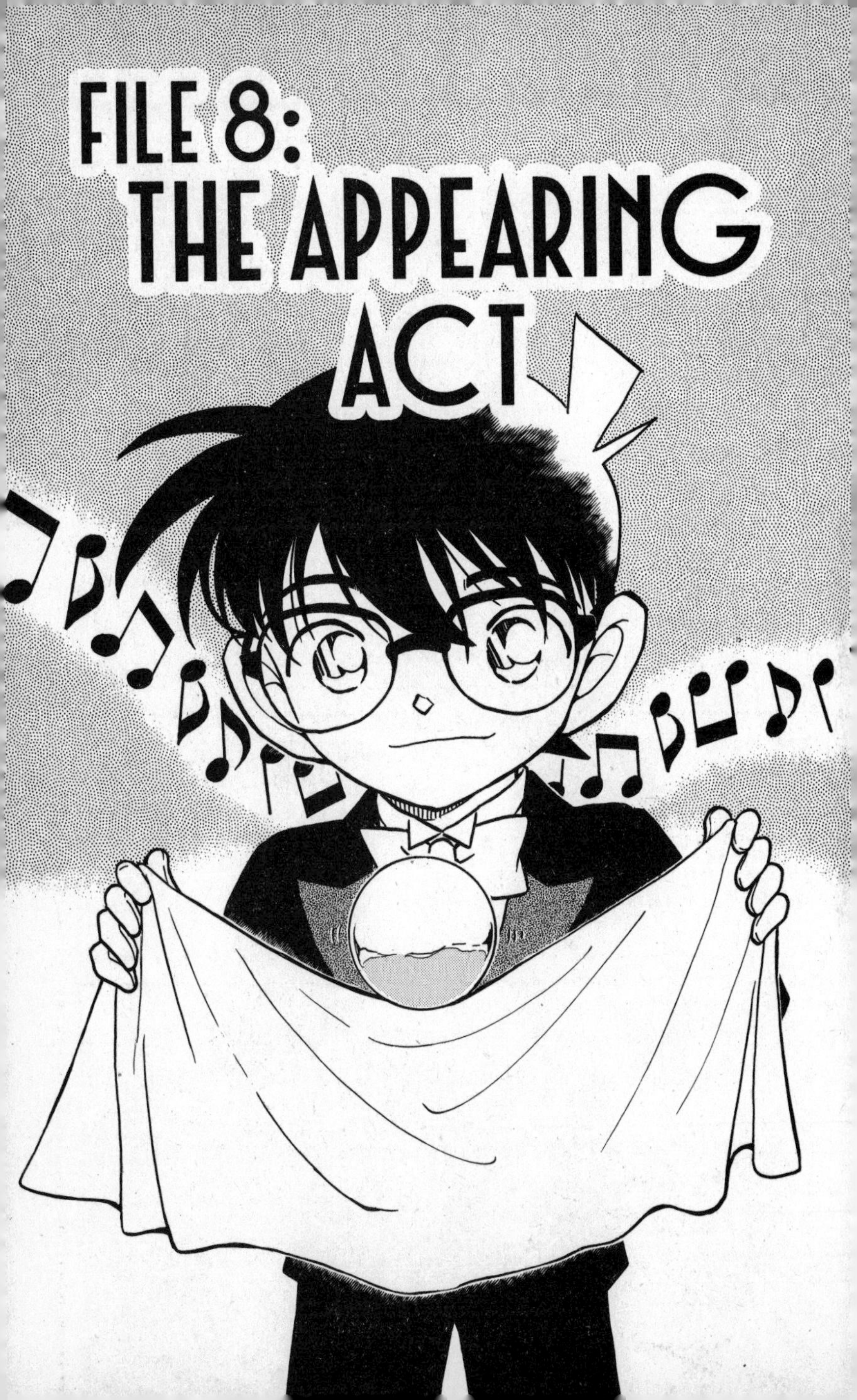
FILE 8:
THE APPEARING ACT

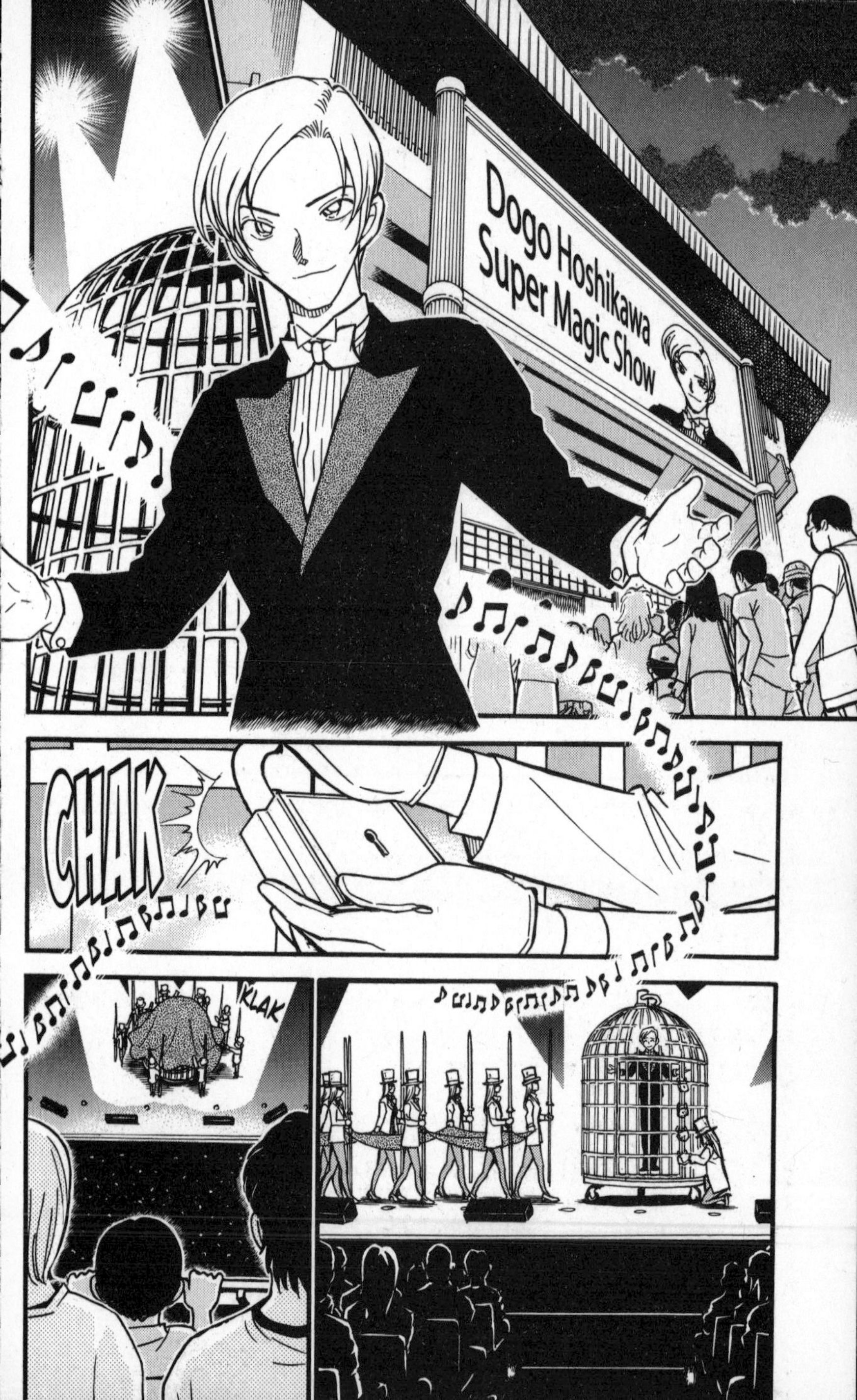
Dogo Hoshikawa
Super Magic Show
CHAK
KLAK

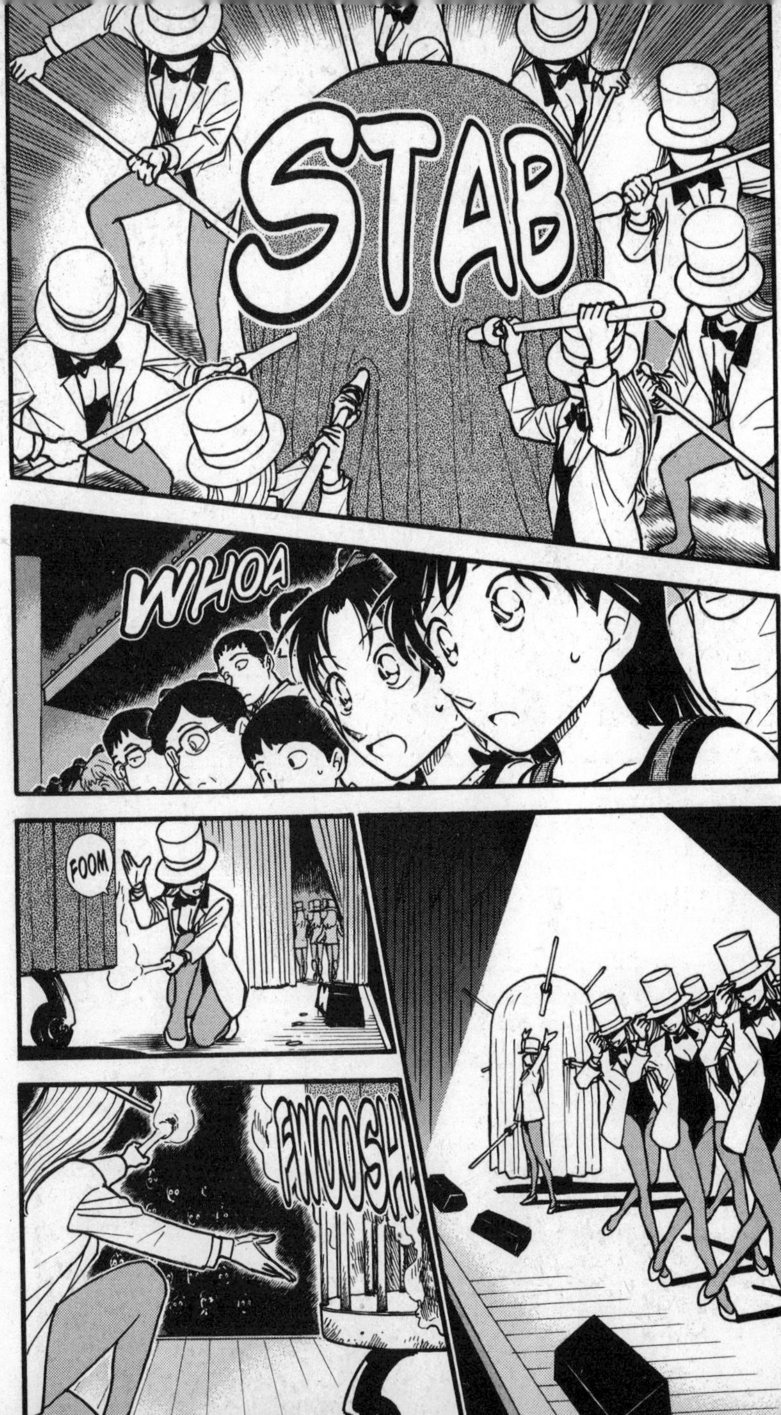
STAB
WHOA
FOOM
FWOOSH

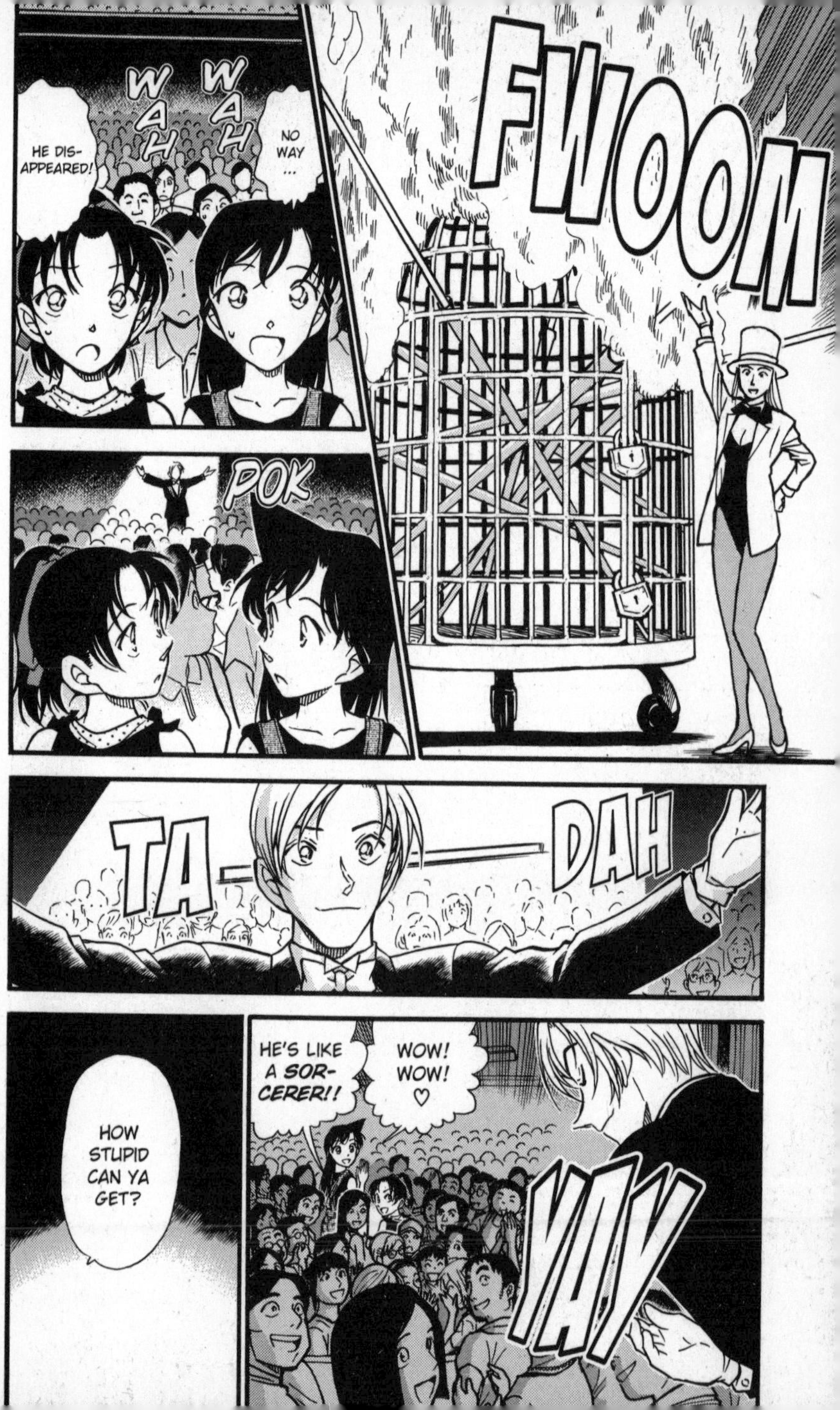
FWOOM
NO WAY ...
WAH
WAH
HE DIS-APPEARED!
POK
TA-DAH
WOW! WOW! ♡
HE'S LIKE A SORCERER!!
YAY
HOW STUPID CAN YA GET?

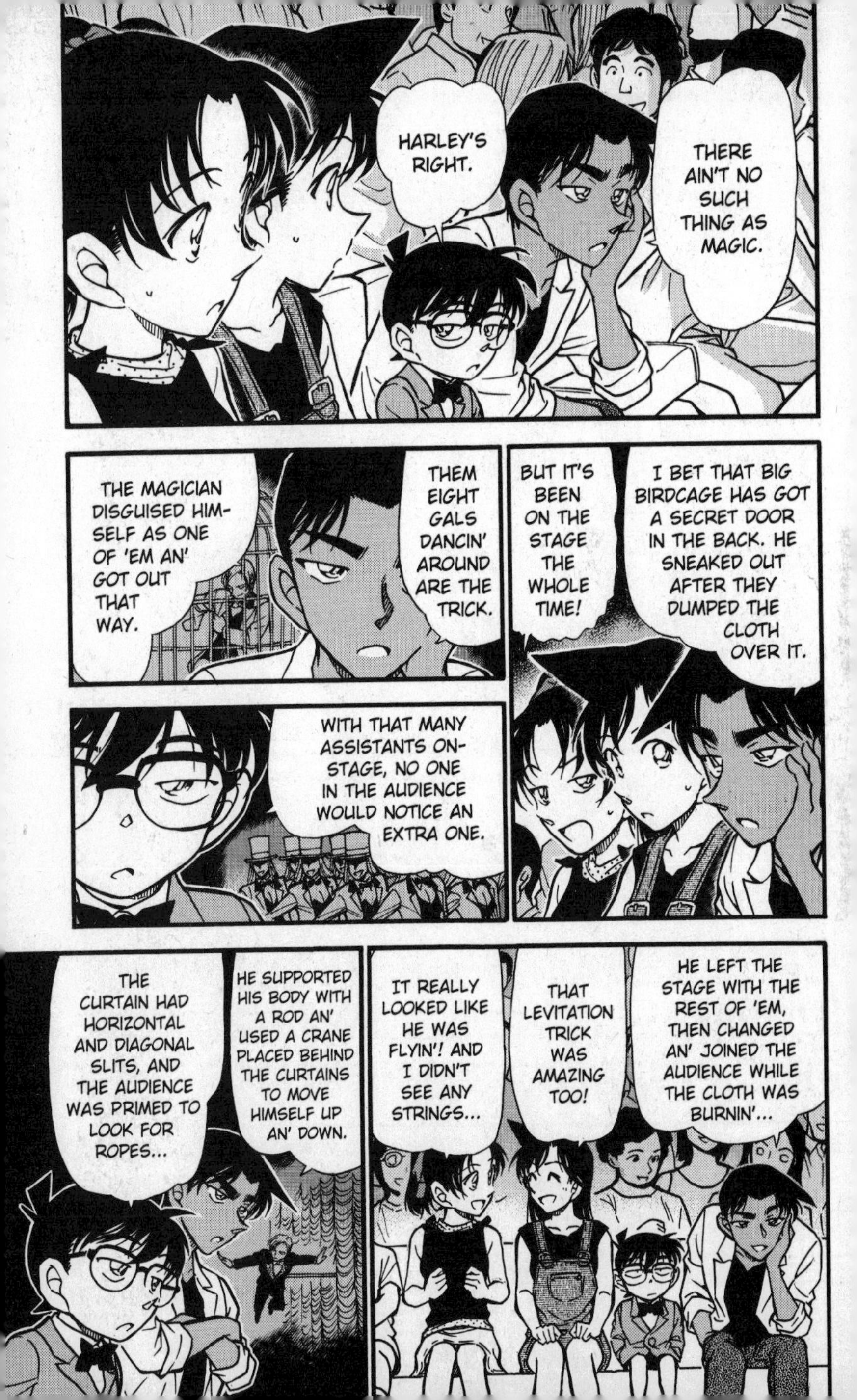
THERE AIN'T NO SUCH THING AS MAGIC.
HARLEY'S RIGHT.
I BET THAT BIG BIRDCAGE HAS GOT A SECRET DOOR IN THE BACK. HE SNEAKED OUT AFTER THEY DUMPED THE CLOTH OVER IT.
BUT IT'S BEEN ON THE STAGE THE WHOLE TIME!
THEM EIGHT GALS DANCIN' AROUND ARE THE TRICK.
THE MAGICIAN DISGUISED HIMSELF AS ONE OF 'EM AN' GOT OUT THAT WAY.
WITH THAT MANY ASSISTANTS ON-STAGE, NO ONE IN THE AUDIENCE WOULD NOTICE AN EXTRA ONE.
HE LEFT THE STAGE WITH THE REST OF 'EM, THEN CHANGED AN' JOINED THE AUDIENCE WHILE THE CLOTH WAS BURNIN'...
THAT LEVITATION TRICK WAS AMAZING TOO!
IT REALLY LOOKED LIKE HE WAS FLYIN'! AND I DIDN'T SEE ANY STRINGS...
HE SUPPORTED HIS BODY WITH A ROD AN' USED A CRANE PLACED BEHIND THE CURTAINS TO MOVE HIMSELF UP AN' DOWN.
THE CURTAIN HAD HORIZONTAL AND DIAGONAL SLITS, AND THE AUDIENCE WAS PRIMED TO LOOK FOR ROPES...

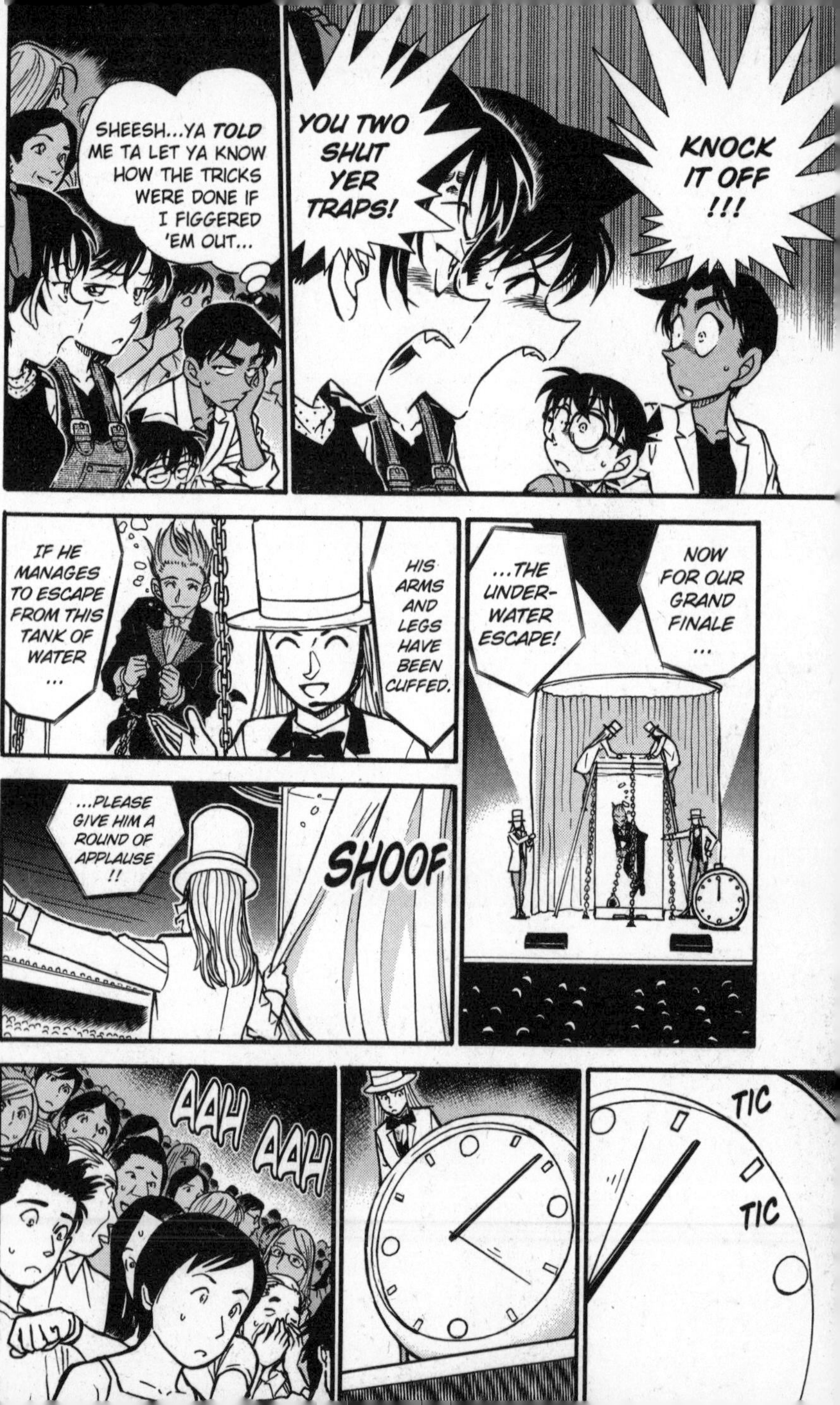
KNOCK IT OFF !!!
YOU TWO SHUT YER TRAPS!
SHEESH...YA TOLD ME TA LET YA KNOW HOW THE TRICKS WERE DONE IF I FIGGERED 'EM OUT...
NOW FOR OUR GRAND FINALE ...
...THE UNDER-WATER ESCAPE!
HIS ARMS AND LEGS HAVE BEEN CUFFED.
IF HE MANAGES TO ESCAPE FROM THIS TANK OF WATER ...
...PLEASE GIVE HIM A ROUND OF APPLAUSE !!
SHOOF
TIC
TIC
AAH
AAH

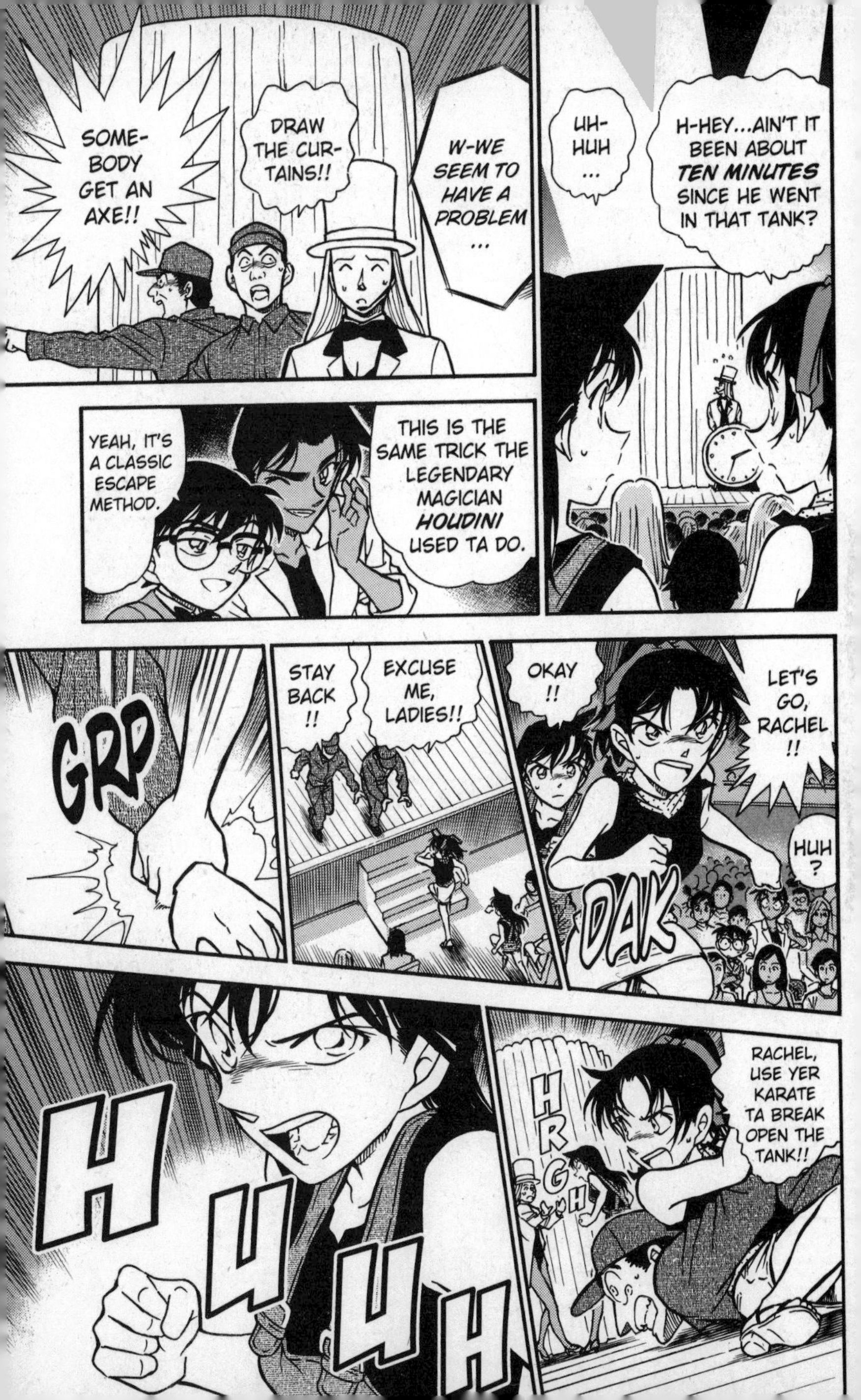
H-HEY...AIN'T IT BEEN ABOUT TEN MINUTES SINCE HE WENT IN THAT TANK?
UH-HUH ...
W-WE SEEM TO HAVE A PROBLEM ...
DRAW THE CUR-TAINS!!
SOME-BODY GET AN AXE!!
THIS IS THE SAME TRICK THE LEGENDARY MAGICIAN HOUDINI USED TA DO.
YEAH, IT'S A CLASSIC ESCAPE METHOD.
LET'S GO, RACHEL!!
OKAY!!
HUH?
DAK
EXCUSE ME, LADIES!!
STAY BACK!!
GRP
RACHEL, USE YER KARATE TA BREAK OPEN THE TANK!!
HRGH
HUUH

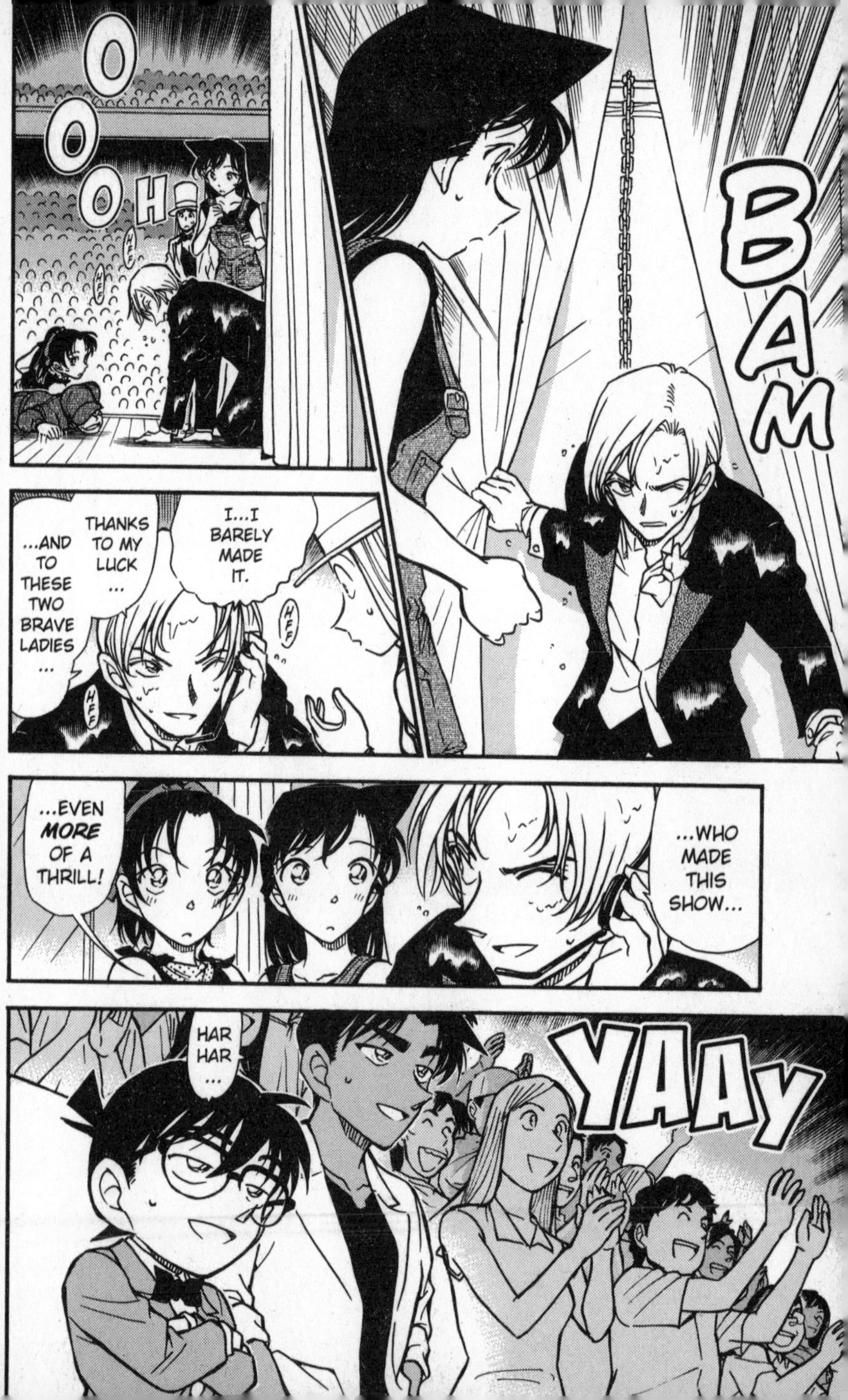
BAM
OOOH
HFF HFF
I...I BARELY MADE IT.
HFF
THANKS TO MY LUCK...
...AND TO THESE TWO BRAVE LADIES...
HFF
...WHO MADE THIS SHOW...
...EVEN MORE OF A THRILL!
YAAY
HAR HAR...

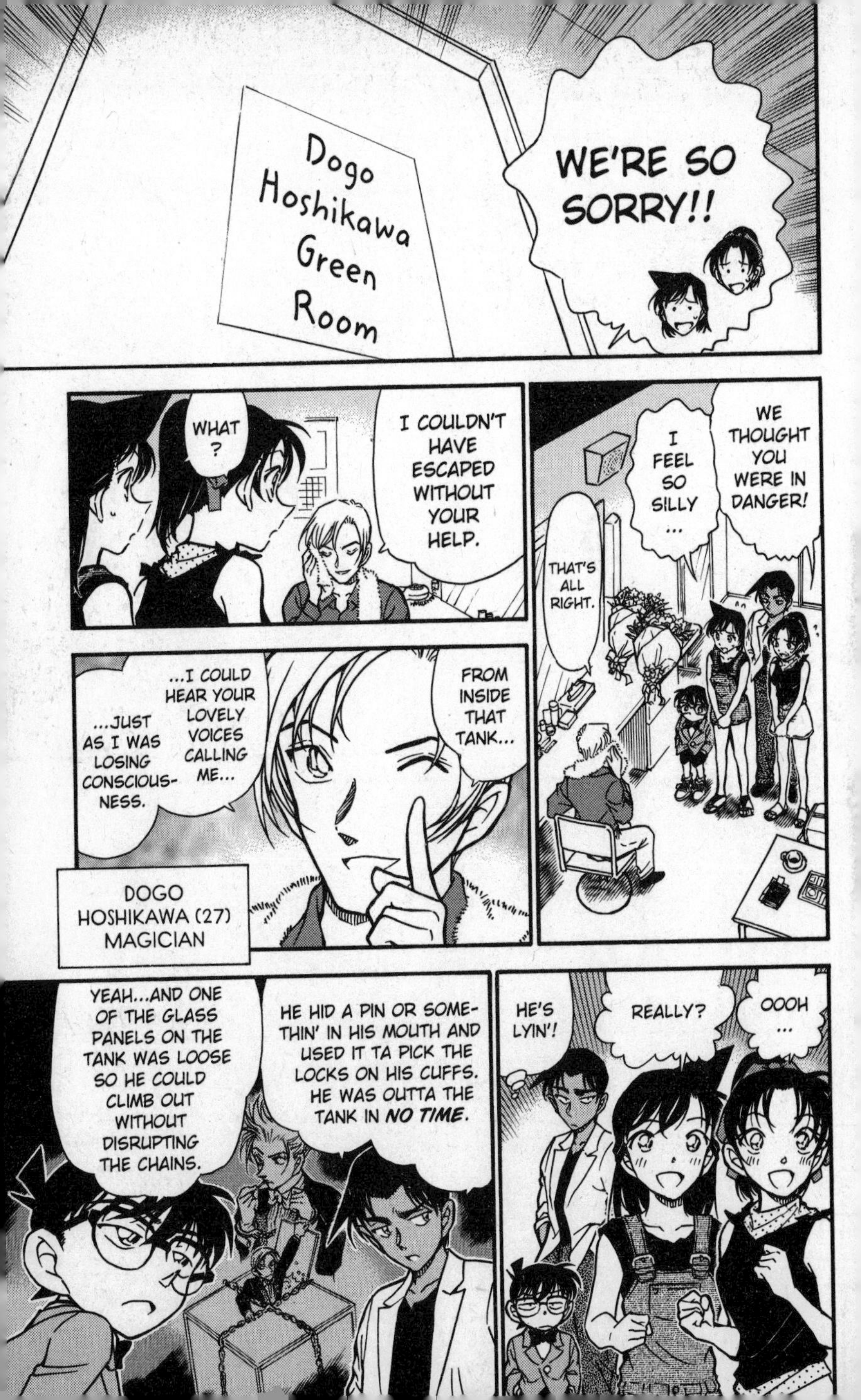
Dogo Hoshikawa Green Room
WE'RE SO SORRY!!
WE THOUGHT YOU WERE IN DANGER!
I FEEL SO SILLY...
THAT'S ALL RIGHT.
I COULDN'T HAVE ESCAPED WITHOUT YOUR HELP.
WHAT?
FROM INSIDE THAT TANK...
...I COULD HEAR YOUR LOVELY VOICES CALLING ME...
...JUST AS I WAS LOSING CONSCIOUS-NESS.
DOGO HOSHIKAWA (27) MAGICIAN
OOOH...
REALLY?
HE'S LYIN'!
HE HID A PIN OR SOME-THIN' IN HIS MOUTH AND USED IT TA PICK THE LOCKS ON HIS CUFFS. HE WAS OUTTA THE TANK IN *NO TIME*.
YEAH...AND ONE OF THE GLASS PANELS ON THE TANK WAS LOOSE SO HE COULD CLIMB OUT WITHOUT DISRUPTING THE CHAINS.

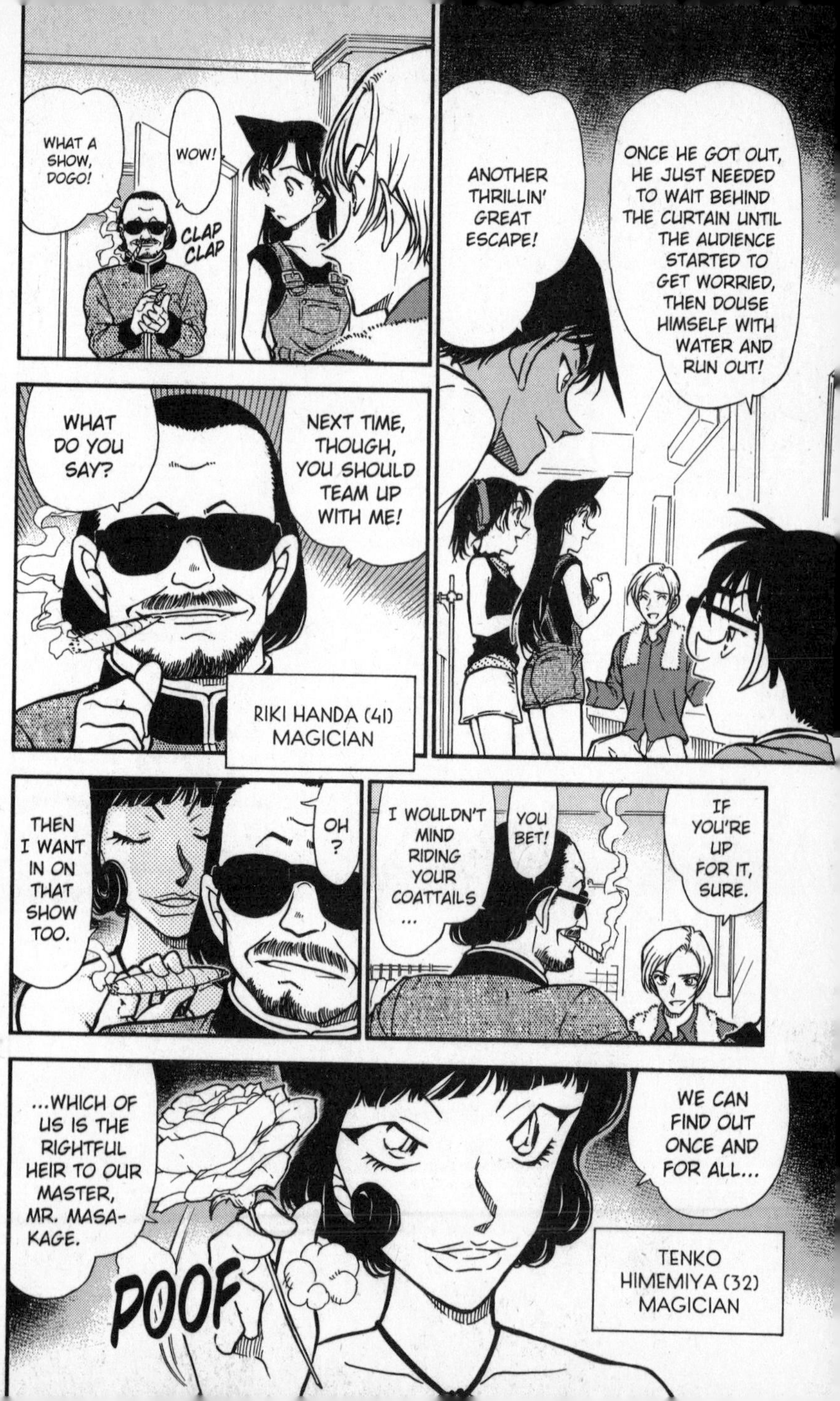
ONCE HE GOT OUT, HE JUST NEEDED TO WAIT BEHIND THE CURTAIN UNTIL THE AUDIENCE STARTED TO GET WORRIED, THEN DOUSE HIMSELF WITH WATER AND RUN OUT!
ANOTHER THRILLIN' GREAT ESCAPE!
WOW!
WHAT A SHOW, DOGO!
CLAP CLAP
NEXT TIME, THOUGH, YOU SHOULD TEAM UP WITH ME!
WHAT DO YOU SAY?
RIKI HANDA (41) MAGICIAN
IF YOU'RE UP FOR IT, SURE.
YOU BET!
I WOULDN'T MIND RIDING YOUR COATTAILS...
OH?
THEN I WANT IN ON THAT SHOW TOO.
WE CAN FIND OUT ONCE AND FOR ALL...
...WHICH OF US IS THE RIGHTFUL HEIR TO OUR MASTER, MR. MASA-KAGE.
TENKO HIMEMIYA (32) MAGICIAN
POOF

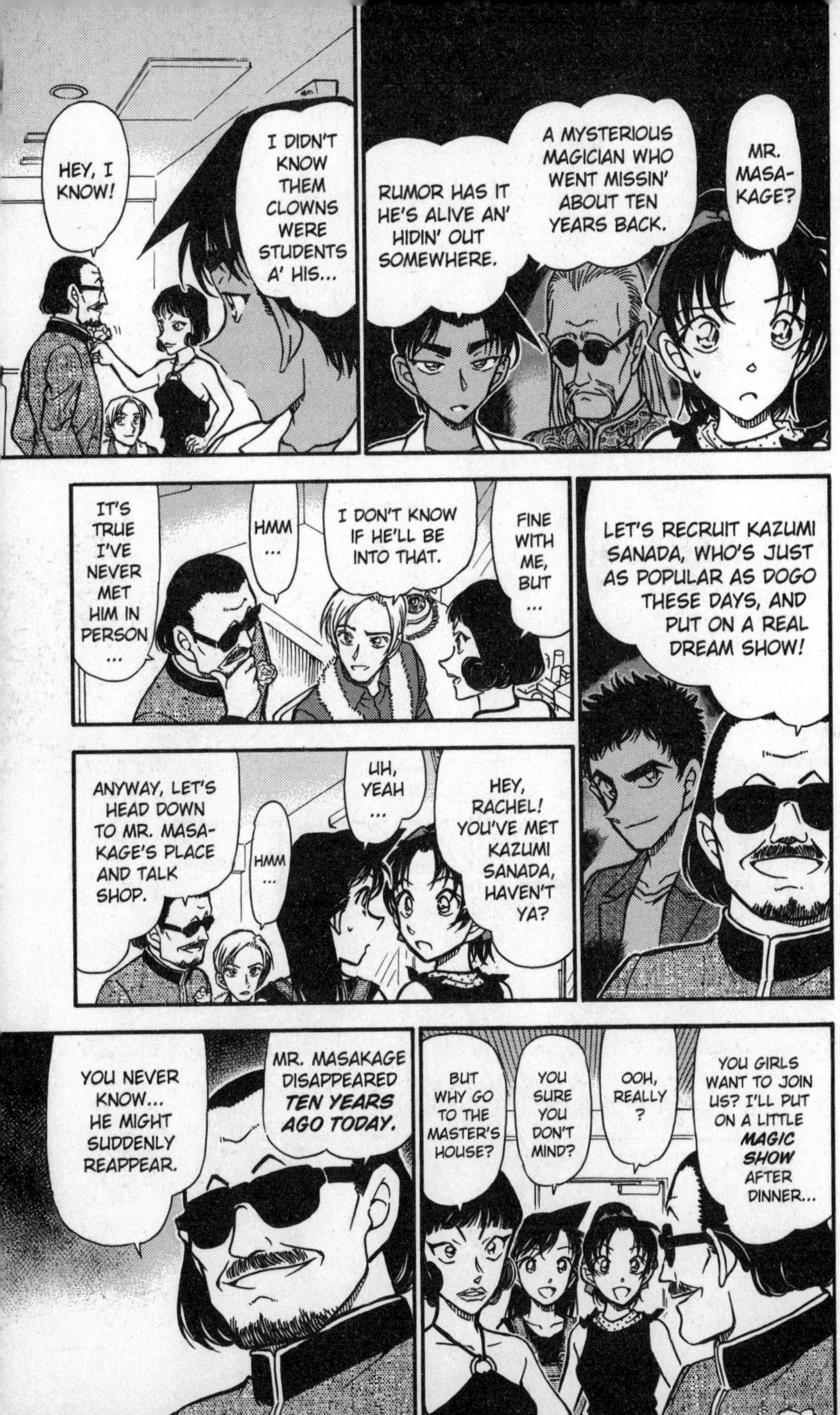
MR. MASA-KAGE?
A MYSTERIOUS MAGICIAN WHO WENT MISSIN' ABOUT TEN YEARS BACK.
RUMOR HAS IT HE'S ALIVE AN' HIDIN' OUT SOMEWHERE.
I DIDN'T KNOW THEM CLOWNS WERE STUDENTS A' HIS...
HEY, I KNOW!
LET'S RECRUIT KAZUMI SANADA, WHO'S JUST AS POPULAR AS DOGO THESE DAYS, AND PUT ON A REAL DREAM SHOW!
FINE WITH ME, BUT...
I DON'T KNOW IF HE'LL BE INTO THAT.
HMM...
IT'S TRUE I'VE NEVER MET HIM IN PERSON...
HEY, RACHEL! YOU'VE MET KAZUMI SANADA, HAVEN'T YA?
UH, YEAH...
HMM...
ANYWAY, LET'S HEAD DOWN TO MR. MASA-KAGE'S PLACE AND TALK SHOP.
YOU GIRLS WANT TO JOIN US? I'LL PUT ON A LITTLE MAGIC SHOW AFTER DINNER...
OOH, REALLY?
YOU SURE YOU DON'T MIND?
BUT WHY GO TO THE MASTER'S HOUSE?
MR. MASAKAGE DISAPPEARED TEN YEARS AGO TODAY.
YOU NEVER KNOW... HE MIGHT SUDDENLY REAPPEAR.

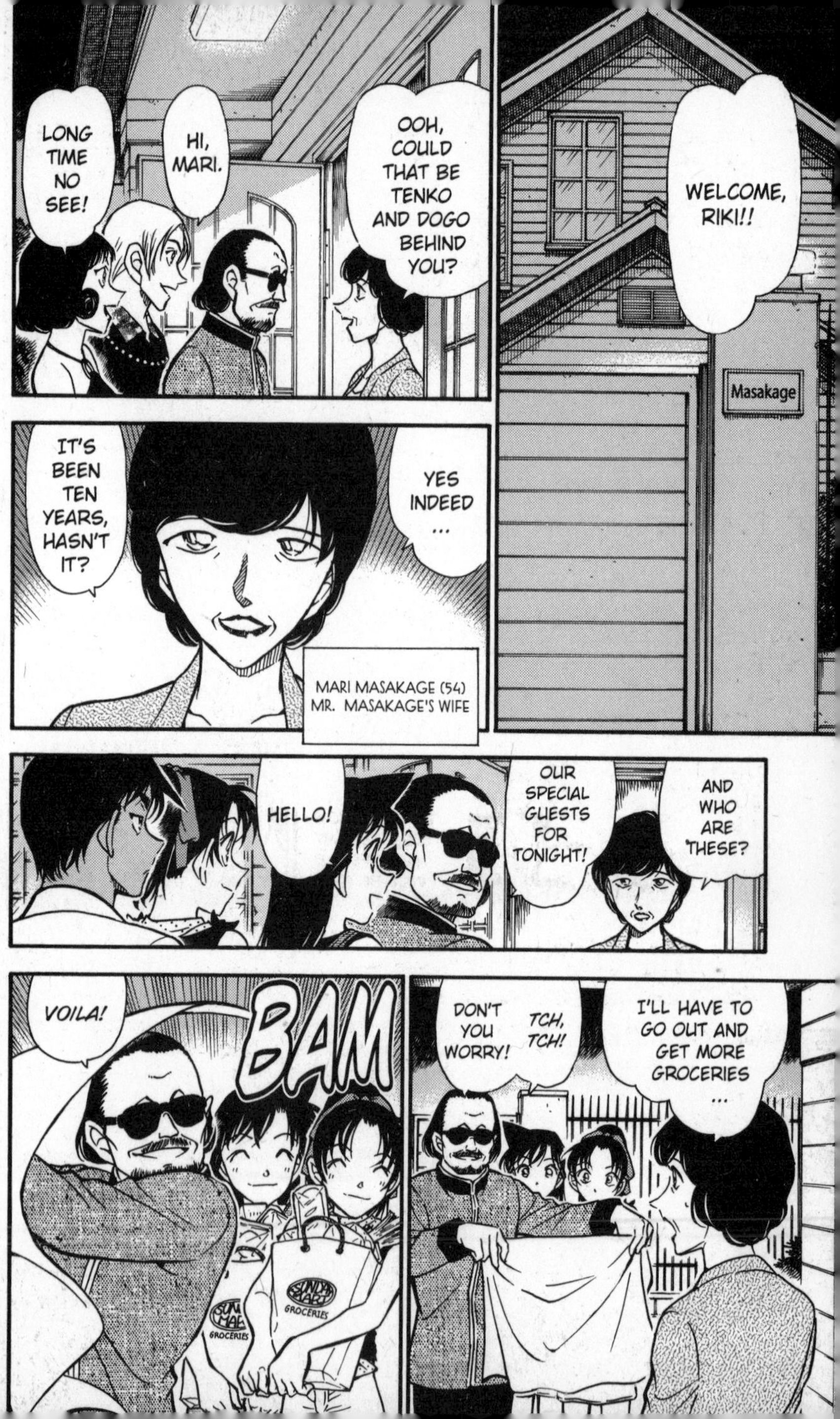
WELCOME, RIKI!!
Masakage
OOH, COULD THAT BE TENKO AND DOGO BEHIND YOU?
HI, MARI.
LONG TIME NO SEE!
YES INDEED ...
IT'S BEEN TEN YEARS, HASN'T IT?
MARI MASAKAGE (54) MR. MASAKAGE'S WIFE
AND WHO ARE THESE?
OUR SPECIAL GUESTS FOR TONIGHT!
HELLO!
I'LL HAVE TO GO OUT AND GET MORE GROCERIES ...
TCH, TCH!
DON'T YOU WORRY!
BAM
VOILA!

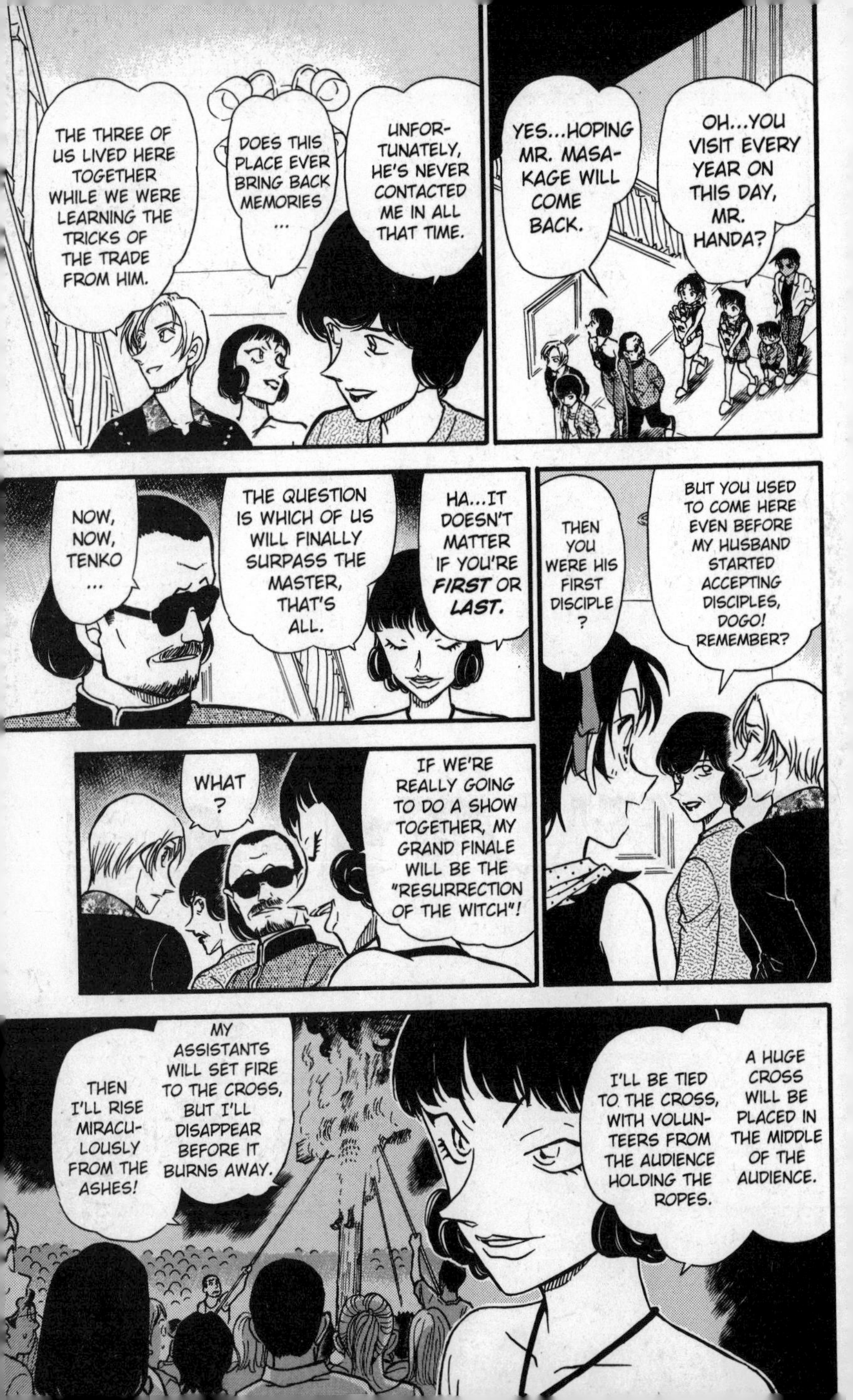
OH...YOU VISIT EVERY YEAR ON THIS DAY, MR. HANDA?
YES...HOPING MR. MASAKAGE WILL COME BACK.
UNFORTUNATELY, HE'S NEVER CONTACTED ME IN ALL THAT TIME.
DOES THIS PLACE EVER BRING BACK MEMORIES...
THE THREE OF US LIVED HERE TOGETHER WHILE WE WERE LEARNING THE TRICKS OF THE TRADE FROM HIM.
BUT YOU USED TO COME HERE EVEN BEFORE MY HUSBAND STARTED ACCEPTING DISCIPLES, DOGO! REMEMBER?
THEN YOU WERE HIS FIRST DISCIPLE?
HA...IT DOESN'T MATTER IF YOU'RE *FIRST* OR *LAST.*
THE QUESTION IS WHICH OF US WILL FINALLY SURPASS THE MASTER, THAT'S ALL.
NOW, NOW, TENKO...
IF WE'RE REALLY GOING TO DO A SHOW TOGETHER, MY GRAND FINALE WILL BE THE "RESURRECTION OF THE WITCH"!
WHAT?
A HUGE CROSS WILL BE PLACED IN THE MIDDLE OF THE AUDIENCE.
I'LL BE TIED TO THE CROSS, WITH VOLUNTEERS FROM THE AUDIENCE HOLDING THE ROPES.
MY ASSISTANTS WILL SET FIRE TO THE CROSS, BUT I'LL DISAPPEAR BEFORE IT BURNS AWAY.
THEN I'LL RISE MIRACULOUSLY FROM THE ASHES!

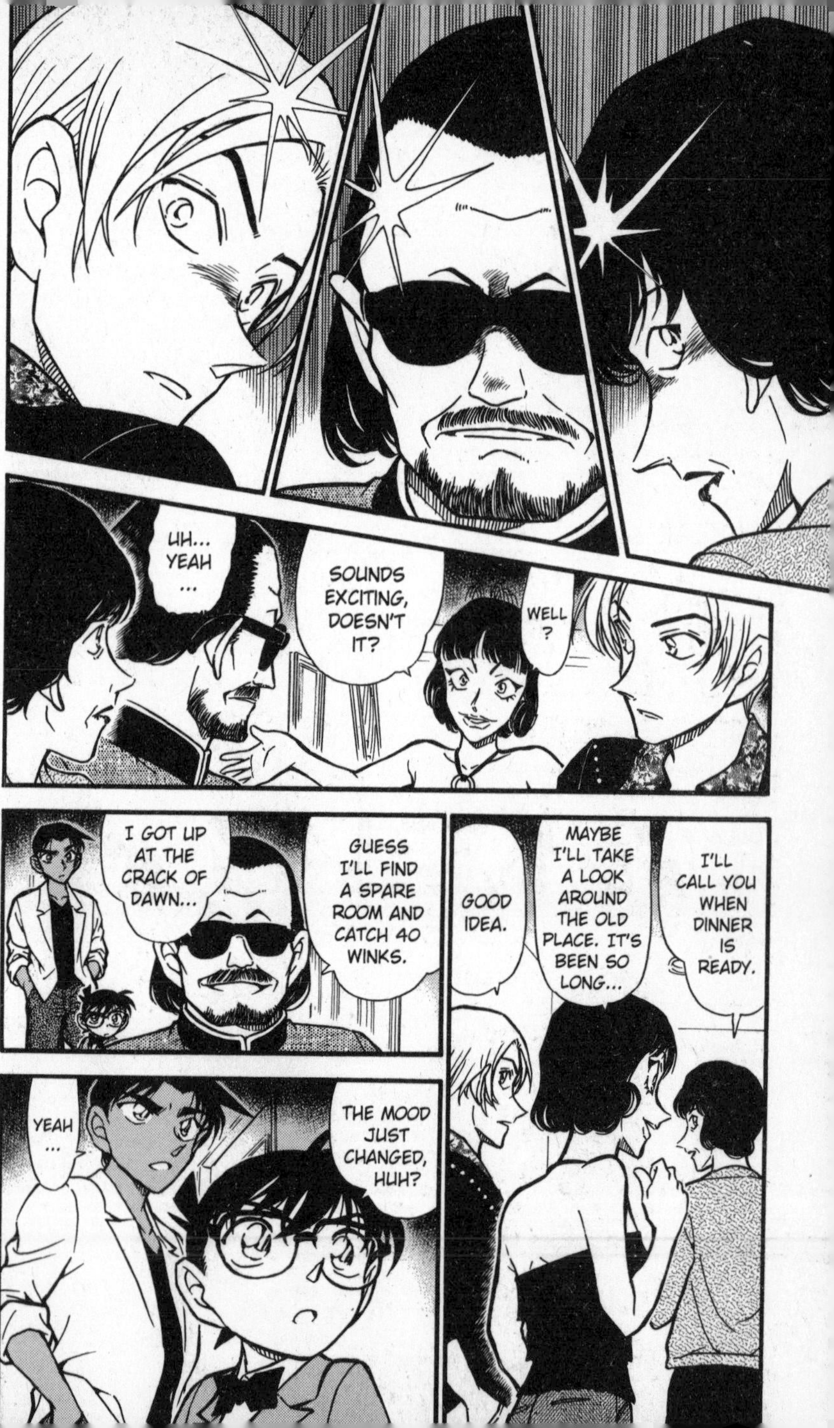
WELL?
SOUNDS EXCITING, DOESN'T IT?
UH... YEAH...
I'LL CALL YOU WHEN DINNER IS READY.
MAYBE I'LL TAKE A LOOK AROUND THE OLD PLACE. IT'S BEEN SO LONG...
GOOD IDEA.
GUESS I'LL FIND A SPARE ROOM AND CATCH 40 WINKS.
I GOT UP AT THE CRACK OF DAWN...
THE MOOD JUST CHANGED, HUH?
YEAH...

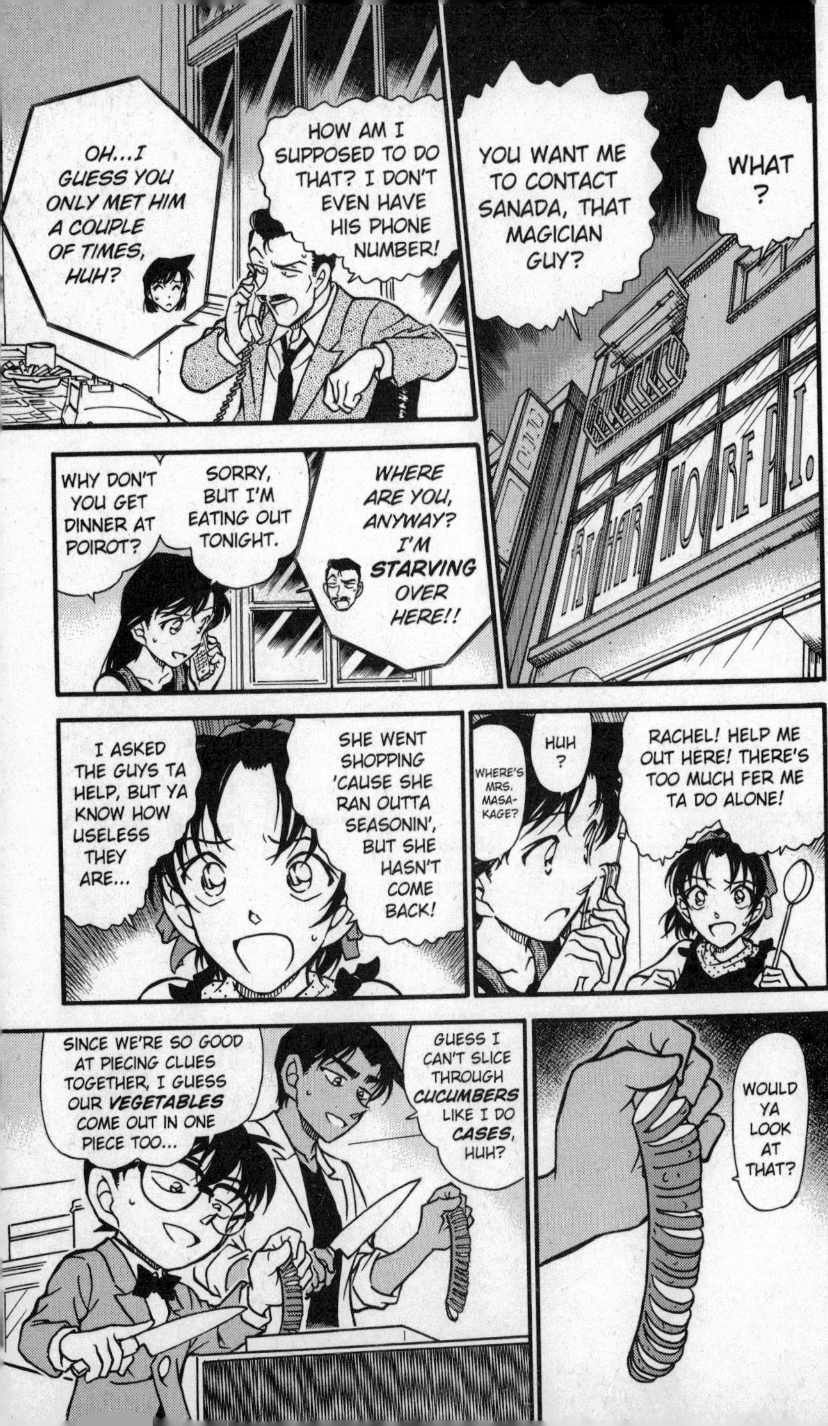
WHAT?
YOU WANT ME TO CONTACT SANADA, THAT MAGICIAN GUY?
HOW AM I SUPPOSED TO DO THAT? I DON'T EVEN HAVE HIS PHONE NUMBER!
OH...I GUESS YOU ONLY MET HIM A COUPLE OF TIMES, HUH?
WHERE ARE YOU, ANYWAY? I'M STARVING OVER HERE!!
SORRY, BUT I'M EATING OUT TONIGHT.
WHY DON'T YOU GET DINNER AT POIROT?
RACHEL! HELP ME OUT HERE! THERE'S TOO MUCH FER ME TA DO ALONE!
HUH?
WHERE'S MRS. MASA-KAGE?
SHE WENT SHOPPING 'CAUSE SHE RAN OUTTA SEASONIN', BUT SHE HASN'T COME BACK!
I ASKED THE GUYS TA HELP, BUT YA KNOW HOW USELESS THEY ARE...
WOULD YA LOOK AT THAT?
GUESS I CAN'T SLICE THROUGH CUCUMBERS LIKE I DO CASES, HUH?
SINCE WE'RE SO GOOD AT PIECING CLUES TOGETHER, I GUESS OUR VEGETABLES COME OUT IN ONE PIECE TOO...

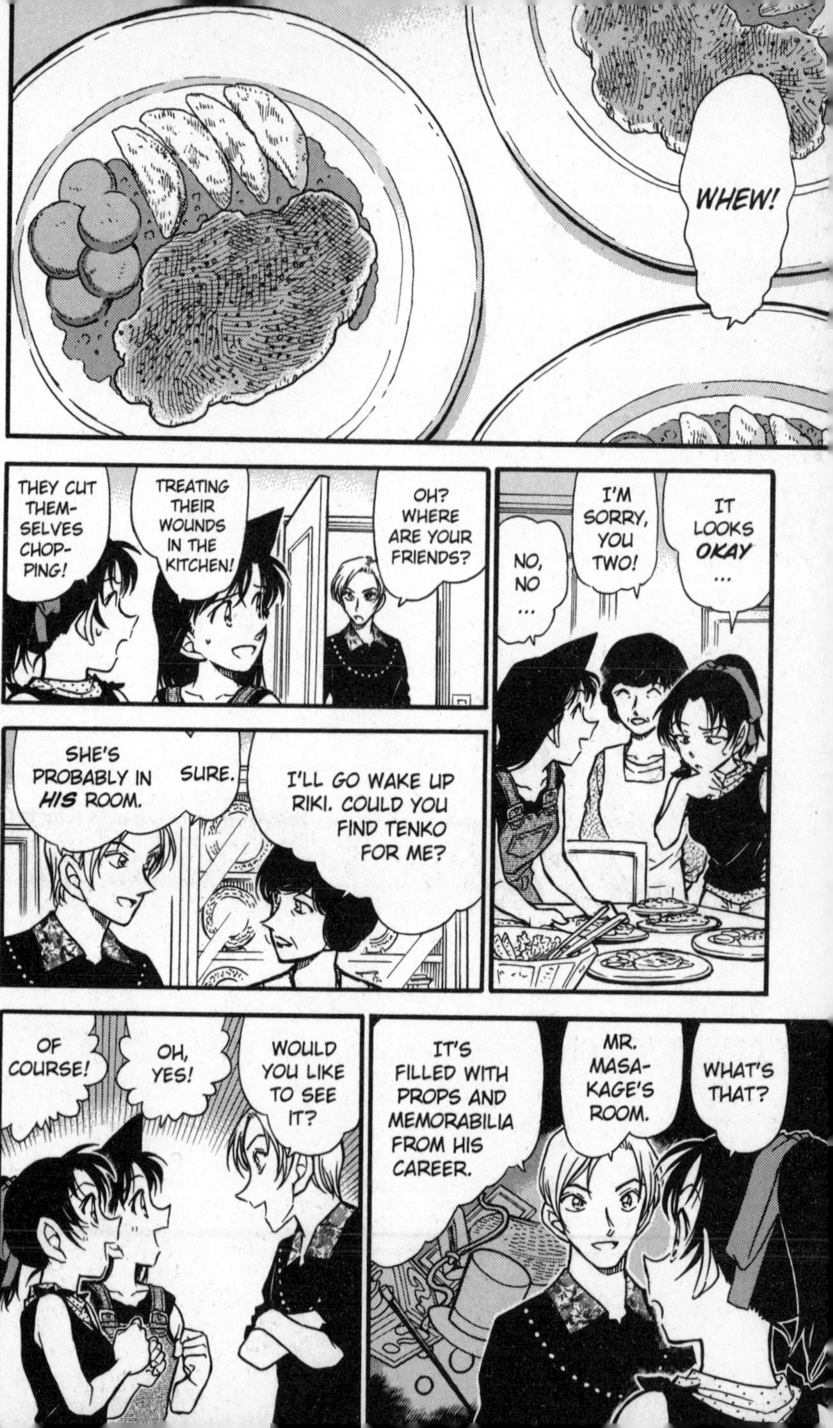
WHEW!
IT LOOKS OKAY ...
I'M SORRY, YOU TWO!
NO, NO ...
OH? WHERE ARE YOUR FRIENDS?
TREATING THEIR WOUNDS IN THE KITCHEN!
THEY CUT THEMSELVES CHOPPING!
I'LL GO WAKE UP RIKI. COULD YOU FIND TENKO FOR ME?
SURE.
SHE'S PROBABLY IN HIS ROOM.
WHAT'S THAT?
MR. MASAKAGE'S ROOM.
IT'S FILLED WITH PROPS AND MEMORABILIA FROM HIS CAREER.
WOULD YOU LIKE TO SEE IT?
OH, YES!
OF COURSE!

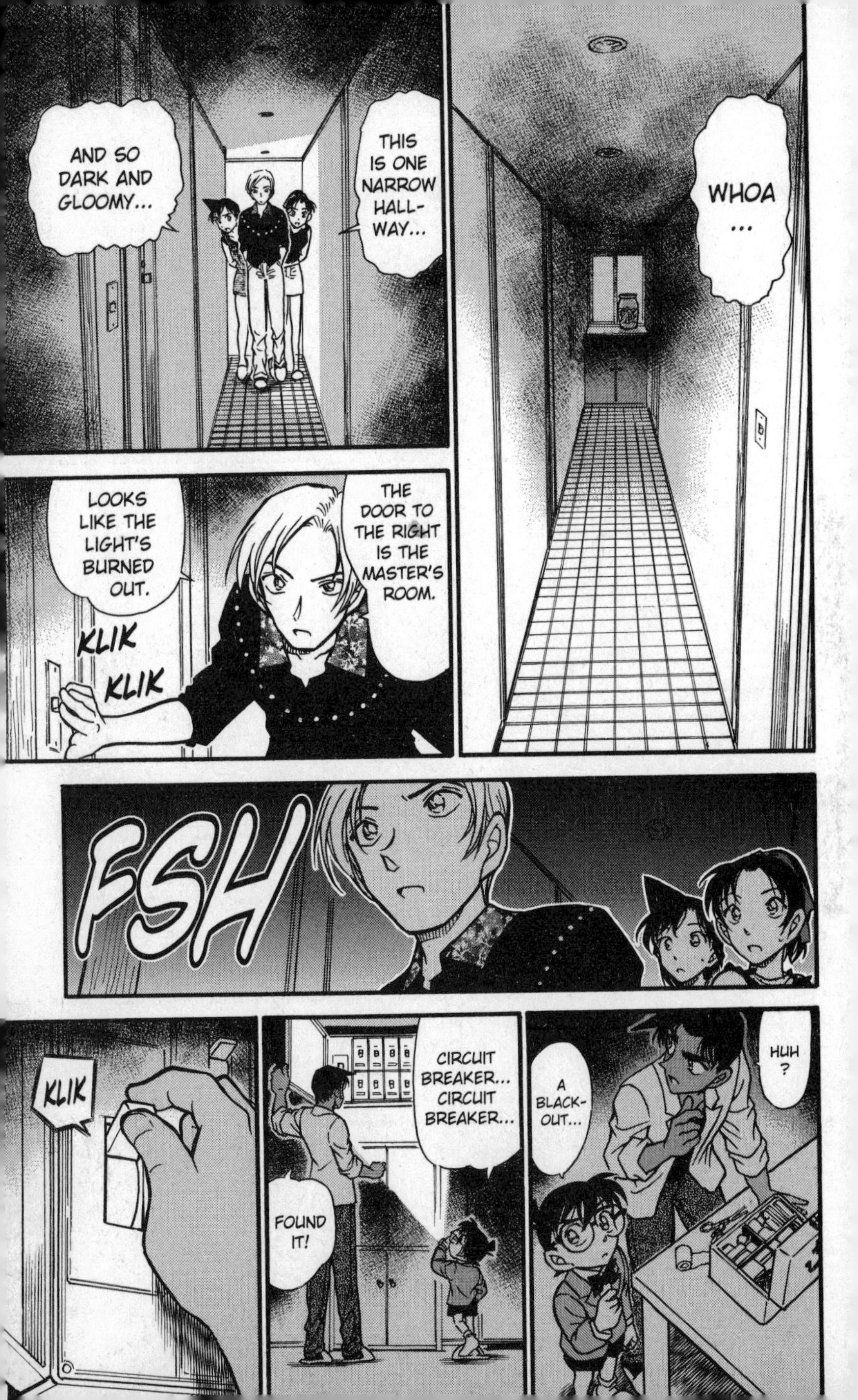
WHOA ...
THIS IS ONE NARROW HALL-WAY...
AND SO DARK AND GLOOMY...
THE DOOR TO THE RIGHT IS THE MASTER'S ROOM.
LOOKS LIKE THE LIGHT'S BURNED OUT.
KLIK
KLIK
FSH
HUH?
A BLACK-OUT...
CIRCUIT BREAKER... CIRCUIT BREAKER...
FOUND IT!
KLIK

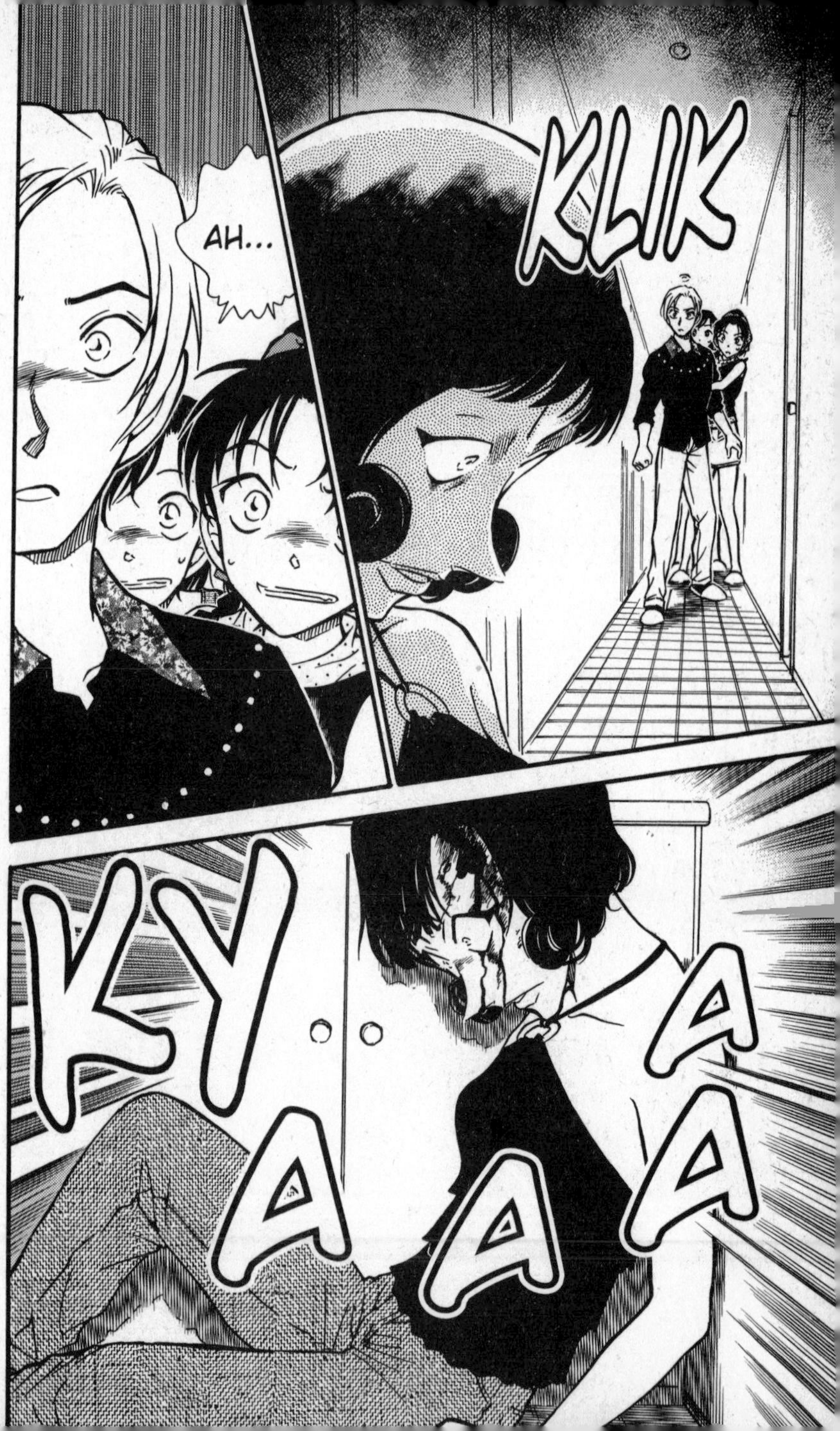
KLIK
AH...
KYAAAAA

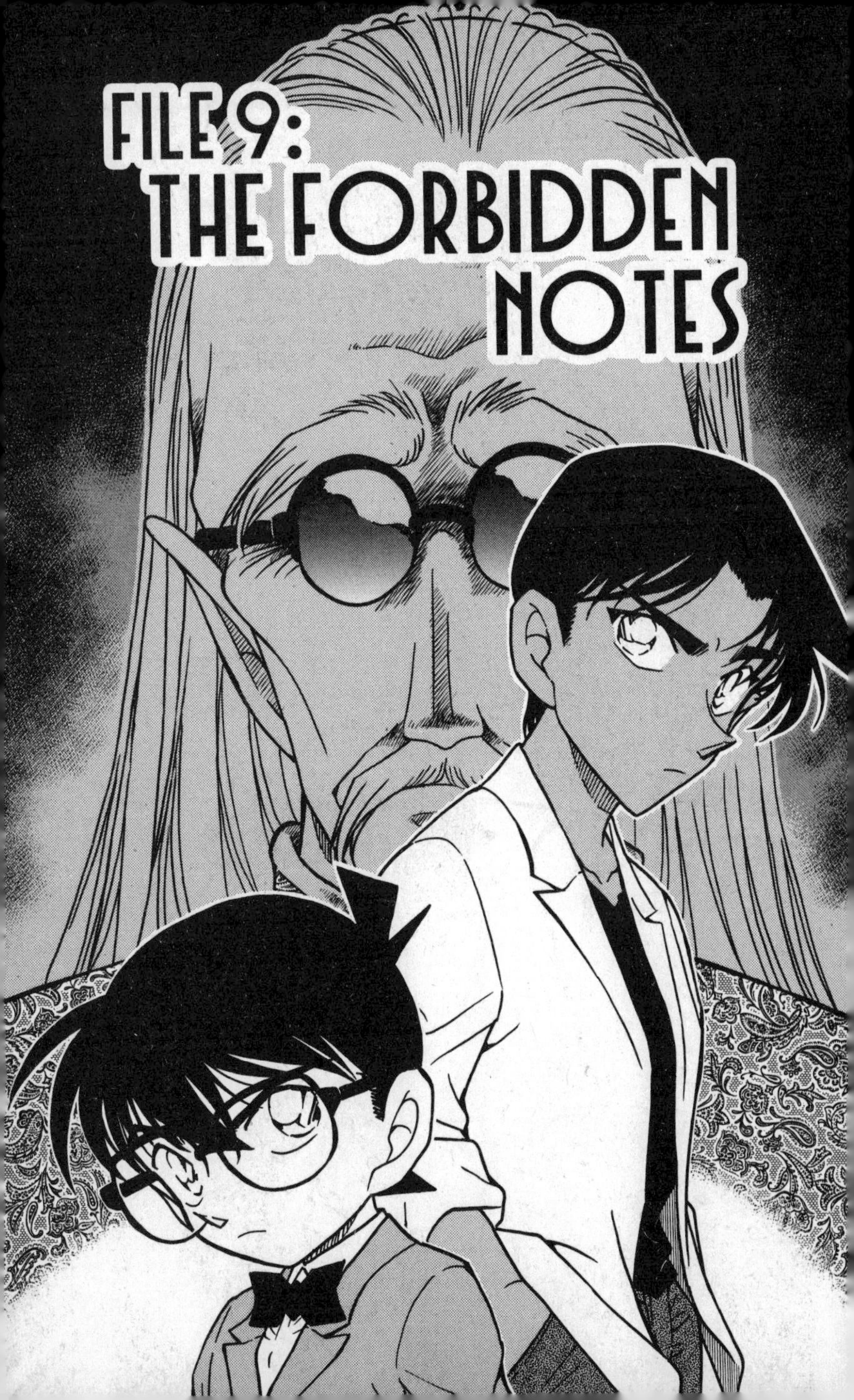
FILE 9:
THE FORBIDDEN NOTES

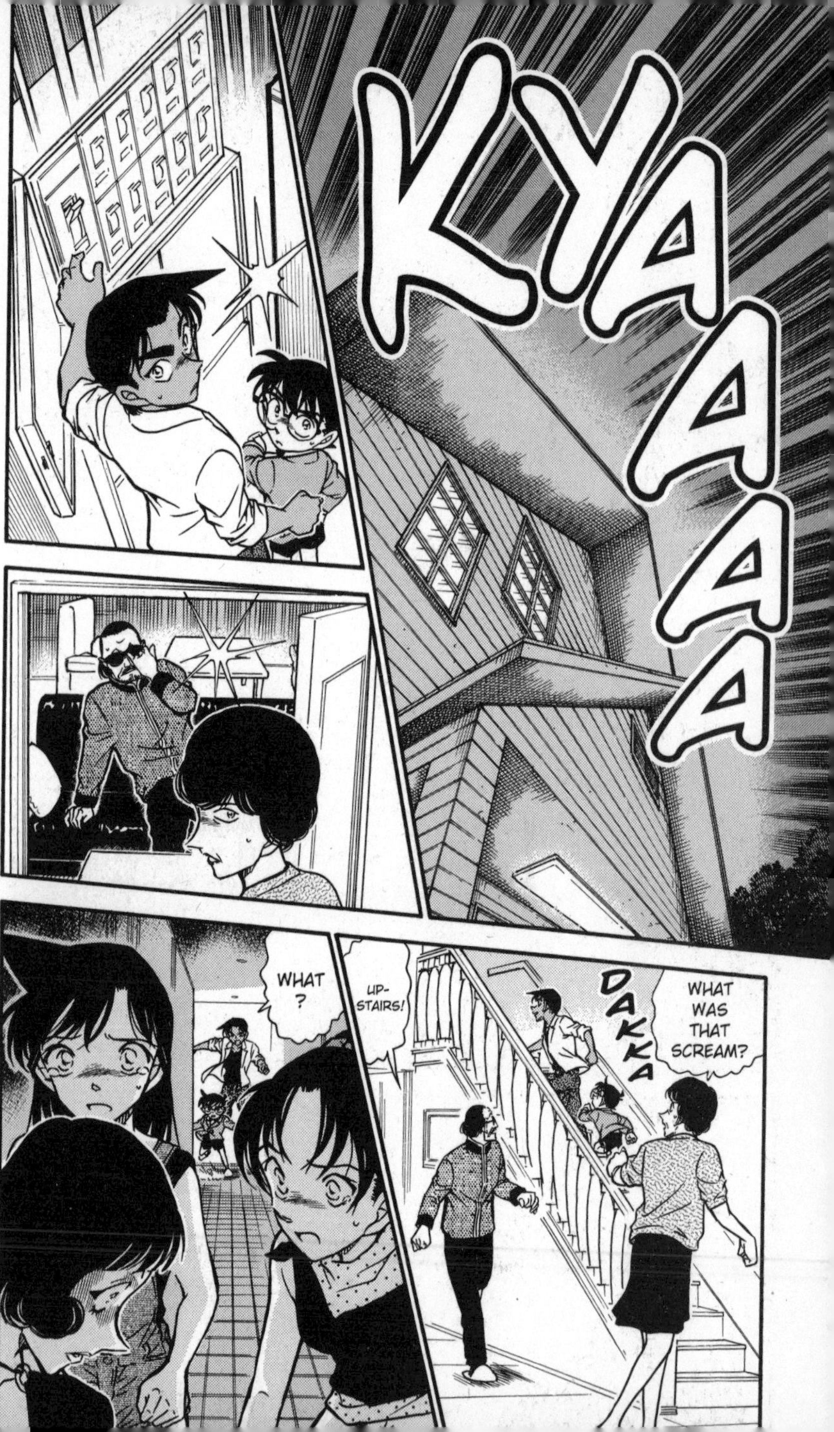
KYAAAAA
WHAT WAS THAT SCREAM?
DAKKA
UP-STAIRS!
WHAT?

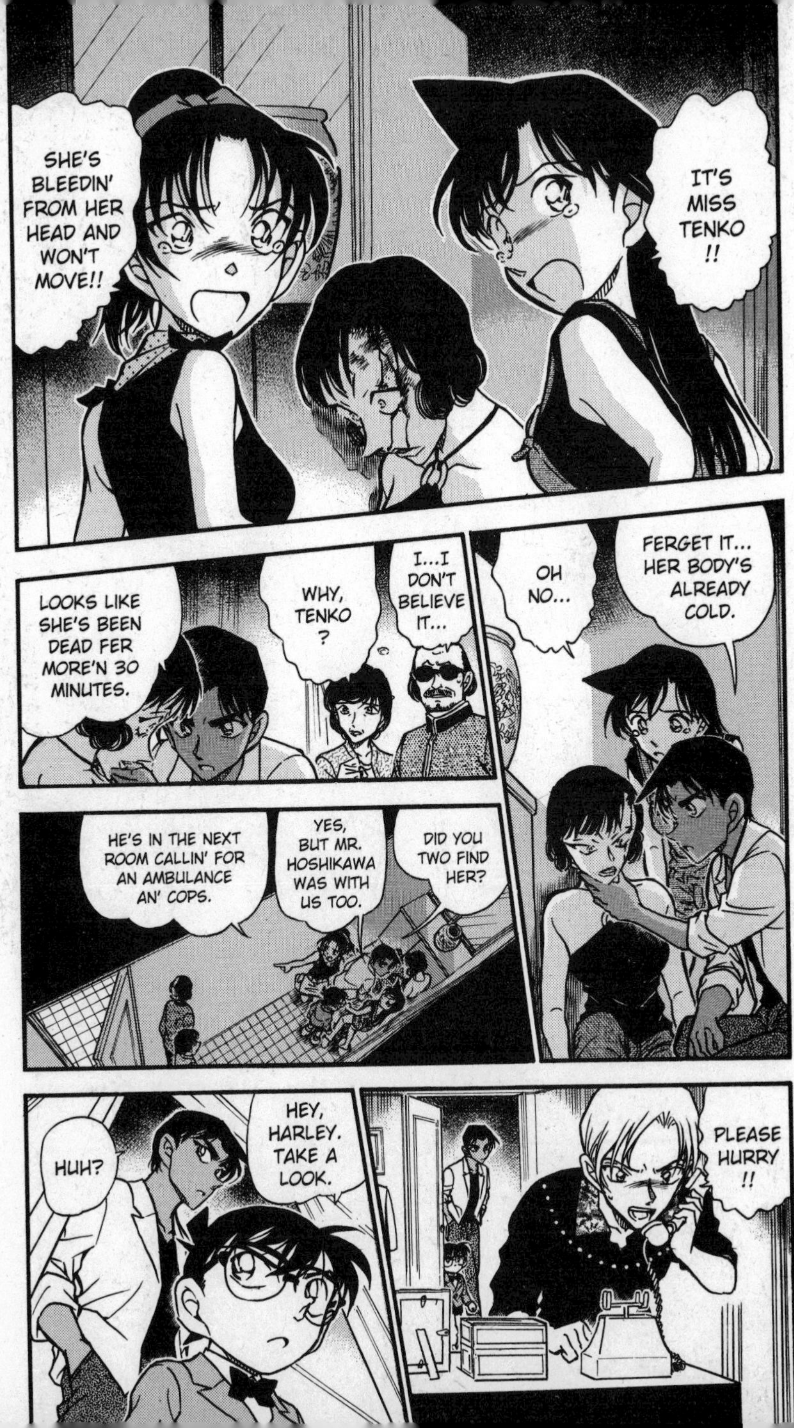
IT'S MISS TENKO !!
SHE'S BLEEDIN' FROM HER HEAD AND WON'T MOVE!!
FERGET IT... HER BODY'S ALREADY COLD.
OH NO...
I...I DON'T BELIEVE IT...
WHY, TENKO ?
LOOKS LIKE SHE'S BEEN DEAD FER MORE'N 30 MINUTES.
DID YOU TWO FIND HER?
YES, BUT MR. HOSHIKAWA WAS WITH US TOO.
HE'S IN THE NEXT ROOM CALLIN' FOR AN AMBULANCE AN' COPS.
PLEASE HURRY !!
HEY, HARLEY. TAKE A LOOK.
HUH?

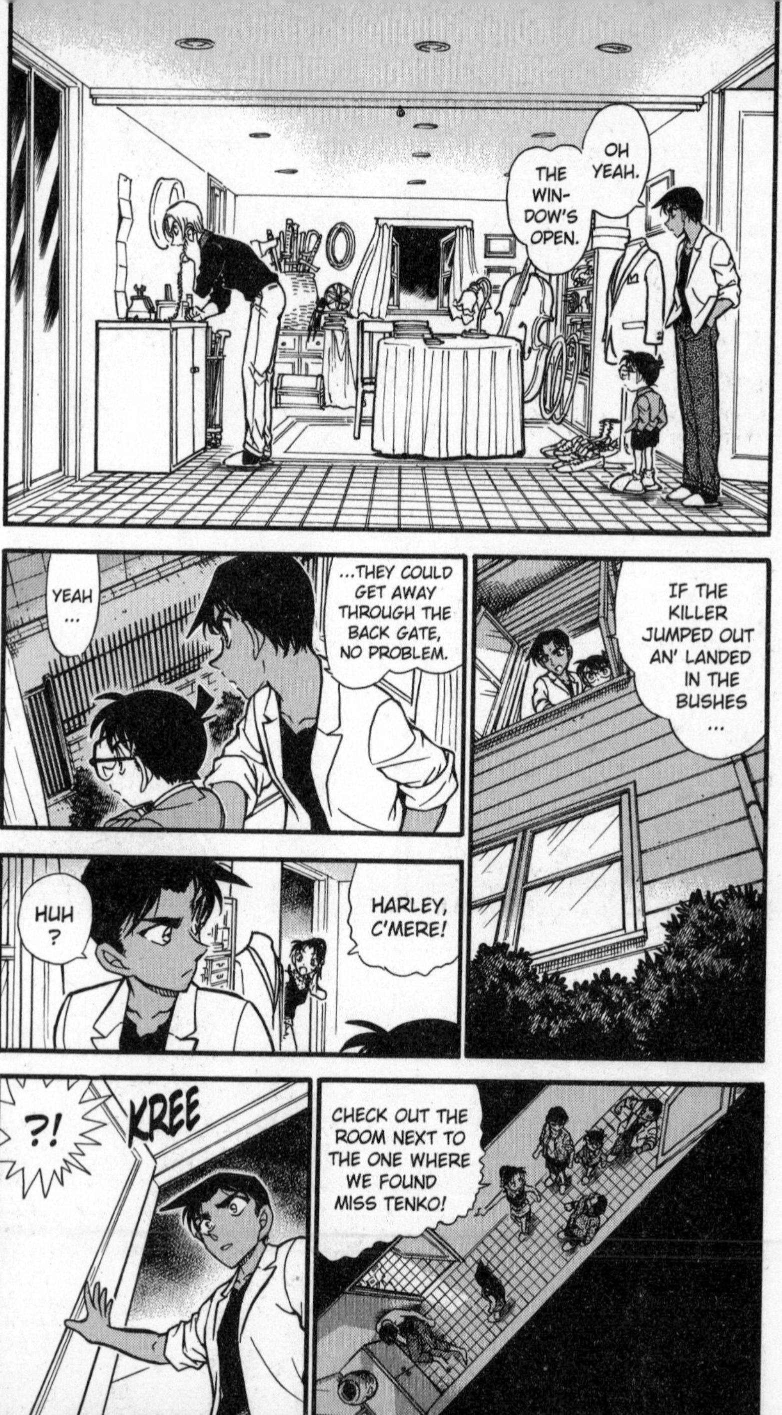
OH YEAH.
THE WIN-DOW'S OPEN.
IF THE KILLER JUMPED OUT AN' LANDED IN THE BUSHES ...
...THEY COULD GET AWAY THROUGH THE BACK GATE, NO PROBLEM.
YEAH ...
HARLEY, C'MERE!
HUH ?
CHECK OUT THE ROOM NEXT TO THE ONE WHERE WE FOUND MISS TENKO!
KREE
?!

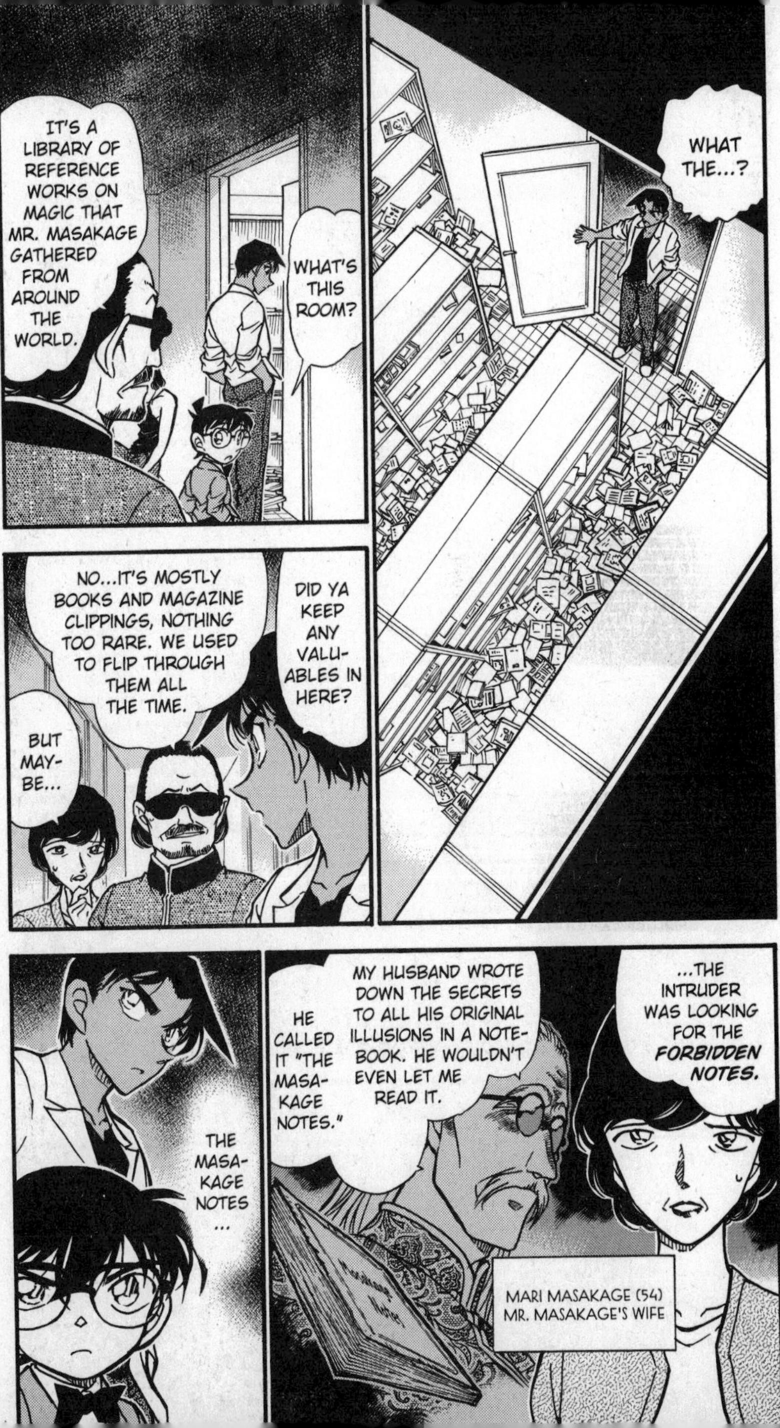
WHAT THE...?
WHAT'S THIS ROOM?
IT'S A LIBRARY OF REFERENCE WORKS ON MAGIC THAT MR. MASAKAGE GATHERED FROM AROUND THE WORLD.
DID YA KEEP ANY VALU-ABLES IN HERE?
NO...IT'S MOSTLY BOOKS AND MAGAZINE CLIPPINGS, NOTHING TOO RARE. WE USED TO FLIP THROUGH THEM ALL THE TIME.
BUT MAY-BE...
...THE INTRUDER WAS LOOKING FOR THE ***FORBIDDEN NOTES.***
MY HUSBAND WROTE DOWN THE SECRETS TO ALL HIS ORIGINAL ILLUSIONS IN A NOTE-BOOK. HE WOULDN'T EVEN LET ME READ IT.
HE CALLED IT "THE MASA-KAGE NOTES."
MARI MASAKAGE (54) MR. MASAKAGE'S WIFE
THE MASA-KAGE NOTES ...

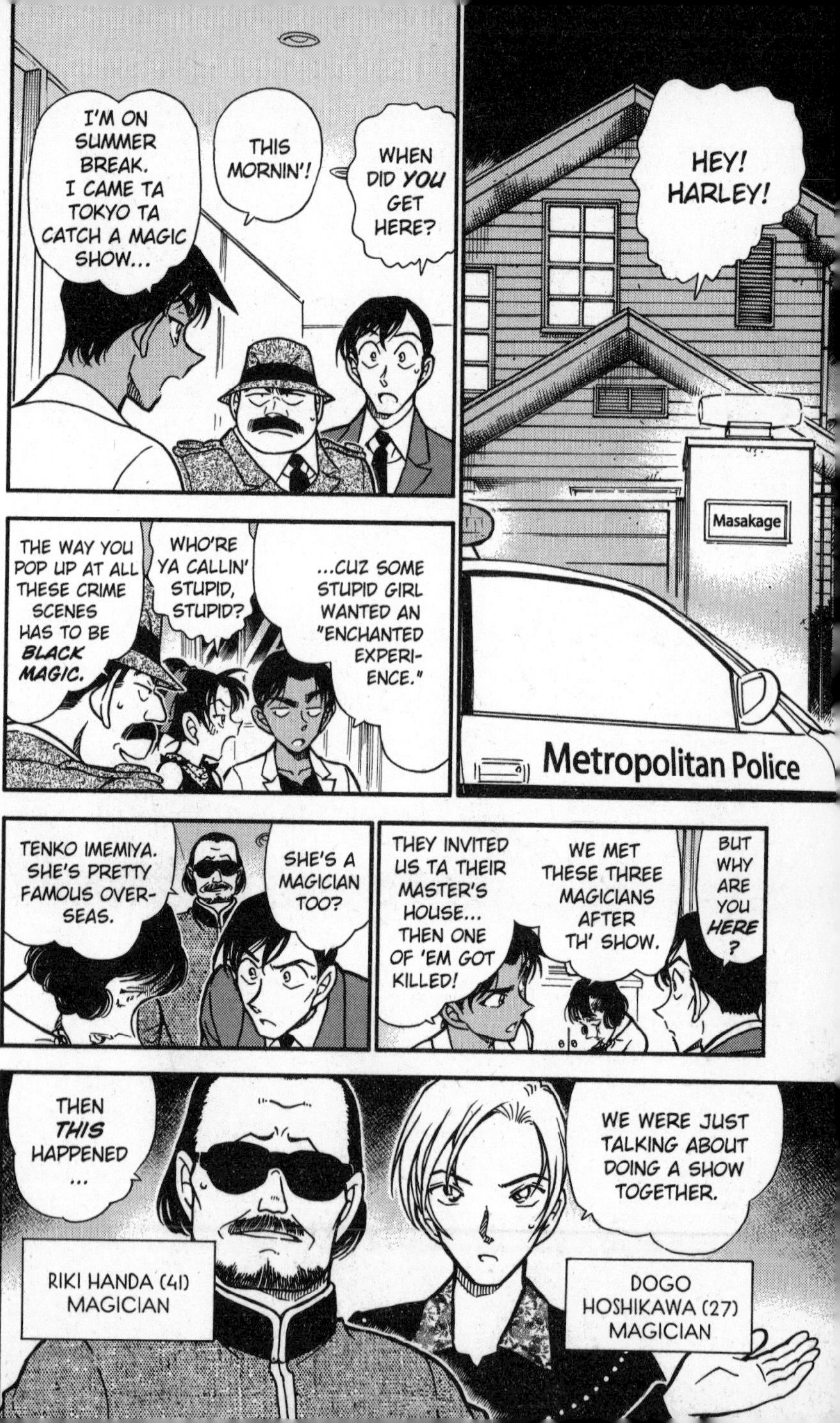
HEY! HARLEY!
Masakage
Metropolitan Police
WHEN DID *YOU* GET HERE?
THIS MORNIN'!
I'M ON SUMMER BREAK. I CAME TA TOKYO TA CATCH A MAGIC SHOW...
...CUZ SOME STUPID GIRL WANTED AN "ENCHANTED EXPERIENCE."
WHO'RE YA CALLIN' STUPID, STUPID?
THE WAY YOU POP UP AT ALL THESE CRIME SCENES HAS TO BE *BLACK MAGIC.*
BUT WHY ARE YOU *HERE*?
WE MET THESE THREE MAGICIANS AFTER TH' SHOW.
THEY INVITED US TA THEIR MASTER'S HOUSE... THEN ONE OF 'EM GOT KILLED!
SHE'S A MAGICIAN TOO?
TENKO IMEMIYA. SHE'S PRETTY FAMOUS OVERSEAS.
WE WERE JUST TALKING ABOUT DOING A SHOW TOGETHER.
DOGO HOSHIKAWA (27) MAGICIAN
THEN *THIS* HAPPENED...
RIKI HANDA (41) MAGICIAN

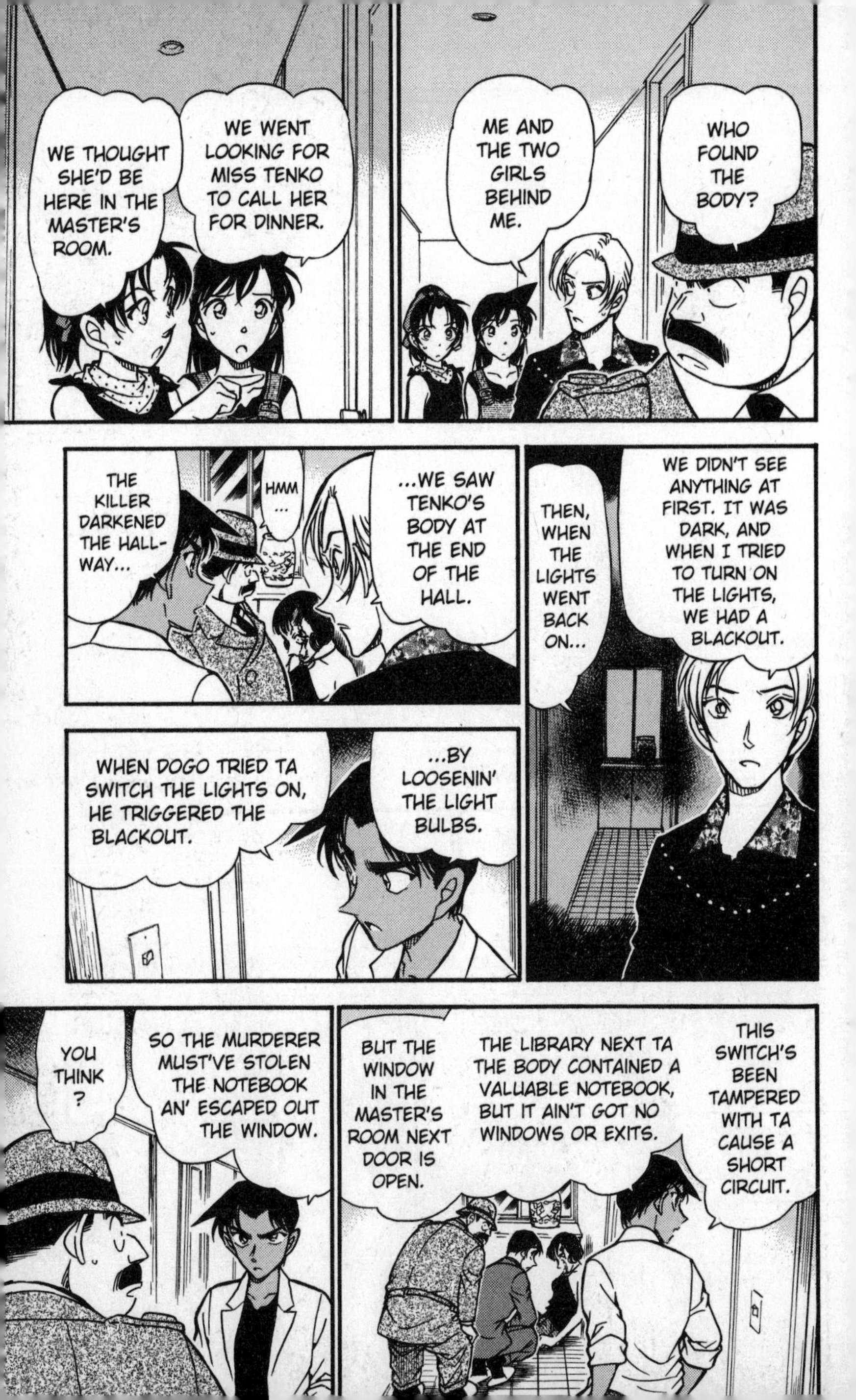
WHO FOUND THE BODY?
ME AND THE TWO GIRLS BEHIND ME.
WE WENT LOOKING FOR MISS TENKO TO CALL HER FOR DINNER.
WE THOUGHT SHE'D BE HERE IN THE MASTER'S ROOM.
WE DIDN'T SEE ANYTHING AT FIRST. IT WAS DARK, AND WHEN I TRIED TO TURN ON THE LIGHTS, WE HAD A BLACKOUT.
THEN, WHEN THE LIGHTS WENT BACK ON...
...WE SAW TENKO'S BODY AT THE END OF THE HALL.
HMM...
THE KILLER DARKENED THE HALL-WAY...
...BY LOOSENIN' THE LIGHT BULBS.
WHEN DOGO TRIED TA SWITCH THE LIGHTS ON, HE TRIGGERED THE BLACKOUT.
THIS SWITCH'S BEEN TAMPERED WITH TA CAUSE A SHORT CIRCUIT.
THE LIBRARY NEXT TA THE BODY CONTAINED A VALUABLE NOTEBOOK, BUT IT AIN'T GOT NO WINDOWS OR EXITS.
BUT THE WINDOW IN THE MASTER'S ROOM NEXT DOOR IS OPEN.
SO THE MURDERER MUST'VE STOLEN THE NOTEBOOK AN' ESCAPED OUT THE WINDOW.
YOU THINK?

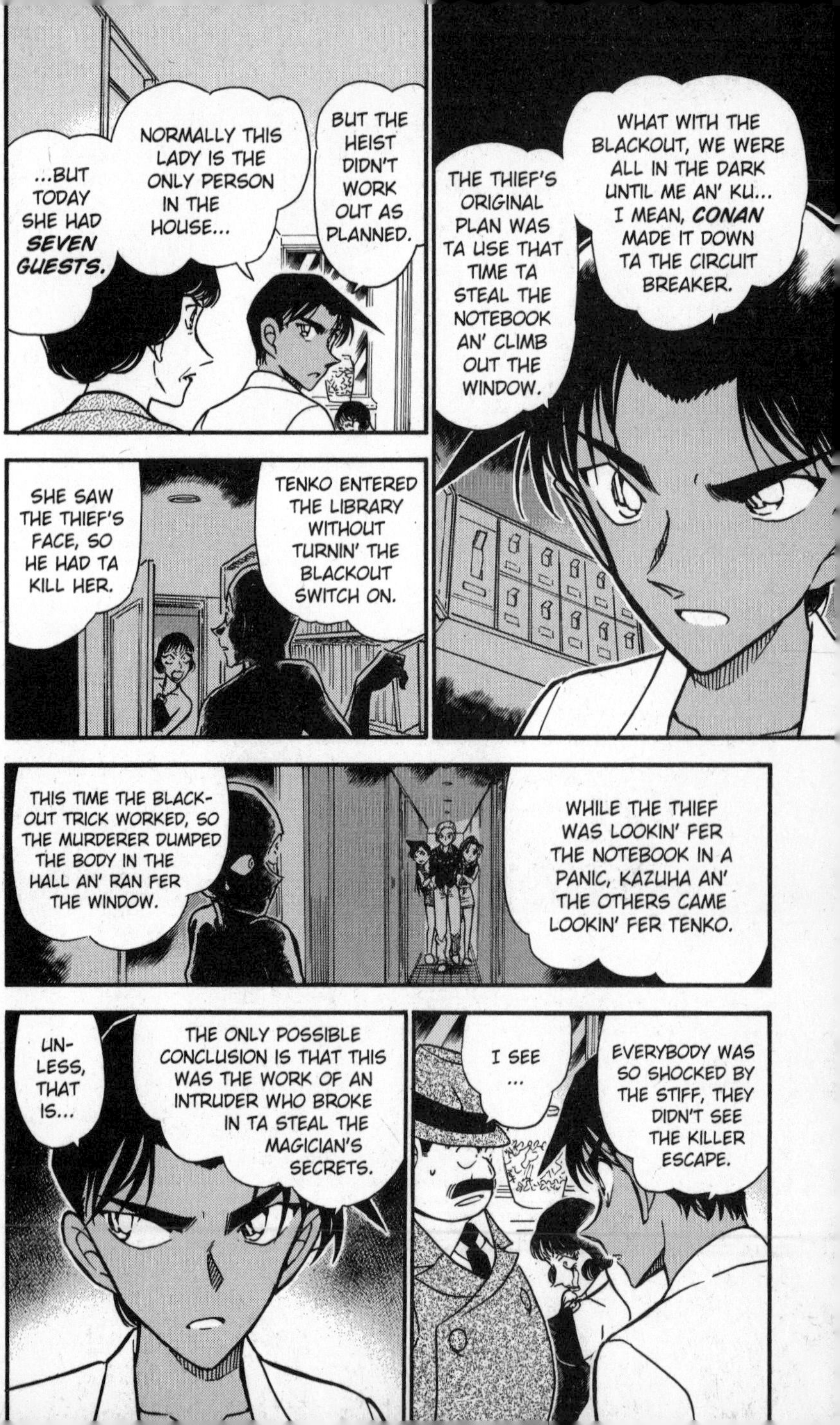
WHAT WITH THE BLACKOUT, WE WERE ALL IN THE DARK UNTIL ME AN' KU... I MEAN, **CONAN** MADE IT DOWN TA THE CIRCUIT BREAKER.
THE THIEF'S ORIGINAL PLAN WAS TA USE THAT TIME TA STEAL THE NOTEBOOK AN' CLIMB OUT THE WINDOW.
BUT THE HEIST DIDN'T WORK OUT AS PLANNED.
NORMALLY THIS LADY IS THE ONLY PERSON IN THE HOUSE...
...BUT TODAY SHE HAD ***SEVEN GUESTS.***
TENKO ENTERED THE LIBRARY WITHOUT TURNIN' THE BLACKOUT SWITCH ON.
SHE SAW THE THIEF'S FACE, SO HE HAD TA KILL HER.
WHILE THE THIEF WAS LOOKIN' FER THE NOTEBOOK IN A PANIC, KAZUHA AN' THE OTHERS CAME LOOKIN' FER TENKO.
THIS TIME THE BLACKOUT TRICK WORKED, SO THE MURDERER DUMPED THE BODY IN THE HALL AN' RAN FER THE WINDOW.
EVERYBODY WAS SO SHOCKED BY THE STIFF, THEY DIDN'T SEE THE KILLER ESCAPE.
I SEE ...
THE ONLY POSSIBLE CONCLUSION IS THAT THIS WAS THE WORK OF AN INTRUDER WHO BROKE IN TA STEAL THE MAGICIAN'S SECRETS.
UNLESS, THAT IS...

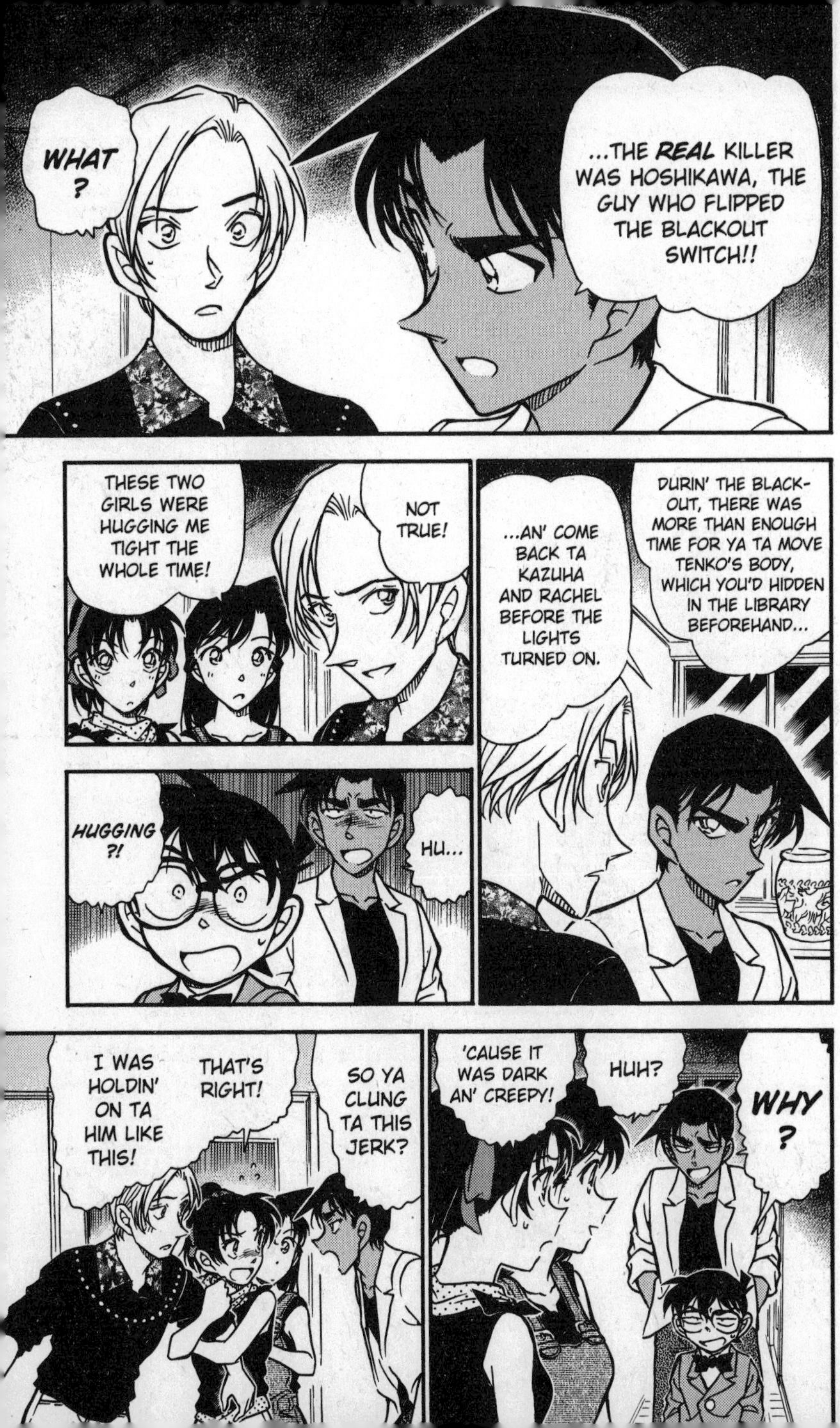
...THE REAL KILLER WAS HOSHIKAWA, THE GUY WHO FLIPPED THE BLACKOUT SWITCH!!
WHAT?
DURIN' THE BLACK-OUT, THERE WAS MORE THAN ENOUGH TIME FOR YA TA MOVE TENKO'S BODY, WHICH YOU'D HIDDEN IN THE LIBRARY BEFOREHAND...
...AN' COME BACK TA KAZUHA AND RACHEL BEFORE THE LIGHTS TURNED ON.
NOT TRUE!
THESE TWO GIRLS WERE HUGGING ME TIGHT THE WHOLE TIME!
HU...
HUGGING?!
WHY?
HUH?
'CAUSE IT WAS DARK AN' CREEPY!
SO YA CLUNG TA THIS JERK?
THAT'S RIGHT!
I WAS HOLDIN' ON TA HIM LIKE THIS!

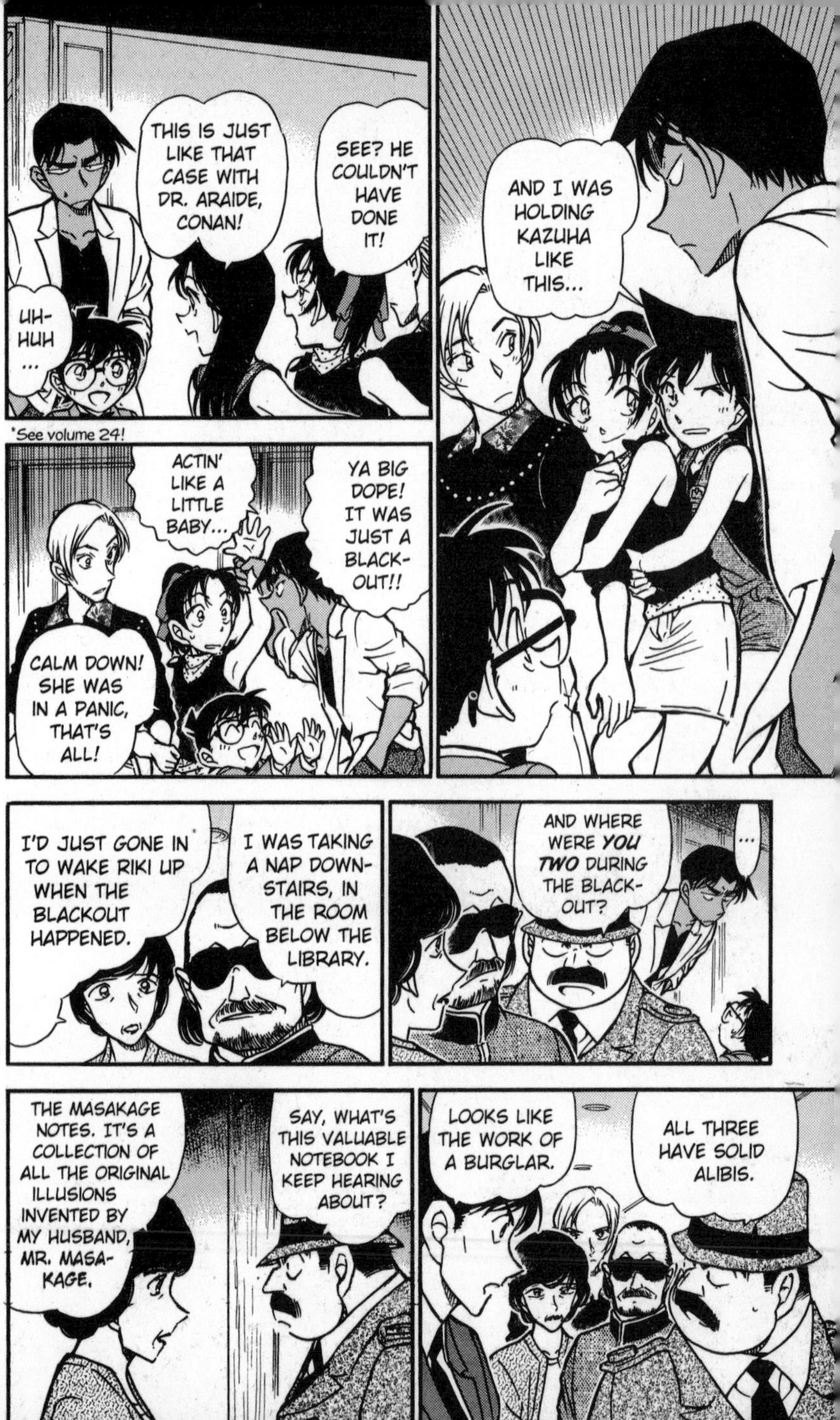
AND I WAS HOLDING KAZUHA LIKE THIS...
SEE? HE COULDN'T HAVE DONE IT!
THIS IS JUST LIKE THAT CASE WITH DR. ARAIDE, CONAN!
UH-HUH ...
*See volume 24!
YA BIG DOPE! IT WAS JUST A BLACK-OUT!!
ACTIN' LIKE A LITTLE BABY...
CALM DOWN! SHE WAS IN A PANIC, THAT'S ALL!
...
AND WHERE WERE *YOU TWO* DURING THE BLACK-OUT?
I WAS TAKING A NAP DOWN-STAIRS, IN THE ROOM BELOW THE LIBRARY.
I'D JUST GONE IN TO WAKE RIKI UP WHEN THE BLACKOUT HAPPENED.
ALL THREE HAVE SOLID ALIBIS.
LOOKS LIKE THE WORK OF A BURGLAR.
SAY, WHAT'S THIS VALUABLE NOTEBOOK I KEEP HEARING ABOUT?
THE MASAKAGE NOTES. IT'S A COLLECTION OF ALL THE ORIGINAL ILLUSIONS INVENTED BY MY HUSBAND, MR. MASA-KAGE.

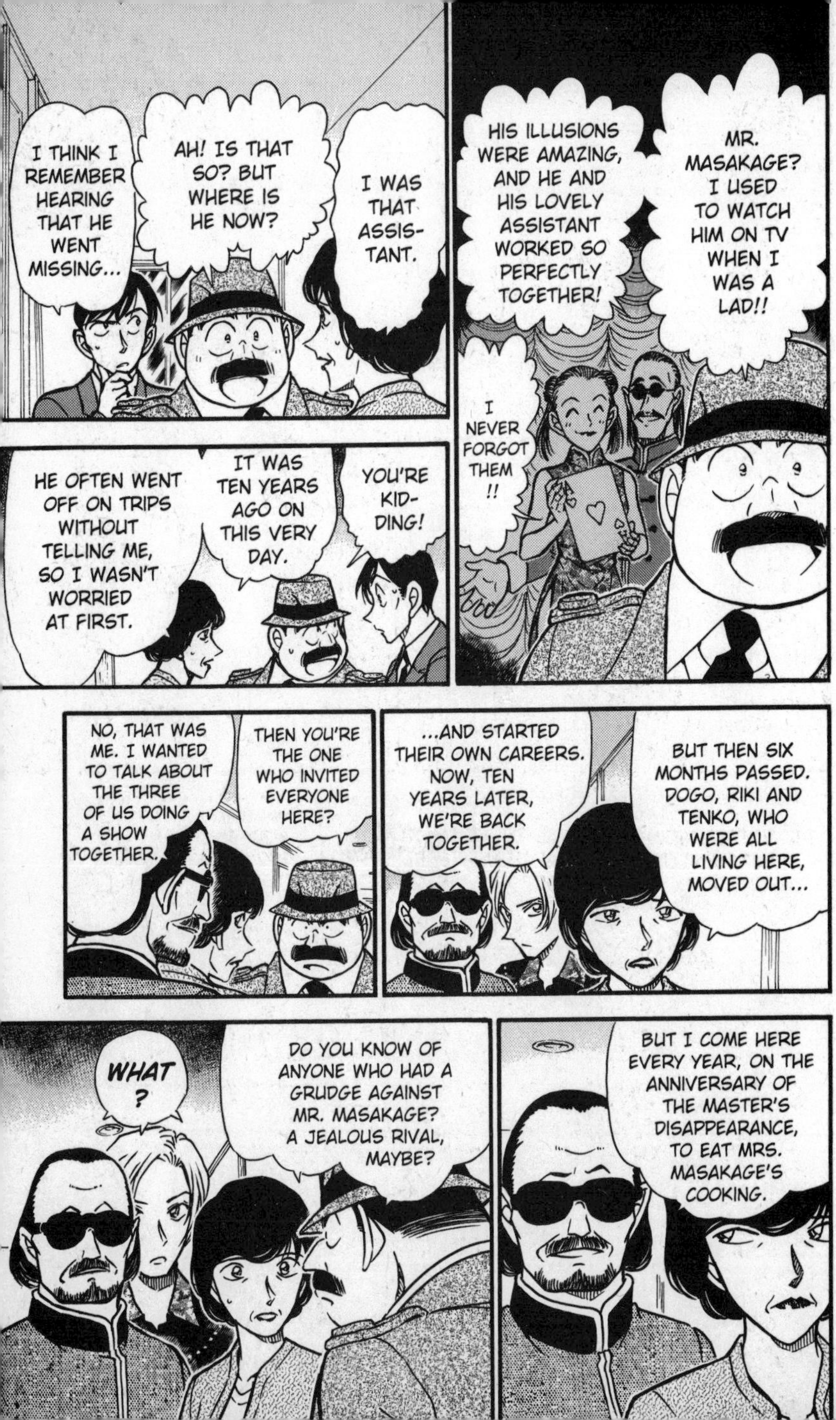
MR. MASAKAGE? I USED TO WATCH HIM ON TV WHEN I WAS A LAD!!
HIS ILLUSIONS WERE AMAZING, AND HE AND HIS LOVELY ASSISTANT WORKED SO PERFECTLY TOGETHER!
I NEVER FORGOT THEM !!
I WAS THAT ASSISTANT.
AH! IS THAT SO? BUT WHERE IS HE NOW?
I THINK I REMEMBER HEARING THAT HE WENT MISSING...
YOU'RE KID-DING!
IT WAS TEN YEARS AGO ON THIS VERY DAY.
HE OFTEN WENT OFF ON TRIPS WITHOUT TELLING ME, SO I WASN'T WORRIED AT FIRST.
BUT THEN SIX MONTHS PASSED. DOGO, RIKI AND TENKO, WHO WERE ALL LIVING HERE, MOVED OUT...
...AND STARTED THEIR OWN CAREERS. NOW, TEN YEARS LATER, WE'RE BACK TOGETHER.
THEN YOU'RE THE ONE WHO INVITED EVERYONE HERE?
NO, THAT WAS ME. I WANTED TO TALK ABOUT THE THREE OF US DOING A SHOW TOGETHER.
BUT I COME HERE EVERY YEAR, ON THE ANNIVERSARY OF THE MASTER'S DISAPPEARANCE, TO EAT MRS. MASAKAGE'S COOKING.
DO YOU KNOW OF ANYONE WHO HAD A GRUDGE AGAINST MR. MASAKAGE? A JEALOUS RIVAL, MAYBE?
WHAT ?

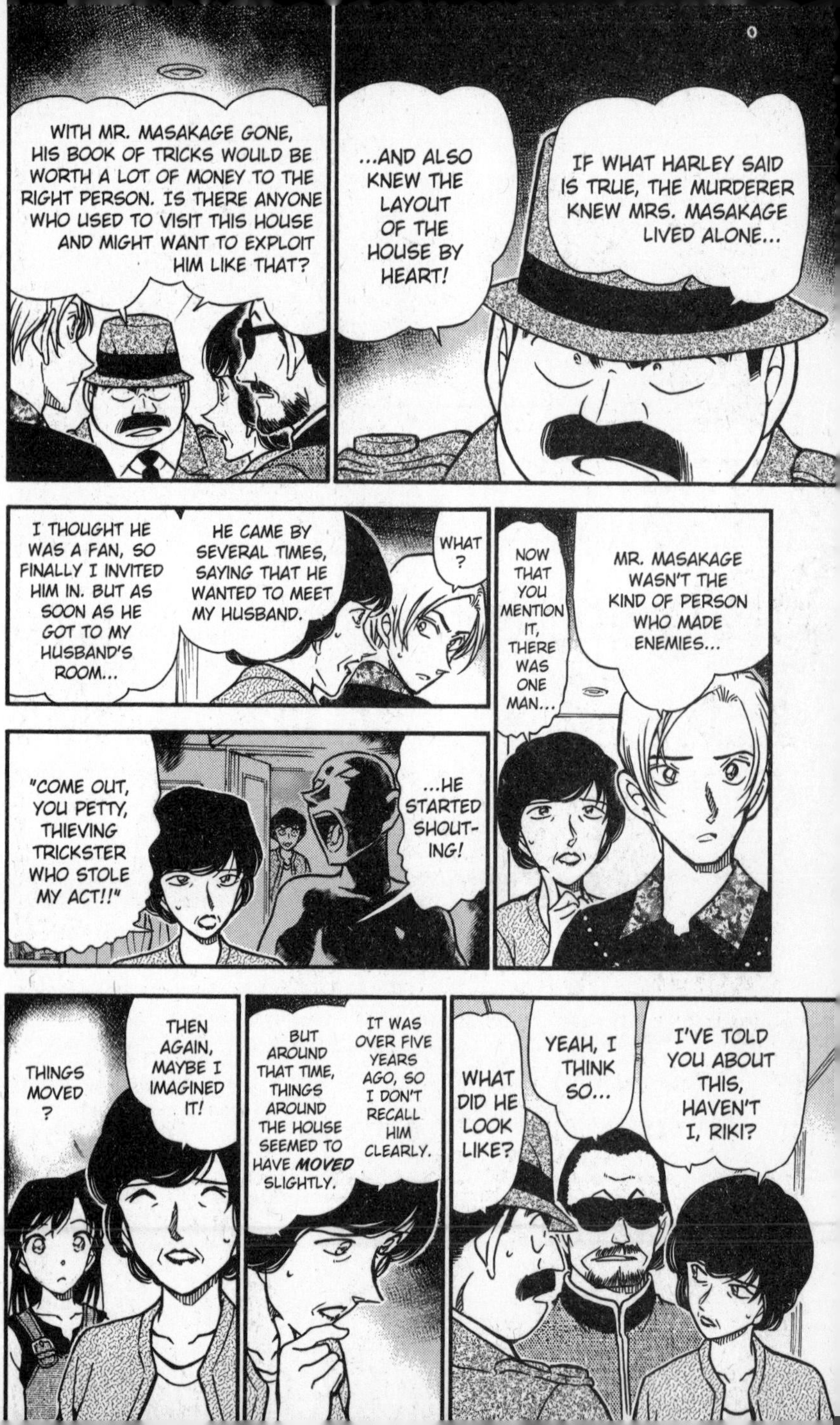
IF WHAT HARLEY SAID IS TRUE, THE MURDERER KNEW MRS. MASAKAGE LIVED ALONE...
...AND ALSO KNEW THE LAYOUT OF THE HOUSE BY HEART!
WITH MR. MASAKAGE GONE, HIS BOOK OF TRICKS WOULD BE WORTH A LOT OF MONEY TO THE RIGHT PERSON. IS THERE ANYONE WHO USED TO VISIT THIS HOUSE AND MIGHT WANT TO EXPLOIT HIM LIKE THAT?
MR. MASAKAGE WASN'T THE KIND OF PERSON WHO MADE ENEMIES...
NOW THAT YOU MENTION IT, THERE WAS ONE MAN...
WHAT?
HE CAME BY SEVERAL TIMES, SAYING THAT HE WANTED TO MEET MY HUSBAND.
I THOUGHT HE WAS A FAN, SO FINALLY I INVITED HIM IN. BUT AS SOON AS HE GOT TO MY HUSBAND'S ROOM...
...HE STARTED SHOUTING!
"COME OUT, YOU PETTY, THIEVING TRICKSTER WHO STOLE MY ACT!!"
I'VE TOLD YOU ABOUT THIS, HAVEN'T I, RIKI?
YEAH, I THINK SO...
WHAT DID HE LOOK LIKE?
IT WAS OVER FIVE YEARS AGO, SO I DON'T RECALL HIM CLEARLY.
BUT AROUND THAT TIME, THINGS AROUND THE HOUSE SEEMED TO HAVE *MOVED* SLIGHTLY.
THEN AGAIN, MAYBE I IMAGINED IT!
THINGS MOVED?

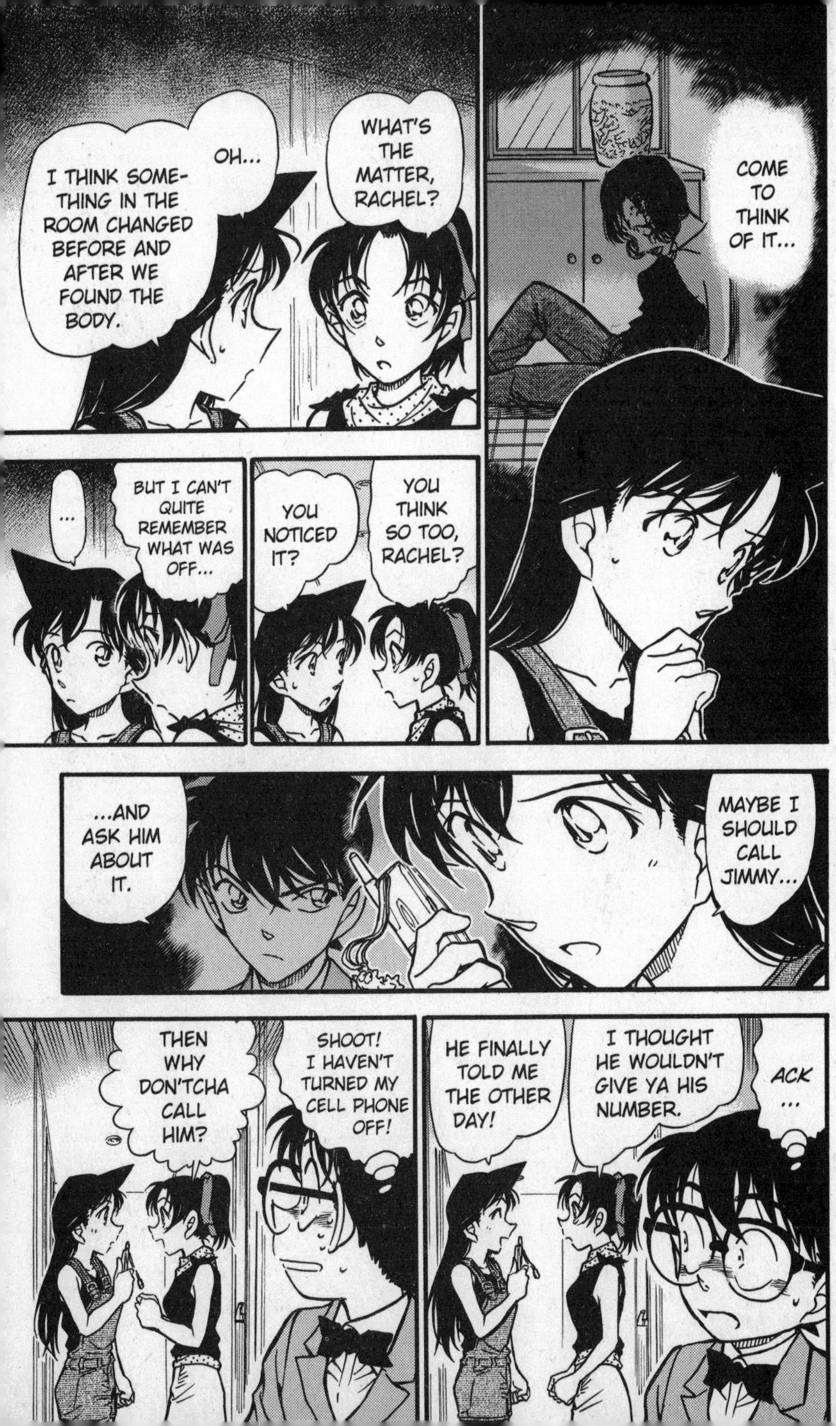
WHAT'S THE MATTER, RACHEL?
OH...
I THINK SOME-THING IN THE ROOM CHANGED BEFORE AND AFTER WE FOUND THE BODY.
YOU THINK SO TOO, RACHEL?
YOU NOTICED IT?
BUT I CAN'T QUITE REMEMBER WHAT WAS OFF...
...
COME TO THINK OF IT...
MAYBE I SHOULD CALL JIMMY...
...AND ASK HIM ABOUT IT.
THEN WHY DON'TCHA CALL HIM?
SHOOT! I HAVEN'T TURNED MY CELL PHONE OFF!
I THOUGHT HE WOULDN'T GIVE YA HIS NUMBER.
HE FINALLY TOLD ME THE OTHER DAY!
ACK...

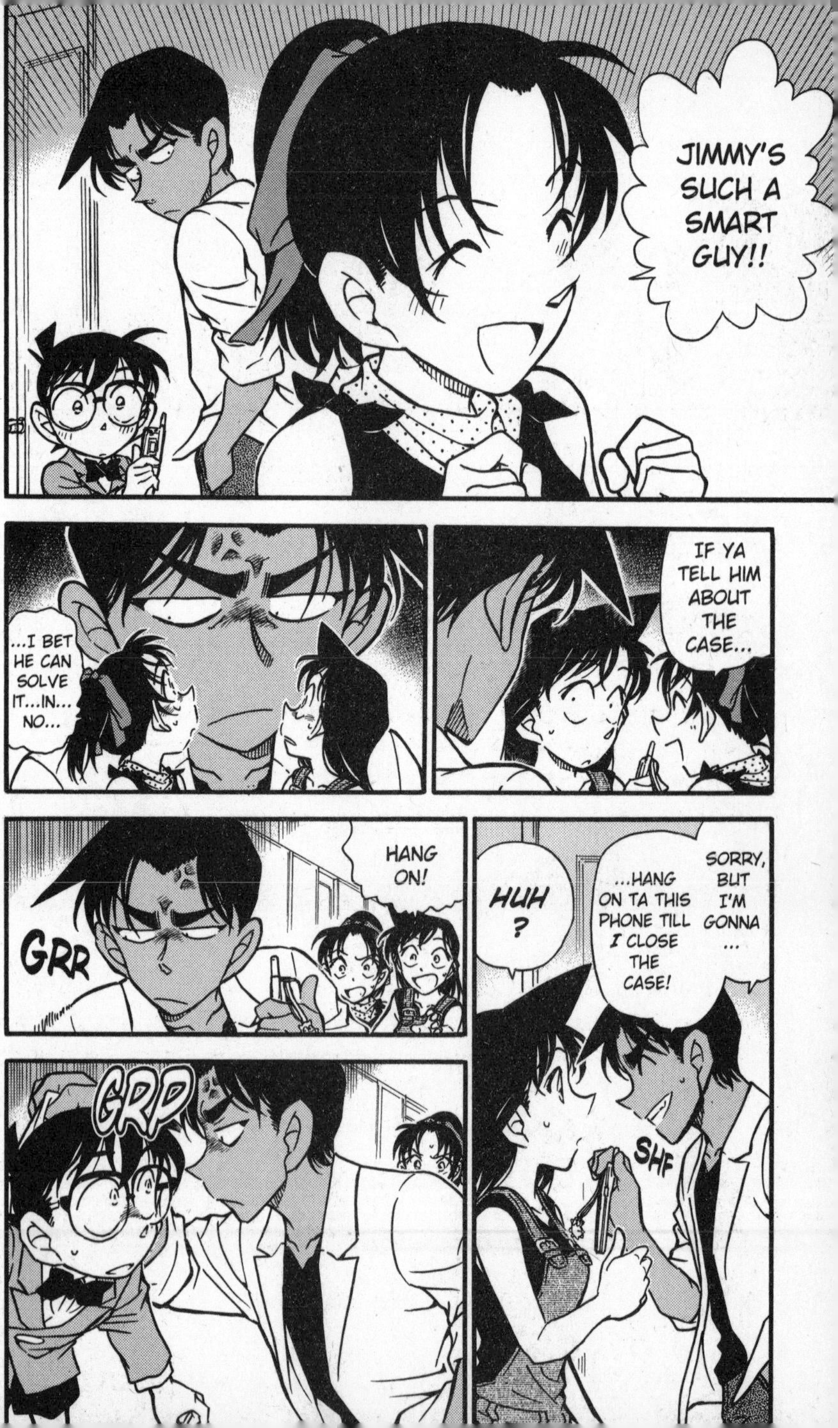
JIMMY'S SUCH A SMART GUY!!
IF YA TELL HIM ABOUT THE CASE...
...I BET HE CAN SOLVE IT...IN... NO...
SORRY, BUT I'M GONNA ...
...HANG ON TA THIS PHONE TILL I CLOSE THE CASE!
HUH ?
SHF
HANG ON!
GRR
GRP

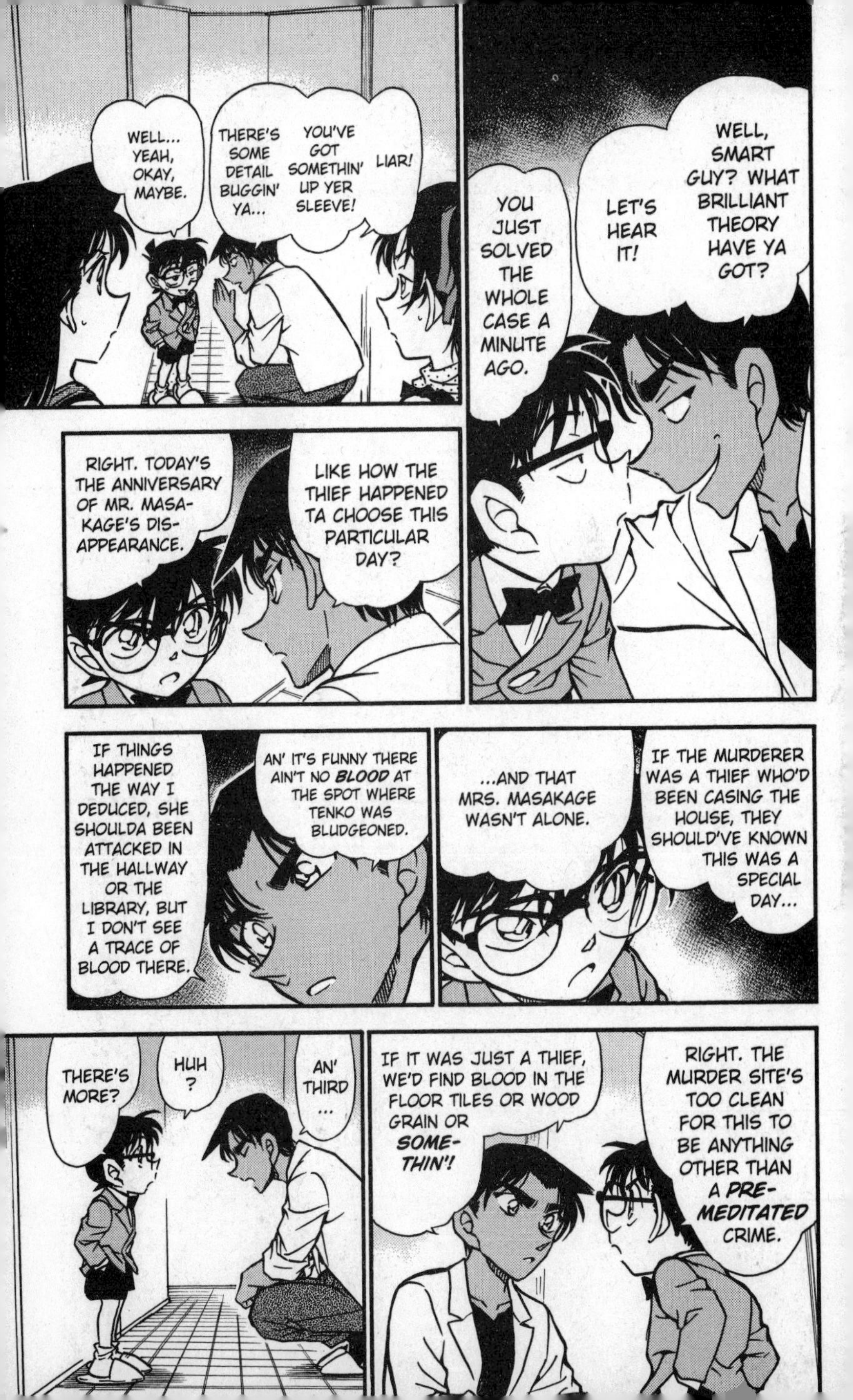
WELL, SMART GUY? WHAT BRILLIANT THEORY HAVE YA GOT?
LET'S HEAR IT!
YOU JUST SOLVED THE WHOLE CASE A MINUTE AGO.
LIAR!
YOU'VE GOT SOMETHIN' UP YER SLEEVE!
THERE'S SOME DETAIL BUGGIN' YA...
WELL... YEAH, OKAY, MAYBE.
LIKE HOW THE THIEF HAPPENED TA CHOOSE THIS PARTICULAR DAY?
RIGHT. TODAY'S THE ANNIVERSARY OF MR. MASAKAGE'S DISAPPEARANCE.
IF THE MURDERER WAS A THIEF WHO'D BEEN CASING THE HOUSE, THEY SHOULD'VE KNOWN THIS WAS A SPECIAL DAY...
...AND THAT MRS. MASAKAGE WASN'T ALONE.
AN' IT'S FUNNY THERE AIN'T NO ***BLOOD*** AT THE SPOT WHERE TENKO WAS BLUDGEONED.
IF THINGS HAPPENED THE WAY I DEDUCED, SHE SHOULDA BEEN ATTACKED IN THE HALLWAY OR THE LIBRARY, BUT I DON'T SEE A TRACE OF BLOOD THERE.
RIGHT. THE MURDER SITE'S TOO CLEAN FOR THIS TO BE ANYTHING OTHER THAN A ***PREMEDITATED*** CRIME.
IF IT WAS JUST A THIEF, WE'D FIND BLOOD IN THE FLOOR TILES OR WOOD GRAIN OR ***SOMETHIN'!***
AN' THIRD...
HUH?
THERE'S MORE?

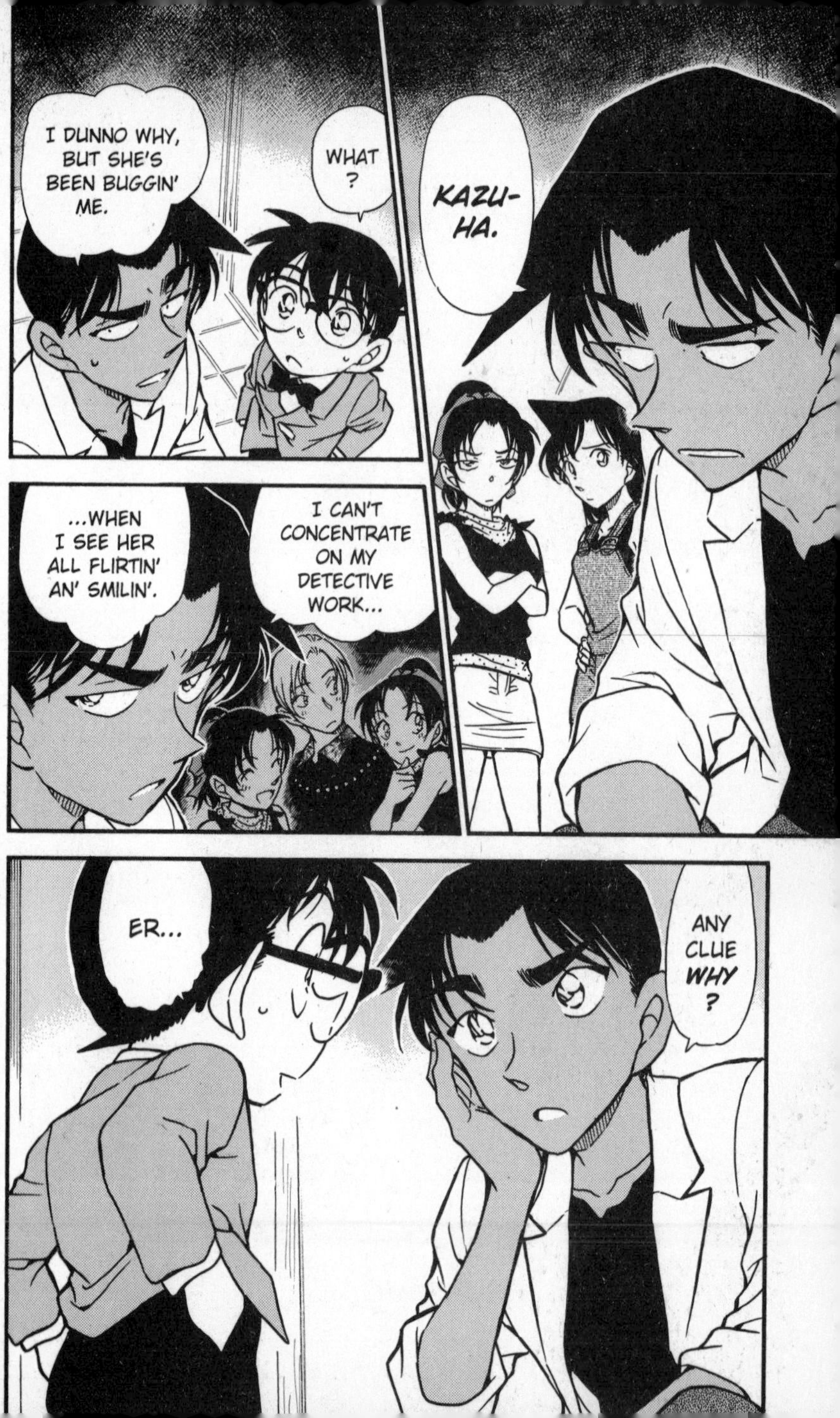
KAZU-HA.
I DUNNO WHY, BUT SHE'S BEEN BUGGIN' ME.
WHAT?
I CAN'T CONCENTRATE ON MY DETECTIVE WORK...
...WHEN I SEE HER ALL FLIRTIN' AN' SMILIN'.
ANY CLUE WHY?
ER...

FILE 10: THE MAGICIAN'S CASTLE

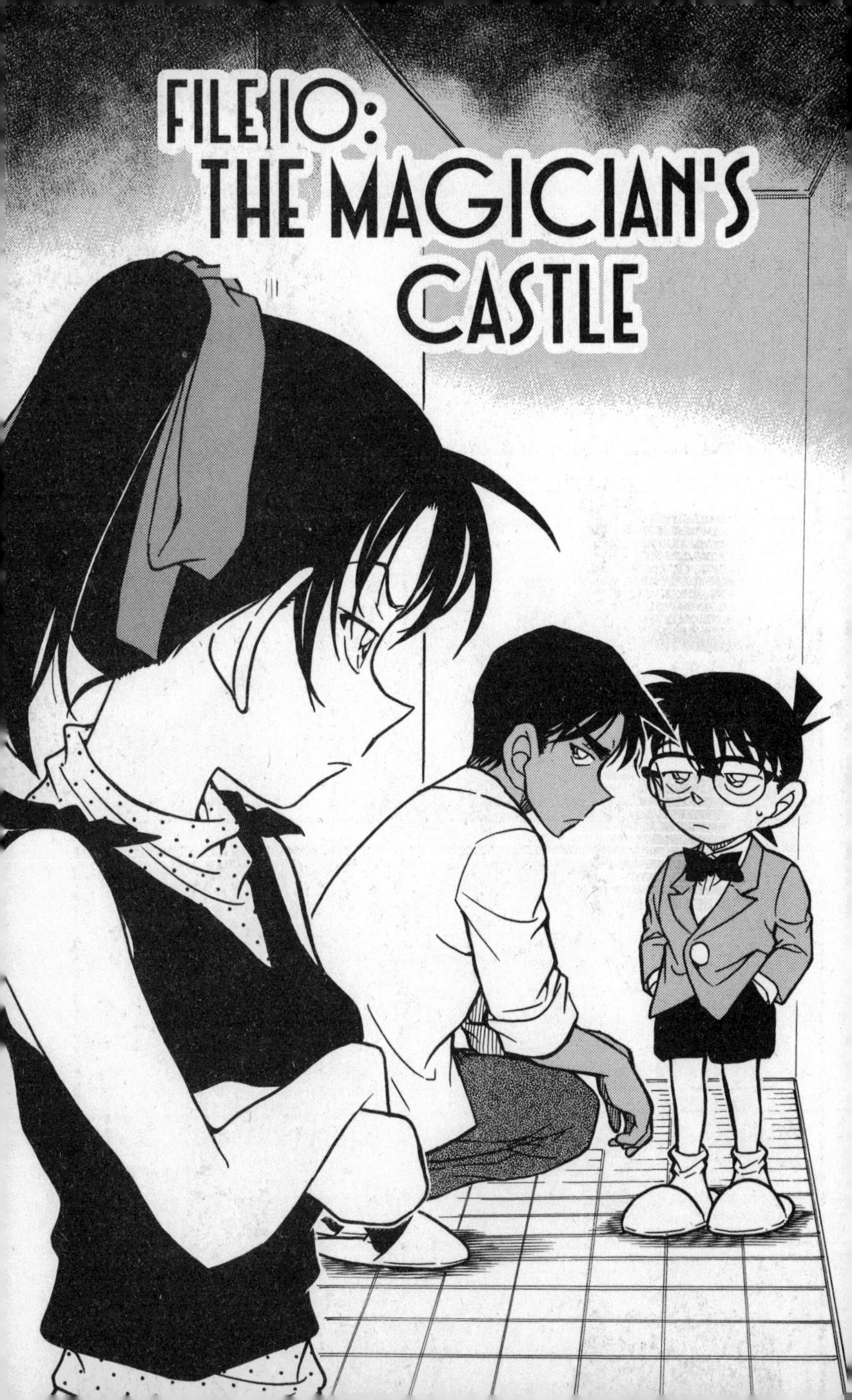

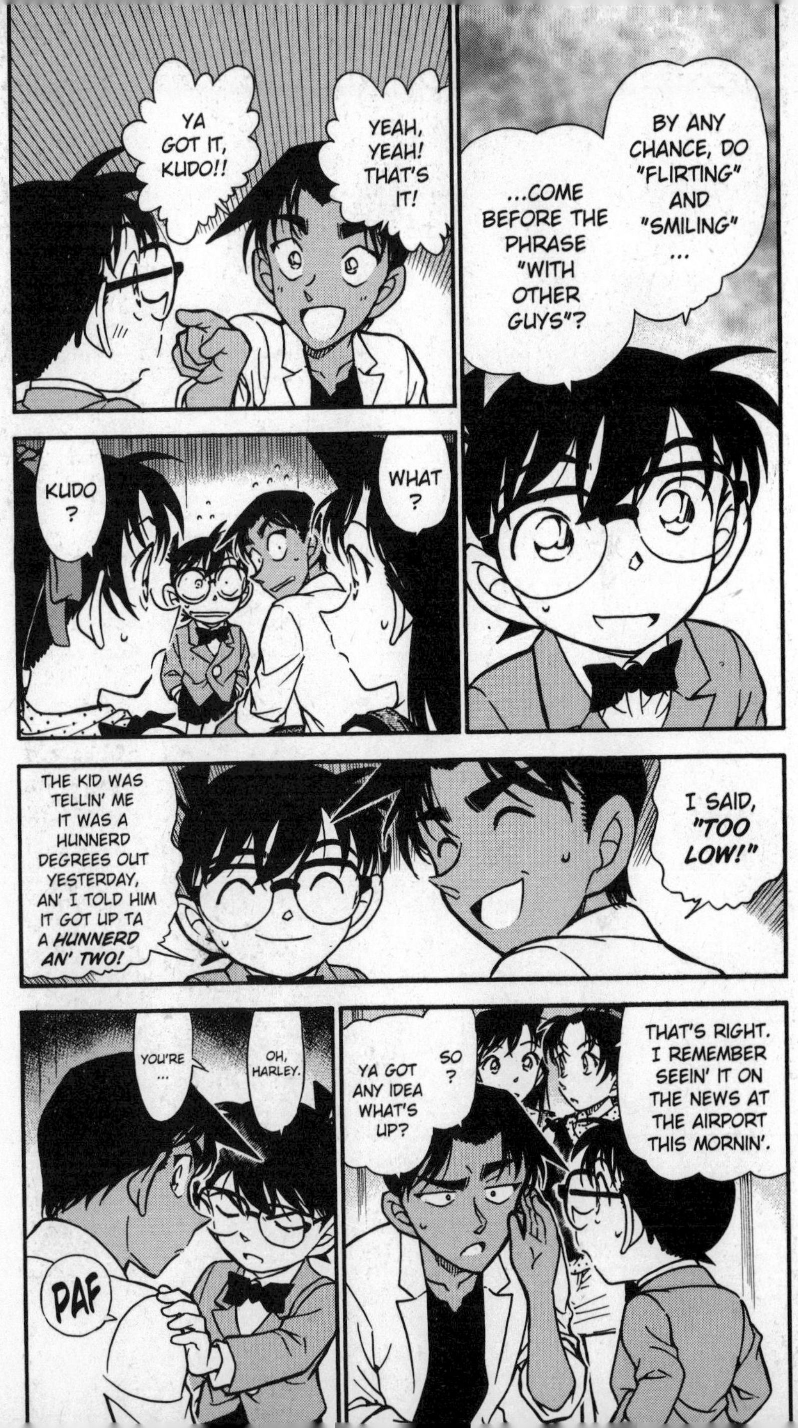
BY ANY CHANCE, DO "FLIRTING" AND "SMILING" ...
...COME BEFORE THE PHRASE "WITH OTHER GUYS"?
YEAH, YEAH! THAT'S IT!
YA GOT IT, KUDO!!
WHAT ?
KUDO ?
I SAID, "TOO LOW!"
THE KID WAS TELLIN' ME IT WAS A HUNNERD DEGREES OUT YESTERDAY, AN' I TOLD HIM IT GOT UP TA A HUNNERD AN' TWO!
THAT'S RIGHT. I REMEMBER SEEIN' IT ON THE NEWS AT THE AIRPORT THIS MORNIN'.
SO ?
YA GOT ANY IDEA WHAT'S UP?
OH, HARLEY.
YOU'RE ...
PAF

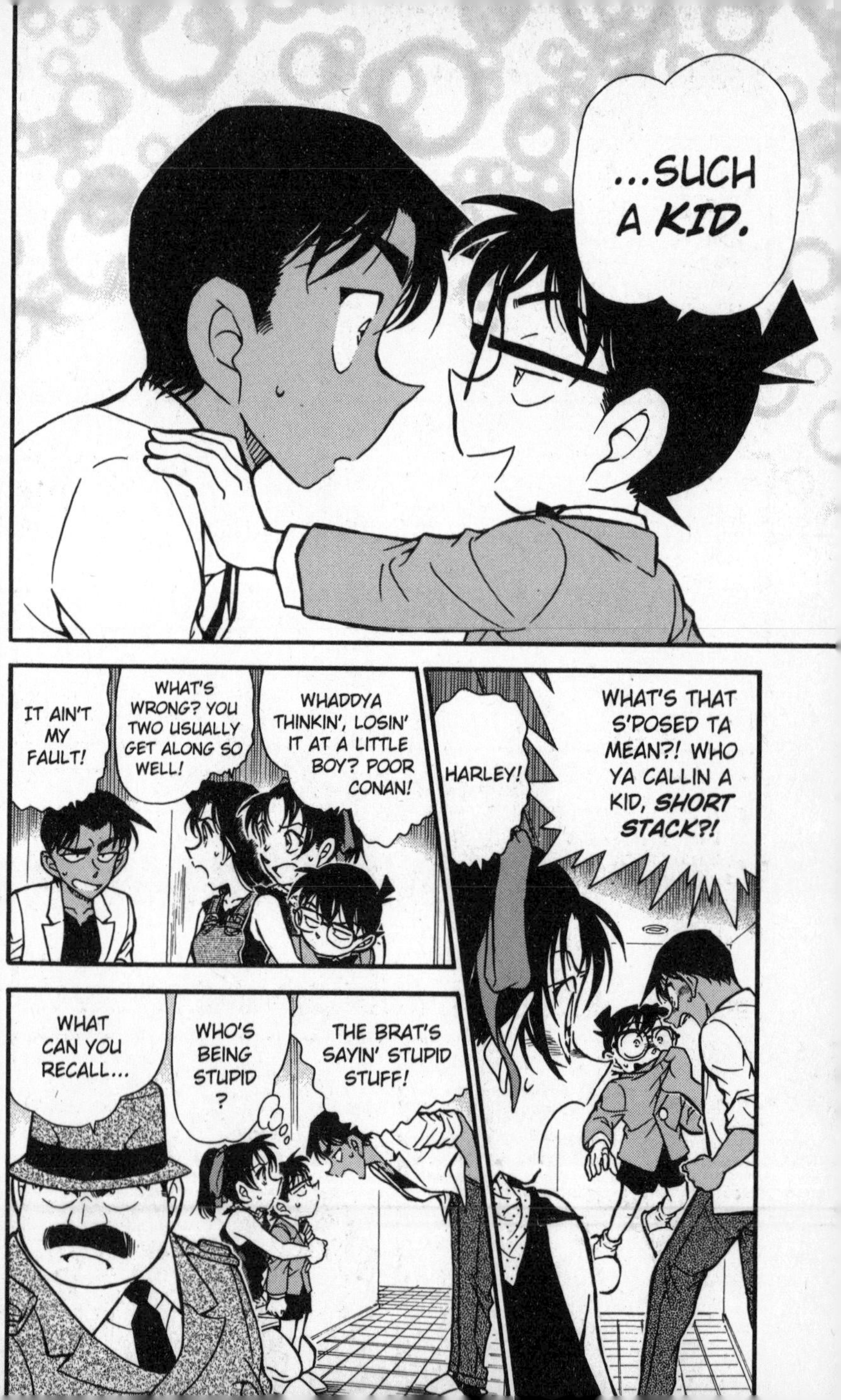
...SUCH A KID.
WHAT'S THAT S'POSED TA MEAN?! WHO YA CALLIN A KID, SHORT STACK?!
HARLEY!
WHADDYA THINKIN', LOSIN' IT AT A LITTLE BOY? POOR CONAN!
WHAT'S WRONG? YOU TWO USUALLY GET ALONG SO WELL!
IT AIN'T MY FAULT!
THE BRAT'S SAYIN' STUPID STUFF!
WHO'S BEING STUPID?
WHAT CAN YOU RECALL...

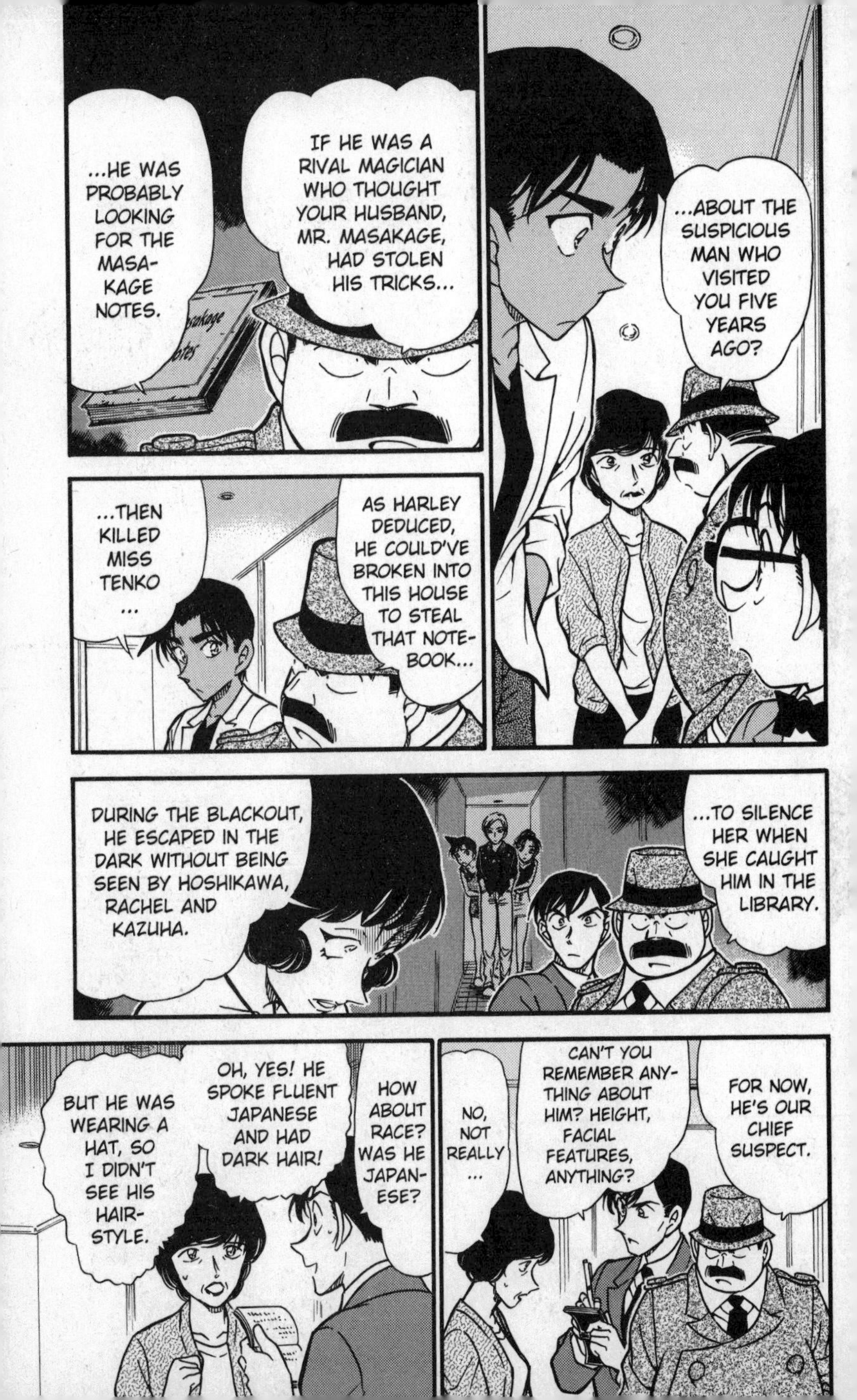
...ABOUT THE SUSPICIOUS MAN WHO VISITED YOU FIVE YEARS AGO?
IF HE WAS A RIVAL MAGICIAN WHO THOUGHT YOUR HUSBAND, MR. MASAKAGE, HAD STOLEN HIS TRICKS...
...HE WAS PROBABLY LOOKING FOR THE MASA-KAGE NOTES.
AS HARLEY DEDUCED, HE COULD'VE BROKEN INTO THIS HOUSE TO STEAL THAT NOTE-BOOK...
...THEN KILLED MISS TENKO ...
...TO SILENCE HER WHEN SHE CAUGHT HIM IN THE LIBRARY.
DURING THE BLACKOUT, HE ESCAPED IN THE DARK WITHOUT BEING SEEN BY HOSHIKAWA, RACHEL AND KAZUHA.
FOR NOW, HE'S OUR CHIEF SUSPECT.
CAN'T YOU REMEMBER ANY-THING ABOUT HIM? HEIGHT, FACIAL FEATURES, ANYTHING?
NO, NOT REALLY ...
HOW ABOUT RACE? WAS HE JAPAN-ESE?
OH, YES! HE SPOKE FLUENT JAPANESE AND HAD DARK HAIR!
BUT HE WAS WEARING A HAT, SO I DIDN'T SEE HIS HAIR-STYLE.

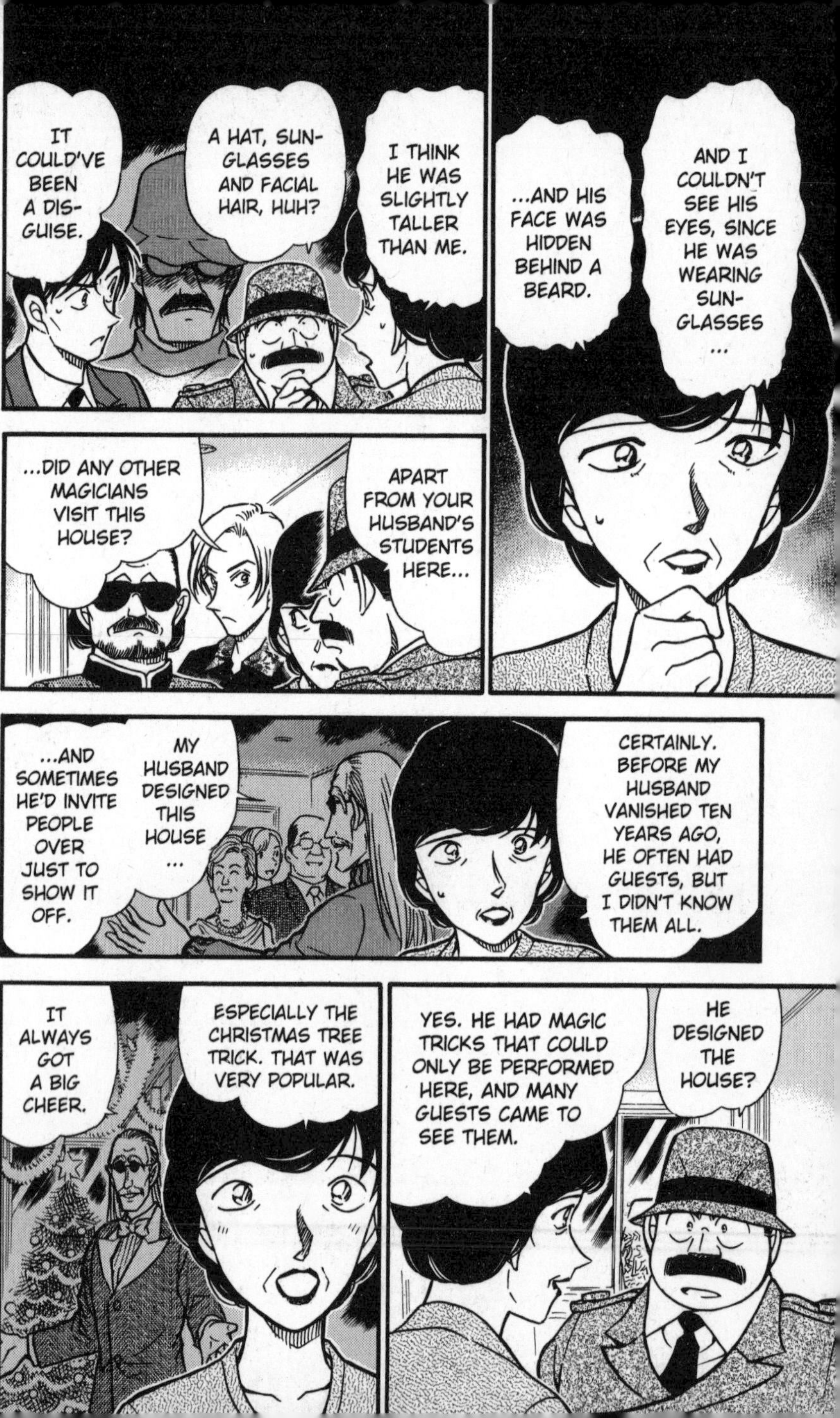
AND I COULDN'T SEE HIS EYES, SINCE HE WAS WEARING SUN-GLASSES ...
...AND HIS FACE WAS HIDDEN BEHIND A BEARD.
I THINK HE WAS SLIGHTLY TALLER THAN ME.
A HAT, SUN-GLASSES AND FACIAL HAIR, HUH?
IT COULD'VE BEEN A DIS-GUISE.
APART FROM YOUR HUSBAND'S STUDENTS HERE...
...DID ANY OTHER MAGICIANS VISIT THIS HOUSE?
CERTAINLY. BEFORE MY HUSBAND VANISHED TEN YEARS AGO, HE OFTEN HAD GUESTS, BUT I DIDN'T KNOW THEM ALL.
MY HUSBAND DESIGNED THIS HOUSE ...
...AND SOMETIMES HE'D INVITE PEOPLE OVER JUST TO SHOW IT OFF.
HE DESIGNED THE HOUSE?
YES. HE HAD MAGIC TRICKS THAT COULD ONLY BE PERFORMED HERE, AND MANY GUESTS CAME TO SEE THEM.
ESPECIALLY THE CHRISTMAS TREE TRICK. THAT WAS VERY POPULAR.
IT ALWAYS GOT A BIG CHEER.

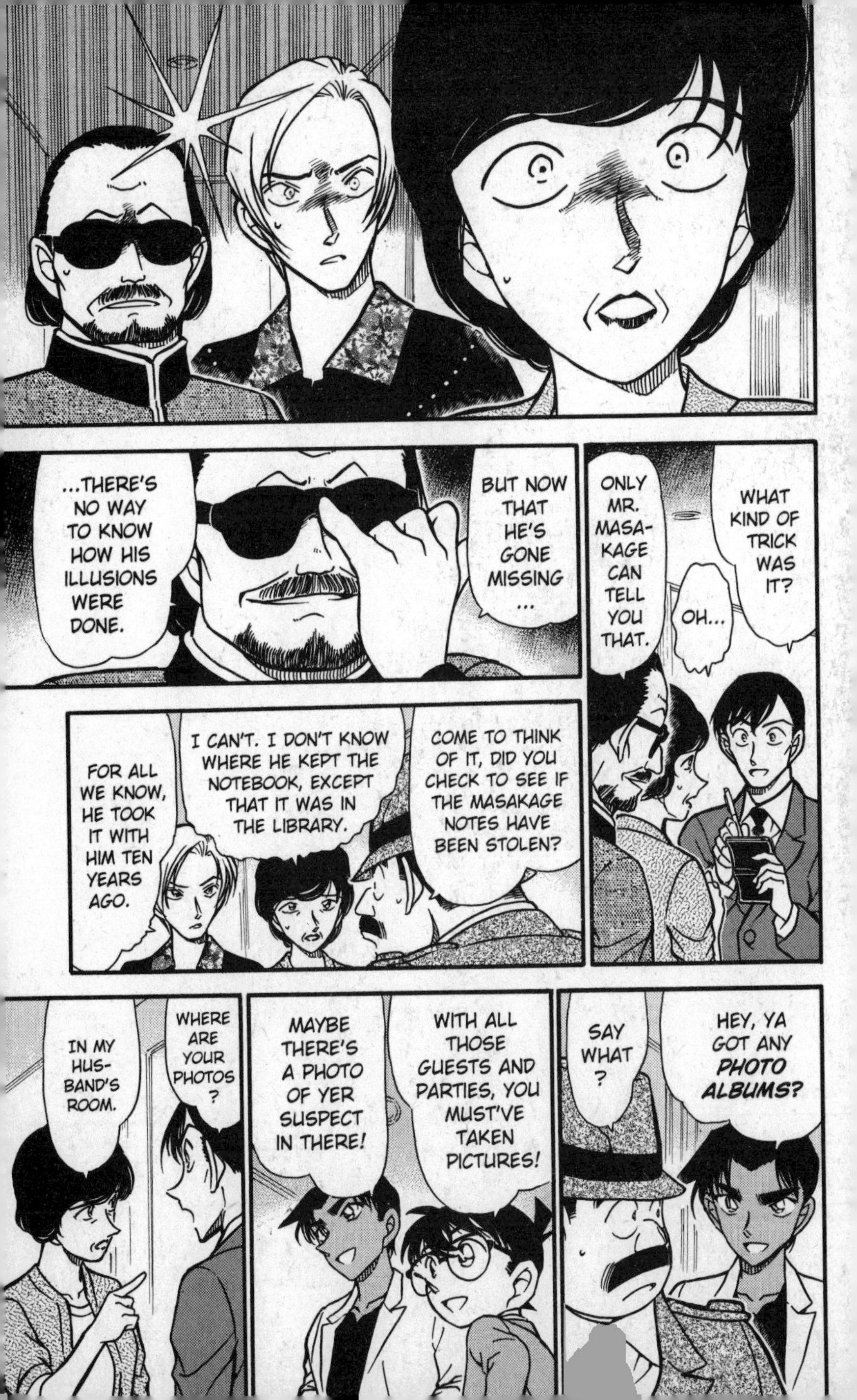
WHAT KIND OF TRICK WAS IT?
OH...
ONLY MR. MASAKAGE CAN TELL YOU THAT.
BUT NOW THAT HE'S GONE MISSING...
...THERE'S NO WAY TO KNOW HOW HIS ILLUSIONS WERE DONE.
COME TO THINK OF IT, DID YOU CHECK TO SEE IF THE MASAKAGE NOTES HAVE BEEN STOLEN?
I CAN'T. I DON'T KNOW WHERE HE KEPT THE NOTEBOOK, EXCEPT THAT IT WAS IN THE LIBRARY.
FOR ALL WE KNOW, HE TOOK IT WITH HIM TEN YEARS AGO.
HEY, YA GOT ANY *PHOTO ALBUMS?*
SAY WHAT?
WITH ALL THOSE GUESTS AND PARTIES, YOU MUST'VE TAKEN PICTURES!
MAYBE THERE'S A PHOTO OF YER SUSPECT IN THERE!
WHERE ARE YOUR PHOTOS?
IN MY HUSBAND'S ROOM.

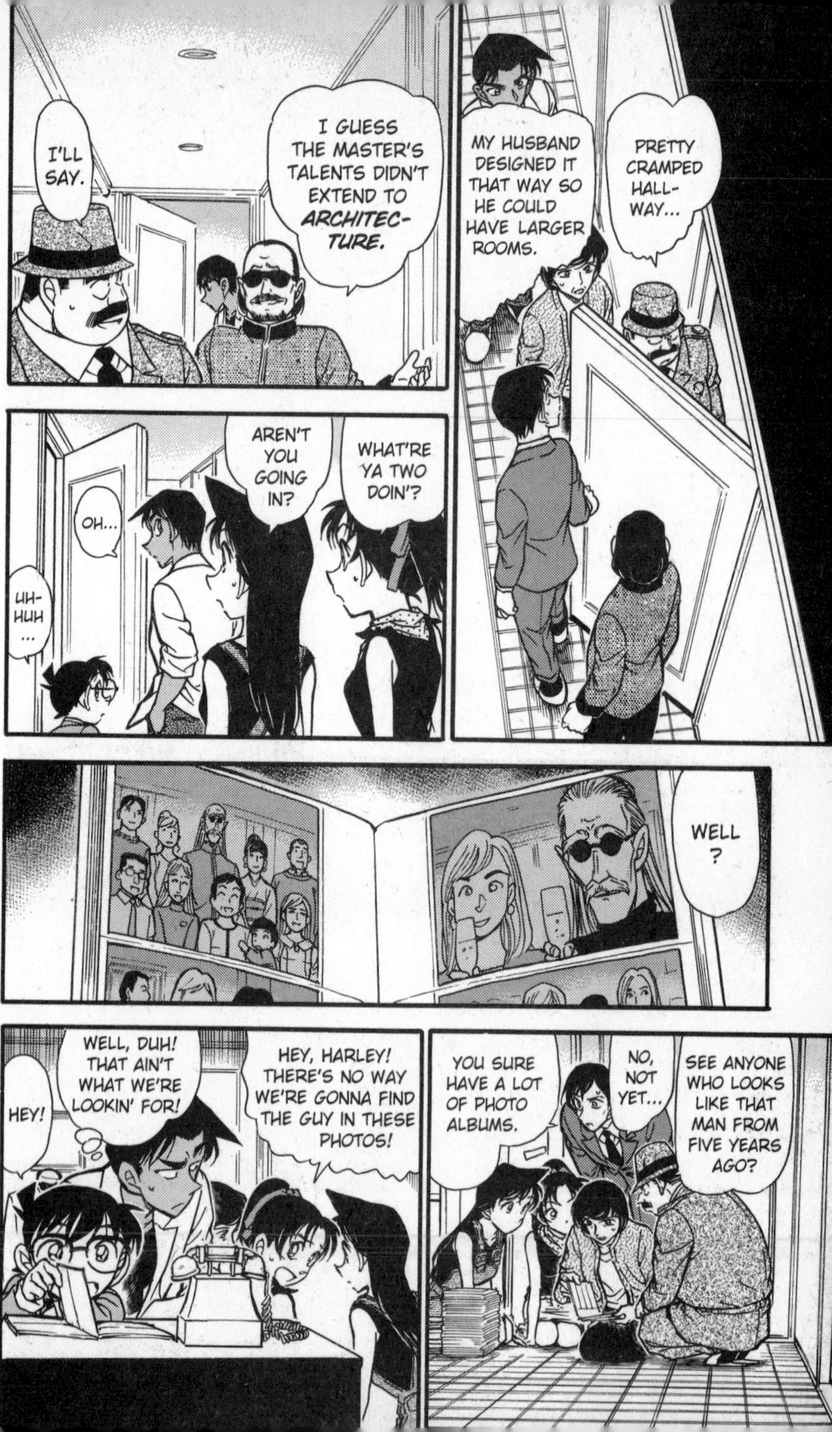
PRETTY CRAMPED HALL-WAY...
MY HUSBAND DESIGNED IT THAT WAY SO HE COULD HAVE LARGER ROOMS.
I GUESS THE MASTER'S TALENTS DIDN'T EXTEND TO *ARCHITEC-TURE.*
I'LL SAY.
WHAT'RE YA TWO DOIN'?
AREN'T YOU GOING IN?
OH...
UH-HUH...
WELL ?
SEE ANYONE WHO LOOKS LIKE THAT MAN FROM FIVE YEARS AGO?
NO, NOT YET...
YOU SURE HAVE A LOT OF PHOTO ALBUMS.
HEY, HARLEY! THERE'S NO WAY WE'RE GONNA FIND THE GUY IN THESE PHOTOS!
WELL, DUH! THAT AIN'T WHAT WE'RE LOOKIN' FOR!
HEY!

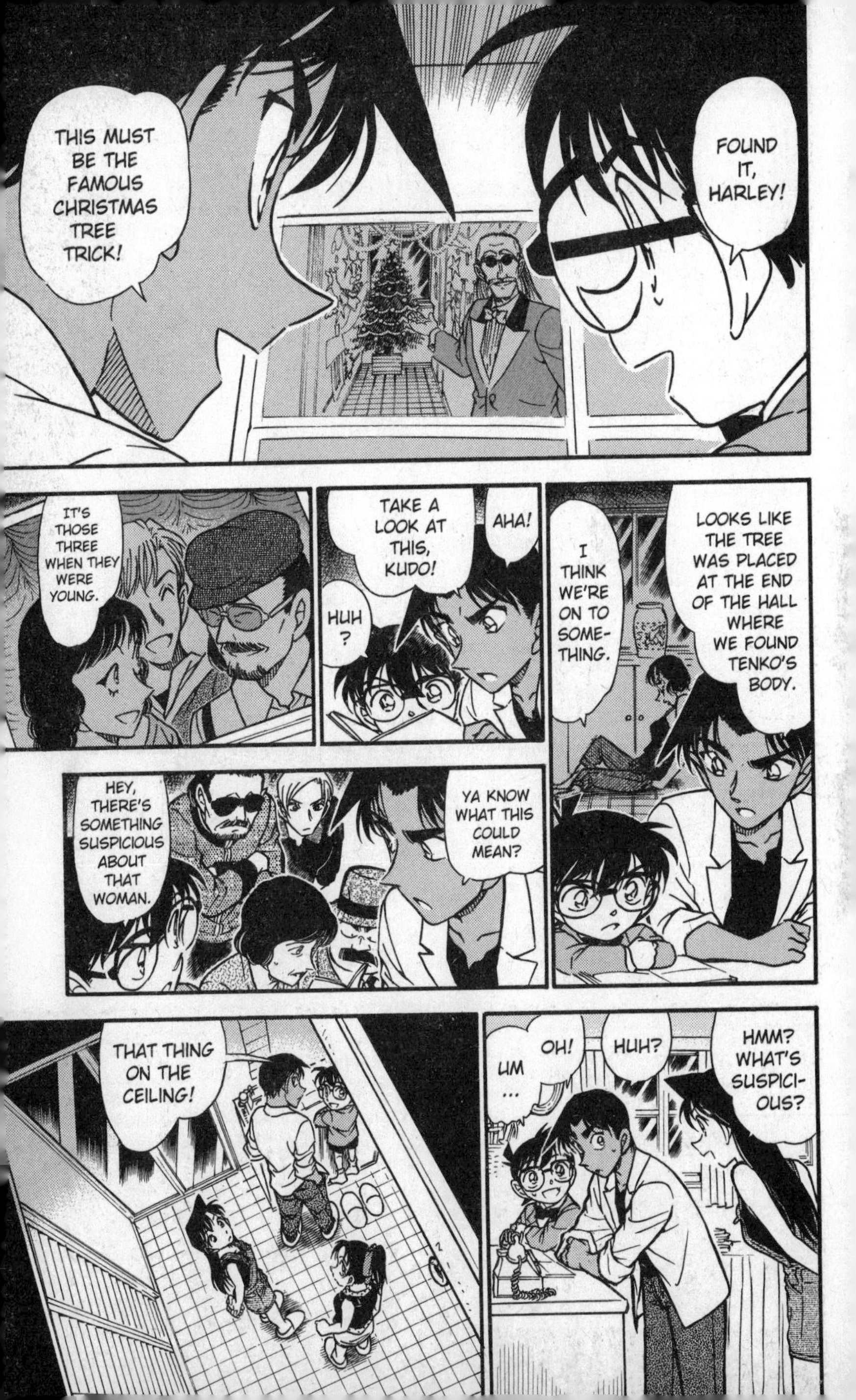
FOUND IT, HARLEY!
THIS MUST BE THE FAMOUS CHRISTMAS TREE TRICK!
LOOKS LIKE THE TREE WAS PLACED AT THE END OF THE HALL WHERE WE FOUND TENKO'S BODY.
I THINK WE'RE ON TO SOMETHING.
AHA!
TAKE A LOOK AT THIS, KUDO!
HUH?
IT'S THOSE THREE WHEN THEY WERE YOUNG.
YA KNOW WHAT THIS COULD MEAN?
HEY, THERE'S SOMETHING SUSPICIOUS ABOUT THAT WOMAN.
HMM? WHAT'S SUSPICIOUS?
HUH?
OH!
UM ...
THAT THING ON THE CEILING!

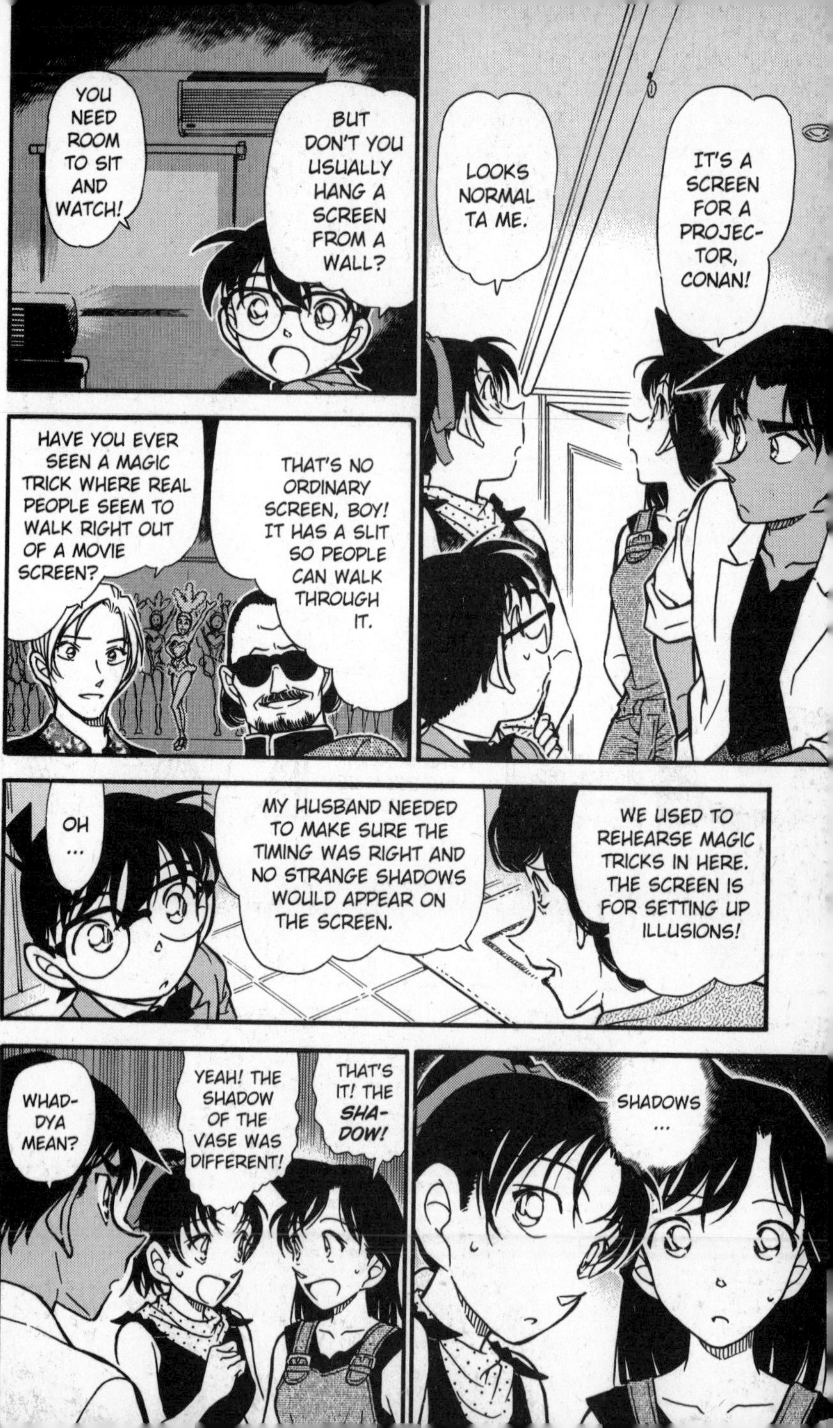
IT'S A SCREEN FOR A PROJECTOR, CONAN!
LOOKS NORMAL TA ME.
BUT DON'T YOU USUALLY HANG A SCREEN FROM A WALL?
YOU NEED ROOM TO SIT AND WATCH!
THAT'S NO ORDINARY SCREEN, BOY! IT HAS A SLIT SO PEOPLE CAN WALK THROUGH IT.
HAVE YOU EVER SEEN A MAGIC TRICK WHERE REAL PEOPLE SEEM TO WALK RIGHT OUT OF A MOVIE SCREEN?
WE USED TO REHEARSE MAGIC TRICKS IN HERE. THE SCREEN IS FOR SETTING UP ILLUSIONS!
MY HUSBAND NEEDED TO MAKE SURE THE TIMING WAS RIGHT AND NO STRANGE SHADOWS WOULD APPEAR ON THE SCREEN.
OH ...
SHADOWS ...
THAT'S IT! THE *SHADOW!*
YEAH! THE SHADOW OF THE VASE WAS DIFFERENT!
WHADDYA MEAN?

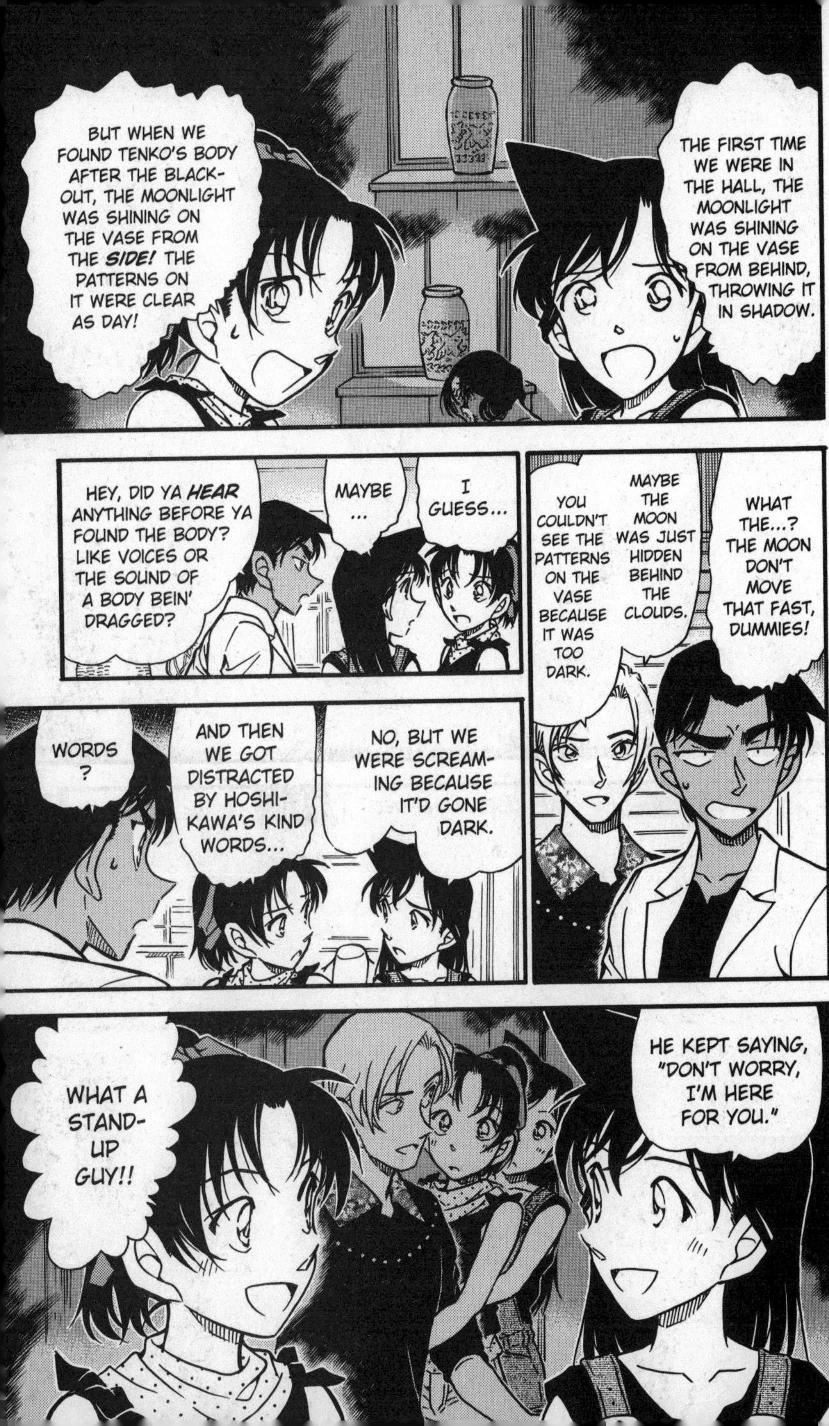
THE FIRST TIME WE WERE IN THE HALL, THE MOONLIGHT WAS SHINING ON THE VASE FROM BEHIND, THROWING IT IN SHADOW.
BUT WHEN WE FOUND TENKO'S BODY AFTER THE BLACK-OUT, THE MOONLIGHT WAS SHINING ON THE VASE FROM THE *SIDE!* THE PATTERNS ON IT WERE CLEAR AS DAY!
WHAT THE...? THE MOON DON'T MOVE THAT FAST, DUMMIES!
MAYBE THE MOON WAS JUST HIDDEN BEHIND THE CLOUDS.
YOU COULDN'T SEE THE PATTERNS ON THE VASE BECAUSE IT WAS TOO DARK.
HEY, DID YA *HEAR* ANYTHING BEFORE YA FOUND THE BODY? LIKE VOICES OR THE SOUND OF A BODY BEIN' DRAGGED?
MAYBE ...
I GUESS...
NO, BUT WE WERE SCREAM-ING BECAUSE IT'D GONE DARK.
AND THEN WE GOT DISTRACTED BY HOSHI-KAWA'S KIND WORDS...
WORDS ?
HE KEPT SAYING, "DON'T WORRY, I'M HERE FOR YOU."
WHAT A STAND-UP GUY!!

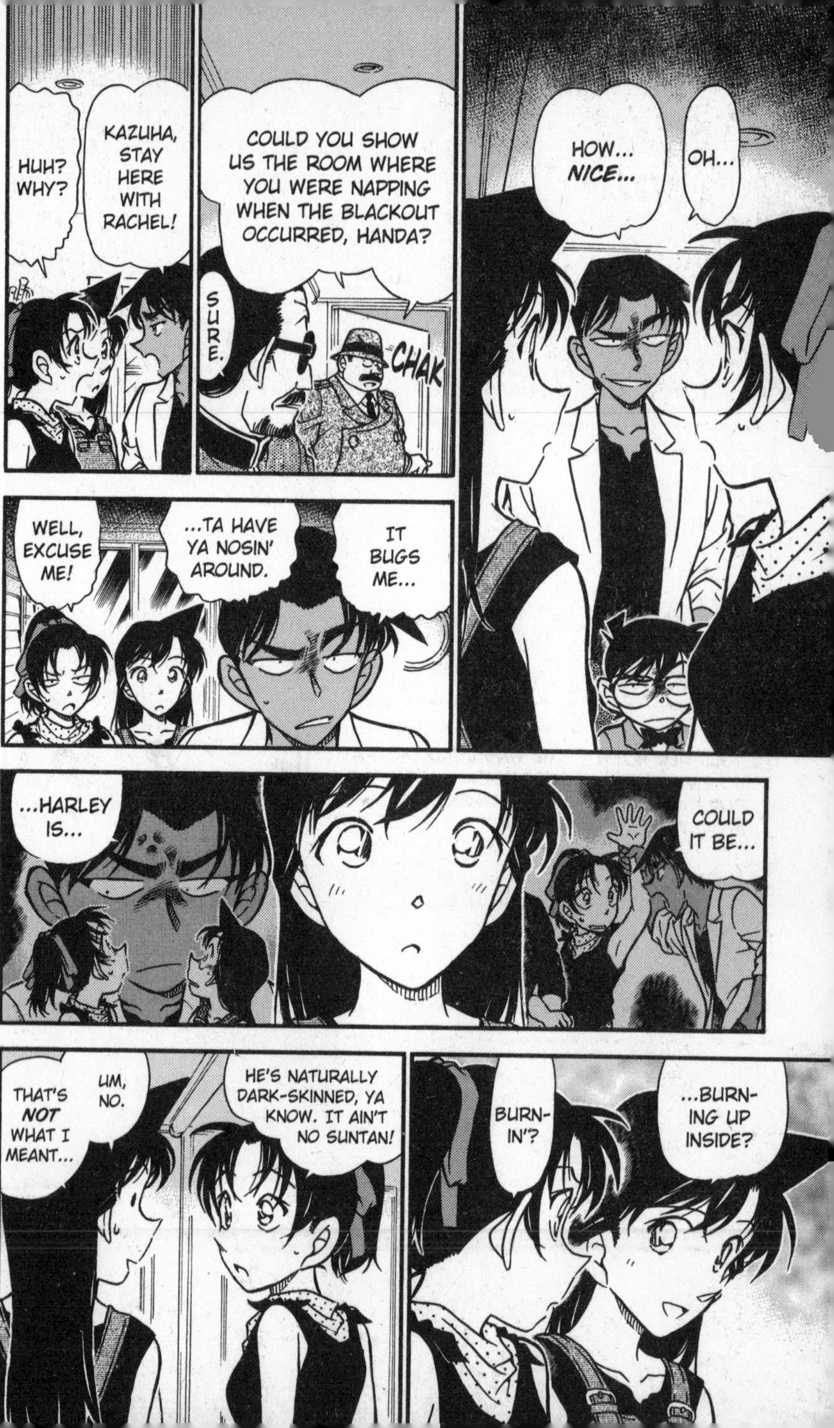
COULD YOU SHOW US THE ROOM WHERE YOU WERE NAPPING WHEN THE BLACKOUT OCCURRED, HANDA?
SURE.
CHAK
KAZUHA, STAY HERE WITH RACHEL!
HUH? WHY?
IT BUGS ME...
...TA HAVE YA NOSIN' AROUND.
WELL, EXCUSE ME!
OH...
HOW... NICE...
COULD IT BE...
...HARLEY IS...
...BURN-ING UP INSIDE?
BURN-IN'?
HE'S NATURALLY DARK-SKINNED, YA KNOW. IT AIN'T NO SUNTAN!
UM, NO.
THAT'S NOT WHAT I MEANT...

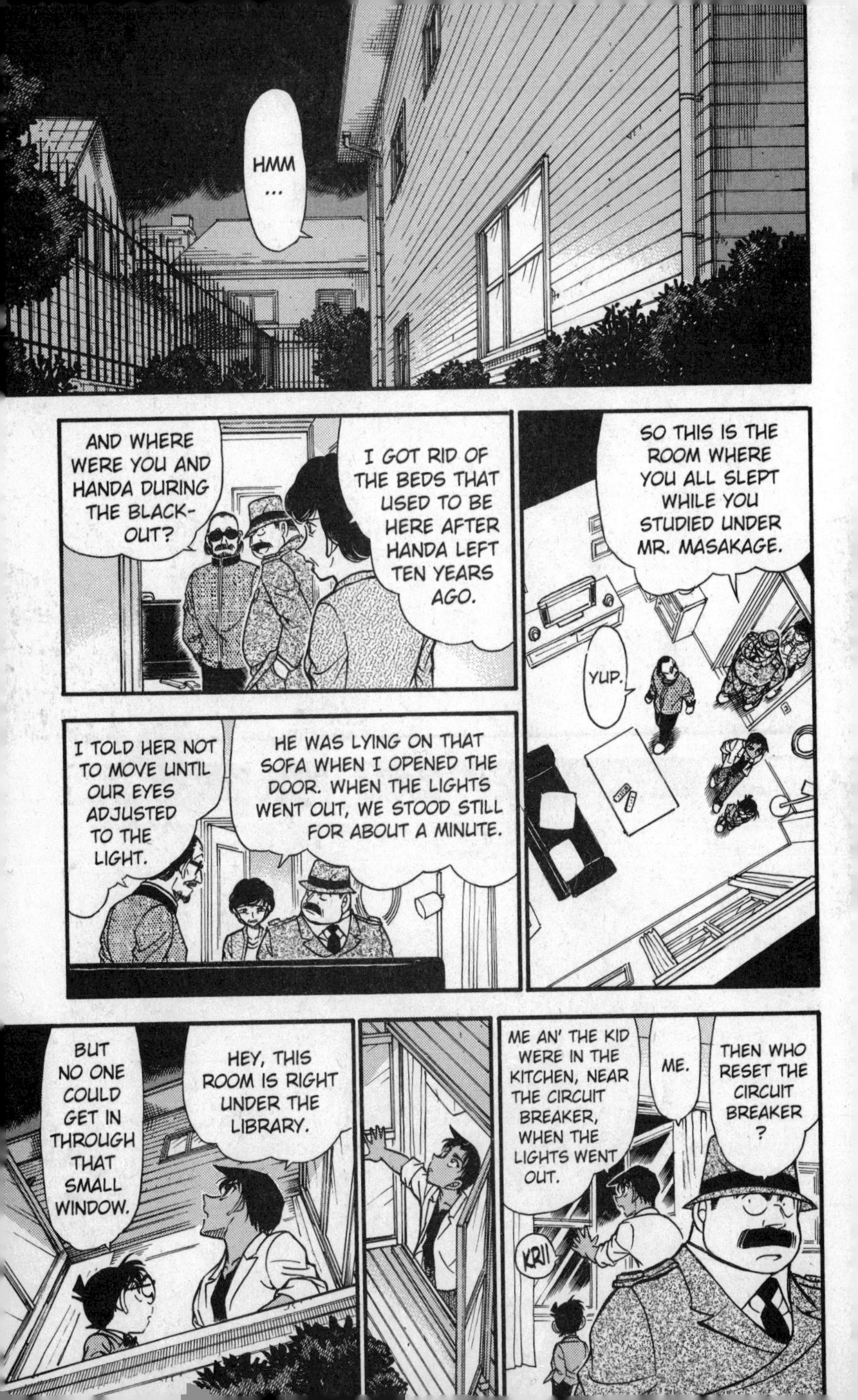
HMM ...
SO THIS IS THE ROOM WHERE YOU ALL SLEPT WHILE YOU STUDIED UNDER MR. MASAKAGE.
YUP.
I GOT RID OF THE BEDS THAT USED TO BE HERE AFTER HANDA LEFT TEN YEARS AGO.
AND WHERE WERE YOU AND HANDA DURING THE BLACK-OUT?
HE WAS LYING ON THAT SOFA WHEN I OPENED THE DOOR. WHEN THE LIGHTS WENT OUT, WE STOOD STILL FOR ABOUT A MINUTE.
I TOLD HER NOT TO MOVE UNTIL OUR EYES ADJUSTED TO THE LIGHT.
THEN WHO RESET THE CIRCUIT BREAKER?
ME.
ME AN' THE KID WERE IN THE KITCHEN, NEAR THE CIRCUIT BREAKER, WHEN THE LIGHTS WENT OUT.
KRII
HEY, THIS ROOM IS RIGHT UNDER THE LIBRARY.
BUT NO ONE COULD GET IN THROUGH THAT SMALL WINDOW.

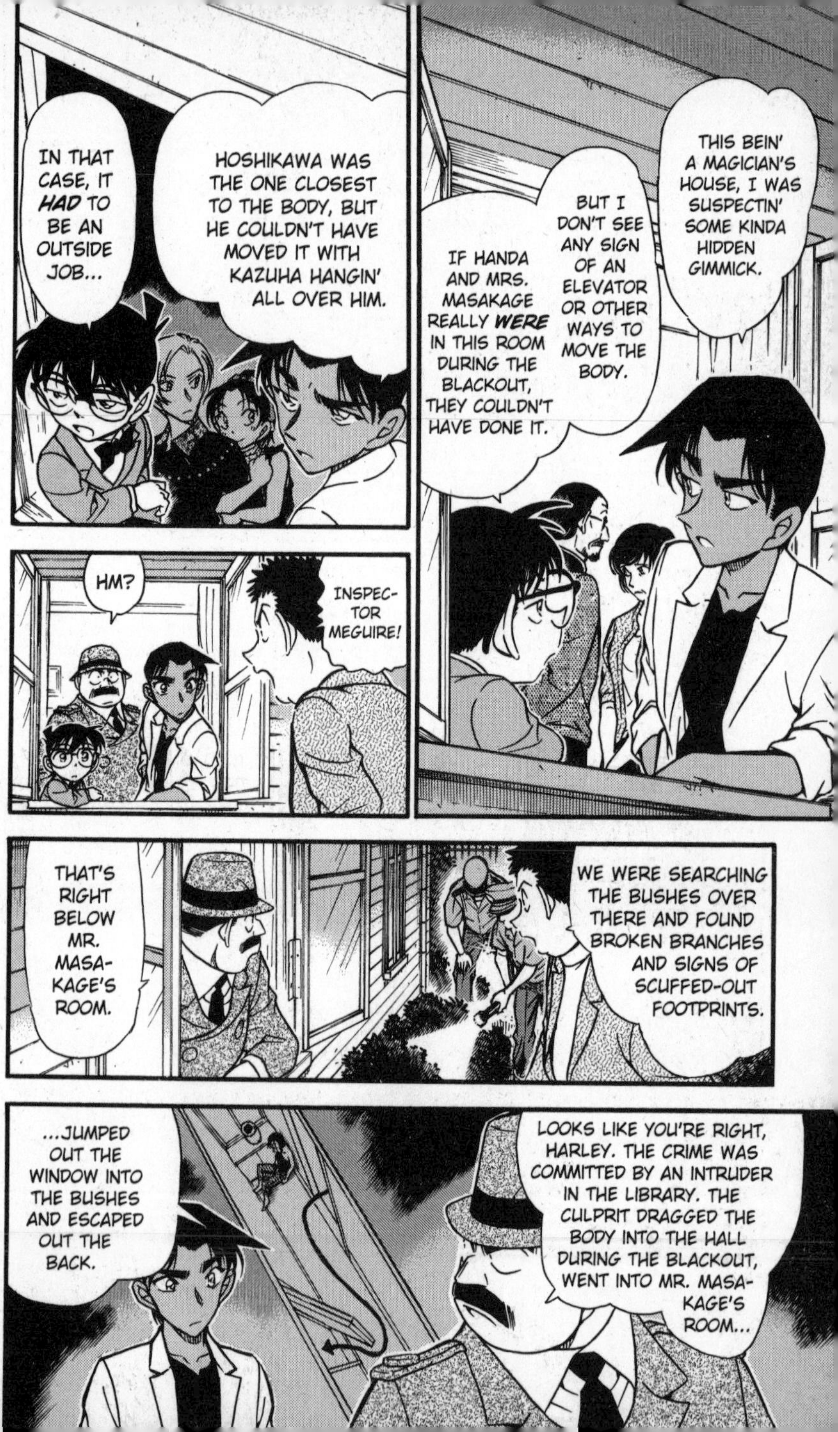
THIS BEIN' A MAGICIAN'S HOUSE, I WAS SUSPECTIN' SOME KINDA HIDDEN GIMMICK.
BUT I DON'T SEE ANY SIGN OF AN ELEVATOR OR OTHER WAYS TO MOVE THE BODY.
IF HANDA AND MRS. MASAKAGE REALLY *WERE* IN THIS ROOM DURING THE BLACKOUT, THEY COULDN'T HAVE DONE IT.
HOSHIKAWA WAS THE ONE CLOSEST TO THE BODY, BUT HE COULDN'T HAVE MOVED IT WITH KAZUHA HANGIN' ALL OVER HIM.
IN THAT CASE, IT *HAD* TO BE AN OUTSIDE JOB...
INSPEC-TOR MEGUIRE!
HM?
WE WERE SEARCHING THE BUSHES OVER THERE AND FOUND BROKEN BRANCHES AND SIGNS OF SCUFFED-OUT FOOTPRINTS.
THAT'S RIGHT BELOW MR. MASA-KAGE'S ROOM.
LOOKS LIKE YOU'RE RIGHT, HARLEY. THE CRIME WAS COMMITTED BY AN INTRUDER IN THE LIBRARY. THE CULPRIT DRAGGED THE BODY INTO THE HALL DURING THE BLACKOUT, WENT INTO MR. MASA-KAGE'S ROOM...
...JUMPED OUT THE WINDOW INTO THE BUSHES AND ESCAPED OUT THE BACK.

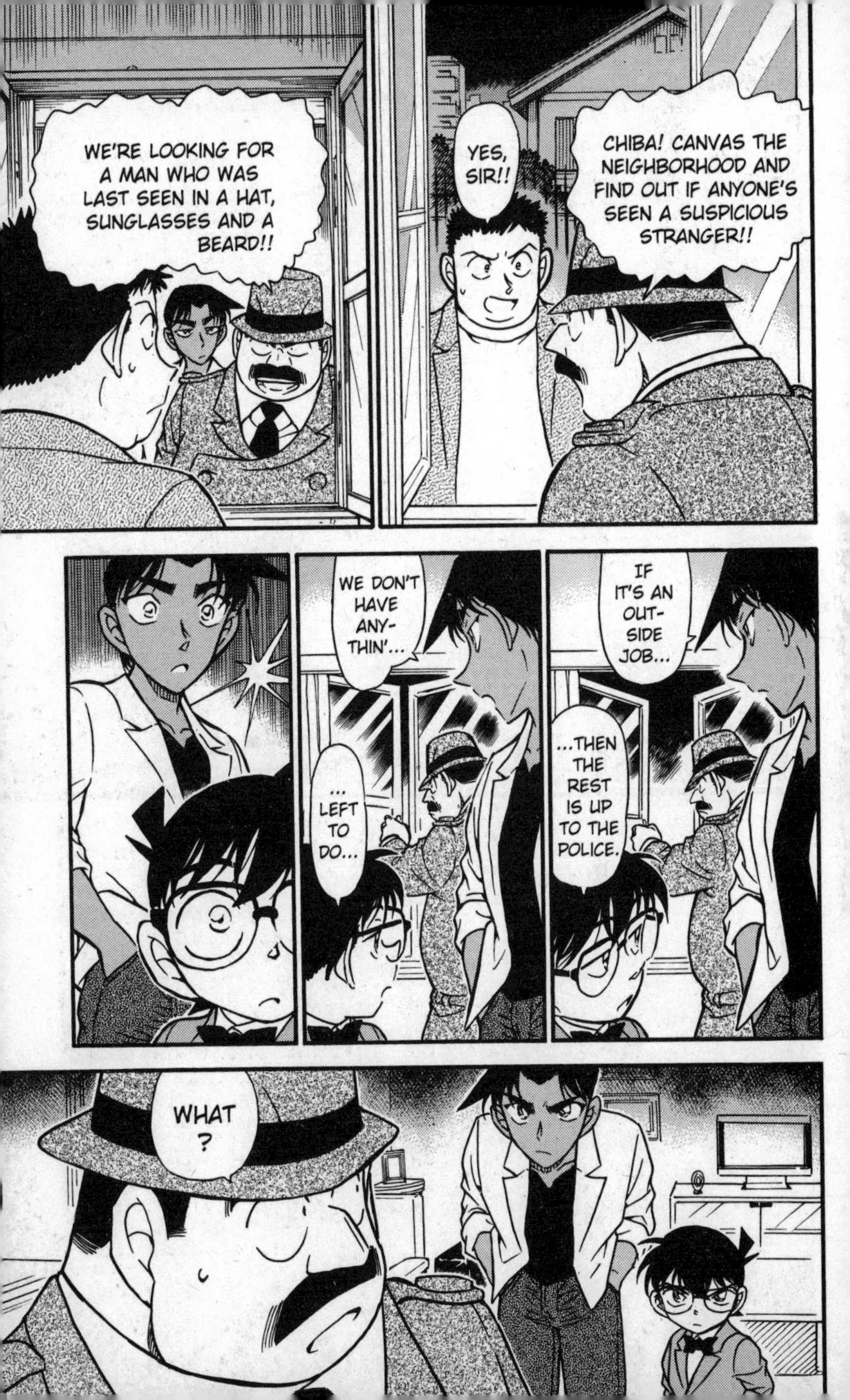
CHIBA! CANVAS THE NEIGHBORHOOD AND FIND OUT IF ANYONE'S SEEN A SUSPICIOUS STRANGER!!
YES, SIR!!
WE'RE LOOKING FOR A MAN WHO WAS LAST SEEN IN A HAT, SUNGLASSES AND A BEARD!!
IF IT'S AN OUT-SIDE JOB...
...THEN THE REST IS UP TO THE POLICE.
WE DON'T HAVE ANY-THIN'...
...LEFT TO DO...
WHAT?

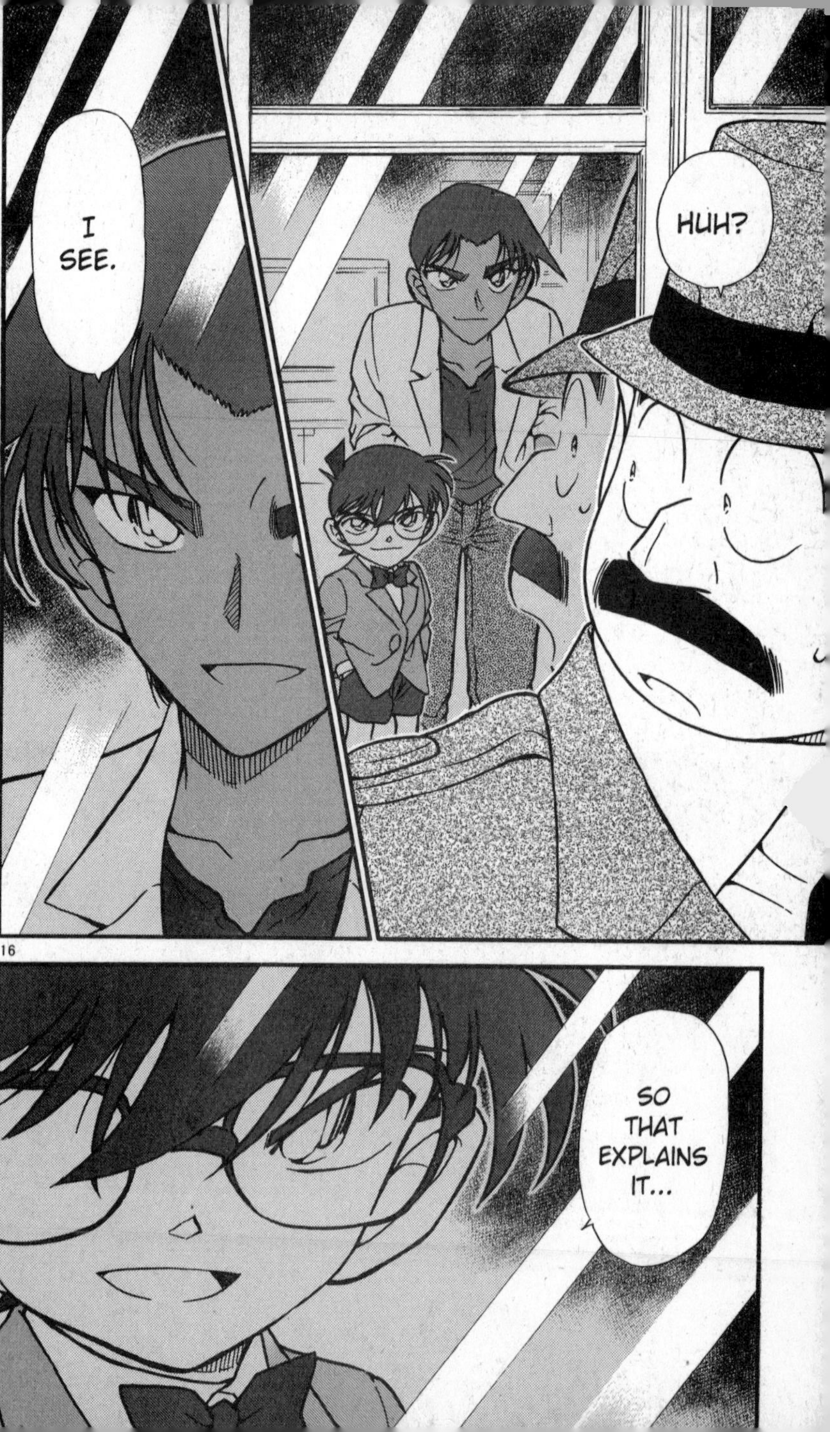
HUH?
I SEE.
SO THAT EXPLAINS IT...

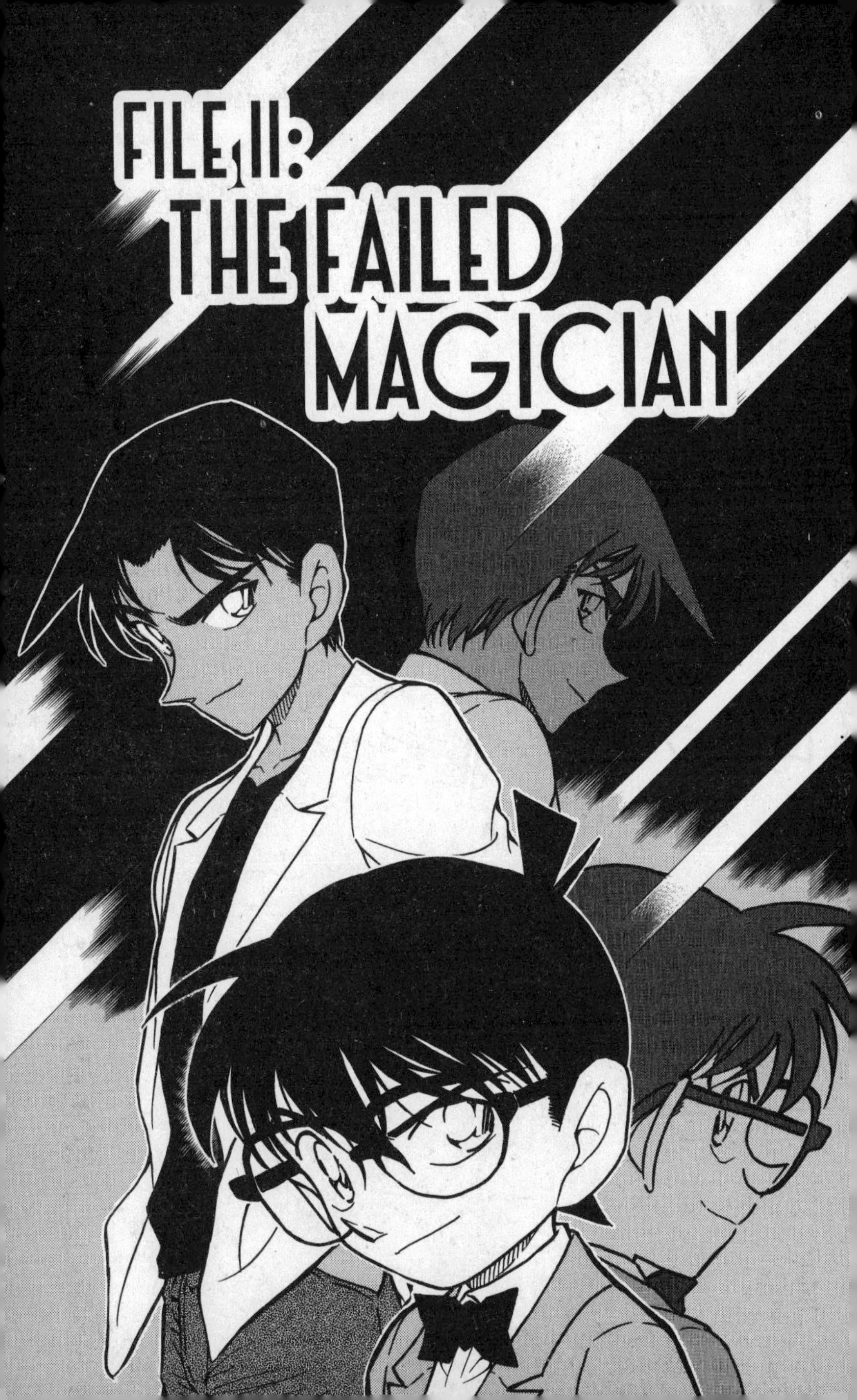
FILE 11:
THE FAILED MAGICIAN

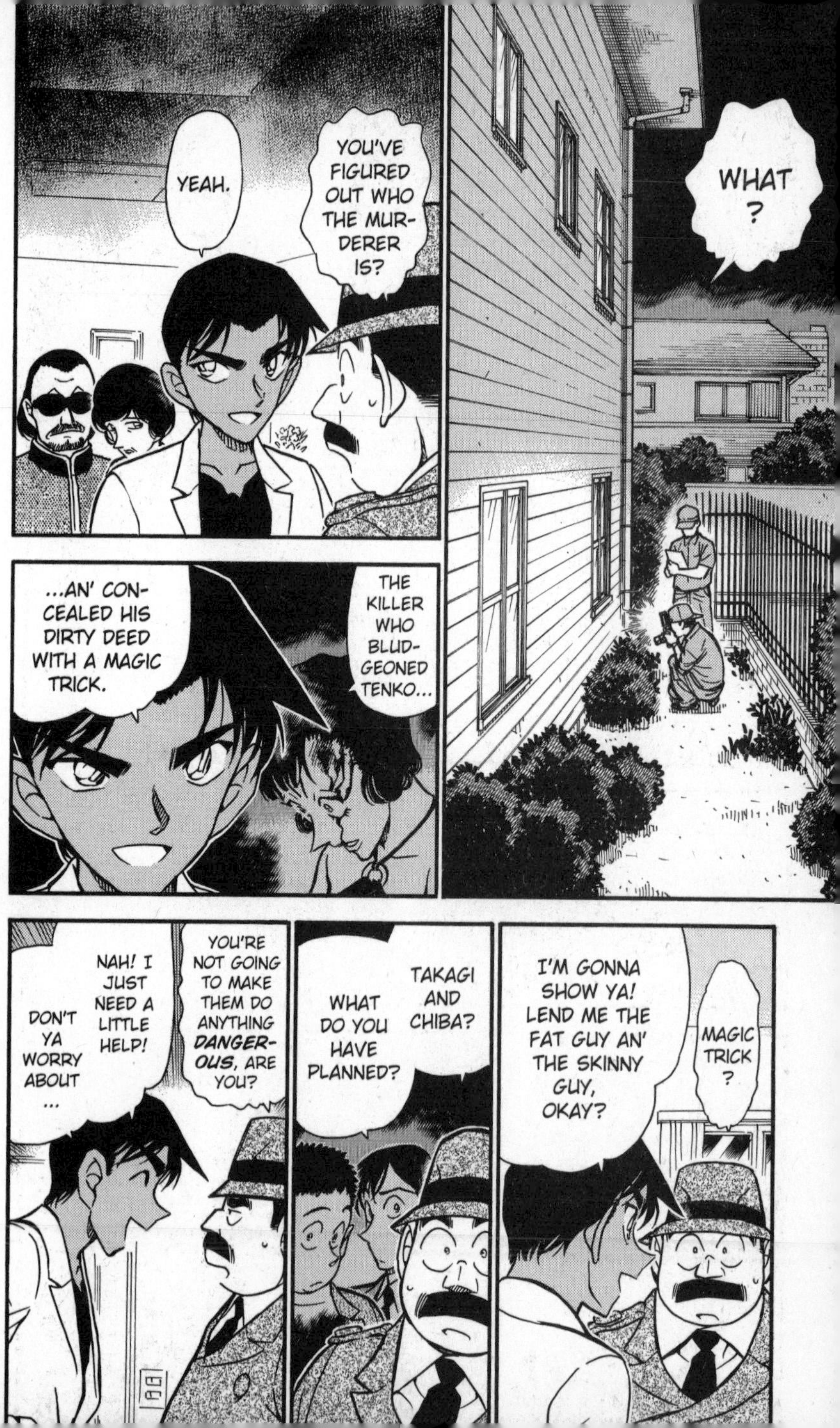
YOU'VE FIGURED OUT WHO THE MURDERER IS?
YEAH.
THE KILLER WHO BLUDGEONED TENKO...
...AN' CONCEALED HIS DIRTY DEED WITH A MAGIC TRICK.
WHAT?
MAGIC TRICK?
I'M GONNA SHOW YA! LEND ME THE FAT GUY AN' THE SKINNY GUY, OKAY?
TAKAGI AND CHIBA?
WHAT DO YOU HAVE PLANNED?
YOU'RE NOT GOING TO MAKE THEM DO ANYTHING *DANGEROUS*, ARE YOU?
NAH! I JUST NEED A LITTLE HELP!
DON'T YA WORRY ABOUT...

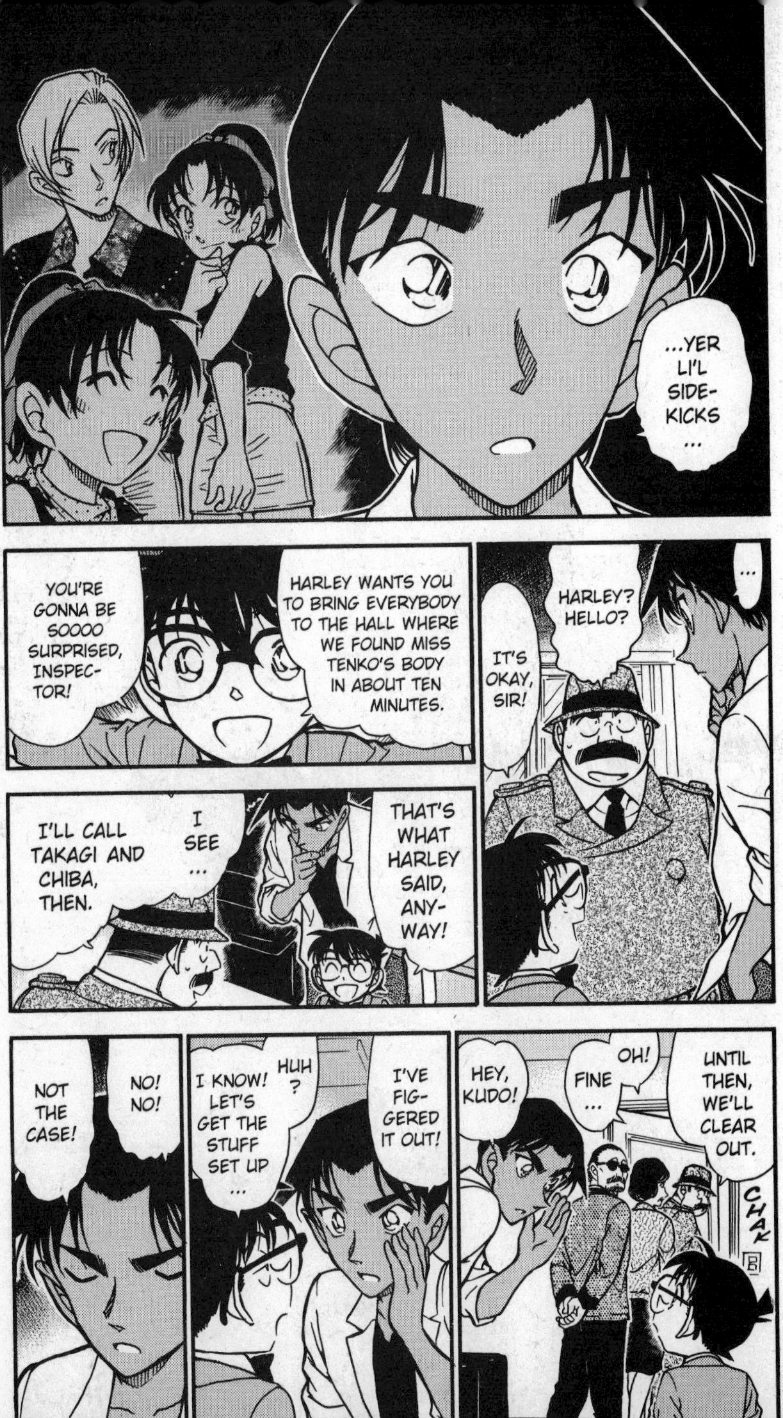
...YER LI'L SIDE-KICKS ...
...
HARLEY? HELLO?
IT'S OKAY, SIR!
HARLEY WANTS YOU TO BRING EVERYBODY TO THE HALL WHERE WE FOUND MISS TENKO'S BODY IN ABOUT TEN MINUTES.
YOU'RE GONNA BE SOOOO SURPRISED, INSPEC-TOR!
THAT'S WHAT HARLEY SAID, ANY-WAY!
I SEE ...
I'LL CALL TAKAGI AND CHIBA, THEN.
UNTIL THEN, WE'LL CLEAR OUT.
CHAK
OH!
FINE ...
HEY, KUDO!
I'VE FIG-GERED IT OUT!
HUH ?
I KNOW! LET'S GET THE STUFF SET UP ...
NO! NO!
NOT THE CASE!

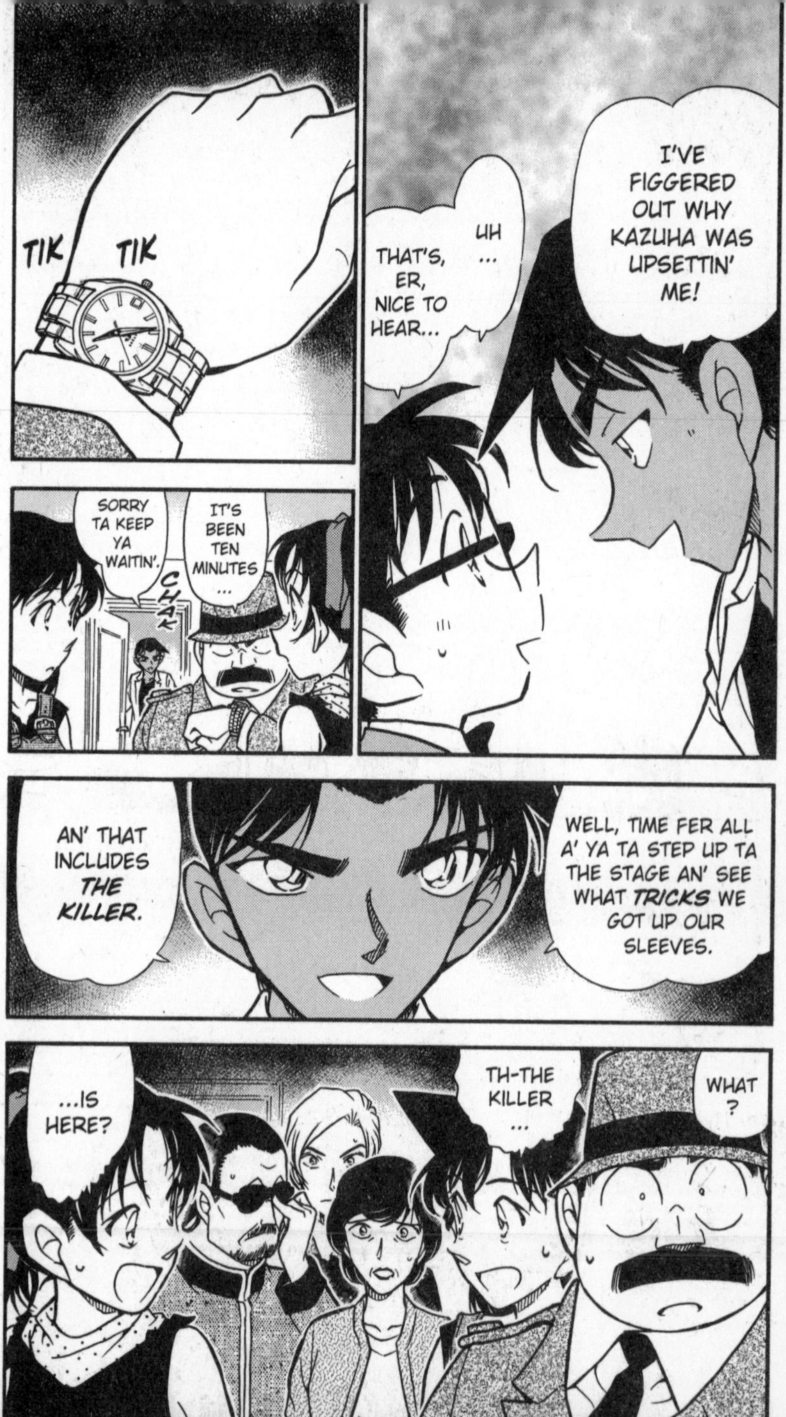
I'VE FIGGERED OUT WHY KAZUHA WAS UPSETTIN' ME!
UH ...
THAT'S, ER, NICE TO HEAR...
TIK TIK
IT'S BEEN TEN MINUTES ...
SORRY TA KEEP YA WAITIN'.
CHAK
WELL, TIME FER ALL A' YA TA STEP UP TA THE STAGE AN' SEE WHAT TRICKS WE GOT UP OUR SLEEVES.
AN' THAT INCLUDES THE KILLER.
WHAT ?
TH-THE KILLER ...
...IS HERE?

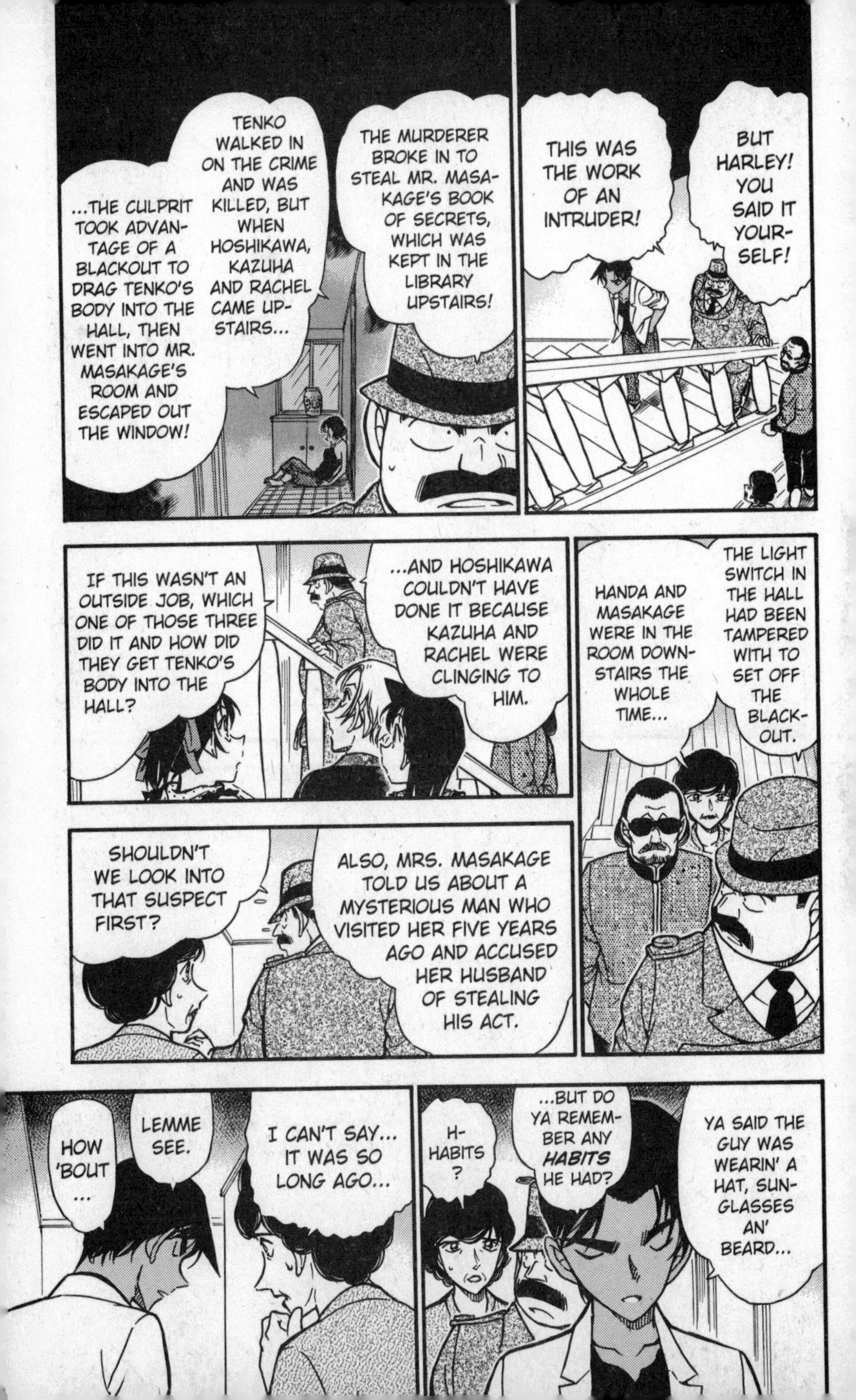
BUT HARLEY! YOU SAID IT YOURSELF!
THIS WAS THE WORK OF AN INTRUDER!
THE MURDERER BROKE IN TO STEAL MR. MASAKAGE'S BOOK OF SECRETS, WHICH WAS KEPT IN THE LIBRARY UPSTAIRS!
TENKO WALKED IN ON THE CRIME AND WAS KILLED, BUT WHEN HOSHIKAWA, KAZUHA AND RACHEL CAME UPSTAIRS...
...THE CULPRIT TOOK ADVANTAGE OF A BLACKOUT TO DRAG TENKO'S BODY INTO THE HALL, THEN WENT INTO MR. MASAKAGE'S ROOM AND ESCAPED OUT THE WINDOW!
THE LIGHT SWITCH IN THE HALL HAD BEEN TAMPERED WITH TO SET OFF THE BLACKOUT.
HANDA AND MASAKAGE WERE IN THE ROOM DOWNSTAIRS THE WHOLE TIME...
...AND HOSHIKAWA COULDN'T HAVE DONE IT BECAUSE KAZUHA AND RACHEL WERE CLINGING TO HIM.
IF THIS WASN'T AN OUTSIDE JOB, WHICH ONE OF THOSE THREE DID IT AND HOW DID THEY GET TENKO'S BODY INTO THE HALL?
ALSO, MRS. MASAKAGE TOLD US ABOUT A MYSTERIOUS MAN WHO VISITED HER FIVE YEARS AGO AND ACCUSED HER HUSBAND OF STEALING HIS ACT.
SHOULDN'T WE LOOK INTO THAT SUSPECT FIRST?
YA SAID THE GUY WAS WEARIN' A HAT, SUNGLASSES AN' BEARD...
...BUT DO YA REMEMBER ANY *HABITS* HE HAD?
H-HABITS?
I CAN'T SAY... IT WAS SO LONG AGO...
LEMME SEE.
HOW 'BOUT ...

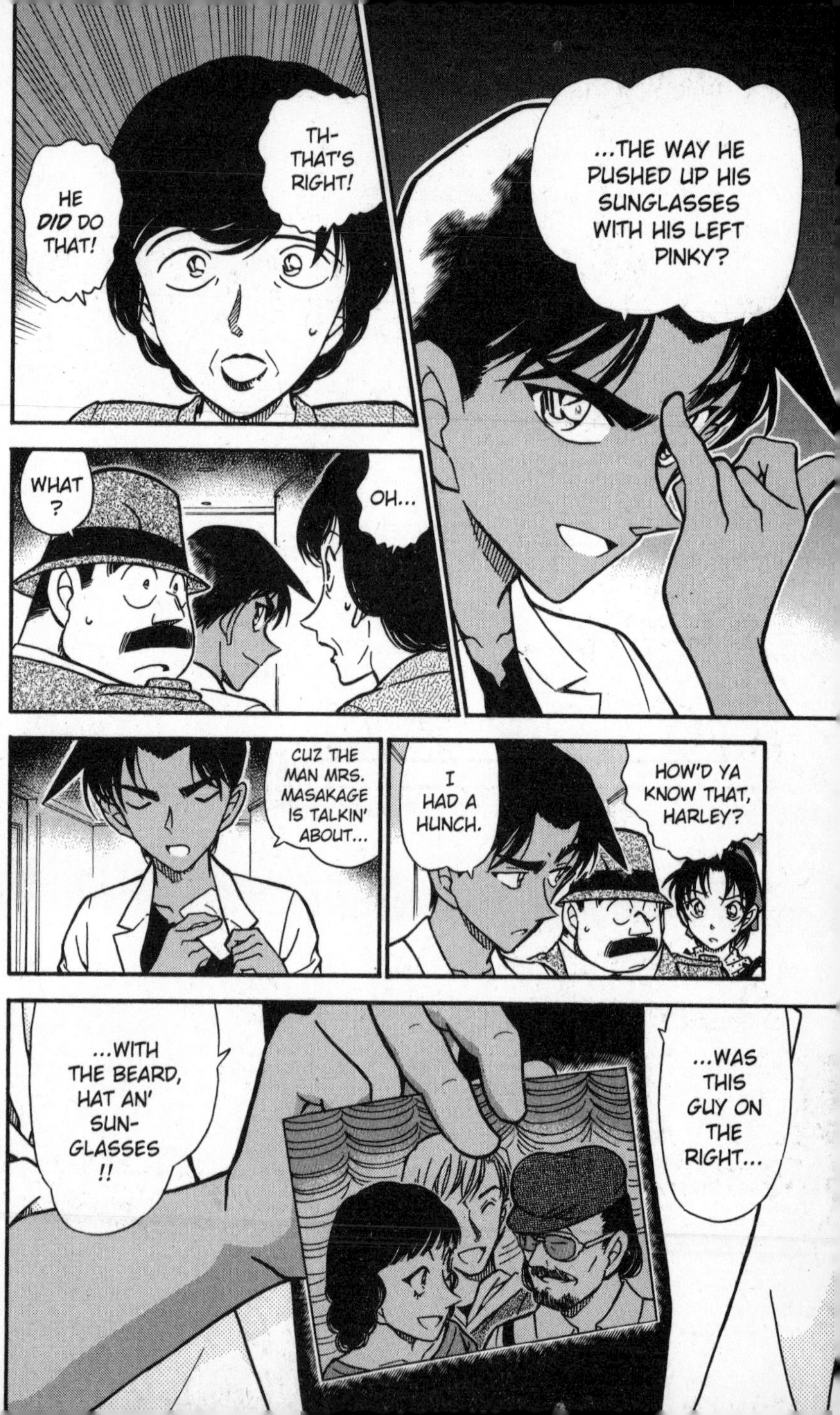
...THE WAY HE PUSHED UP HIS SUNGLASSES WITH HIS LEFT PINKY?
TH- THAT'S RIGHT!
HE *DID* DO THAT!
OH...
WHAT?
HOW'D YA KNOW THAT, HARLEY?
I HAD A HUNCH.
CUZ THE MAN MRS. MASAKAGE IS TALKIN' ABOUT...
...WAS THIS GUY ON THE RIGHT...
...WITH THE BEARD, HAT AN' SUN-GLASSES!!

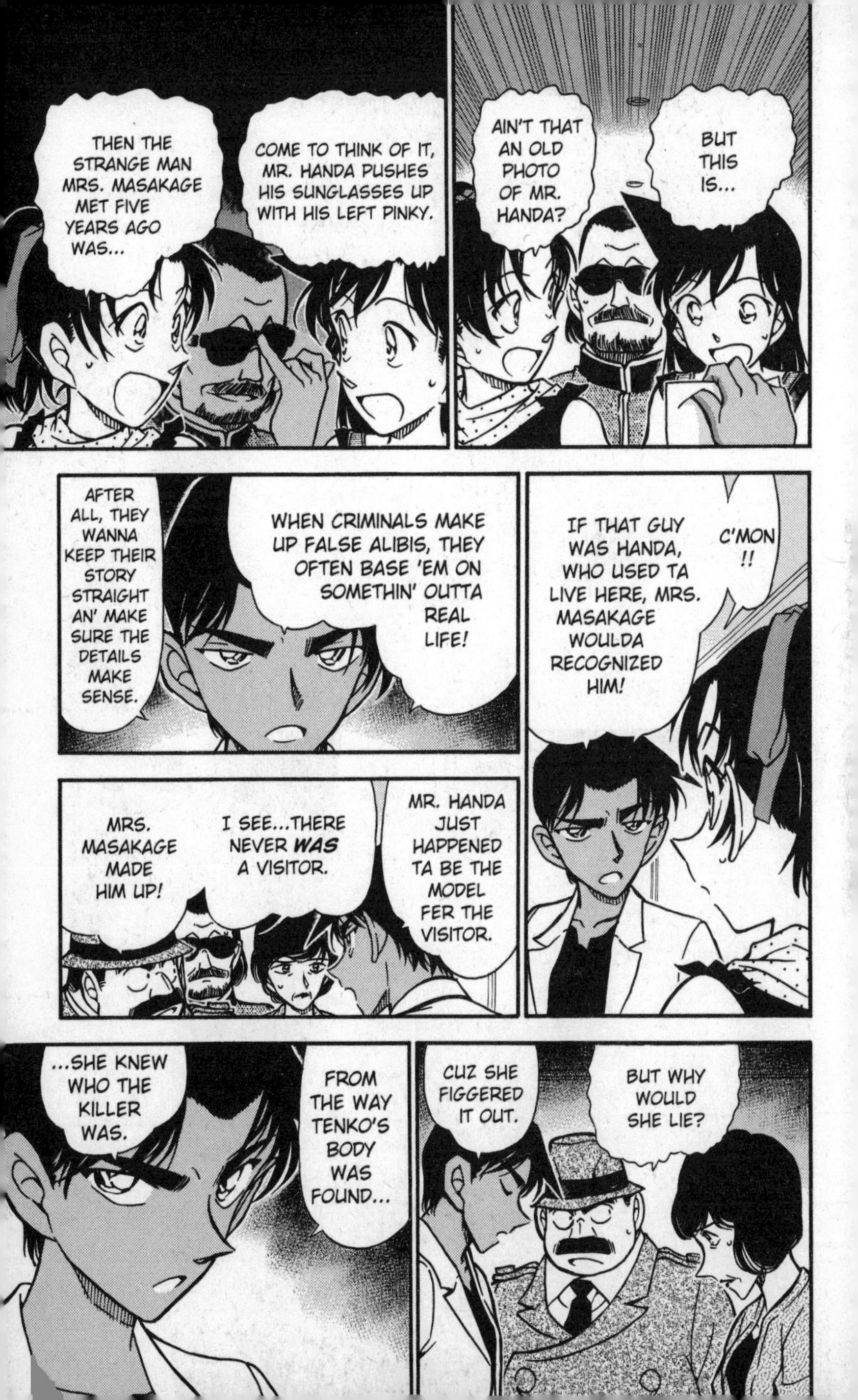
BUT THIS IS...
AIN'T THAT AN OLD PHOTO OF MR. HANDA?
COME TO THINK OF IT, MR. HANDA PUSHES HIS SUNGLASSES UP WITH HIS LEFT PINKY.
THEN THE STRANGE MAN MRS. MASAKAGE MET FIVE YEARS AGO WAS...
C'MON !!
IF THAT GUY WAS HANDA, WHO USED TA LIVE HERE, MRS. MASAKAGE WOULDA RECOGNIZED HIM!
WHEN CRIMINALS MAKE UP FALSE ALIBIS, THEY OFTEN BASE 'EM ON SOMETHIN' OUTTA REAL LIFE!
AFTER ALL, THEY WANNA KEEP THEIR STORY STRAIGHT AN' MAKE SURE THE DETAILS MAKE SENSE.
MR. HANDA JUST HAPPENED TA BE THE MODEL FER THE VISITOR.
I SEE...THERE NEVER *WAS* A VISITOR.
MRS. MASAKAGE MADE HIM UP!
BUT WHY WOULD SHE LIE?
CUZ SHE FIGGERED IT OUT.
FROM THE WAY TENKO'S BODY WAS FOUND...
...SHE KNEW WHO THE KILLER WAS.

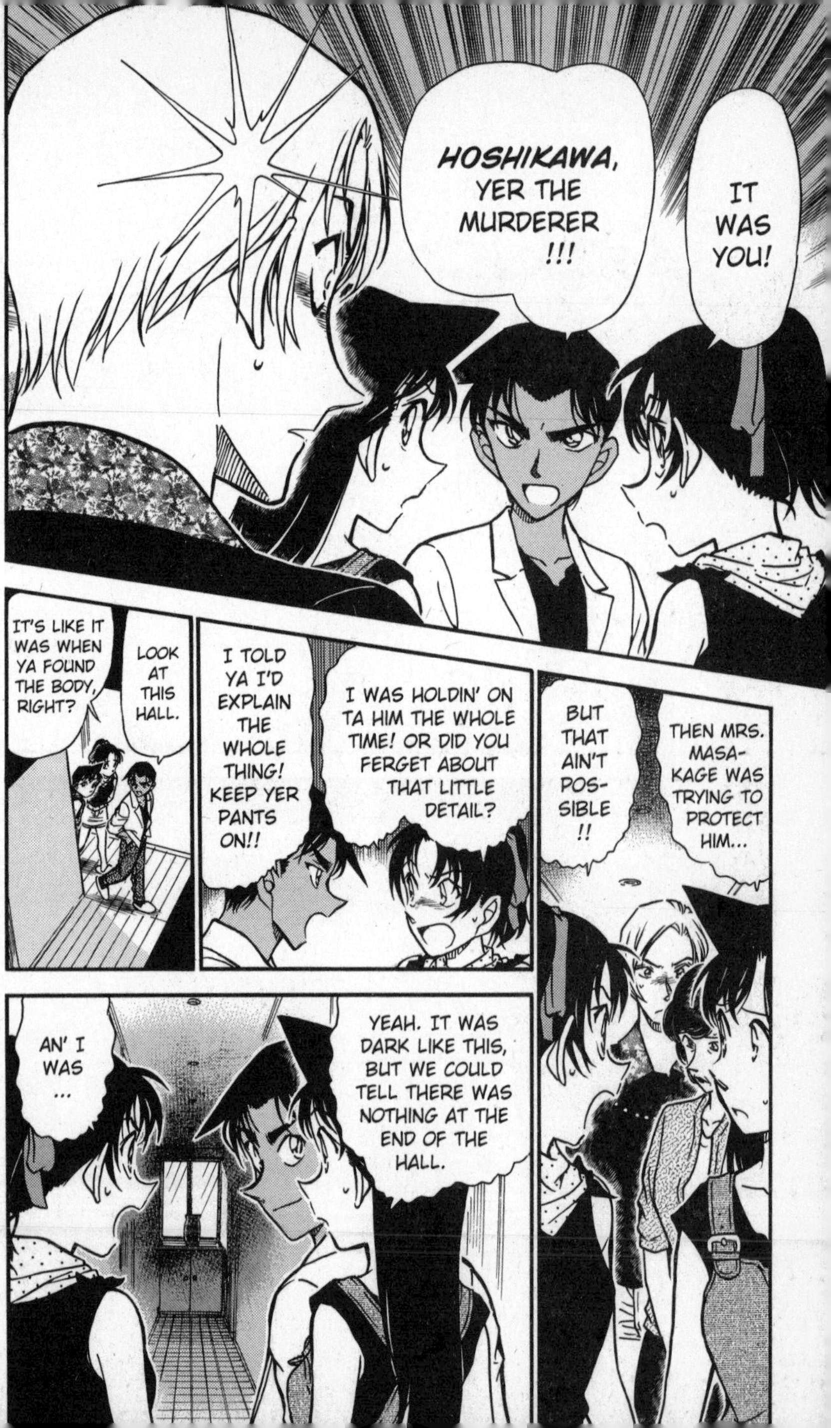
IT WAS YOU!
HOSHIKAWA, YER THE MURDERER !!!
THEN MRS. MASA-KAGE WAS TRYING TO PROTECT HIM...
BUT THAT AIN'T POS-SIBLE !!
I WAS HOLDIN' ON TA HIM THE WHOLE TIME! OR DID YOU FERGET ABOUT THAT LITTLE DETAIL?
I TOLD YA I'D EXPLAIN THE WHOLE THING! KEEP YER PANTS ON!!
LOOK AT THIS HALL.
IT'S LIKE IT WAS WHEN YA FOUND THE BODY, RIGHT?
YEAH. IT WAS DARK LIKE THIS, BUT WE COULD TELL THERE WAS NOTHING AT THE END OF THE HALL.
AN' I WAS ...

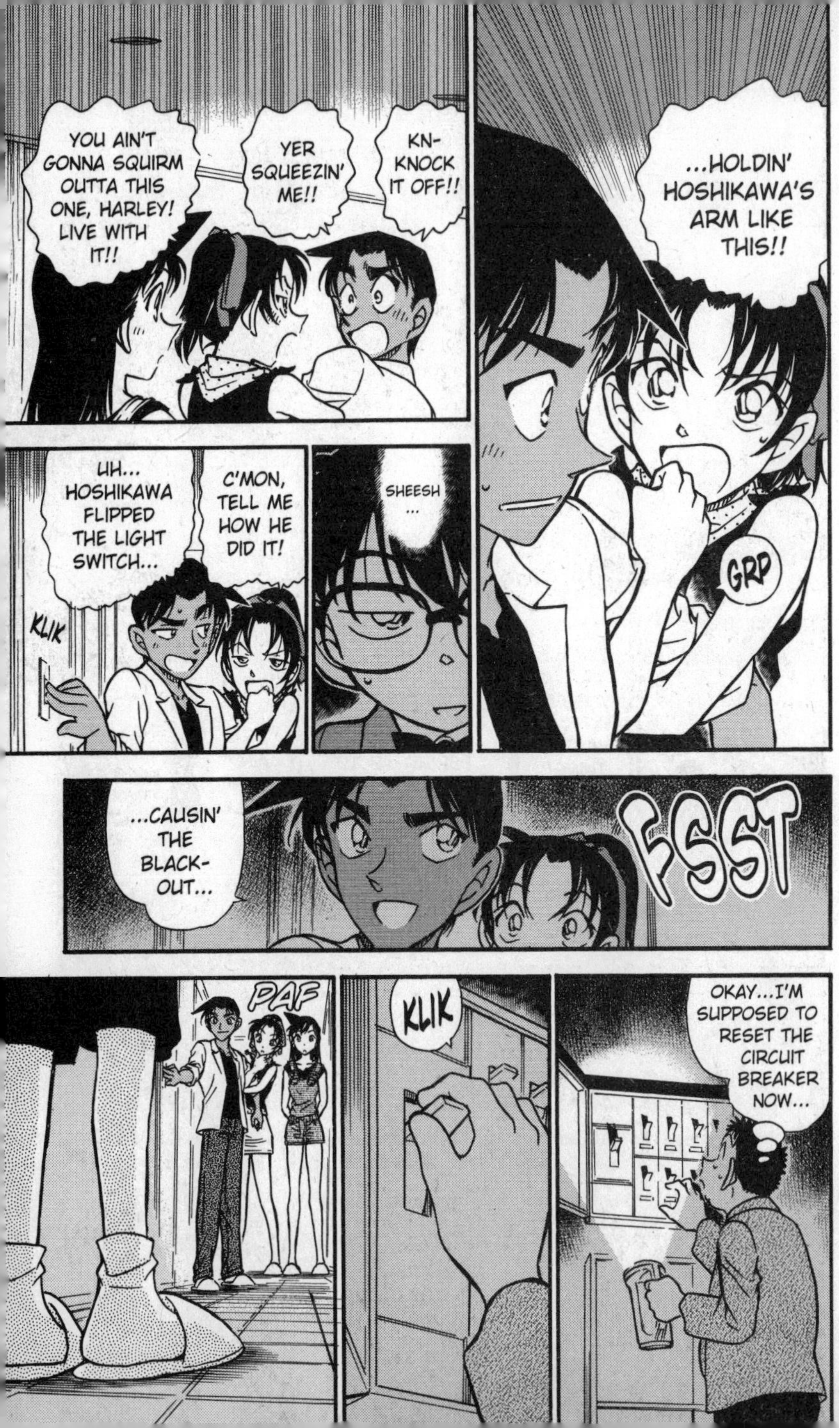
...HOLDIN' HOSHIKAWA'S ARM LIKE THIS!!
GRP
KN-KNOCK IT OFF!!
YER SQUEEZIN' ME!!
YOU AIN'T GONNA SQUIRM OUTTA THIS ONE, HARLEY! LIVE WITH IT!!
SHEESH ...
C'MON, TELL ME HOW HE DID IT!
UH... HOSHIKAWA FLIPPED THE LIGHT SWITCH...
KLIK
FSST
...CAUSIN' THE BLACK-OUT...
OKAY...I'M SUPPOSED TO RESET THE CIRCUIT BREAKER NOW...
KLIK
PAF

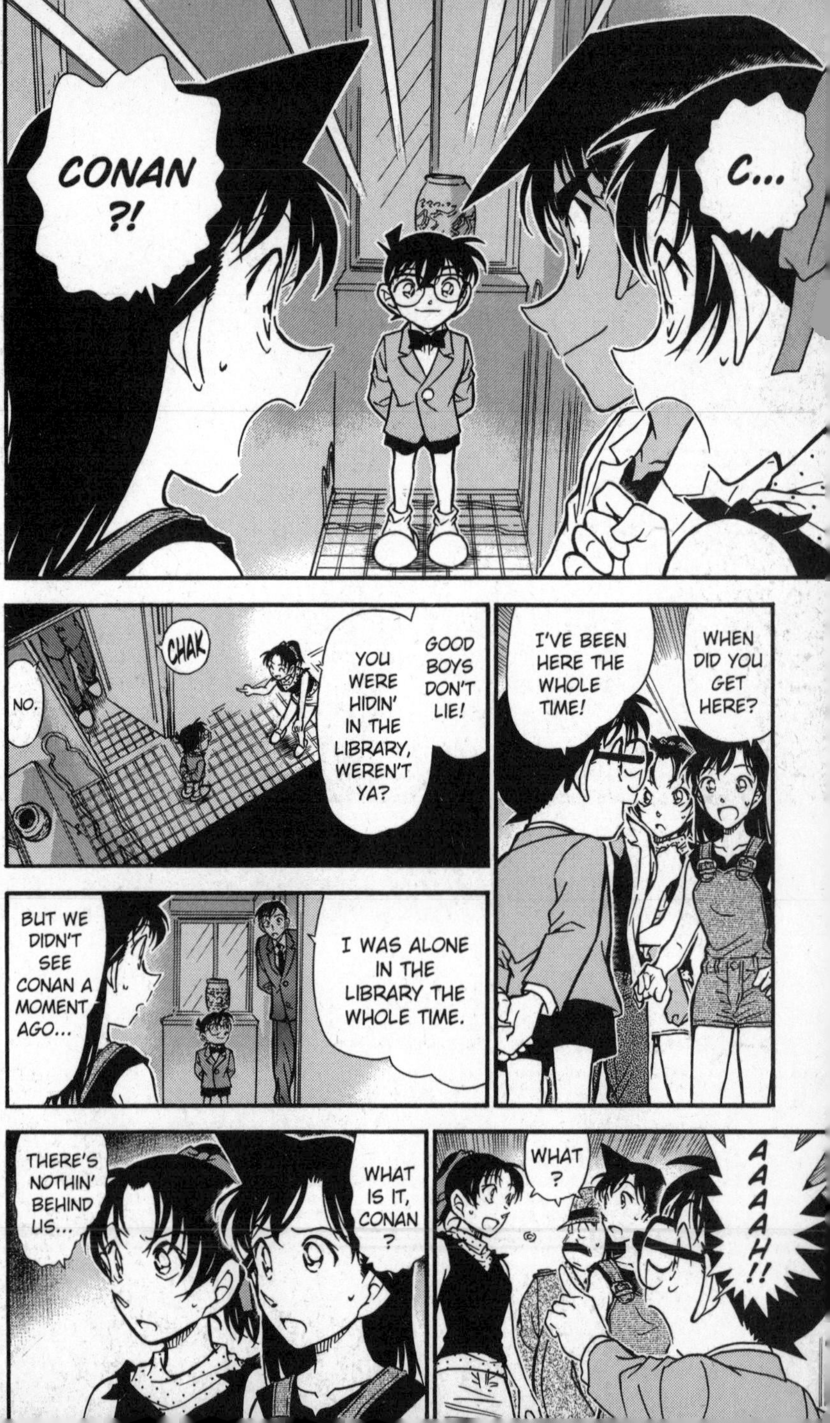
C...
CONAN ?!
WHEN DID YOU GET HERE?
I'VE BEEN HERE THE WHOLE TIME!
GOOD BOYS DON'T LIE!
YOU WERE HIDIN' IN THE LIBRARY, WEREN'T YA?
CHAK
NO.
I WAS ALONE IN THE LIBRARY THE WHOLE TIME.
BUT WE DIDN'T SEE CONAN A MOMENT AGO...
AAAAH!!
WHAT?
WHAT IS IT, CONAN?
THERE'S NOTHIN' BEHIND US...

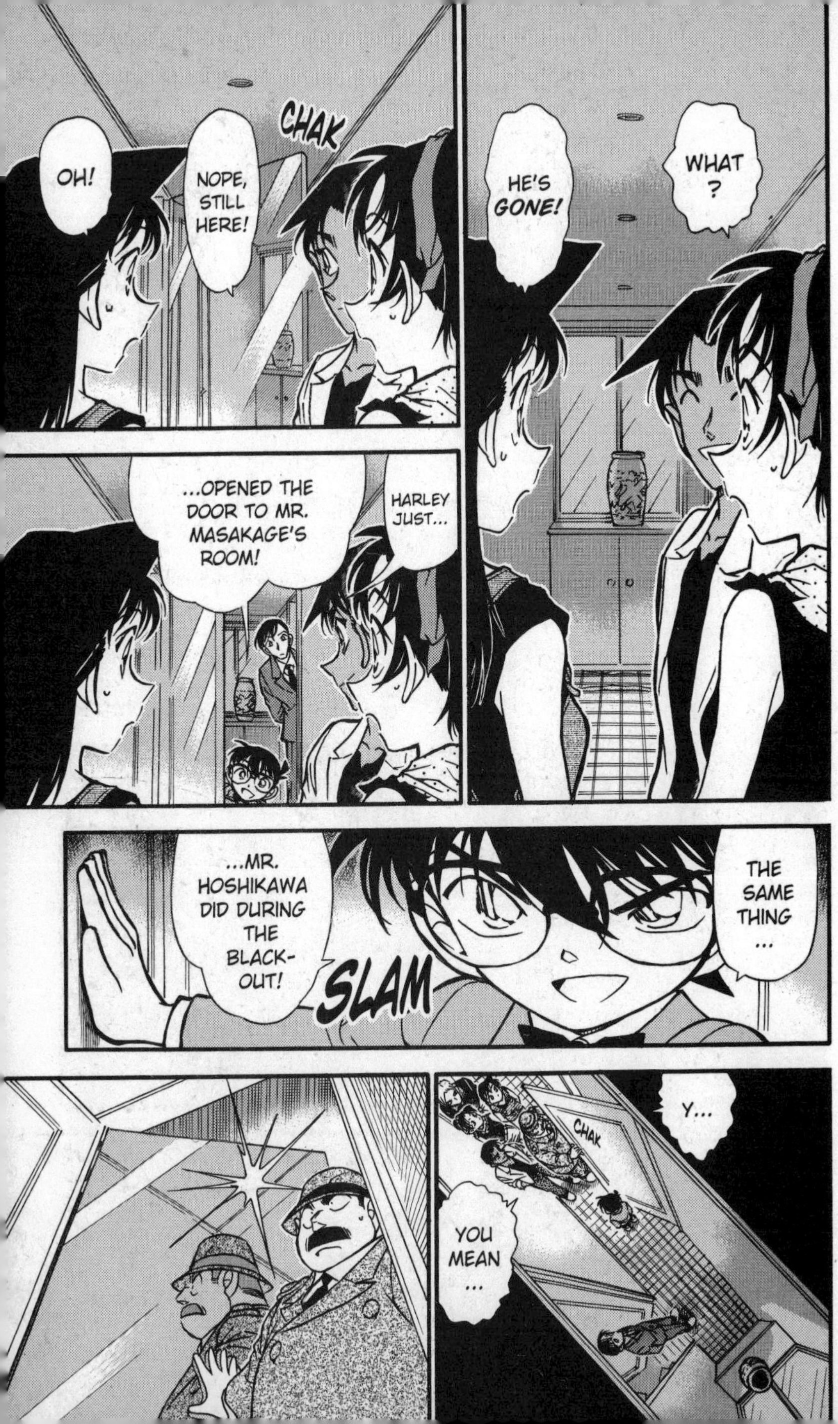
WHAT ?
HE'S GONE!
CHAK
NOPE, STILL HERE!
OH!
HARLEY JUST...
...OPENED THE DOOR TO MR. MASAKAGE'S ROOM!
THE SAME THING ...
...MR. HOSHIKAWA DID DURING THE BLACK-OUT!
SLAM
Y...
CHAK
YOU MEAN ...

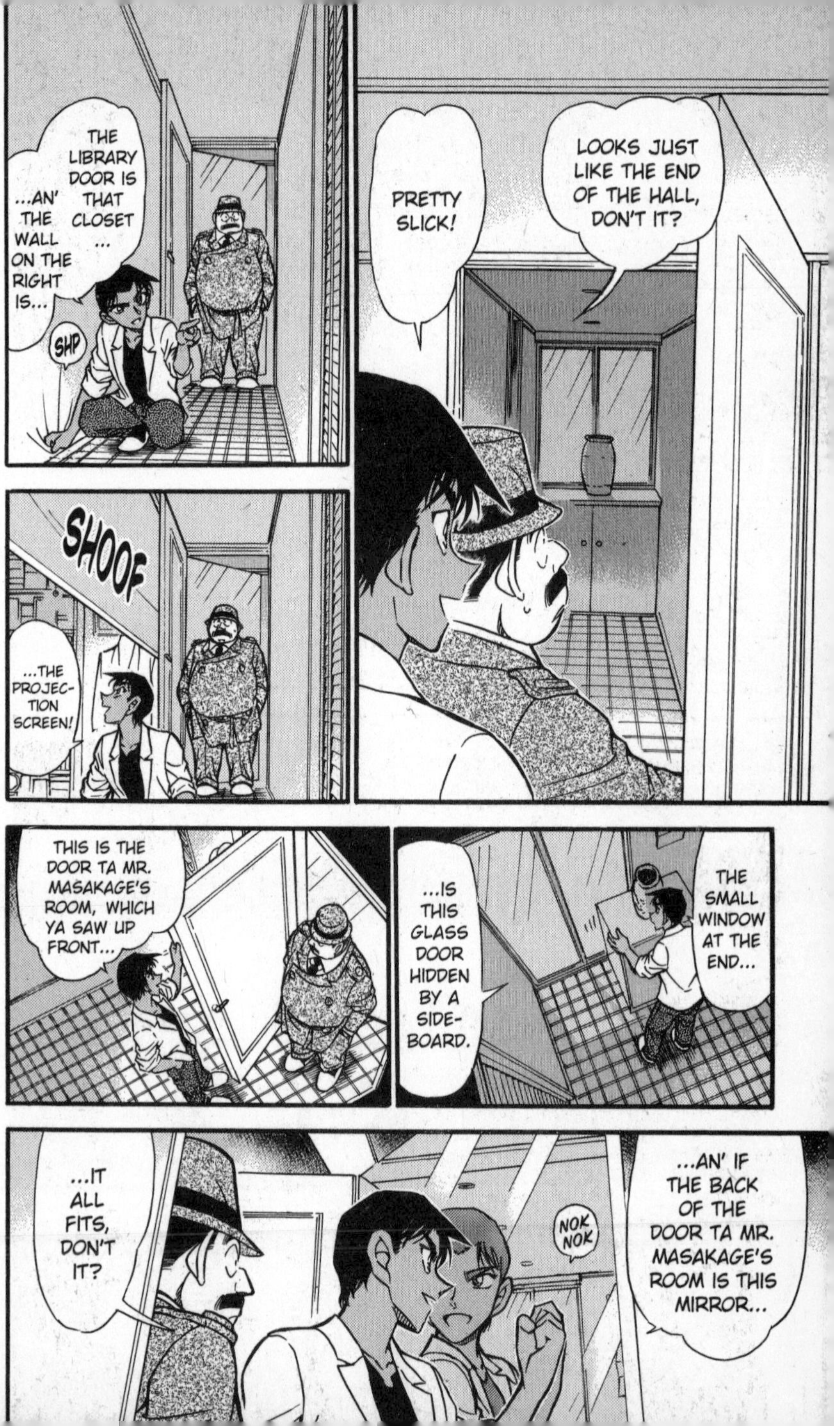
LOOKS JUST LIKE THE END OF THE HALL, DON'T IT?
PRETTY SLICK!
THE LIBRARY DOOR IS THAT CLOSET ...
...AN' THE WALL ON THE RIGHT IS...
SHP
SHOOF
...THE PROJECTION SCREEN!
THE SMALL WINDOW AT THE END...
...IS THIS GLASS DOOR HIDDEN BY A SIDEBOARD.
THIS IS THE DOOR TA MR. MASAKAGE'S ROOM, WHICH YA SAW UP FRONT...
...AN' IF THE BACK OF THE DOOR TA MR. MASAKAGE'S ROOM IS THIS MIRROR...
NOK NOK
...IT ALL FITS, DON'T IT?

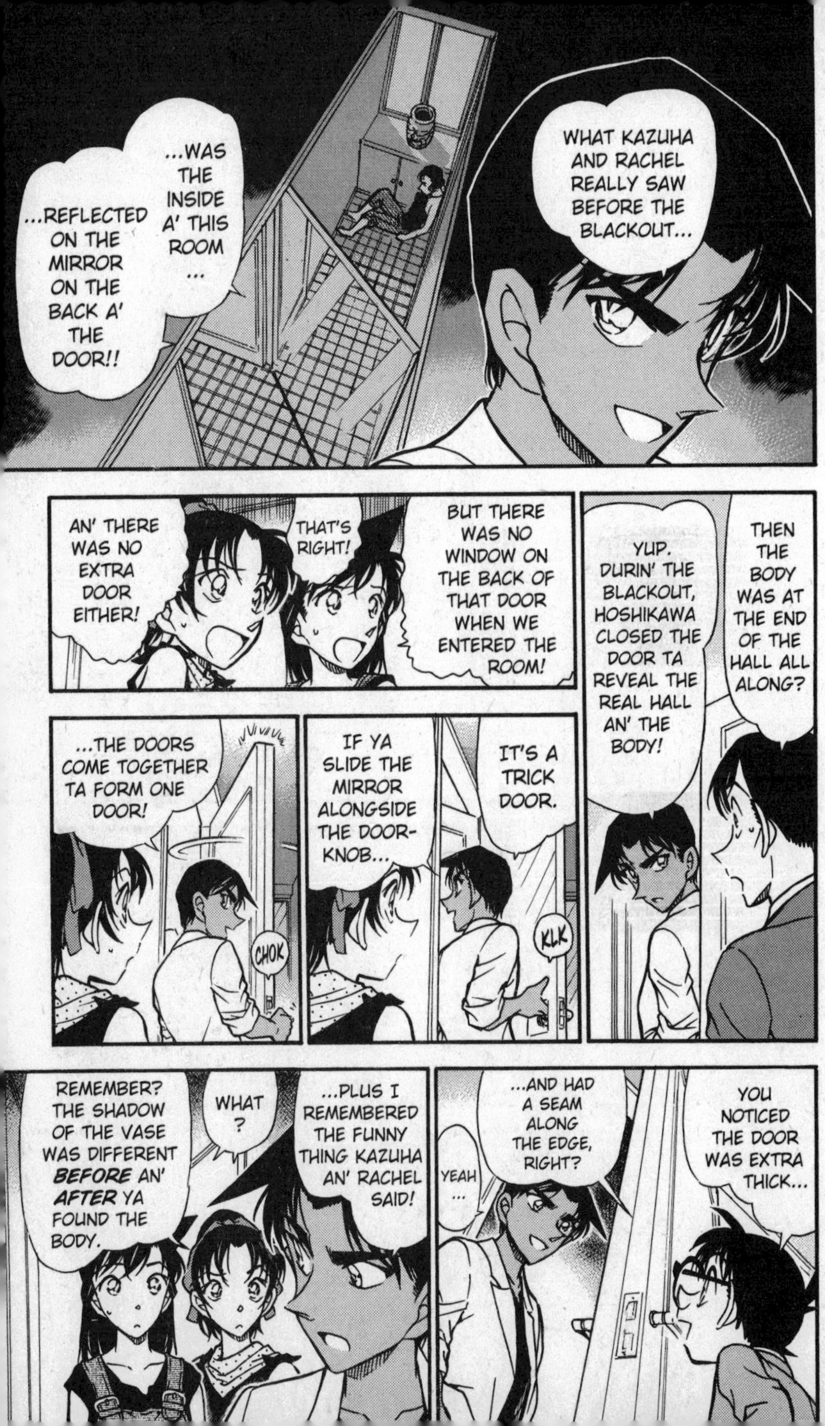
WHAT KAZUHA AND RACHEL REALLY SAW BEFORE THE BLACKOUT...
...WAS THE INSIDE A' THIS ROOM ...
...REFLECTED ON THE MIRROR ON THE BACK A' THE DOOR!!
THEN THE BODY WAS AT THE END OF THE HALL ALL ALONG?
YUP. DURIN' THE BLACKOUT, HOSHIKAWA CLOSED THE DOOR TA REVEAL THE REAL HALL AN' THE BODY!
BUT THERE WAS NO WINDOW ON THE BACK OF THAT DOOR WHEN WE ENTERED THE ROOM!
THAT'S RIGHT!
AN' THERE WAS NO EXTRA DOOR EITHER!
IT'S A TRICK DOOR.
IF YA SLIDE THE MIRROR ALONGSIDE THE DOOR-KNOB...
KLK
...THE DOORS COME TOGETHER TA FORM ONE DOOR!
CHOK
YOU NOTICED THE DOOR WAS EXTRA THICK...
...AND HAD A SEAM ALONG THE EDGE, RIGHT?
YEAH ...
...PLUS I REMEMBERED THE FUNNY THING KAZUHA AN' RACHEL SAID!
WHAT ?
REMEMBER? THE SHADOW OF THE VASE WAS DIFFERENT ***BEFORE*** AN' ***AFTER*** YA FOUND THE BODY.

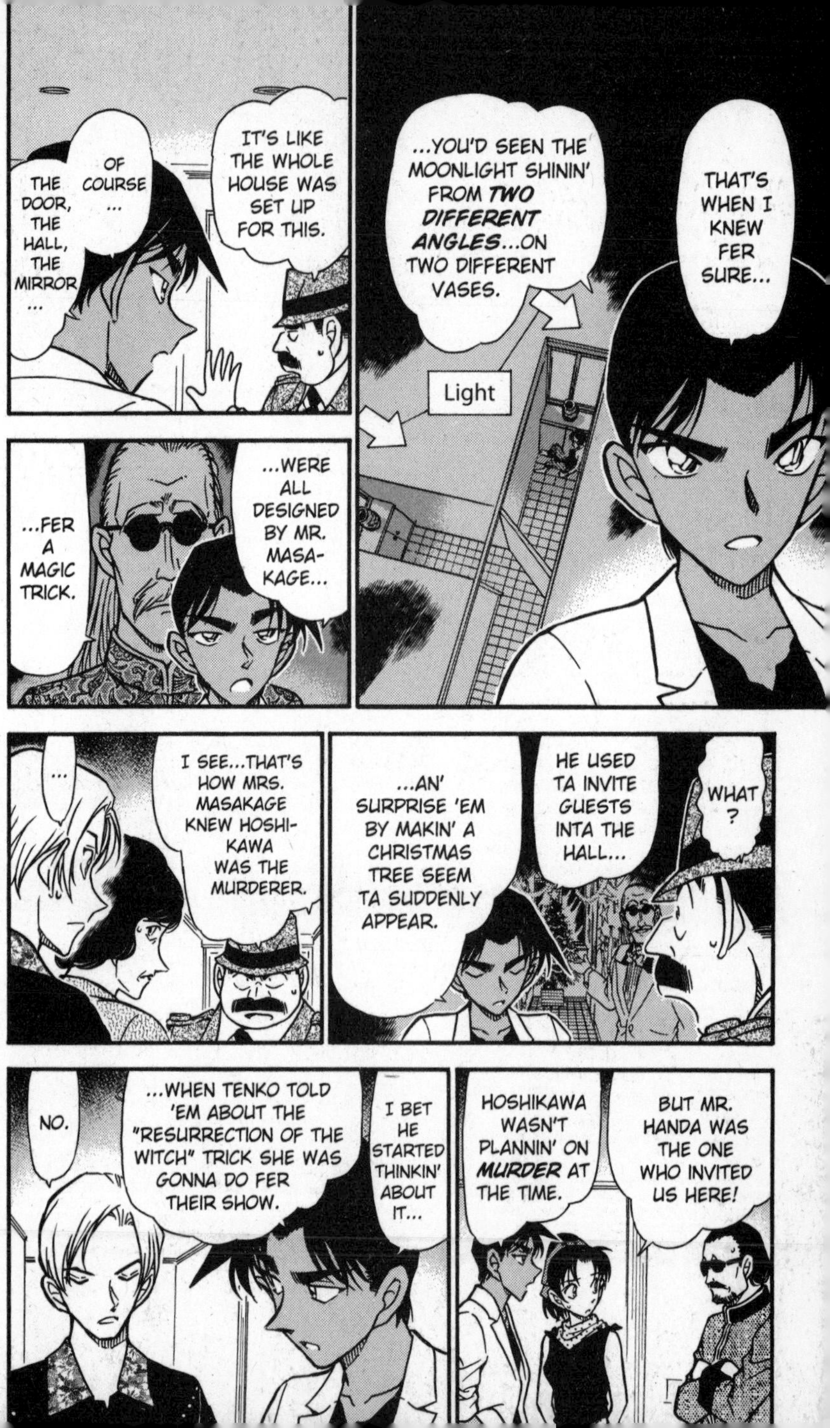
THAT'S WHEN I KNEW FER SURE...
...YOU'D SEEN THE MOONLIGHT SHININ' FROM TWO DIFFERENT ANGLES...ON TWO DIFFERENT VASES.
Light
IT'S LIKE THE WHOLE HOUSE WAS SET UP FOR THIS.
OF COURSE...
THE DOOR, THE HALL, THE MIRROR...
...WERE ALL DESIGNED BY MR. MASAKAGE...
...FER A MAGIC TRICK.
WHAT?
HE USED TA INVITE GUESTS INTA THE HALL...
...AN' SURPRISE 'EM BY MAKIN' A CHRISTMAS TREE SEEM TA SUDDENLY APPEAR.
I SEE...THAT'S HOW MRS. MASAKAGE KNEW HOSHIKAWA WAS THE MURDERER.
...
BUT MR. HANDA WAS THE ONE WHO INVITED US HERE!
HOSHIKAWA WASN'T PLANNIN' ON MURDER AT THE TIME.
I BET HE STARTED THINKIN' ABOUT IT...
...WHEN TENKO TOLD 'EM ABOUT THE "RESURRECTION OF THE WITCH" TRICK SHE WAS GONNA DO FER THEIR SHOW.
NO.

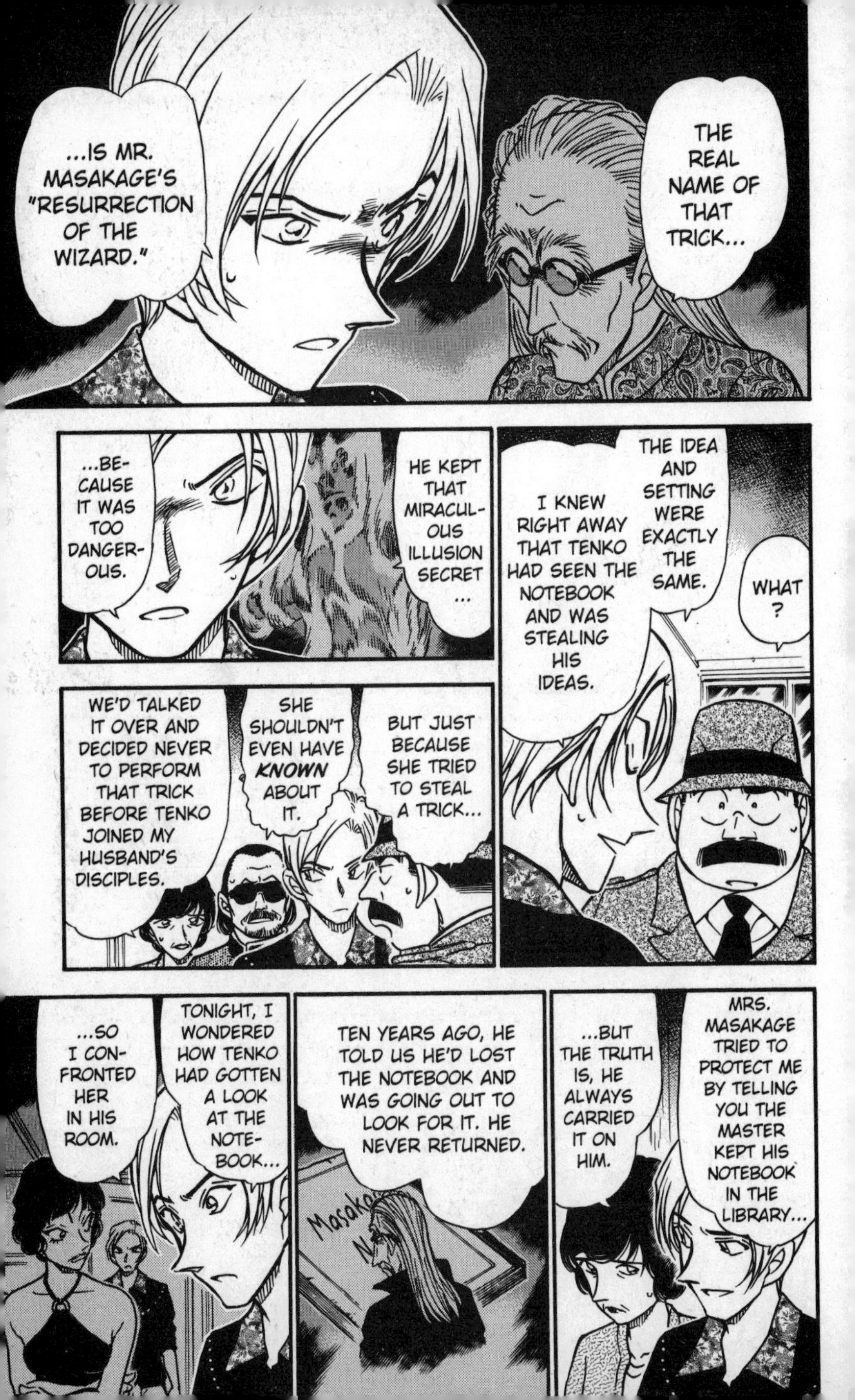
THE REAL NAME OF THAT TRICK...
...IS MR. MASAKAGE'S "RESURRECTION OF THE WIZARD."
THE IDEA AND SETTING WERE EXACTLY THE SAME.
I KNEW RIGHT AWAY THAT TENKO HAD SEEN THE NOTEBOOK AND WAS STEALING HIS IDEAS.
WHAT?
HE KEPT THAT MIRACULOUS ILLUSION SECRET...
...BECAUSE IT WAS TOO DANGEROUS.
BUT JUST BECAUSE SHE TRIED TO STEAL A TRICK...
SHE SHOULDN'T EVEN HAVE ***KNOWN*** ABOUT IT.
WE'D TALKED IT OVER AND DECIDED NEVER TO PERFORM THAT TRICK BEFORE TENKO JOINED MY HUSBAND'S DISCIPLES.
MRS. MASAKAGE TRIED TO PROTECT ME BY TELLING YOU THE MASTER KEPT HIS NOTEBOOK IN THE LIBRARY...
...BUT THE TRUTH IS, HE ALWAYS CARRIED IT ON HIM.
TEN YEARS AGO, HE TOLD US HE'D LOST THE NOTEBOOK AND WAS GOING OUT TO LOOK FOR IT. HE NEVER RETURNED.
TONIGHT, I WONDERED HOW TENKO HAD GOTTEN A LOOK AT THE NOTEBOOK...
...SO I CONFRONTED HER IN HIS ROOM.

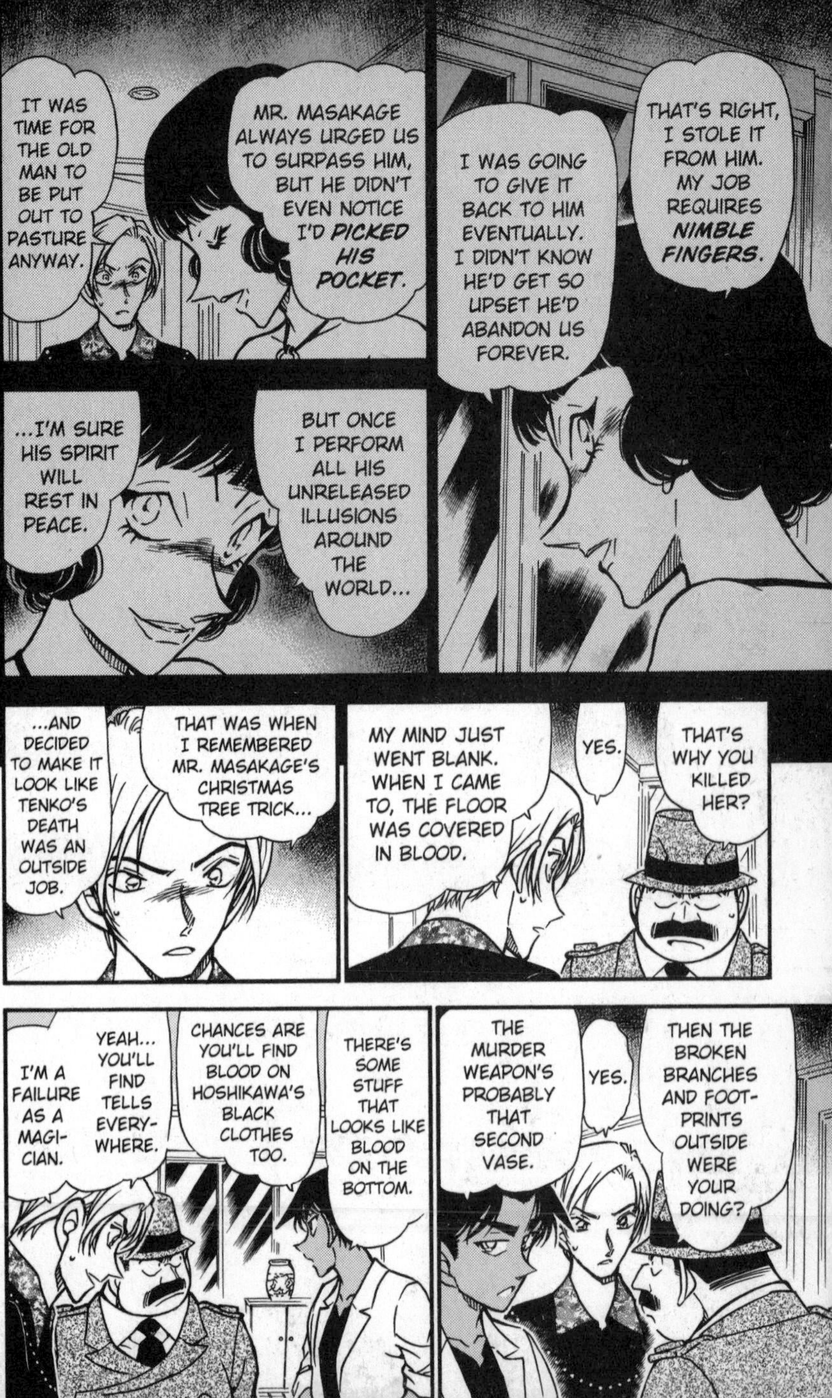
THAT'S RIGHT, I STOLE IT FROM HIM. MY JOB REQUIRES NIMBLE FINGERS.
I WAS GOING TO GIVE IT BACK TO HIM EVENTUALLY. I DIDN'T KNOW HE'D GET SO UPSET HE'D ABANDON US FOREVER.
MR. MASAKAGE ALWAYS URGED US TO SURPASS HIM, BUT HE DIDN'T EVEN NOTICE I'D PICKED HIS POCKET.
IT WAS TIME FOR THE OLD MAN TO BE PUT OUT TO PASTURE ANYWAY.
BUT ONCE I PERFORM ALL HIS UNRELEASED ILLUSIONS AROUND THE WORLD...
...I'M SURE HIS SPIRIT WILL REST IN PEACE.
THAT'S WHY YOU KILLED HER?
YES.
MY MIND JUST WENT BLANK. WHEN I CAME TO, THE FLOOR WAS COVERED IN BLOOD.
THAT WAS WHEN I REMEMBERED MR. MASAKAGE'S CHRISTMAS TREE TRICK...
...AND DECIDED TO MAKE IT LOOK LIKE TENKO'S DEATH WAS AN OUTSIDE JOB.
THEN THE BROKEN BRANCHES AND FOOT-PRINTS OUTSIDE WERE YOUR DOING?
YES.
THE MURDER WEAPON'S PROBABLY THAT SECOND VASE.
THERE'S SOME STUFF THAT LOOKS LIKE BLOOD ON THE BOTTOM.
CHANCES ARE YOU'LL FIND BLOOD ON HOSHIKAWA'S BLACK CLOTHES TOO.
YEAH... YOU'LL FIND TELLS EVERY-WHERE.
I'M A FAILURE AS A MAGI-CIAN.

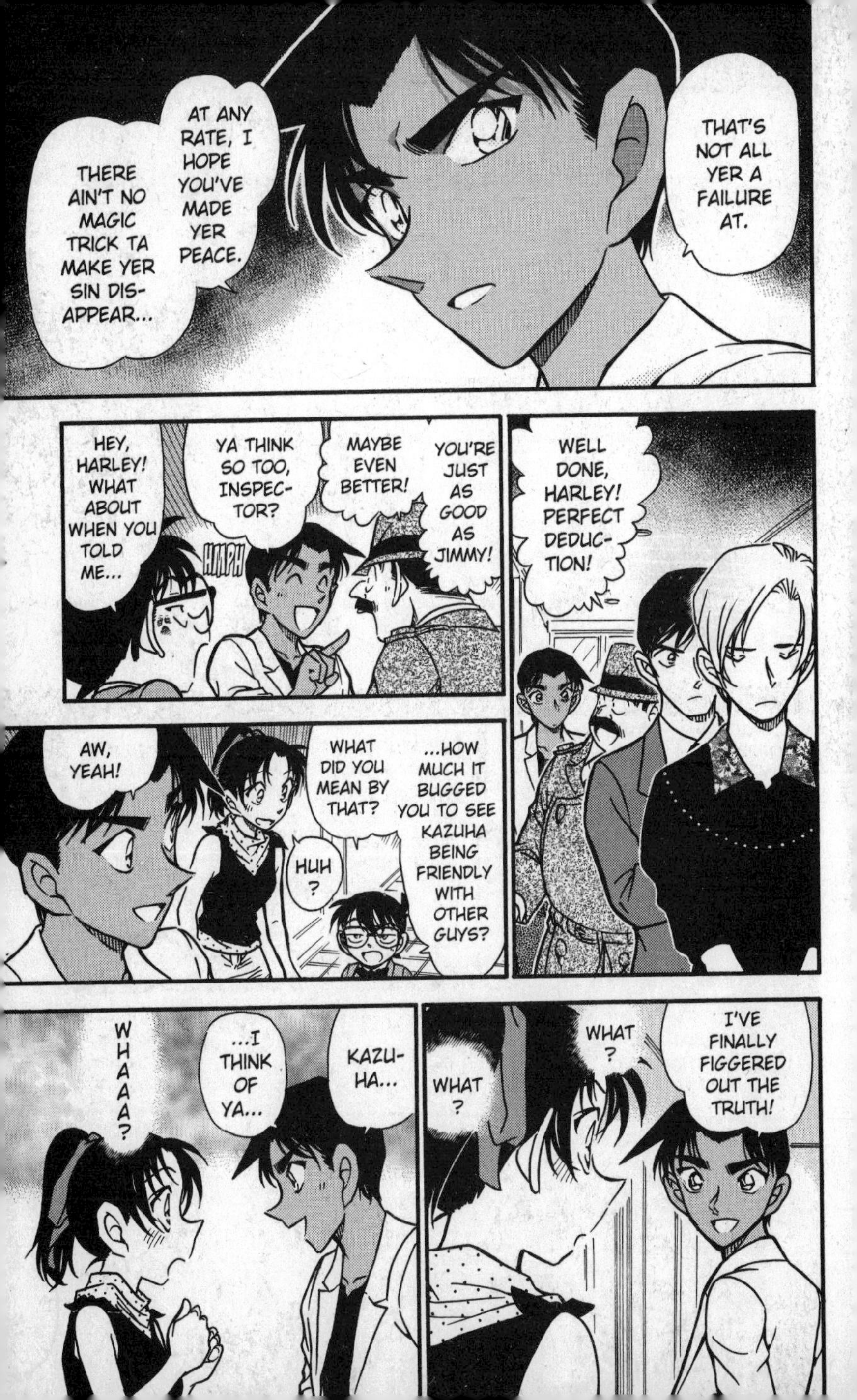
THAT'S NOT ALL YER A FAILURE AT.
AT ANY RATE, I HOPE YOU'VE MADE YER PEACE.
THERE AIN'T NO MAGIC TRICK TA MAKE YER SIN DIS-APPEAR...
WELL DONE, HARLEY! PERFECT DEDUC-TION!
YOU'RE JUST AS GOOD AS JIMMY!
MAYBE EVEN BETTER!
YA THINK SO TOO, INSPEC-TOR?
HMPH
HEY, HARLEY! WHAT ABOUT WHEN YOU TOLD ME...
...HOW MUCH IT BUGGED YOU TO SEE KAZUHA BEING FRIENDLY WITH OTHER GUYS?
WHAT DID YOU MEAN BY THAT?
HUH?
AW, YEAH!
I'VE FINALLY FIGGERED OUT THE TRUTH!
WHAT?
WHAT?
KAZU-HA...
...I THINK OF YA...
WHAAAA?

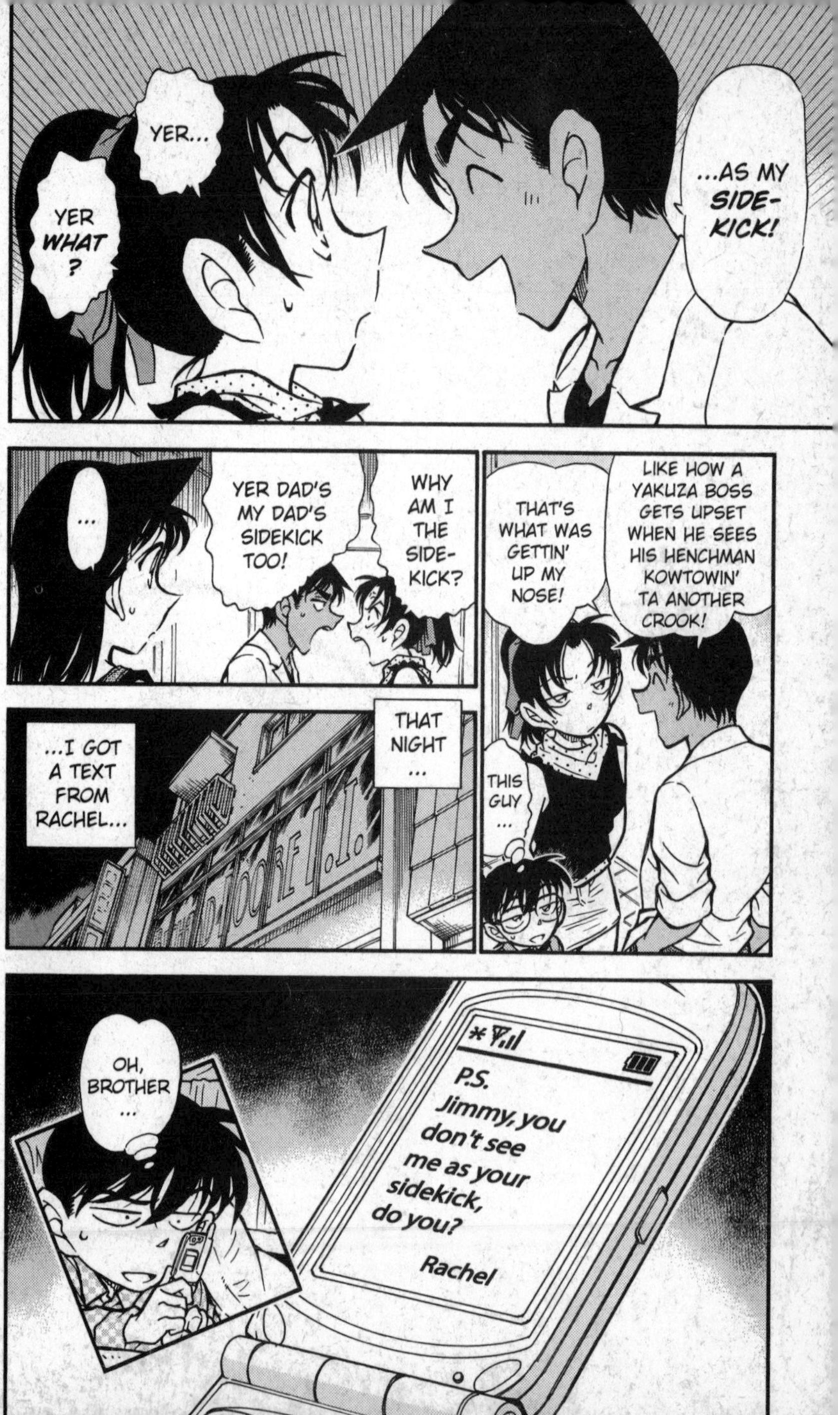
...AS MY SIDE-KICK!
YER...
YER WHAT ?
LIKE HOW A YAKUZA BOSS GETS UPSET WHEN HE SEES HIS HENCHMAN KOWTOWIN' TA ANOTHER CROOK!
THAT'S WHAT WAS GETTIN' UP MY NOSE!
THIS GUY ...
WHY AM I THE SIDE-KICK?
YER DAD'S MY DAD'S SIDEKICK TOO!
...
THAT NIGHT ...
...I GOT A TEXT FROM RACHEL...
P.S. Jimmy, you don't see me as your sidekick, do you? Rachel
OH, BROTHER ...

Hello, Aoyama here.

Did you see it? The 2004 Summer Olympics in Athens? Whoa, I was surprised by all the consecutive wins for Japan! Gold! Gold!! And more gold!!!

But what awed me the most was Matsuzaka, the pitcher for Japan's baseball team. He caught a comebacker on his right arm but continued to pitch as if nothing had happened. I'd like to give him a gold medal for that.

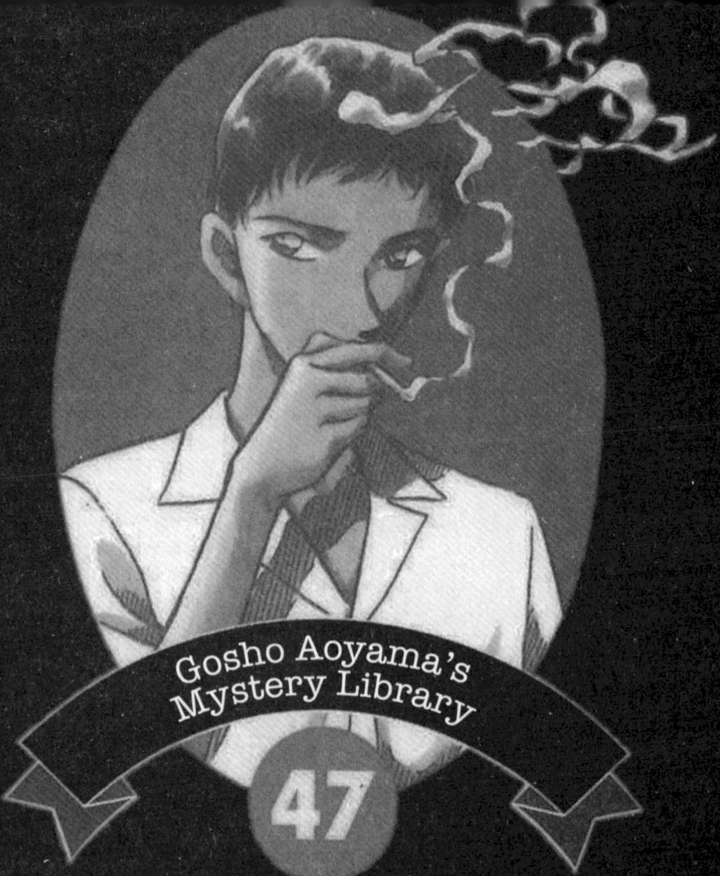
Gosho Aoyama's
Mystery Library
47

YUICHIRO GODA

Being a detective is a tough and lonely job...and Yuichiro Goda fits that image to a T! Born in Osaka, Goda is a detective with the International Investigation division of the Metropolitan Police. Tall with short hair and a narrow, youthful-looking face, he's in his thirties and divorced. People describe him as a "rocky cliff" because he's so cold and harsh, seemingly without a spark of warmth.

Goda's greatest weapon in solving a case is his endurance! He chases the truth, wearing out the soles on his white shoes, with the tenacity he acquired as a mountain climber. The only person he trusts is prosecutor Yusuke Kano, a friend from his college days. Since Kano is also his ex-brother-in-law, they have a rather complex relationship, but their deep friendship remains unchanged.

Kaoru Takamura, Goda's author, hated writing as a child because she had sloppy handwriting. She started writing novels after she acquired a computer as an adult. I even have trouble typing texts into my cell phone, so I guess I'll never match her.

I recommend *Marx's Mountain*.